The Dawning of American Drama

Recent Titles in
Contributions in Drama and Theatre Studies

Radical Stages: Alternative History in Modern British Drama
D. Keith Peacock

A Search for a Postmodern Theater: Interviews with Contemporary Playwrights
John L. DiGaetani

The Age of *Hair*: Evolution and Impact of Broadway's First Rock Musical
Barbara Lee Horn

The Gymnasium of the Imagination: A Collection of Children's Plays in English, 1780-1860
Jonathan Levy

Every Week, A Broadway Revue: The Tamiment Playhouse, 1921-1960
Martha Schmoyer LoMonaco

The Simple Stage: Origins of the Minimalist *Mise-en-Scène* in the American Theater
Arthur Feinsod

Richard's Himself Again: A Stage History of *Richard III*
Scott Colley

Eugene O'Neill in China: An International Centenary Celebration
Haiping Liu and Lowell Swortzell, editors

Toward an Aesthetics of the Puppet: Puppetry as a Theatrical Art
Steve Tillis

George Sand's *Gabriel*
Gay Manifold

Confronting Tennessee Williams's *A Streetcar Named Desire*: Essays in Critical Pluralism
Philip C. Kolin, editor

Challenging the Hierarchy: Collective Theatre in the United States
Mark S. Weinberg

The Dawning of American Drama

*American Dramatic Criticism,
1746–1915*

Edited and Compiled by
Jürgen C. Wolter

Contributions in Drama and Theatre Studies, Number 51

Greenwood Press
Westport, Connecticut • London

Library of Congress Cataloging-in-Publication Data

The Dawning of American drama : American dramatic criticism, 1746-1915
/ edited and compiled by Jürgen C. Wolter.
   p.   cm. – (Contributions in drama and theatre studies, ISSN 0163-3821 ; no. 51)
   Includes bibliographical references and index.
   ISBN 0-313-29028-8 (alk. paper)
   1. Theater – United States – Reviews.   2. Dramatic criticism – United States.   3. American drama – History and criticism.   I. Wolter, Jürgen.   II. Series.
PN2221.D38   1993
792.9'5'0973 – dc20   93-19129

British Library Cataloguing in Publication Data is available.

Copyright © 1993 by Jürgen Wolter

All rights reserved. No portion of this book may be reproduced, by any process or technique, without the express written consent of the publisher.

Library of Congress Catalog Card Number: 93-19129
ISBN: 0-313-29028-8
ISSN: 0163-3821

First published in 1993

Greenwood Press, 88 Post Road West, Westport, CT 06881
An imprint of Greenwood Publishing Group, Inc.

Printed in the United States of America

The paper used in this book complies with the
Permanent Paper Standard issued by the National
Information Standards Organization (Z39.48-1984).

10 9 8 7 6 5 4 3 2 1

Contents

1. Introduction — 1

2. The American Theatre As Seen by Its Critics:
   A Historical Survey: From the Devil's Den to the Nation's Temple — 9

   1746–1789: Struggling for a Foothold — 9
   1790–1860: Defining Morality As Utility — 11
   1860–1915: Continuity and the Debate over Realism — 18

3. An Anthology of American Dramatic Criticism, 1746–1915:
   Jeremiads and Eulogies — 25

4. Chronological List of Dramatic Criticism in
   American Periodicals, 1746–1915 — 273

5. Alphabetical List of the Periodicals Consulted — 297

6. Selected Bibliography on the History of the
   American Drama and Theatre before 1915 — 305

7. Index of Names and Key Terms — 311

1

Introduction

Even though the quantity and quality of twentieth-century American drama is now widely recognized, the American drama of the eighteenth and nineteenth centuries still seems to be reserved for the eccentric specialist.[1] With the exception of the plays available in the standard editions,[2] the bulk of American drama written and produced prior to O'Neill is virtually unknown. This obscurity is even more true of dramatic criticism, especially that which was written before the movement toward realism at the end of the nineteenth century. Merrill G. Christophersen's statement of 1956 is still valid today: "Most historians of American dramatic criticism seem to have decided that they have no subject matter extending behind a time barrier set up somewhere around 1870."[3] And even with regard to the dramatic criticism of the advocates of stage realism, Brenda Murphy argues that scholars have not given it sufficient attention either.[4]

To a certain extent the neglect seems to be justified by the low standard both of the plays and the criticism. Poe, for example, complained: "How absolute is the necessity now daily growing, of rescuing our stage criticism from the control of illiterate mountebanks, and placing it in the hands of gentlemen and scholars!"[5] And as late as 1908 Frank Moore Colby stated that "no American dramatic critic has thus far in our history published a volume that was particularly worth reading."[6]

The lack of intellectual depth in the majority of the critical discussion of early American drama and theatre is, however, more than counterbalanced by the spontaneity of these firsthand accounts. The best of them reflect the heated debates over the direction theatre and drama in America ought to take. The periodicals were mirrors of public taste, as, for example, the name of Stephen Cullen Carpenter's short-lived monthly *The Mirror of Taste and Dramatic Censor* (Philadelphia, 1810–11) attempted to indicate, and the standards their critics expounded were extremely influential; their polemics are part of the moral and cultural disputes of the nation.[7] Thomas Hamilton, who toured the United States at the beginning of the nineteenth century, confirmed that "the influence and circulation of newspapers is great beyond anything ever known in Europe. In truth, nine-tenths of the population read nothing else.... Newspapers penetrate to every crevice of the Union."[8] And de Tocqueville's characterization of American journalists can fully be applied to most American theatrical critics: "Only the journalists strike me as truly American. They are certainly not great writers, but they speak the country's language and they make themselves heard."[9] In this sense, the periodicals of the eighteenth and nineteenth centuries are a treasure house of cultural memorabilia, which have not been readily available for teaching and research purposes because the periodicals have not been investigated systematically. This book aims to fill these lacunae. For the first time, it provides researchers with a number of bibliographical lists as well as teachers with an anthology of the most representative and illuminating texts from 170 years of dramatic criticism in America.

The "Chronological List of Dramatic Criticism in American Periodicals, 1746 to 1915," Chapter 4, is the nucleus of this book. It is the result of a systematic study of over 150 American periodicals. On the basis of a comprehensive list of American theatrical and literary journals before 1915, which I compiled from the recent bibliographies of American periodicals,[10] I scrutinized those journals that are still extant and generally available in the microfilm collections *American Periodicals 1741–1900* (Ann Arbor, MI: University Microfilms International, 1979) and *American Theatre Periodicals of the Nineteenth and Early Twentieth Centuries* (Reading, PA: Research Publications, 1989). An alphabetical list of the periodicals I checked is given in Chapter 5. My study of these periodicals resulted in the selection of the almost five hundred articles I list chronologically in Chapter 4; they are especially valuable in that they represent the fierce debate over the role of the drama in America's cultural history. Since few early American critics would meet modern standards, I approached the periodicals with a broad definition of criticism.

The most interesting texts from this "Chronological List of Dramatic Criticism" are reprinted in the "Anthology of American Dramatic Criticism, 1746–1915" (Chapter 3). This collection is a documentary history of the changing attitudes of Americans toward their drama and theatre from the eighteenth to the early twentieth century. Critics here write a cumulative history of the American stage as they witnessed it, each from his own personal perspective and in response to the particular interests of his time. The texts outline the social rise of the actor from the despised outsider stigmatized for the immorality of his profession to the admired star who sets the standards in fashion and language; they trace the controversial evaluations of the "devil's institution" and present the various endeavors to establish realism on the American stage; they report on the manifold attempts to reform the theatre through moral censorship, parliamentary action, or organizations for actors and audiences alike.

Finally, they contribute to our understanding of the development of theatrical criticism in the United States and demonstrate that it followed the main tendencies in the nation's cultural, literary, and critical debate in the eighteenth and nineteenth centuries. In prerevolutionary times public discussion started as a religious controversy over morality, then, in the formative decades before the Civil War, turned into the quest for an adequate expression of the American national character on the stage, and, finally, attempted to redefine American drama and theatre in terms of national reality and individual experience. All writers acknowledged the European, especially English, origins of American drama and theatre, but they differed radically in their views about what use Americans should make of these origins and how closely American dramatists, managers, and actors should adhere to the norms set by their non-American counterparts.

A "Selected Bibliography on the History of the American Drama and Theatre before 1915" (Chapter 5) points to further research opportunities. The emphasis is on bibliographies and general studies with the main focus on dramatic criticism. It highlights the fact that our knowledge about early American theatre criticism is still very scanty. Historical surveys are only included in my list if they were written by contemporaries (i.e., by critics who witnessed the development of the American theatre before 1915). In addition I list a few modern histories that are important because of their extensive research of pre-1915 sources.

The bibliographical lists and the anthology are framed by a "Historical Survey" and "Index of Names and Key Terms" (Chapters 2 and 7). The survey presents a descriptive analysis of the texts in the anthology and outlines in detail the critical debate about theatre and drama in America. The index refers not only to the texts reprinted in Chapter 3, but to all the articles listed in the "Chronological List of Dramatic Criticism." The survey and the index supplement each other by giving different ways of approaching the material collected in Chapters 3 and 4.

In preparing this book, I have been guided by these two objectives:

1. As a sourcebook for courses on the history of the American theatre it aims to bring to life the prolonged dawning of the American drama, to outline America's continued quest for a national drama and theatre, and to provide a survey of the development of dramatic criticism in America. For over a century dramatists and critics alike were in search of "a drama of our own, based on our own manners, habits, characters, and political institutions."[11] Since I wanted to reconstruct this search, I was primarily interested in articles with an American perspective (i.e., articles that reflect American attitudes and values and try to define the future of the nation's drama and theatre). The texts collected here provide a survey of the changing attitudes of Americans toward

their drama and theatre from the eighteenth century to 1915, that is, from the first appearance of periodicals on the American literary market to the middle of that "formative decade"[12] when the Provincetown Players and other enthusiasts, inspired by European developments, inaugurated a new epoch on the American stage. The texts present the various arguments put forward both for and against drama and theatre in almost two hundred years of American criticism. In addition, they give graphic descriptions of the early American theatre, which some transformed into a zoological exhibition, a drinking saloon, or a whorehouse, and they offer suggestions for the improvement of its morals, its architecture (e.g., its safety and ventilation), but also its frequently rioting members of the audience.

2. Since I also aimed to provide a tool for further research on the beginnings of American drama and theatre, my search was focused on early and unretrieved material. Consequently, I checked many early periodicals whose names do not indicate any connection with the American theatre and discovered a substantial amount of relevant material in journals not listed in Carl J. Stratman's bibliography of *American Theatrical Periodicals.* In addition, I included the better-known criticism by authors like Irving, Poe, and Whitman. There was no risk of duplicating texts gathered in the few existing anthologies of American theatrical criticism because they made only very limited use of pre-1915 material.[13]

These objectives account for the fact that I was more interested in representative articles reflecting widely accepted attitudes and values than in critiques of individual performances that were often mere puffery, anyway. Therefore, I consulted weeklies and monthlies, with only a few exceptions: In my anthology I reprint Joseph Tisdale's 1767 speech to the Boston House of Representatives because of its revolutionary anticlerical argumentation, and, in my bibliography, I list John Edwards's "warning to sinners" of 1812 as an outstanding example of early nineteenth-century anti-theatre pamphlets as well as the *New York Evening Post* reports on the Astor Place Riots because of their circumstantiality. As a rule, therefore, I did not consult daily newspapers because their coverage was limited to the facts of a particular theatrical event; naturally, they were not interested in a general discussion of the state and future of the American drama and theatre. My reading corroborated Clayton Hamilton's statement that "most newspapers, and even many magazines, report plays as they report base-ball games."[14] Finally, I was not concerned with historical surveys, biographical sketches of actors, or articles on the opera.

I retain the language and spelling of the original versions with all their timeworn idiosyncracies and silently emended only obvious typographical errors. However, I have deleted the typographical emphasis frequently given to names (by italics or inverted commas) and standardized the writing of titles; I use italics throughout where the originals use small capitals, boldface, or inverted commas. Because of the futility of such an endeavor in most cases, I have not attempted to establish the identities of the numerous anonymous authors, following Nina Baym's example: "Reviews were almost always anonymous, and since I am interested in a body of critical opinion rather than in individual personalities, I have usually left them so."[15] While the bibliography gives the titles of articles as they are in the original, in the text collection I have replaced uninformative titles such as "The Drama," "The Theatre," and "The Stage" with my own, which in many cases use phrases from the article in question. Frequently, I have made the author's argumentation more concise by deletions; in particular, I have deleted plot summaries of plays. My deletions or annotations are indicated by [...]; if the original text used brackets, I have changed them to parentheses.

The texts are arranged in chronological order to illustrate both the continuity of some critical concerns over the centuries (most importantly the questions of morality and the decline of the drama) and the gradual change in attitudes as well as national aspirations. The numbers preceding the texts refer to the bibliography, as do the numbers in brackets in the introduction.

I am grateful to the Ministerium für Wissenschaft und Forschung in Nordrhein–Westfalen for financial support over several years and to the staff of the libraries at the Bergische Universität–Gesamthochschule Wuppertal, at the John F. Kennedy Institut, Berlin, as well as at the Niedersächsische Staats- und Universitätsbibliothek, Göttingen, for invaluable assistance. I wish to express my gratitude to Alfred Weber for unflagging support and valuable advice and to Ulrich Halfmann for amicable encouragement. I should also like to thank Philip Kolin and Irmgard Wolfe of the University of Southern Mississippi, Hattiesburg, for providing texts not available in Europe, Angelika Lotz, Michael Windgassen, Thomas Göhler, and Ute Pantenburg for substantial help with both the manuscript and the bibliography, and Ingrid Hinz–Hildebold and Isa Wendler of the Wuppertal University Library, who valiantly wrestled with microforms of varying format and quality, striving to make readable copies.

NOTES

1. Walter J. Meserve, "The State of Research in American Theatre History," *Theatre Survey* 22 (1981): 125–31.

2. For a list of anthologies, see Walter J. Meserve, *American Drama to 1900: A Guide to Information Sources* (Detroit: Gale, 1980), 15–21.

3. Merrill G. Christophersen, "Early American Dramatic Criticism," *Southern Speech Journal* 21 (1956): 195.

4. Brenda Murphy, *American Realism and American Drama, 1880–1940* (Cambridge: Cambridge University Press, 1987), x.

5. E. A. Poe, "Walsh's Didactics," *Southern Literary Messenger* (May 1836), reprinted in *The Complete Works of E. A. Poe*, ed. James A. Harrison (New York: Society of English and French Literature, 1902), vol. 8: 322.

6. Frank Moore Colby, "A Model for Dramatic Critics," *Forum* 39 (April 1908): 551.

7. Patricia Marks, *American Literary and Drama Reviews: An Index to Late 19th Century Periodicals* (Boston: Hall, 1984), xi, concurs: "Such periodicals, which both guided and reflected the taste of the reading public, are an important cultural record."

8. Thomas Hamilton, *Men and Manners in America* (Edinburgh, 1833), vol. 2: 73–74.

9. A. de Tocqueville, *Democracy in America*, trans. George Lawrence (New York: Harper & Row, 1966), 439.

10. Most helpful were: Carl J. Stratman, *American Theatrical Periodicals, 1798–1967: A Bibliographical Guide* (Durham, NC: Duke University Press, 1970), Edward E. Chielens, *American Literary Magazines: The Eighteenth and Nineteenth Centuries* (Westport, CT: 1986), Edward E. Chielens, *The Literary Journal in America to 1900: A Guide to Information Sources* (Detroit: Gale, 1975), Jayne K. Kribbs, *An Annotated Bibliography of American Literary Periodicals, 1741–1850* (Boston: Hall, 1977), and Walter J. Meserve, *An Emerging Entertainment: The Drama of the American People to 1828* (Bloomington: Indiana University Press, 1977) [with a list of newspapers and periodicals, 1714–1828, pp. 326–28]. For further sources, see my selected bibliography.

11. Preface to J. K. Paulding and William Irving Paulding, *American Comedies* (Philadelphia, 1847), quoted in *The Literary World* 1 (27 Feb. 1847): 88–89.

12. Richard Moody, "Theatre U.S.A., 1909–1919: The Formative Decade," *Theatrical Touring and Founding in North America*, ed. L.W. Conolly (Westport, CT: Greenwood, 1982), 113–33.

13. Barrett H. Clark, *European Theories of the Drama, with a Supplement on the American Drama*, rev. Henry Popkin (New York: Crown, 1965), lists only a few critical essays from the nineteenth century. Alan S. Downer, *American Drama and Its Critics. A Collection of Critical Essays* (Chicago: Chicago University Press, 1965), contains only one article from the nineteenth century: Herne's "Art for Truth's Sake in the Drama" (1897), and two articles from the period before 1915: Howells's "Some New American Plays" (1904), and Eaton's "Our Infant Industry" (1908). In L. L. Harris, *19th-Century Literature Criticism*, 2 vols. (Detroit: Gale, 1982), William Dunlap and William Wells Brown are the only early American dramatists represented; the focus is on the critical reception of these authors' works up to our times. Montrose J. Moses and John Mason Brown, eds., *The American Theatre as Seen by Its Critics. 1752–1934* (1934; rep. New York: Cooper Square, 1967), has only very little material from the period before 1852.

14. Clayton Hamilton, "Organizing an Audience," *The Bookman* 34 (1911): 166. In "What Is Wrong with the American Drama?" *The Bookman* 39 (1914): 317, Hamilton wrote: "With less than a dozen exceptions, the newspapers and even the magazines of this country treat the theatre as 'news' and refuse to recognize the drama as an art."

15. Nina Baym, *Novels, Readers, and Reviewers: Responses to Fiction in Antebellum America* (Ithaca, NY: Cornell University Press, 1984), 7. Only in a few

cases do we know the identity of the author; Poe and Whitman were among the first to sign their criticism. William Winter, one of the most influential critics of his age, wrote for the New York *Albion* under the pseudonym "Mercutio" in the 1860s. See Tice L. Miller, *Bohemians and Critics. American Theatre Criticism in the Nineteenth Century* (Metuchen, NJ: Scarecrow, 1981), 70ff. Acorn in the *Spirit of the Times* was the pseudonym of James Oakes. Where available, I have, of course, made use of research on identifying anonymous contributors, such as: Ralph M. Aderman, "Contributors to the *American Quarterly Review*, 1827–1833," *Studies in Bibliography* 14 (1961): 163–76; M. A. De Wolfe Howe, *Journal of the Proceedings of the Society Which Conducts* The Monthly Anthology & Boston Review (Boston: Boston Athenaeum, 1910).

2

The American Theatre As Seen by Its Critics: A Historical Survey: From the Devil's Den to the Nation's Temple

1746–1789: STRUGGLING FOR A FOOTHOLD

Remarkably, the Southern colonies never enacted laws to prohibit the building of a theatre or the public performance of a drama; drama in colonial New England on the other hand was a major target of Puritan prejudices. In New England, the drama, just as the novel, was considered dangerously nonconformist because it constructed a world of the imagination, which, for many members of the community, was more attractive than the world of God's creation. In addition, any form of entertainment was considered a waste of time that should be much better employed in religious investigations. However, since the drama, in contrast to the privacy of novel-reading, is dependent on public performances and as such on the institution of the theatre, it was soon made an object of controversies in New England courts and local parliaments: the issue was not only, as it was with the novel, whether it should be tolerated, but whether theatrical entertainment and the establishment of a theatre building should be legalized.

Because of the public context of the theatre it received much more attention than the novel. Church annals and records of colonial courts document that drama and theatre had become issues of public concern as early as 1665, when the actors who had presented *Ye Bare and Ye Cubb* were summoned before the court of Accomac County, Virginia. However, true to Southern tolerance for entertainment and belles lettres, the justices acquitted the actors.[1] In Calvinist New England the profession met with much less sympathy, and as soon as magazines started to be published there in the eighteenth century, they were immediately pushed to the forefront of the public war of words. However, irrespective of their attitude, almost all the arguments for the condemnation or toleration of theatrical performances used moral criteria.

The enemies warned against the "Lewdness or Impiety of most of the Plays" and commented on the "infamous Characters of the Actors and Actresses" *[1]*. If they had to concede that a few plays were acceptable, they were quick to make a distinction between the drama and the theatre, denouncing the custom of having serious plays followed by "scandalous Farces" and having "a painted Strumpet" perform "inhumanly impudent Dances and Songs" between the acts; by this "ingenious Contrivance" the managers, they argued, prevented the good effects that may have been achieved by a properly moral play. They also pointed out that by tolerating a theatrical troupe society would prove itself hypocritical and inconsistent in its religion because it would support "one Order of Men for the Propagation of Virtue and Religion, and another for the Destruction of them" [1].

The supporters of the stage refuted these accusations as being based on superstition and on a misconception of God, who had given man his senses not only to use them, but also to enjoy them. Furthermore, it was for them not so much a religious and moral question, but rather a social and political one, because it had direct consequences for the individual's rights, his life, liberty, and pursuit of happiness [3]. A ban on theatrical entertainment would "abridge the natural right of every freeman, to dispose of his time and money, according to his own taste and disposition, when not obnoxious to the real interests of society" [7]. They also perceived very clearly that fundamentally the issue was that of the rights of a minority in a democratic society; if the majority could dictate the entertainment of a minority, it could also dictate other details of the lives of the citizens: "the same authority which proscribes our amusements, may, with equal justice, dictate the shape and texture of our dress, or the modes and ceremonies of our worship" [7].

The advocates of the theatre took the clergy particularly severely to task because, as they saw it, the campaign against the theatre was mounted by the clergy for their own interest, not for Christ; the clergy were afraid of losing their political influence to people who had "a more effectual method to improve the morals, and excite sentiments of virtue and religion." The witch trials vividly illustrated, they argued, where undue dominance by the clergy might lead [4]. Furthermore, they emphasized its potential moral, cultural, and political benefits: not only did the theatre engage the "powers of the soul in the cause of virtue" [4] and tend to the "refinement of manners and the polish of society," but it was also "a natural and necessary concomitant of our [national and political] independence" [7].

The controversy over the legalization of theatres became less prominent after the Revolutionary War, although most of the earlier arguments were taken up time and again in the continuing debate over the propriety of the stage. With the repeal of the 1774 anti-theatre act and the burgeoning national self-confidence after the Revolution, the situation changed: most of the major cities constructed theatres or dedicated buildings to theatrical performances, and dramatic entertainment became part of the staple amusement of all classes of American society. The question was no longer whether playhouses and dramatic troupes should be tolerated, if not supported, but rather what the specific tasks of the drama and theatre in the newly established American society were and how an indigenous American drama should differ from its European models.

Naturally, communities seldom decided unanimously for or against the theatre, and even the Puritan anti-theatre stronghold of Boston was divided over this question, as is testified by the uproar of indignation in the New Exhibition Room in December 1792, when the sheriff stopped a performance of *The School for Scandal* and arrested the manager *[65]*. Political leaders and public representatives, even presidents, first and foremost George Washington, patronized the theatre. Nonetheless, even as late as 1854 theatrical entertainment was unlawful at any time in Connecticut, while Massachusetts forbade dramatic performances on Saturdays and Sundays *[247]*. However, when in 1854 the new Boston Theatre opened, *Gleason's* proudly announced: "The old prejudices against theatrical entertainments have been swept away by the enlightened spirit of the age, and there is no longer a doubt of their moral tendency, among persons of sound judgment" *[248]*. To a large extent this was wishful thinking, as the moralizing anti-theatre arguments of the first phase were continually taken up well into the early years of the twentieth century.

1790–1860: DEFINING MORALITY AS UTILITY

In the first half of the nineteenth century the main critical concern was the decline of the stage and the quest for genuinely American departures. Fundamentally, the public debate was still based on the old conception entertained by its friends and enemies alike that the theatre had to be a moral and didactic institution. However, the conception of morality gradually changed from a religious to a social context: morality was no longer solely defined by reference to God and the Bible. Now the theatre began to be regarded as moral if it was useful and instructive, that is, if it taught a value system accepted in America and thus served American nationalism, and if it subscribed to a new conception of realism—for example, in the historical accuracy of the mise-en-scènes. The stage still had to be "a School of Reform," but now it was called upon to adapt itself to the American situation, to reflect American follies and to teach American virtues *[144]*. In short, the definition of morality moved away from universalism and idealism toward nationalism and realism.

Abolitionists versus Apologists

The prerevolutionary debate about the morality and didacticism of the stage was constantly revived, and only very rarely were new arguments put forward. The abolitionists of the anti-theatre faction simply repeated their by now timeworn tirades, castigating playgoing as a waste of time and money and a first step toward moral ruin; time and again they referred to the barrooms and the presence of licentious women to prove that the theatre was a school for scandal, indeed, teaching intemperance, lasciviousness, and "extravagance in dress" *[115]*. Some still echoed the Puritan abhorrence of fiction as a lie of the depraved human mind.²

In contrast, the apologists' eulogies were more ingenious. Not only did they postulate the moral usefulness of the theatre, provided it was strictly regulated, but they also reasoned that since everybody needed a "relaxation from labour," the theatre was to be preferred to the tavern or the gaming table *[32]*. The critic of *The Knickerbocker* *[138]*, probably for the first time in American dramatic criticism, defined the sociopsychological functions of what others criticized as the marvels, perplexities, or absurdities of the stage world. In addition to specifying the moral, cultural, intellectual, national, and educational benefits of the theatre, he clearly realized the escapist and thus placatory function of the stage world for the less well-off members of the audience, who otherwise "may grow dissatisfied at viewing their relative position in society." By offering dream-world solutions to the insuperable problems of their daily lives and by depicting a feigned world that countervailed their dismal everyday experience, the stage marvels provided a safety valve for dissatisfaction and assured social peace in America.

The defenders of the stage also referred to the theatricality of the church service, and some even compared the stage to the pulpit and the drama to a sermon, because they used similar strategies and had similar propitious effects *[24]*. Others compared its educational function to that of the press; both, they asserted, were equally necessary for publicly conveying "the productions of the comparatively wise . . . to the comparatively ignorant" *[13]*. And they called upon the abolitionists to patronize the theatre so that "by their presence they might check the further encroachments of immorality"; women especially should attend theatrical performances because of their refining influence on men *[39]*.

In some cases, the apologists had to admit that some of the arguments of the anti-theatre moralists were justified, and they even used the abolitionists' rebukes for their own purposes: They explained the depravity of plays by the fact that (1) they were written by British dramatists, members of a "luxurious and corrupt" nation, and (2) they mirrored a human society that was "a deluge of crimes and miseries" *[11]*. They argued that an improvement of the theatre required higher moral standards in society which, in turn, might be encouraged by the drama. If the stage represented the depraved world, it was all the more useful because here the wise came into contact with it "without danger of infection"; here they learned where to find the weeds they wanted to pluck *[12]*.

A frequent side effect of this view of the stage as an instrument of public education was a severe mutilation of the original text, so that, as the critic of the *Anglo American* complained with regard to *Richard III* at the Park Theatre (1846), "half the acted text is not Shakspeare's *at all*" *[199]*. Others replied to such strictures that in order to be successful on the modern stage, all old plays, even Shakespeare's, had to be adapted to the modern language and to modern taste *[200, 201, 215]*. Some critics even demanded that Shakespeare's plays should be confined to the closet since they did not conform to the current, mostly Aristotelian rules for plays—these should have few scenic changes, respect the unities, and rely on the effects of the scenic and the spectacular *[254]*. For the Richmond *Magnolia Weekly* of 1864 most of Shakespeare's dramas and tragedies in general were unsuitable for another reason: in times of war it was the duty of the theatre to provide escapist relaxation by avoiding scenes of death and giving preference to farces *[279]*. In addition, for this paper the theatre was extremely helpful in keeping up the spirit of the Confederate Army.

Nationalism and the Drama

For many critics of this second phase of the drama in America the question of the theatre's national utility in the newly established republic became paramount. It was regarded as an important "instrument for the formation of national character" *[113]*. For some the evolution of a new American man (in the sense of Crèvecoeur) called for a specifically American comedy: "We have foibles peculiar to ourselves, which seem to require the assistance of the laughing muse." *[8]* Many demanded a national drama, which they defined not only as a drama on American incidents and manners, but also as one that inspired a flamboyant patriotism *[104]*. Suggestions for possible subjects for native playwrights were legion. To consider tragedy, critics most frequently proposed the hostilities between the early settlers and the Indians *[113]*, which they deemed better suited than the still too recent Revolutionary history. For comedy they saw a much wider field in national peculiarities. And even if the subject was not American, a play had to propagate American democratic values; under no circumstances should the author allow the slightest doubt about his patriotism *[124]*.

The American theatre had to reflect democratic ideals not only in the plays it produced, but also in its policy of pricing and style of acting: For instance, *Gleason's* demanded uniform prices because classification of seats by gradation of admission fees was considered undemocratic *[248]*. And Edwin Forrest was praised for creating an American school of acting, which embodied the democratic spirit of the national character *[216]*. The events of the Astor Place Riots in May 1849 testified that the masses regarded the theatre as a battlefield where the nation and its representatives had to be defended.

Anti-British sentiments had always been strong in the American theatre, although English actresses and actors were highly admired. Some nationalists argued that the decline of the theatre in America resulted from its servility to English theatrical fashion. It could only improve if managers and audiences stopped kowtowing to English taste. As a first step in this necessary process of separation it was suggested to make America's stage an "asylum" for the best traditional dramatists, because the English had rejected them in favor of the "puerilities of Spectacle" [68]. Some critics even contended that plays that had been successful on the English stage were not necessarily suitable for production in the United States because of the different standards Americans entertained [96].

Many tried to support American authors and foster the beginnings of an American drama in whatever ways they could. Therefore, a play dealing with national events or written by an American was never received objectively, let alone condemned, although critics were well aware of the considerable faults of the sometimes naive and crude productions [16]. Audiences were also willing to applaud unreservedly the daring of the endeavor rather than the quality of the achievement [19, 99].

As early as 1809 it was recognized that the lack of a copyright law impeded the development of a genuinely American drama because the aspiring playwright could not expect adequate recompense [40]. Many were confident that the passing of such a law by Congress in 1856 would finally give birth to a "permanent and respectable national drama" [253]. Some even suggested a tariff on imported plays to protect American drama against European competition [105].

Another difficulty American dramatists had to face was that the managers and actors, who for a long time were almost exclusively English, apparently refused to accept dramas that too openly propagated American (i.e., anti-British) sentiments and values [61]. Many critics, however, realized that the greatest barrier to an American drama was the inveterate prejudice in favor of anything that originated in England or France. It was due to this bias that the numerous American plays nonetheless written frequently met with contemptuous neglect.

With the passing of strident patriotism, the concept of a national drama was redefined: nationalism was no longer synonymous with spread-eagle chauvinism, but it came to mean "American originality" as contrasted with English conventionality. A national—or as most critics preferred to write, a native—drama was to depict "the new revelations of thought and experience" in the United States and had to be inspired by American democracy [160]. The tragedy of an average human life, for instance, was considered more appropriate for the American stage than the tragedy of kings and nobles, and American equality would provide domestic tragedy with new heroes: "the schoolmaster is one of the modern heroes" [160]. As regards comedy and farce the diversity of life in America and its multicultural society was thought to be a particularly rich mine. Critics with such a nationalist perspective praised Anna Cora Mowatt's *Fashion* (1845) because of its genuinely American moral: it showed "how the poorest and humblest may be noble, while the rich and aristocratic may be contemptible" *[195]*. Soon, however, originality was limited to new spectacular effects brought about by an elaborate stage mechanism, plots and characters followed a stereotyped pattern, especially so in dramas on national incidents or ethnic types.

It was also due to this change in the definition of theatrical nationalism that an American drama was no longer necessarily a vehicle for partisan politics *[162]*, although a dramatist was expected to respect the patriotic feelings of his or her audience *[222]*. But generally, in the middle of the nineteenth century, a national drama no longer meant a patriotic, but rather a "local" drama, in other words one "drawn from national sources," illustrating "periods and events in American History," or presenting "the features of national peculiarities, habits and manners" *[211]*. The critic of the *American Whig Review* went even further in warning against nationalism turning into parochialism and argued that American drama did not depend on the dramatists' choice of American localities or subjects, but on the literary quality of their dramatic treatment *[243]*.

The Theatre's Impact on Society

In addition to the moral and patriotic arguments in favor of an American drama and theatre, critics emphasized other manifest advantages: A theatre would not only provide a representative and decorative building for the recreation of the general public, attract visitors (and their custom and money), reduce the contrast between town and country, create jobs, and increase public revenue, but it would also offer destitute women a proper means of earning money *[9]*. This early argumentation from 1792 was taken up more than half a century later by M. D. Conway, who explained that the theatre provided well-paid employment for hundreds of people, spent more money than "all the Churches and Schools combined," meant better business for all trades in the community, and attracted strangers and their money. He also claimed that the theatre was the only democratic art form, and he was one of the first to put forward feminist arguments: In the theatre alone "full justice [was] done to woman, to both her labor and her intellectual dignity," only here was it "clearly understood that women [had] souls," and only here did a woman receive just payment that made her independent and saved her "from her most terrible temptation" *[272]*.

Once the usefulness of theatre for American society was more generally accepted, the social position of actors and actresses changed considerably and positively. Respectable citizens even attended meetings of the Dramatic Fund Association, founded in 1848 *[223]*. Some actors began to earn large fortunes, and actresses could now become independent and retire while still quite young *[247]*; in general, they became respected as useful and integrated members of society. But the militant tone in which, for instance, *The Albion* celebrated the first anniversary of the association (1849) *[223]* or in which *Putnam's* described the actors' social standing *[247]* suggests that a large part of the public still held an inveterate bias against the "agents of vice."

Toward Realism

In their search for additional proof of the potential usefulness of the theatre, critics pointed out that it could provide language lessons because of its influence on pronunciation and delivery and, more importantly, history lessons, because historical tragedies, if produced without "anachronisms" in their costuming, provided "the most accurate information, upon particular subjects of ancient history" *[30, also 67]*. These were the first arguments in favor of stage realism. Since historical instruction became generally accepted as one of the major duties of the stage, the repeated call for more realistic (i.e., historically accurate) properties and lifelike scenery was a standard point of criticism after 1815. In addition to this demand for realism of the mise-en-scène, there was also, very rarely though, an increasing demand for probability and authenticity of action and characterization in the melodramas. This was most obvious in the continued debate over the unacceptability of the soliloquy *[80]*.

One purpose of stage realism was, of course, to facilitate the identification of the audience with the world created on the stage. This fourth-wall realism was a prerequisite for the success of the burlesque in the 1840s, since the burlesque destroyed the unity of the dream world by caricature and ridicule. Because of its alienation devices some critics found fault with it. *The Knickerbocker*, for example, condemned it for disenchanting the members of the audience by familiarizing them with the mechanical tricks of the theatre *[174]*.

The Decline of the Drama

Another standard topic of critics was the much lamented decline of the drama. Some investigated its causes and found a "dearth of talent" *[112]*, the star system *[104]*, the commercialism of managers *[43]*, the prevalence of spectacles, the predilection for novels and magazines, and the competition from private parties *[112]*. The critic of *Emerson's Magazine and Putnam's Monthly* *[264]* attributed the "feebleness" of American drama to the fact that women were not granted an influential position in public life equal to that of men.

They were "powerless," "accounted inferior," and were restricted to the domestic circle so that dramatic authors had no models for their female characters; consequently their "women are either viragoes or imbeciles"; and the critic declared that there could be no American tragedy unless women were permitted to enjoy the republican principle of equality.

The defeat of the legitimate drama by melodrama, hippodrama, and acrobatic exhibitions was deplored time and again *[78]*, but obviously without much success. Traditional plays became almost the exotic exceptions and were produced on only a few stages, whereas the new forms of entertainment became the staple amusement of the playgoing masses. By some, melodramas were severely reprehended for the lack of lifelikeness in their plots and characters *[79]*. Audiences, however, were not irritated by the unrealistic inconsistencies of the melodramas. On the contrary, they were delighted by the nightly victory of heroic virtues over vicious depravity and clamorously relished the last minute resolutions of seemingly insuperable diffulties with the help of a deus ex machina. The *Spirit of the Times* even concluded that a drama, in order to be successful with the masses, must be "extravagant," rather than realistic *[173]*.

A strong critical concern in this second phase was the star system, which many held responsible for the decline of the stage *[104]*. Critics were undecided whether the system was to be blamed on the managers, who were accused of being only interested in financial gains, on the public, who demanded sensational novelty in all aspects, even in that of the cast, or on the actors themselves, on their "pride and vanity" *[177]*. Whatever the cause, the system had a disastrous effect on the quality of new plays, which had to be tailored to the specialties of the star; old plays were crippled accordingly.

The decline of the theatre by the introduction of sensational melodrama caused many a critic to resign and many a journal to discontinue its theatre column, for they were dissatisfied at writing weekly reports "upon performances which are remarkable for nothing but ignorance and stupidity, or wilful violations of common sense and propriety" *[83]*. Others had always kept a considerable distance from the theatre building because of the potential contagion of diseases, "dissipation and ruin" *[110]*. However, they agreed with the moral arguments in favor of the *drama* and therefore recommended the reading of the older plays, but warned against attending stage performances.

Suggestions for Improvement

The debate over how the American theatre should be improved was sharply divided among those who thought that the acknowledgment of the common inheritance of England and America was essential and that the best London productions should be imported *[73]*, and those who maintained that an unconditional separation from English theatrical decadence was necessary for a genuinely American departure in drama.

To terminate the decline of the drama and elevate it again to its early nineteenth-century level of quality, most critics advocated the return to the system of stock companies. Some suggested the elimination of afterpieces and demanded that actors, scenepainters, and property men serve the play again, not vice versa *[246]*. The Rev. Dr. Bellows, one of the most renowned spokesmen for the theatre in mid-century America, even blamed the immorality of the theatre on "the withdrawal . . . of the moral and religious portion of the community . . . from the pleasure-loving resorts of the people," and he called upon clergymen and leading citizens to patronize the theatre in order to improve it. In his enthusiastic defense of stage entertainment he even smeared his own profession by arguing that the theatre, being only a "mirror of bad times," had "no serious vices of its own . . . like the Church, with hypocrisy and arrogance" *[265]*.

Dramatic Criticism

As theatre grew in size and support, newspapers and journals paid increasing attention to theatrical events, demanding free admission for their critics and soliciting advertisements from the managers who, in turn, could expect indiscriminately positive notices. Conversely, managers rewarded favorable critiques with well-paid insertions, free tickets, and other gratuities. Puffing was very common, and some, as Whitman observed, wrote their reviews before the play discussed was even performed [204]. Not every critic was so conscientious as Poe, who went to see *Fashion* several times before he wrote his review. Very soon the more serious critics reproved the low quality of the press notices of their dishonest and incompetent colleagues and reprimanded the widespread practice of puffing *[125, 282]*. Frequently they expounded the responsibilities of the dramatic critic, which one of them defined as "to check [the drama's] abuses, to refine its character, and render it subservient to purposes of moral good" [129]. So in this second phase dramatic criticism and the stage were judged with the same categories of usefulness.

1860–1915: CONTINUITY AND THE DEBATE OVER REALISM

After the Civil War, the debate over the characteristics of what constituted a genuinely American drama was, of course, continued. It developed in the direction it had taken after the redefinition of theatrical nationalism, and consequently Brander Matthews argued against the conception of American drama as a local art and in favor of its universality *[316]*. Others, in contrast, still claimed that an American play had to present American characters in an American setting and should be "thoroughly American in tone" *[341]*.

Morality

The controversy over the morality of theatrical entertainment was taken up again and again with very much the same arguments that had been current before the Civil War. The majority of the critics still regarded the theatre as a school of moral instruction and, for example, entreated Jefferson to make his *Rip Van Winkle* "a veritable temperance-lecture" *[326]*. Even if the attitude toward the representation of immorality on the stage changed with the realist movement, fundamentally the realists at the end of the nineteenth century were as didactic as the moralists at its beginning, for their "mission" still was "to interest and to instruct" *[381]*. However, in order to achieve these ends they did not stop short of breaking moral and social taboos, and so their plays were unacceptable to the conservative majority of the public. Many Americans were not prepared to follow Edward Harrigan's argumentation that, since vice and sin were obvious elements of modern life, they had to be represented on the stage, although in the end virtue should always be triumphant *[348]*. Alfred Hennequin testified to the prevalence of a conventional taste and asserted that nothing but poetic justice would be accepted by an American audience, who would not even consent to having serious social problems or "delicate questions" *[354]* discussed on the stage. In contrast, feminists thought that the stage should give much more space to the treatment of the pressing problems of contemporary society such as the alarmingly high number of divorces, the struggle for women's suffrage, the position of "women in the professions," or "the sudden awakening of the sheltered woman to a knowledge of prostitution and venereal diseases" *[490]*. Clayton Hamilton was among the few who disapproved of such "journalistic plays" not on moral, but on literary grounds: by "allying their work with journalism our playwrights are withholding it from literature." Otherwise he defended these dramas on topical issues against charges of indecency and clearly preferred them to superficial plays that treated no problems at all *[484]*.

Marc Klaw of the theatrical syndicate was the most outspoken critic of the persistent charge that the theatre had to assume a moral and educational obligation to society. He maintained that there had never been a demand by the public to be educated, and the theatre, being run on strictly commercial rules, had always tried to meet the demands of the public *[420]*. In an equally provocative denial of another theatrical assumption, he asserted that the theatre in America was not a public institution, but a private enterprise, financed by private capital. Consequently, the public had no right to dictate to the managers, nor was the theatre entitled "to dictate to public taste." Howells also attacked the conception that the theatre had to moralize: "They have no scruple in luring you to the theater and then letting you realize that you are as in a church, under a machine-gun fire of homilies from a pulpit that calls itself a stage" *[494]*. Reading about such a controversy we feel taken back into the eighteenth century.

Redefining Realism

The call for realism or, as some now preferred to term it, naturalism or veritism, became more persistent in this third phase. Critics realized that the smaller stages in the recently erected theatre buildings permitted the performance of more social and private plays—in contrast to the grand heroism of the drama of the past—and they welcomed the increase in familiarity because it was more appropriate for the age. However, they complained that the opportunities were not used, that actors, for example, kept on hitching and strutting instead of walking like ordinary human beings. In general, whereas realism in the second phase was defined as authenticity and probability, it now denoted a fidelity to the common lives of average contemporary people. Consequently, the plot was required to be based on the everyday experience of the common man and represent "the manners of the time" *[286]*. Whereas the aim of the melodrama and spectacle was to make the audience laugh and forget about reality outside the theatre, the new drama that critics (not audiences, though) now increasingly demanded was to address the intellect of the audience and to remind them of real life.

Some critics, however, found the detailed depiction of the ordinary life of the common man and woman not very exciting *[309]*. Alfred Hennequin faulted the new movement because it meant the death of drama; he argued that many of the conventions the advocates of naturalism wanted to abolish were essential to the stage and that naturalism in the theatre was demanded by writers of prose fiction who were "not at home in stageland" *[360]*. Boucicault also doubted the premise of the naturalist arguments and flatly denied "that the drama is, or ever was intended to be, a copy of Nature" *[358]*.

The call for dramatic realism brought about the so-called society comedies, which, in many cases, used pre–Civil War theatre conventions and developed them, sometimes even to a more or less obnoxious extreme. The use of background music was extended *[287]*, the showy elements became more dazzling, the dresses of fast women in gaudy burlesques more daring. The critic of the *Galaxy* summarized and faulted these tendencies: "The current drama seems to develop . . . in two directions—first, into the millinery plays, and secondly, into the railroad smash-up plays" *[310]*. As a rule, productions were now mounted with extraordinary "pictorial splendour of . . . setting" and unprecedented historical accuracy *[300]*. The mania for realistic scenery resulted in "real fountains, real cascades, real trout-streams" on the mid-century stage where, of course, everything had to be practicable *[304]*. Edward Harrigan was proud of his minutely photographic realism and that he was able to name the real-life models for his interior scenes *[348]*. William Gillette rejected the photographic realism of the society plays as "actualism" and advocated a return to "the principle of suggestiveness" *[348]*.

The Decline of the Drama

The complaints about the decline of the drama continued unabated, just as the search for its reasons did, although occasionally there was now the flat denial of a degradation of the stage and the announcement that theatres were improving *[329]*. Augustin Daly boldly stated: "The status of the theatre was never as good as it is at present" *[348]*. Only very rarely were new ideas and arguments proffered. Boucicault, in his explanation of the causes of the decline of the theatre, on the one hand repeated the widely accepted opinion that nineteenth-century intellect had assumed functions other than literary or aesthetic; it was occupied by explorations and inventions instead. On the other hand he blamed the state of the theatre on the newspapers; as people were increasingly "busy in commercial affairs" they turned to the newspapers to furnish them with ready-made opinions; the man of literary inclinations became a newspaper critic who had to turn out opinions on a daily basis, and "this eternal diarrhoea of thought ... debilitated his mental system" and the stress forced him "to cover with pertness of style his baldness of treatment" *[325]*.

With the beginning of the new century the major blame for the decadence of the drama was assigned to the theatrical syndicate, although at first critics had to concede that the monopoly led to a considerable improvement in the commercial side of the theatre: productions showed a higher standard of scenery and actors worked under better conditions *[400]*. But, as Belasco, who valiantly fought the syndicate, convincingly demonstrated, the pernicious potential of the system was soon developed to the extreme *[419]*.

Suggestions for Improvement

Occasionally, critics and influential theatre people suggested remedies. F.A.A. Mathews advocated public censorship by granting "absolute copyright" *[372]* to the dramatic writer, who could then consent to the printing of his plays without risk; the reading public would function as a censor by not attending or warning against attending performances of plays of which it did not approve. Howells even recommended institutionalized censorship; the Board of Education should examine all the plays to be staged and "forbid those ethically or aesthetically bad" [380]. Generally critics emphasized the public's responsibility for the state of the drama. Time and again it was blamed for its patronage of the degraded theatre, thus making itself an accomplice of vice. Some feminists called upon women to use their influence as "the dominant force in all social laws" and thus to "set the standard for plays" [404].

Others sought salvation in a change of the theatrical system of the nation. Some critics proposed the establishment of a representative National Theatre, which, according to James S. Metcalfe, would be educationally instrumental in the purification of speech and the refinement of manners [423]. Charles Meltzer saluted Conried's project of a New Theatre prematurely as the realization of this dream of a National Theatre *[434]*. Boucicault even suggested founding "a university of the arts" *[358]*. Many others demanded endowed theatres after the European model, with the only difference that the American independent theatres would, of course, have to be financed by private donations *[369]*, and these numerous appeals did not go unheeded, since in the 1890s the papers report many projects for endowed theatres.

New Beginnings

Just as Tyler's *The Contrast* (1787) in the first phase of American dramatic criticism and Mowatt's *Fashion* (1845) in the second were hailed as inaugurating the much longed for American Drama, Herne's *Margaret Fleming* (1891) was received with equal enthusiasm as "an epoch-marking drama," "a bold innovation" *[361]*. Interestingly enough, in his eulogium the critic of *The Arena* saw the great merit of the play in its "utility," a term that had been at the center of theatrical criticism in America since the beginning of the century. *Margaret Fleming*, for him, proved the theatre an effective and powerful means of social "progress and reform" *[361]*. Hamlin Garland, although also full of praise for the play's unconventionality, found it not sufficiently radical, because of its still too contrived plot *[363]*. Others harshly contradicted the encomia and criticized the "sociological fads" of the new movement *[364]*. They agreed that realism was just another word for vulgarity *[369]*.

Due to the changes in the American theatre at the turn of the century, the number of articles that tried to predict the future of the American drama increased. Of particular interest is Helen Potter's prophecy, inspired by socialism, that the stage will "become again ... the best friend of the proletariat" *[390]* and that the "new hero" of the new century will be "a worker" who, on the stage, will move in "his own environment." William Mailly also emphasized the sociological relevance of the future drama *[437]*.

A new departure was the moving-picture show, which was seen as an inevitable result of the machine age *[456]*. Interestingly enough, its early reception was as divided as that of the drama had been over a hundred years before.

Again some leveled charges of immorality because they foresaw homes corrupted and children stealing in order to obtain the admission fee [456].

The first decade of the twentieth century was especially fertile for the American drama. George Jean Nathan reported about a "play-writing mania" [453], caused, however, not by artistic or literary inspiration but by manifest financial interests, as the theatre was supposed to offer the shortest way to a large fortune. Clayton Hamilton commented upon an undue demand for plays and an "over-production" generated by an excessive number of theatres [454]. In a similar manner John Corbin complained that "with the multiplication of theatres the drama has become a machine-made commodity handled wholesale" [485].

Since this surfeit of plays and productions was solely motivated by commercial interest, it could obviously not lead to a reform of American drama and theatre. Salvation had to be sought outside the established theatre business, as the agents of the numerous theatrical experiments clearly perceived. In a "revolt against Broadway" [485], theatre enthusiasts tried to improve the drama and the theatre by organizing the public and thus ensuring the success of what they conceived to be good plays; by a system of recommended patronage the numerous drama leagues throughout the country exercised the public censorship Howells and others had encouraged. The most radical revolt against Broadway, however, was recommended by Howells, who turned his back on all theatrical entertainment, preferring to read a play at home [494].

Critics who closely observed American drama and theatre in the second decade of the twentieth century repeatedly prophesied an imminent and decisive turn away from the theatre as a business and toward drama as an art. In 1913 Clayton Hamilton, an acquaintance of James O'Neill, felt that American drama was "in a state of transition" [484]; in 1910 he had predicted that "the conditions [for a new beginning] are ripe, and all that is needed is the men; and it is one of the miracles of destiny that when great work is ready to be done, the necessary men arise to do it" [459]. Sheldon Cheney, in 1914, also noticed promising signs [488]. *The Nation* even saw a great chance for the drama in the extremely popular moving-picture shows; they endangered only the profit-seeking theatre and could lead to an ultimate separation of the drama from its greatest enemy, commercialism [496]. The history of American drama proved these prophets right: O'Neill and the Provincetown Players were preparing to pave a new way for American drama and theatre.

NOTES

1. Walter J. Meserve, *An Emerging Entertainment: The Drama of the American People to 1828* (Bloomington: Indiana University Press, 1977), 16.
2. "Theatre," *The Friend* (Albany) 1 (Aug. 1815): 53–54.

3

An Anthology of American Dramatic Criticism, 1746–1915: Jeremiads and Eulogies

[1] [The Wickedness of the Theatre]
The American Magazine and Historical Chronicle [1746]

Should I pretend to give a View of the Wickedness of the Theatre, I should not know where to begin, or to what Length the Subject would carry me. For whether I insisted on the Lewdness or Impiety of most of the Plays themselves, on the infamous Characters of the Actors and Actresses, on the scandalous Farces they commonly tag the gravest Plays with, or, above all, on the inhumanly impudent Dances and Songs, with which they lard them between the Acts; I say, which soever of these Particulars I insisted on, each of them would furnish Matter for a great many Pages; and much more, if I should enter upon a full View of them all. Indeed the Theatre is at present on such a Footing in *England*, that it is impossible to enter it and not come out the worse for having been in it; for, now-a days, a good Play is no other than a Trap to draw in the Modest and Innocent to a Love of Theatrical Entertainments: And the Minds of the Spectators are not the safer from being polluted and debauched, tho' the Play itself be in the main decent & modest; since the ingenious Contrivance of the Managers entirely prevents the good Effect of any worthy Sentiment expressed in the Play, by introducing a painted Strumpet at the End of every Act, to cut Capers on the Stage in such an impudent and unwomanly Manner, as must make the most shocking Impressions on every Mind; and, lest the Audience should chance in spite of all this to carry away somewhat that might make their Hearts the better, a ludicrous and shameless Farce concludes the whole, and with one Stroke erases all the little Traces of virtuous Sentiments that were formed by the Play itself.

I only beg leave to ask you, my dear Countrymen, for what Purpose you support a sacred Order of Men to teach you the pure and holy Laws of the Christian Religion, and at the same Time encourage by your Countenance and your Riches a Sett of the very Dregs of Human Nature, who make it their Business to debauch your Minds by their lewd Compositions and wanton Gesticulations, to fill them with impure and vile Ideas, and to disappoint the most diligent Endeavours of a Christian Ministry? Surely it can never be consistent with common Sense to support in the same Country one Order of Men for the Propagation of Virtue and Religion, and another for the Destruction of them; to maintain one Sett of People for promoting a Reformation of Manners, and another for promoting an universal Corruption.

It is the Saying of a great Man of the last Age, That upon some Accounts it were better that wicked Men would fairly renounce Christianity, than continue to profess it, and at the same Time disgrace it by their scandalous Lives. And indeed it could be no such Matter of Grief to good Men to see a Nation of *Barbarians* over run with Vice and Debauchery, as to see this Kingdom, once illustrious for its Purity in Doctrine and Practice, celebrated for its Martyrs, and which pretends to be the grand Bulwark of the Protestant Religion; to see this Kingdom, I say, thus sunk to a Pitch of Wickedness and Lewdness in its publick Entertainments, which at *Athens*, where they worshipped the unknown God, would have thrown the celebrated Diversions of the Stage into utter Disgrace.

And are these the favourite Pleasures that so wholly ingross and bewitch a Christian Nation, that we cannot live without them, even while an Enemy is laying waste our Country, and is expected every Hour at our very Gates [the reference is to King George's War]? For my part, I cannot say I am sure, whether, if it had been our miserable Fate to have had our Metropolis burnt to the Ground, and the Inhabitants put to the Sword by the Rebels, they would not have found us upon their Arrival engaged in hearing Musick and seeing Plays, and whether Numbers had not been sent by them directly from the Play-house into another World.

That I may not appear singular in my Sentiments upon Theatrical Entertainments, I will add the Judgments of a few (out of innumerable that might be inserted) of the wisest Men of ancient and modern Times, which will strengthen what I have said.

[Here the author quotes Plutarch, Cicero, Bishop Burnet, and Archbishop Tillotson.]

[3] [Arguments in Favor of the Theatre]
The New England Magazine of Knowledge and Pleasure [1758]

Theatrical Representations *not* condemned; the harmless Recreations of the *over-righteous* indulged; and a *high-strained Compliment* to uncharitable Clergymen.

When Tyranny *with* Superstition *join'd,*
As that *the Body,* this *enslav'd the Mind:*
Much was believ'd, *but little* understood,
And to be dull *was constru'd to be* good:
All comic Entertainments *were decry'd*
By superstitious Fear and gloomy Pride.

1. That there should be some gloomy Spirits in all Sects averse to Theatrical Representations in general, is not to be wondered at: But if these have inveighed against Plays, they have likewise as bitterly inveighed against each other's religious Principles and Practices: And if they have agreed in condemning the *Theatre*, they have likewise agreed in condemning very innocent Things; as the wearing of *Perriwigs*, the taking of *Snuff*, and the smoaking of *Tobacco*. Where *Superstition* mixes with Religion, she frequently paints the Deity as a sour morose Being, disgusted with Chearfulness and Gaiety in his Children, offended with their Amusements and Diversions, and delighted only with Penance and Mortification. Her Votaries are often fighting against Nature and Reason; embracing Things that are painful because they are disagreeable; and denying themselves innocent Gratifications, because they are pleasing. But the bountiful Creator has given Man an *Eye* to be delighted with beautiful Appearances, an *Ear* to enjoy Harmony, and a *Taste* to relish not only the Variety of Food intended him, but every Convenience and even *Elegance* of Life. We are here happily situated in a *free Country*, under a *good Prince*, and a *mild Government*; and it is not at present unlawful for any Man, or Sett of Men, to be entertained in any Manner not injurious to their Neighbours.

2. If there are any among us, that chuse to cloister themselves up in Cells, because Sun-shine, Air, and Liberty are pleasing to Human Nature; if any chuse Silence or discordant Sounds, because the Sense of Hearing is delighted with Musick; if any will whip themselves because Nature is averse to Pain; if they will watch and pray at Mid night, because they are then most sleepy; or fast all Day, because they are then most hungry; they may do so; and let us by no Means grudge them these their harmless Diversions. On the other Hand, let not those who have fettered themselves by their own too rigid Rules, (and therefore cannot enjoy Entertainments of a more agreeable Kind, how much soever they desire them) envy those that have preserved their Liberty, nor endeavour to deprive them of it.

[4] [The Moral Usefulness of Plays]
The Speech of Joseph Tisdale [1767]

[. . .] THEATRES have ever been countenanced in all free and civilized countries, and when plays are under good regulation, they are of admirable use, by carrying conviction into the mind with such irresistable force and energy, as to engage the whole faculties and powers of the soul in the cause of virtue; and the same faculties and powers will also be engaged in stifling vice in its first principles, or in its feeble beginnings; this is not too much to be attributed to a *Tragedy*:—what can be more engaging and instructive to the mind, than to see Cato represented dying for his country? What more soothing to the mind after the fatigues of a day, than to see the representation of friends; the delicate and constant fathers; just children; tender, grateful and affectionate wives, faithful and obliging?—We ought to be very careful, and take care, that we drive not our youths from such noble amusements to the practice of something much more shameful and destructive, though perhaps more secret. [. . .] Need I say any thing more to impress upon this honorable assembly an opinion of an entertainment so pregnant with blessings?—Methinks I have said enough: But I have still something further [. . .]. Since I have been upon the stage of action, I have observed the clergy in general have made it their business to cry down all kinds of *Theatrical performances*; and it is not to be wondered at, since there is such a temporal interest depending upon their doing of it; if they had not done it, possibly there might by this time have risen up a set of people, that would have taken a more effectual method to improve the morals, and excite sentiments of virtue and religion, than what they have done:—A set of people I say, might have risen up, that would have taught the people in general, to have thought too wisely for the temporal interest of the clergy; but I dont say too wisely for the interest of Christ.—I have sometimes thought we seem to conduct as though we were about to set up and establish the kingdom of Christ by laws of our own making, which never can be done: it is not the warden law nor a *thousand white staff men* that will do it, nor prevent its being set up, where it is to be set up, neither will the law; for the kingdom of Christ takes its course like lightning, and it is not to be directed by man, nor by the laws of men.—But to return more immediately to the point in question, and before I proceed any further, I shall acknowledge I never saw a *Play* acted in my life, therefore I am not so well able to let forth the beauty, the excellency, and the usefullness they are of to mankind in general, as though I had seen them acted; I have only had the advantage of reading them, and I dont imagine that my reading them has taught me to dispise religion, virtue nor honesty; but rather taught me to be more in favour of them; all this is the effect it has had upon me.—I should not have said so much was it not that I apprehend that the clergy were at the bottom of this motion; and I have no notion of having the general court rul'd by the clergy, while I have a seat here.—In ancient times the clergy did as they pleas'd with the general court; then Quakers were hanged for witches; and they had a curious method of trying them, by binding them and throwing them into the water; if they could swim bound, they were taken out and hanged for witches, if not, they were only drowned;—this is some of the good fruits that arise by the general court's being rul'd and dictated by the clergy of old. [. . .]

[6] [Votes and Proceedings of the Continental Congress]
The Boston Gazette and Country Journal [1774]

[. . .] To obtain redress of these grievances, which threaten destruction to the lives, liberty, and property of his Majesty's subjects in North-America, we are of opinion, that a non-importation, non-consumption, and non-exportation agreement [. . .] will prove the most speedy, effectual, and peacable measure:—And therefore we do, for ourselves, and the inhabitants of the several Colonies, whom we represent, firmly agree and associate under the sacred ties of virtue, honor, and love of our country, as follows:
[. . .]
Eight. That we will in our several stations encourage frugality, economy, and industry; and promote agriculture, arts, and the manufactures of this country, especially that of wool; and will discountenance and discourage, every species of extravagance and dissipation, especially all horse-racing, and all kinds of gaming, cock fighting, exhibitions of shews, plays, and other expensive diversions and entertainments. [. . .]

[7] [Report of a Committee of the Assembly of Pennsylvania, on Licencing a Theatre in Philadelphia]
The American Museum, or, Universal Magazine [1789]

[. . .] The committee have had to withstand the force of a very serious and important objection made to the stage, that it has ever been a great corrupter of the public morals; but this position, as one of a speculative nature, is not capable of complete demonstration—it is even doubted whether it is to be maintained; the better opinion seems to be, that dramatic pieces, in common with other works of taste and sentiment, tend to the general refinement of manners and the polish of society, than which nothing can be more favourable to the growth of the virtues.

In this regard, it may be said, that men, in appearance the farthest removed from the influence of the stage, have obligations to it, which they neither perceive nor own.

But your committee have been led to contemplate the stage as the great mart of genius, and as such, a natural and necessary concomitant of our independence.—We have cast off a foreign yoke in government, but shall still be dependent for those productions of the mind, which do most honour to human nature, until we can afford due protection and encouragement to every species of our own literature.

In these sentiments, your committee offer the following resolution:

<u>Resolved</u>, That a special committee be appointed to bring in a bill to licence a theatre in or near the city of Philadelphia for dramatic representations.

To the general assembly of Pennsylvania.

The memorial and petition of the people called quakers, in the city of Philadelphia, Respectfully sheweth,

That at the early settlement of Pennsylvania the preservation of the morals of the inhabitants was considered, by the legislature, essential to the well-being and prosperity of the community, and many wise laws were enacted for the suppression of vice and immorality, which appeared to them likely to be greatly promoted by stage entertainments, wherever they were permitted; and accordingly, the assemblies passed divers acts from time to time, to prohibit them, although disallowed by the rulers in Great Britain, who then exercised a controul over the legislature here; their exceptions being founded on maxims of mere human policy, rather than virtuous considerations.—Nevertheless, the virtue of the people, for a considerable time, manifested such an abhorrence of those ensnaring diversions, that the stage actors did not find it their interest to prosecute their corrupting employment. And, since the late revolution, the legislature, actuated by laudable motives, enacted a law, entitled, *An act for the prevention of vice and immorality, and unlawful gaming, and to restrain disorderly sports and dissipation*, passed in 1786, (for a repeal of which a petition was presented to the late house of assembly by Lewis Hallam and John Henry, in behalf of themselves and other comedians) notwithstanding which, in defiance of its authority, regardless of the penalties, and in contempt of government, those delusive scenes have, in the course of last summer, been exhibited, and, as appears by public advertisements, are of late renewed.

Other persons, also, promoters of licentiousness, at the same time continued amusements among the people of the like pernicious tendency. Whereupon, affected with concern that these exhibitions should be revived at any time, but more especially when a stagnation of commerce, a scarcity of money, and a great appearance of a failure of the staple of this country, from the alarming destruction of our wheat by an unusual insect, require a serious attention to an improvement in every moral and religious duty: an address was presented to the executive council on the eighteenth day of the seventh month last, setting forth our just apprehensions, respecting such entertainments, which are not founded on mere speculative opinion; it being not only the sense of divers persons, conspicuous for wisdom and virtue, resulting from their religious observation and experience, but supported by incontrovertible fact. [. . .]

Influenced by a sense of duty, and a sincere regard for the youth and others of the present day, we are engaged to request your serious attention to the premises, and that you may reject the application of the said Lewis Hallam and John Henry, however supported by plausible, though fallacious pretensions.

And we earnestly desire the same laudable zeal which influenced your predecessors in their virtuous endeavours to preserve the morals of the people from depravity, may induce you to reject an offer, which proposes to raise a revenue by so currupt a practice, at the risque of the virtue, happiness, and solid reputation of the people.

And lastly, that you will make such further provision, for the due execution of the law before mentioned, as also to prevent jugglers, mountebanks, rope-dancers, and other immoral and irreligious entertainments, as, under the direction of best wisdom, you may see meet. [. . .]

To the honourable the general assembly of Pennsylvania, the subscribers, being a committee of the dramatic association, on behalf of themselves and the many citizens, who have prayed for a repeal of any law, or part of a law, that prohibits dramatic entertainments, beg leave, with the utmost respect, to submit the following representation:

[. . .]

The drama is now a subject of earnest discussion; from a topic of private conversation, it has become the object of legislative decision, and contending parties are formed, on the one hand denying, and on the other asserting, the propriety of tolerating the stage.

Let us, therefore, for a moment suppose, that in wisdom, virtue, fortune, and patriotism, these parties are equal—are there any collateral circumstances which can then determine the weight of argument? Here truth dictates a reflexion, on which we appeal to the candour of this honourable house.

Those, who wish the establishment of the drama, desire a thing, which it is in the power of their opponents, deeming it an evil, to avoid, even after it is established; and which, at all events, intrudes upon no right, and interferes with no privilege. But those who wish the prohibition of the drama, seek to deprive their opponents of what they consider as a rational enjoyment, and, by their success, will abridge the natural right of every freeman, to dispose of his time and money, according to his own taste and disposition, when not obnoxious to the real interests of society.

[. . .]

We do not conceive it to be necessary, at this time, to suggest to your honourable house, the arguments which have been employed in favour of the drama, by the wisest and most virtuous characters, in the most enlightened nations. Nor shall we attempt to deny, that men of a similar description, have controverted the utility of the institution. It is enough for our purpose, that the difference of opinion is so evident, as to render the subject, in that respect, a matter of mere speculation; for in addressing the wisdom of the legislature, while, on the one hand, we cannot admit, that a theatre is the temple of vice, we presume not to insist that it is the school of virtue. As a rational amusement, it is the object of our wishes; and the whole force of our reasoning is directed only to shew, that those who regard it in a contrary light, are not entitled to controul our sentiments, or to compel the adoption of what they profess. If, indeed, a mere difference of opinion, shall be thought a sufficient foundation to curtail our rights, and diminish our enjoyments, the boasted liberality of the present age, will be eclipsed by a comparison with the [illegible] bigotry of the middle centuries; and the same authority which proscribes our amusements, may, with equal justice, dictate the shape and texture of our dress, or the modes and ceremonies of our worship.

This, however, is an evil, which, we are confident, cannot receive the countenance of a legislature, elected to protect and insure the equal rights of the citizens of a free commonwealth. [. . .]

[8] [Royall Tyler's *The Contrast*, 1787]
The Universal Asylum and Columbian Magazine [1790]

The situation of our country hitherto has been such, as would not admit of cultivating every part of knowledge. Most men have been assiduously employed in gaining a subsistence; and those few, who have devoted themselves to science, have necessarily been more engaged in the acquisition of what may be strictly termed useful knowledge, than of that which is more properly called ornamental. Poetry and the drama have been little attended to. Some specimens have indeed been given of the former, which shew that a poetic genius is not denied to America; and there is every reason to expect that, as we become more at leisure to contemplate the numerous scenes of our extensive territory, where grandeur, beauty, and novelty are combined, poetic imaginations will be formed amongst us, which will rival the celebrated bards of the eastern continent. Many incidents of the late revolution, when time shall have spread over them the mantle of obscurity, will afford excellent subjects for sublime and pathetic tragedy. And it does not appear chimerical to assert, that the comic muse may fix among us, under peculiarly favourable circumstances. In Europe, comedy, like every other species of writing, has been carried to such an extent, as almost to have exhausted the subject matter. Scarcely a character has escaped the notice of the comic writers of the present or former days. Hence they are reduced now to this alternative, either to draw characters which are not in nature, or to atone for the want of novelty in character, by novelty of sentiment. The former practice is frequently ridiculous, and sometimes disgusting; the latter has produced a motley species of writing, which might be termed, tragedy without bloodshed.

As the state of society and manners in America differs materially from those in Europe, new characters must necessarily be produced, of which the dramatic writer may avail himself. We have here people from every part of Europe, whose manners are variously intermixed and blended, producing a compound entirely unknown in Europe. We have foibles peculiar to ourselves, which seem to require the assistance of the laughing muse. Satire does not seem suited to our genius. We cannot bear its lash. It would rather aggravate than reform. But we may perhaps be laughed out of our follies.

The comedy before us levels its attack principally against a character, which is not yet very frequent amongst us, a travelled American, who returns to his native country, with a sovereign contempt for its customs and manners, and a firm attachment to foreign vices and follies. [. . .]

The characters are well drawn, and well preserved. No one is, perhaps, entirely new, except that of Jonathan, a plain, untutored Yankee. [. . .]

The dialogue is sprightly, and correct. There are many excellent strokes of wit and humour; and some admirable sentiments well expressed. The reader will not find the continued flashes of wit, of the comedies of the last century, nor an uninterrupted succession of hacknied sentiments, which tires and disgusts us in the modern comedy. This seems to steer a middle course between the two. In some respects, we could wish that it bore less resemblance to the comedies of Charles II. reign, as there are some passages which border on indelicacy.

We cannot by any means pronounce this a perfect comedy. Little or no adherence has been paid to rules. It approaches in some degree to those performances, which have been called, farces in five acts. But as it is the first American attempt at this species of composition, and as it may induce others to follow and improve upon it, we think it worthy of the public attention, and cheerfully add our tribute of applause, to that which has been already bestowed by the public on this performance, at its different representations. [. . .]

[9] [Economic and Other Reasons for Establishing a Theatre]
The Massachusetts Magazine [1792]

[Review of the book:] *Effects of the Stage on the Manners of a People, and the propriety of encouraging and establishing a virtuous Theatre.* By a Bostonian. Printed by Young and Etheridge.
[. . .]
The Theatre will invite foreigners to reside in Boston, and leave much money therein.

Invites Spectators from the adjacent towns, etc. many of whom will be induced to purchase their wares and merchandise.

Proposes to save the cash carried out to commencement, and will bring much money into town.

The building will furnish employ to mechanicks, artificers and labourers, and thus half maintain their families and many such, after finished.

Obtains without cost, a grand ornamental building, the pride of America, which, beside the purpose of a Theatre, will serve for many other uses.

The building, when paid for, will become the property of the town, and bring in a large clear revenue.

Which will operate as a remission of poor rates.

The entries, piazza, etc. will afford the most pleasant walk for the healthy gentlemen and ladies, and expedite the recovery of the valetudinary.

The tendency of this Theatre is to reform manners, enforce good order, suppress mobs, etc. etc. etc.

Proposes relaxations from hard labour, study, business, etc. as well by games, lectures, etc. as by the Theatre.

Withdraws from taverns, alehouses, gaming houses, and bad houses, those who have formerly haunted such places, and will render them detestable.

Preserves the indigent helpless female from the necessity of earning bread by improper means.

Attempts to establish harmony, love and esteem between the country and the town, by shewing that they mutually help and enrich each other, and that though the merchant hath some fine shewy advantages, that nature hath amply compensated all these to the country, nay more, hath been partial to them, and it gives them an invitation to come and partake with their brethren in town at the feast of souls.

Proposes games and sports to strengthen the body, and to awake a spirit of emulation, serving to invigorate the mind and give it confidence in its own powers.

The military evening exercises and lectures, will tend to form soldiers in time of peace, will prevent invasions, and become a strong defence in time of war.

The incomes from this Theatre are intended to establish manufactures that shall become great national objects—To employ the able and maintain the helpless poor.

Such manufactures will employ multitudes of people in every part of the state, increase the demand for provision, for iron, hemp, flax, and all other things necessary to carry on such works.

Will invite tradesmen and manufacturers from Europe, multiply the number of inhabitants, and increase the wealth and power of the state in like proportion.

[11] [The Theatre "hurtful to morals and happiness"]
The Weekly Magazine [1798]

To ascertain the tendency of plays is by no means difficult. There is no more powerful mode of winning the attention, and swaying the passions of mankind. Mental power is quite a different consideration from the moral application of that power. Genius affords no security from error. The writers of plays have been generally necessitous and profligate. They have therefore written under the influence of wrong conceptions of duty and happiness; and, in order to effect their purpose, which was gain, have deemed themselves obliged to humour the caprices and pamper the vicious appetites, of those who frequent these spectacles.

This surely is no inequitable statement of the motives of dramatic writers. A very slight acquaintance with plays will convince us that this is the fact. It is equally easy to account for it: Nay, the circumstances of mankind have been such as to render this effect unavoidable. Our pieces are the productions of British writers. That this nation is luxurious and corrupt; that the progress of commerce and refinement have widely diffused the plagues of luxury and poverty; that those classes of the people who chiefly frequent the theatre are the opulent and voluptuous on the one hand, and, on the other, the ignorant and debauched, will surely be readily admitted. That dramatic writers have seldom been distinguished by purity of morals; that they have written to supply their pecuniary cravings, and have therefore studiously accommodated themselves to the circumstances of the times and the taste of their audience, is no less incontestible. [...]

It is commonly observed that the plays of a later period [i.e., after the reign of Charles II] are less impure. It must be owned that manners have improved since that period, but the improvement is extremely slight. The tragedies are pompous, and, to the majority of theatrical spectators, totally unmeaning. Kings and nobles, of some remote age, and acting upon maxims foreign to the experience of men of the present times and of middling classes, speaking a language as unintelligible as Greek, and raving about thrones and mistresses, are not very edifying examples to the multitude. The comedies are strings of incidents occurring among persons of a polished rank in society, interlarded with the blunders of the ignorant, and the vices of the poor; and embellished with spurious or obscene wit. The farces are replete with broad mirth, low buffoonery, and pictures, which for their vulgarity and grossness, are well adapted to the taste of the majority of play-goers.

[...] It is sufficiently manifest that the influence of these exhibitions, so far as that influence ought to be ascribed to the nature of the scene exhibited, is hurtful to morals and happiness. [...]

[...] Artful seducers, specious profligates, lying valets, female votaries of voluptuousness and vanity, in the form of prodigal coquets and pert chambermaids, compose, for the most part, the theatrical world. It is easy to see what inexpressible advantage actors must derive from laboriously imprinting on their memory and feelings the sentiments peculiar to all these characters!

One of the merits of popular dramas is, that they are genuine copies of life and manners. This merit cannot be denied to them. Let no man look upon the world with an accurate and comprehensive scrutiny. The spectacle will drive him into madness. Whither shall he look and not find a deluge of crimes and miseries? All the baneful passions, subversive of our own happiness and that of others, rage without control in the present condition of human society. They are powerfully delineated on the stage, and are regarded by the infatuated multitude with delight and applause. But this perhaps is an unreasonable view of the subject. The fidelity of theatrical representation is one thing: The influence of this profession on an actor is another. [. . .]

[. . .] It has been said, that time and money spent at the play-house would be spent at brothels and taverns, if theatres were unknown. This is a mistake. The play-house has ever been found to be an avenue to the taverns and the stews. The habits of dissipation and expence which this amusement has an evident tendency to foster, are favourable to all the more flagitious misapplications of our time. [. . .]

[. . .] It is likewise certain that there are numerous ways in which time and money may be used, within the reach of every one, more advantageous than this, and which, therefore, it is our duty to prefer. [. . .]

[12] [The Stage "an avenue to the knowledge of the actual state of mankind"]
The Weekly Magazine [1798]

[. . .] Plays are pictures of the world, and the world abounds with error and vice. What more can be said on the subject? It seems idle to talk about the injuries which arise from contemplating the world. What alternative have we? Because every part of the world is tainted with follies and crimes, shall we hide ourselves with hermits in a wilderness, and estrange ourselves from human intercourse?

History is a tissue of crimes and calamities. Its authors are at least of as dubious integrity and as liable to mistaken views as the dramatic writers. This will hardly be alleged as a reason why the volumes of history should be heaped upon a funeral pyre. [. . .]

No small gratification is afforded by the skilful imitation of the actors. Abstracted from the moral tendencies or properties of the scene, there is nothing ignoble or pernicious in the delight which poetry and eloquence are adapted to communicate. Whatever disapprobation we may feel for the sanguinary tyrant, or the drunken soldier, we may laudably indulge our admiration at the creations of the poet, and the personifications of the actor. Music too, is a theatrical appendage which it is no argument of wisdom to despise.

The scene, considered apart from the invention and actor, cannot have an hurtful tendency. To exterminate vice and error is the good man's business. For this end he must view the world as it is. He must inspect it closely and impartially. To pluck up weeds it is requisite to know where they are to be found, and in what consists their hurtfulness or inutility. Now, perhaps, no imagination can conceive an avenue to the knowledge of the actual state of mankind, which combines so many advantages as this. In no conceivable way can a dollar and two hours be employed with the same success. Books and second hand information are tedious, cumbrous, and delusive mediums; but here we may examine for ourselves; we may come in contact with vice, as it were, without danger of infection; and the impressions that are made are eminently forcible and vivid. It is evident, therefore, that theatrical establishments are useful to the wise. [. . .]

[13] [The Theatre As a Means of Instruction of the Ignorant]
The Weekly Magazine [1798]

[. . .] Perhaps it will be found that the press and the stage are the two great engines by which man is to be snatched out of ignorance: that the first is the most valuable is not to be doubted, principally from that assuredness which it has given to the progress of science, that mound which it has raised against the retrograde movement of mind; but there are advantages which the stage possesses in its turn, which render it a powerful and consequently a valuable auxiliary. The time may arrive when the stage shall be no longer necessary; perhaps we can form no idea of a period when the press will be useless: but at present, that the productions of the comparatively wise should be presented to the comparatively ignorant, through every possible medium, seems to be highly desirable, and it will scarcely be denied that instruction may be and is conveyed by dramatic representations to many, who from habit or other causes, scarcely ever look within the binding of a book or beyond the advertisements and daily occurrences of a news-paper. [. . .]

The stage has many striking resemblances to the press. Ought we to prohibit printing because by its means every kind of error is propagated? Ought we to annihilate the press because superstition, from thence, discharges incessantly her poisoned and barbed arrows? [. . .]

[16] [National Sentiments Compensate for Dramatic Defects of a Play]
The Monthly Magazine, and American Review [1800]

The 25th of November, the anniversary of that auspicious day when the troops of a foreign enemy, after many years possession, evacuated our city, was celebrated at the Theatre, by recalling to the minds of a very numerous audience, the first proof which Americans gave of that firm attachment to liberty which led them to seek death in its defence.

All the numerous defects of the play of *Bunker-Hill* were amply compensated by the enthusiasm of the audience.

[19] [American Plays to Be "exempted from the severity of criticism"?]
The American Review, and Literary Journal [1801]

In a country where literature is yet in its infancy, it may be deemed proper that those labours which are meant to contribute towards its support and improvement, should not only be exempted from the severity of criticism, but should be received with kindness and encouragement.

This sentiment, however, must be confined to such productions as discover unequivocal marks of a mind worthy of cultivation, and should by no means be extended into a general license to every trifling retailer of puns and witicisms to arrogate to himself the rights of authorship. Whilst, therefore, we are careful not to exercise a fastidious nicety over the first offerings of merit, and thus discourage the future efforts of genius, we cannot too soon examine and expose the pretensions of those who vainly aspire to rank themselves among the writers of the age. Whatever allowance ought justly to be made in favour of the inexperience of our countrymen, yet, unless this discrimination be strictly observed, public taste is in great danger of becoming utterly depraved. If every thing that is American is, on that account, to be screened from censure, one of the most powerful inducements to human exertion is, in a great measure, destroyed; for emulation must cease where commendation is alike bestowed on all. [The author then gives a plot summary of W. Winstanley, *The Hypocrite Unmasked*, New York, 1801.]

We read this play with a sincere desire of finding something in it worthy of selection and commendation; but we have read in vain. [. . .]

[21] [Introduction of the Melodrama to America]
The Weekly Visitor, or Ladies' Miscellany [1803]

[. . .] The public attention was somewhat excited by the following paragraph introduced by the manager in the bill.

The MELO–DRAME, being new to the English and American stage, it may be necessary to observe, that in this species of dramatic composition, instrumental Music is introduced occasionally during the pauses in the dialogue, with a view of heightening the effect, and aiding the expression of those passions which occupy the scene: the present admirable piece [i.e., Thomas Holcroft's *A Tale of Mystery*, 1802] may be considered as the first experiment to introduce a new species of Drama: on the English stage it has succeeded beyond calculation; and it is presented to the public of New–York, under the strongest impression, that it will contribute in an eminent degree to their rational pleasures.

[24] [The Drama As Propitious As the Sermon]
The Companion and Weekly Miscellany [1805]

[...] Theatrical performances have long been a subject of declamation, amongst christians, under a belief, that they are pregnant with the most outrageous incentives to vice. Applauding the moral and religious examples of these pious people, I respectfully beg leave to differ from them in sentiment, and declare my respect for the drama. If they will take a peep into the ancient philosophers, they will find, that theatrical performances were held in the highest veneration by them; for, sensible of the inadequacy of school, and pulpit precepts alone, they had recourse to the Drama, in order that the various characters of life might be represented to their pupils, in the most pertinent point of view; such as the Miser and Spendthrift; the Debauchee and Glutton, the Prodigal and Grotesque; together with all immoral practices and vicious habits; so as to excite in the youthful mind, an abhorrence of vice and immorality; for, by acting their parts well, the *personae dramatis* inculcated prejudice against such characters; which, no doubt, has a moral and edifying tendency. Theatrical performances, therefore, from their first institution, appear to have been designed to expose and ridicule vice, and, consequently, to inculcate virtue; inasmuch, as they point out deviations from decency, and reprehend the errors of all classes before their faces; which, indeed, often strike home with great force.

The reverend doctors instruct virtue and admonish vice, by dint of sermons, replete with edifying references to the holy scriptures, and invitations to pursue the infallibility, both scriptural and personal, of the Saviour of the world; which is conducive to great good. On the other hand, in my opinion, theatrical performances have a powerful tendency to check many growing follies of youth—warn them against vicious habits, by exhibiting to their view, the miscarriages of those who, unrestrained by prudence, fall victims to their immoral practices, gusts of passion and anger, which prevail, in a greater or less degree, in all grades of life: indeed, mankind are too subject to the bias of fashion and folly; and therefore, it is absolutely necessary and pertinent, that they should be checked when unruly passions unhinge their reason.

If those good christians, who declaim against dramatic performances, as "being a battery against religion," will draw aside the veil of prejudice, and open their minds to conviction, they will acknowledge, that some of the most pious and learned characters of antiquity allowed themselves free access to, and encouraged theatrical exhibitions. [...]

If necessary, I could quote various other testimony from sacred history to prove, that the drama first originated in religion. [. . .]

[30] [The Stage As Language and History Adviser]
The Emerald, or, Miscellany of Literature [1806]

[. . .] In particular the influence of Theatrical performances on pronunciation and delivery, is strikingly great. People in general have no determinate idea of propriety in the utterance of language, and are ready to receive any impression as a standard, which an eminent actor may be disposed to stamp. Hence arises the necessity of keeping check on Stage pronunciation; and hence too results the great effect which injudicious acting *may* have on the public taste. It should therefore be a primary principle with the Manager to suffer nothing but pure English to be uttered from the Boston Stage; and in laying his *emphasis*, the actor should be careful of conveying the most complete sense, of which the sentence pronounced may be susceptible. [. . .]

But this is not all. [. . .] Let these lines too be impressed on the attention of the performers,

> A nation's *taste* depends on you,
> Perhaps a nation's *virtue* too.

While the Manager therefore, is attentive to his own interest, he must also consult the effects, which his representations may be calculated to produce. Do not let him *merely* think of his purse, and be contented to vend that commodity which will sell best [. . .].

In tragedy he should often exhibit the best historical pieces, by which the scope of common knowledge is enlarged, and the usurpation of forgetfulness is resisted. Perhaps the most accurate information, upon particular subjects of ancient history, is that which is obtained after seeing some of our best tragedies performed. As a subject of polite literature, plays should be consulted for the purity of their style, their acumen of thought, and elegance of expression. All rant, fustian and bombast should be carefully avoided; and in time the public taste may be recalled to true discriminations of passion, instead of being led away by the pomp of shew, and declamatory vehemence.

In comedy, it should be the manager's endeavor, not to suffer any obscenity or indecency to be uttered; or any appearance of buffoonery to be observed. These catches of vulgar admiration "betray a very pitiful ambition in the fool that uses them." The *dress* in comedy should be nicely observed; let every performer be in *character*, as respects the fashion at the period represented, as well as the individual appearance. Any anachronisms in this particular, betray palpable ignorance, and are at the same time disgusting to the mind of a man of sense. [. . .]

[32] [The "Propriety of Establishing a Theatre" in Albany]
The Guardian [1807]

[. . .] I am not disposed to defend the theatre against *all* the objections which may be offered: many are undoubtedly well founded; and it would indeed be rather remarkable that an institution so universally encouraged in all polished nations, should not be chargeable with some abuses and defects.

But in considering this subject, we ought to take society as *it is*, not as it *ought to be*. We should not suffer the *abuse* of a thing to be urged against the *intended use* of it. If a theatre under strict and proper regulation may be made conducive to the *rational* amusement and instruction of man, it is a fair deduction in its favour. I do admit that theatres in *small towns* are unnecessary, and perhaps hurtful; but I do contend that in *large cities and towns*, they are necessary and useful.

Let us for a moment consider the nature and constitution of man. Man, through necessity and habit is a *social animal*; prompted by the dictates of nature and his imperious wants, he becomes *industrious*. Industry necessarily requires relaxation from labour, and in these hours of relaxation, his propensities for amusement, for society, are naturally rekindled. He resorts to the tavern—for there he hopes to find company and past-time, calculated to fill up the leisure he enjoys. Or to the gaming-table—for there he hopes to find, super-added to his other enjoyments, the prospect of *profit*. Or he indulges in other exercises, hurtful to his morals and destructive to his constitution. Every man in society (with scarce an exception) will devote a portion of his time and money to amusements, either more or less innocent or criminal. The only question then is, into what channel shall these invincible propensities be directed—and whether in this view of the subject, a theatre is not less exceptionable than any other species of amusement?—Nay, whether will it not tend to divert the thoughtless and giddy from plunging into criminal and destructive excesses?

I lay aside for the present, any argument to be derived from the morality and instruction frequently inculcated and exhibited on the stage, but view it as an amusement, either *harmless*, or as not producing any *positive good*, farther than the prevention of greater *positive evil*. But when to this may be added, that the stage frequently operates as a corrector of morals, where *vice* is held up in all its deformity, and *virtue* arrayed in all her beauty, the argument in favour of a theatre becomes doubly forcible. [. . .]

[33] [Reply: The Stage "neither useful nor innocent"]
The Guardian [1808]

Sir,

THROUGH the medium of the *Guardian*, you have submitted to its readers "Thoughts on establishing a Theatre in this city." I propose, through the same channel, briefly to examine what you have already written on the subject of Theatres in general; and shall probably follow you thro' your future numbers.

Like all other advocates for the stage, you insist, that in treating of it, we must consider it not as it in reality is, but as it might be. By this subterfuge of its advocates, all who oppose the stage, are obliged to combat a mere shadow, an imaginary something which never had existence; which probably never will, and never can exist. The abuse of the stage seems to be inseparable from its use. If it be otherwise, how does it happen that they have at all times, and in all places existed together? If there are any exceptions, why do not the advocates for the drama point them out.—Show us what you call "a well regulated Theatre." Among the many schemes and projects daily offered to the consideration of the public, why has there never been any attempt to point out a way to bring the stage to a "proper regulation?" In what does a well regulated stage consist? Will you reform the attendants? There is need enough of this [. . .] as you have represented them. You make them all tavern-haunters, gamblers, or otherwise grossly immoral: and so anxious were you to do this, that you have, whether wilfully or otherwise I know not, made all mankind such. This is taking society "not as it ought to be" in earnest. And those drinkers, gamblers, and the rest, are to be sent to the Theatre to—be reformed! And when so reformed, they are to come in as an *item*, in constituting "a well regulated Theatre." But I am anticipating. You are to treat hereafter of the "morality and instruction frequently inculcated and exhibited on the stage."

But perhaps this "proper regulation" is to consist in the *plays* themselves. We must bear in mind, however, that the plays must be adapted to the taste of the spectators; that is, drinkers, gamblers, &c. We know that where attempts have been made to reform the stage, by selecting *good plays*, the Theatre has been deserted, and the managers obliged to abandon the attempt. But suppose it otherwise, what plays will you select which shall be brought in as an *item* in constituting "a well regulated Theatre?" Will you take *Pizzaro*, the *Stranger*, and *John Bull*, where the spurious virtues are blazoned out, and the genuine thrown in the back ground and degraded? In the one is a bold and sentimental strumpet, whom the passions of lust and jealousy prompt to follow the adventures of her paramour. In the other an adultress, who had forsaken her amiable husband, and lived in criminal commerce with her seducer. In the last is the daughter of a humble tradesman; she suffers herself to be seduced by the son of a baronet, flies from the roof of her fond and most affectionate father, and afterwards is united in marriage to the despoiler of her virtue.—And these ladies are the prominent characters of the respective pieces, and instead of being held up instructive warnings to others, are contrived to be made the objects of our sympathy, esteem, and admiration. If this selection does not please you, make one [. . .] to suit yourself.

But for the sake of argument, I will grant you for a moment, what you and your brethren of the drama so uniformly contend for—this something, nothing, called "a Theatre under strict and proper regulations." Such a Theatre you contend, and in the number now under consideration, attempt to prove, "may be conducive to the rational amusement of man." Amusement, to be rational, I contend, and you admit, must be innocent, or "harmless." You must also admit, that mere amusement or diversion cannot be innocent unless it be proper and necessary. To deny this is to destroy the very idea of recreation, and to contend that the chief end of man is amusement.

Need of recreation is much less than people commonly apprehend. Those who stand in need of it, may be divided into two sorts—such as are employed in bodily labor—and such as have their spirits often exhausted by study, and application of mind. For the first of these, a mere cessation from labor is sufficient for refreshment: of the other, only a very small number of them will choose the recreation of the stage; bodily exercise and social converse (which may be found at other places besides the tavern and gaming-table) answering the purpose much better. Ninety-nine of a hundred who attend the Theatre, do not stand in need of recreation at all. Their time may hang heavily upon them, but this arises, not from labor, but from idleness.

Further, the stage is an improper, that is to say, an unlawful recreation to all without exception, because it consumes too much time. If recreations are only lawful because necessary, they must surely cease to be lawful when they are no longer necessary. Whoever considers the time necessary to prepare for attending and the time of actual attendance at the Theatre, must acknowledge that it is more than is proper to be sacrificed to recreation. This holds peculiarly in the recreation of mind. No man ever yet returned from the Theatre with his mind strengthened and better qualified for doing his duty as a man, much less as a christian, in consequence of his attendance there. On the contrary, it is commonly of such length as to produce satiety and weariness itself, and actually to require rest and refreshment, to recruit the exhausted spirits.

The stage is further improper as a recreation because it agitates the passions too violently and interests too deeply, so as, in some cases, to bring people into a real, while they behold an imaginary distress. Whatever either requires or causes a strong application of mind, is contrary to the intention of recreations. [. . .]

Perhaps arguments drawn from the expense of attending the Theatre might be treated with contempt by those who know no other use of money, than to feed and pamper their appetites. I shall therefore only say, that as the recreation of the stage is neither useful nor innocent, the expense of attending it must be at least a useless expense.

As to your argument, that a Theatre is necessary, as it affords an asylum for the *tavern-haunter* and the *gambler*, it is really too futile to need a reply. I can hardly believe you were sincere when you advanced it. If a refuge for such characters is really wanted, perhaps a mad-house would be the more suitable one; or if they are not reformed it is to be apprehended that they will too soon be obliged to join a large company of their unhappy associates, who are already assembled in a capacious building, in the city of New-York.

The possibility, or even certainty of a person's doing well in one place, does not itself prove the innocence of their frequenting another place. Because a man goes to a tavern or gambling-house, is it conclusive that we must build and support a Theatre? Will these tavern-haunters and gamblers come to the Theatre? And if they come, will they abandon the tavern and gaming-table? Experience proves the contrary.—Of all characters, the players themselves are generally most given to gambling and intemperance, as well as other vices. And those who frequent Theatres learn from that attendance to frequent other places of dissipation: for at the Theatre they acquire a taste for every disgraceful vice.

[39] [Improvement of the Theatre by Attendance of Clergy and Females]
Something [1809]

The Drama will engage a considerable portion of our attention; nor shall we forget that the authors of its institution in our mother country were ecclesiastics, that the preachers of the Gospel were the first and originally the only actors in the Drama, and that it was introduced to give a more impressive effect to the doctrines of morality and Christianity.

However changed in its nature or effect, it must still be regarded as an object of high consideration in its influence over the public mind, and consequently claiming and deserving the support of all enlightened societies. They who fear it as an instrument of evil tendency, (if their sincere wishes for general amendment have equal energy with their professions) should think it their duty to attend dramatic representations, that by their presence they might check the further encroachments of immorality, for the stern countenance of virtue will easily make vice retire ashamed: while they who think it has a moral influence, should present themselves as guardians to that moral influence, and by their sanction promote its permanency.

If the aged, the wise, and the good *will* give up that control over dramatic representations, which a public should always possess as an essential right, to the young, the thoughtless, and the profligate, what can be expected but that authors, managers, and actors will endeavour to please the deputed agents of authority, instead of the authority itself?

Without entering into a discussion of the wisdom of those measures which, public or private, have continued to banish the greater part of our clergy from theatrical representations, we shall only point out and lament the effect. [. . .]

Another apparent cause of an incorrectness of conduct sometimes discernible among those who compose part of the audience of the Boston Theatre is the exclusion of females from the pit. It cannot but be acknowledged that in all societies not absolutely depraved, the presence of females refines the moral conduct of men, or at least checks for the period their depraved habits.

[40] [Meager Recompense for American Playwrights Because of Copyright Reasons]
The Rambler's Magazine [1809–10]

[. . .] What is the fate amongst us of a poor *aspirant* after fame in the walks of the drama? His production is delivered into the hands of men capable perhaps of examining the correctness of a *leger*, but totally incompetent to the task of judging of literary merit. Admitting that a piece be put in rehearsal, that it be played, and that the public receive it favorably; the author receives an invitation to dinner, in company with a host of the manager's parasites, and is *be-praised* and *be-thanked* for the services he has rendered to the theatre until his head runs round, and then is dismissed with a general invitation to repeat his visit at every convenient opportunity.

Here then is the harvest the poor devil of an author reaps on this side the Atlantic, after four or six months' seclusion and labor. [. . .]

A manager here, like a bookseller, grows fat on the brains of Europeans, drinks his wine out of their skulls, and is careless of meddling with those of his own countrymen. For this there are a *thousand* reasons; one of which will preclude the necessity of enumerating the other nine hundred and ninty-nine—*he pays nothing for the former, and he would have to PURCHASE the latter.*

[43] [The "miserable economy" of Managers]
The Cabinet [1811]

[. . .] No local observation is more just in its application or more generally extended than that, though the theatre has been supported during the present season by a liberality of patronage far exceeding all anticipation or hope; yet that the management has been dictated by a penny-wise economy, and by a system of low cunning, equally removed from every feeling of gratitude, and of reciprocity. This meanness is discoverable in respect to the *performers, musicians*, and the *general economy of the house*; and this deception or cunning, is to be found in the various expedients which have been adopted to coerce the favourers of the stage respecting box tickets since the arrival of Mr. Cooke in Boston. We shall offer a few observations upon each of these topicks of controversy.

As to performers, the company is miserably deficient both in respect to number as well as merit, which was rendered evident during the performance of *Richard the Third*; for not only was Mr. Cooke not well supported by those with whom he was more immediately concerned, but some performers were obliged to personate two parts in the same play; candle snuffers were made, in *vile robes* to represent nobility, and the whole army of Richard and Richmond, and the tribe of citizens of London altogether were represented by about five supernumeraries. The whole illusion of the scene was destroyed by this miserable economy. Thus Richard addresses the mayor and citizens of London, represented by Mr. Dickenson and a candle snuffer behind him, as "*sage grave men*;" and Richmond having *two* men with him for an army makes them both soldiers and generals in the same breath. But not only in respect to supernumeraries does this saving spirit appear; it is evident from their pretensions, that the corps of regular performers are obtained at a very cheap rate; and however these ladies and gentlemen may have been puffed into notice by the friends of the theatre in the newspapers, their merits among the people at large, are by no means equivocal. [. . .]

But whatever apology can be assigned, respecting the performers, there is certainly none which can be applied to the miserable state of the *Orchestra*, a state which the managers have had abundant opportunity to improve; but which has not only been grossly neglected but wilfully neglected. [. . .] Under the present regulations of the managers, the Orchestra, outrages all principles of taste and musical science. [. . .]

The arrangements of the other departments of the house are equally despicable and mean. The front lights, which have been during this season almost without crystals, throw so dim a lustre upon the reflectors, that the foreground of the stage is hardly illuminated sufficiently to discern the face of a performer the distance of four boxes from the scene. This inconvenience, added to the smoke which rises from the most execrable oil, which is burned, together with the side lights, dim with "ineffectual fire," affords a proper subject of serious complaint. In addition to this, the coldness of the house in severe weather, for want of early and sufficient fires, renders it dangerous for ladies to venture thither at all, much more, to appear there dressed with taste, elegance, and fashion. The boxes too are not in a fit situation for the reception of ladies; they are neither washed, nor properly swept. [. . .]

[44] [Continuation of Preceding Complaint]
The Cabinet [1811]

The arrival of Mr. Cooke in this place, was considered quite an epoch in the theatrical history of Boston, and the attention of the publick was naturally excited to witness the uncommon powers of a performer, whose reputation in Great Britain had spread beyond that of perhaps any other actor in the kingdom.—The managers taking advantage of this state of the pulse of publick anxiety, determined to make the favourers of theatrical representation, pay as dearly as possible for the *priviledge of supporting the theatre*. As they had announced a play to be performed on Wednesday evening, without the attraction of Mr. Cooke's abilities, they executed a trick by which every ticket in the boxes were *forced* upon those persons who intended to see Mr. Cooke perform upon subsequent nights. They therefore advertised in the Wednesday newspapers, that places might be taken, for all the nights of Mr. Cooke's performance, at eleven o'clock *that day*, provided tickets were also purchased for Wednesday night, when Mr. Cooke did *not* perform. By this contemptible avarice, the managers in effect enhanced the *price* of the box tickets, to one dollar and eleven cents each, calculating the whole nine nights of the engagement. But in many instances they have done infinitely worse, for the managers after having coerced the holders of places, in this way, advertised, that if they failed to call and take their tickets previous to four o'clock of the day of any performance, not only should the tickets for that *particular* evening be sold, but for every other night during the engagement of Mr. Cooke. [. . .]

But besides the coercion of those persons who obtained seats during the *whole first engagement* of Mr. Cooke, the system of exclusion which such a priviledge created, deserves singular reprobation. The managers determining to sell their tickets on Wednesday evening, for no adequate consideration, well knowing that certain friends of theatrical amusements would on such peculiar occasions take them at any rate, disregarded that fair dealing which the town had an undoubted right to demand, and thereby deprived the great bulk of the community of access to an amusement ostensibly supported by publick favour, and depending upon publick patronage. It may be considered an incontrovertible principle, that all possible equality should be given to all classes of citizens, in the participation of the pleasure derivable from publick exhibitions. The course which the managers followed respecting the community, was as distantly removed from equality on one hand, and fair dealing on the other, as it is possible to imagine. [. . .]

Whilst therefore we are insulted with such a deplorable corps of regular performers, and such an ill assorted jumble of musicians to compose an orchestra, at a time when the managers have been repeatedly solicited, and have had abundant opportunity to improve both; and whilst the general economy of the house is such as to endanger the health of female visitors, and disgrace those who superintend it, we hope they may be made to feel the force of general disapprobation in the coldness of general neglect. Nor will the deception practised upon the friends and supporters of the theatre, upon Mr. Cooke's arrival, pass without due retaliation, if when the *personal benefits of the managers arrive*, the publick will so far resent the imposition, as entirely to withdraw their countenance from men, who could dare openly to wrest from our generosity what could never have been claimed from our justice.

PUBLICK RETRIBUTION

[54] [Order in the Theatre]
The Polyanthos [1812]

WANTED—A gentleman to act as *Master of Ceremonies* at the Boston Theatre. The business will be to keep silence in the box lobbies during the performance, to preserve, if possible, decorum among the *bucks* in the boxes, to keep *gentlemen* from wiping the mud of their boots upon the drapery of ladies who happen to be on the seat before them, to confine the *grog-sellers* to their *north room*, and to assist those *young blades* to find the outside of the theatre that have drank too much to stay within. Any one disposed to undertake this employment, will receive the sincere thanks of those who go to be amused with the performances, and ought to receive a prompt engagement and a good salary from the PROPRIETORS and MANAGERS.

[61] [Difficulties an American Playwright Has to Face]
The National Register [1816]

It is to be regretted that the American drama is so little attended to. There is, perhaps, no country that affords so fine a field as this for the exercise of dramatic talent. The freedom of our political institutions, the variety and diversity of character which is to be found in the United States, and the unrestrained liberty of speech, which tends to develope all the peculiarities and excentricities of our nature, must afford an unbounded field for the exertions of the dramatic muse. The prejudices, however, which exist against the productions of our domestic authors, and the rage for every thing European, will have a tendency to retard the exertions of American genius; & while it reflects on the patriotism of our citizens, contributes, in no small degree, to check the growth of our literature. Several efforts have been made to overcome these absurd and deleterious prejudices, but they have been ineffectual. The stage, that source of refined and rational amusement, has been resorted to by a very few American writers, who have furnished dramatic pieces more with a view to their own amusement and to excite a national taste, calculated to overcome the prejudices already mentioned, than for any purpose of pecuniary emolument. Among these are Messrs. Barker, Ingersoll, Waterston, &c. who have furnished dramatic pieces for the stage, and who have already almost outlived their reputation. The former of these gentlemen, who has perhaps justly been denominated the American dramatist, from his having devoted more of his leisure to the stage than any other American, has produced some pieces of considerable merit, and much superior to many of the European dramas that have been received in this country with great *eclat*. The last of his dramatic productions is *Marmion*, the plot of which is borrowed from Scott's poem of that name; and this, with all its intrinsic merit, to the disgrace of the country, he was obliged to get the managers to announce as a European production, and as such, was, of course, received with great applause and approbation. Such are the shifts to which American writers, however laudible and patriotic their motives may be, are compelled to resort to preserve their productions from silent neglect, or instant damnation. But there are other difficulties which an American writer for the stage has to encounter, of a more unyielding character. The stage is closed against our domestic dramas, and it is not without much difficulty the managers can be at all prevailed upon to bring them out. If, however, the writer is even so fortunate as to obtain the consent of our anglo-American managers to bring his piece on stage, he is obliged to submit to their dictatorial arrogance, or royal pruning knife, with which they disfigure and mutilate the finest sentiments and best diction of his play. I understand that the most patriotic sentiments of Mr. Waterson's *Battle of Orleans*, which was performed in this city last summer, the manager struck out, because they were quite too American for the palates of English players; and the prologue, written by Mr. Colvin, Mrs. Entwisle refused to speak, because it bore too hard on her country. If these are facts, and I have no reason to doubt them, it will be a long time before the American drama will be able to succeed. For however excellent they may be in plot, in sentiment, and in manners, it will not be possible to overcome immediately the torrent of prejudice and the current of difficulties they have to encounter. The American dramatist who writes for his own amusement, or with a view to add to the literary reputation of his country, for he never receives any pecuniary emolument, will certainly not submit to the exclusion of the finest sentiments of his play, merely because they are patriotic; and will not stoop to beg an English player (and we have scarcely any that is not) to spare his piece, and gratify the feelings of his audience by the repetition of those sentiments that are dear to every lover of his country. The feelings of these anglo-American managers must, indeed, be very delicate, that can induce them to insult an American audience by the expression of the most monarchical, British and royal sentiments, while they positively refuse to utter those of an American character, because, forsooth, though it would gratify their audience, it would offend their sensibility. These are some of the difficulties the American writer has to encounter, and until they can be removed there is but little probability of acquiring any thing like dramatic reputation. To effect this object, so desirable in its nature—this slavish *dependence* on foreign literary supplies, which is so extensively felt in this country, must be destroyed, and the stage, now closed, must be entirely free to the dramatic productions of the American muse. We have been long enough a nation to produce dramatists, and I presume no one will say there is a deficiency of genius. Let us strive then to overcome this melancholy apathy, and remove those numerous difficulties I have enumerated as retarding the progress of the American drama, and paralizing the exertions of American genius.

[64] [Failure of the Pittsburgh Theatre a Triumph of Morality]
The Weekly Recorder [1816]

It is stated in a Pittsburgh paper of the 12th instant, that the Theatre in that city had been open nearly a fortnight; and the managers, though they had used every exertion to please in the selection of their pieces, had not been able to pay the contingent expenses of the House.

This fact deserves to be recorded and published. It is highly honourable to the taste and character of that city. It shews that the inhabitants are not disposed, in a wanton and prodigal manner, to waste their time and money on amusements, which are not only unprofitable, but highly pernicious in a moral point of view. Their conduct in neglecting the theatre is worthy of general imitation. If the inhabitants of all our cities and towns were to conduct in the same way, one great cause of licentiousness and immorality would cease to operate. Theatres, probably, would soon be converted into academies and churches, and stage-players forced to abandon their unlawful profession, and turn their attention to some other business for sustenance.

[65] [The Boston Anti-Theatre Law of 1750 and an Instance of Its Application in 1792]
The Boston Weekly Magazine [1816]

[A historical survey of the theatre in Boston]
We now give the Law to which we alluded in our first number. [. . .]
An Act to prevent Stage Plays and other Theatrical Entertainments.
For preventing and avoiding the many and great mischiefs which arise from public stage-plays, interludes and other theatrical entertainments, which not only occasion great and unnecessary expences, and discourage industry and frugality, but likewise tend generally to increase immorality, impiety and a contempt of religion:

Sect. 1. Be it enacted, &c. that from and after the publication of this act no person or persons whosoever shall or may, for his or their gain, or for any price or valuable consideration, let or suffer to be used and improved any house, room or place whatsoever, for acting or carrying on any stage-plays, interludes or other theatrical entertainments, on pain of forfeiting and paying for each and every day or time such house, room or place shall be let, used or improved contrary to this act, twenty pounds.

Sect. 2. And be it further enacted, that if at any time or times whatsoever from and after the publication of this act, any person or persons shall be present as an actor in, or spectator of any stage-play, interlude, or theatrical entertainment in any house, room or place where a greater number of persons than twenty shall be assembled together, every such person shall forfeit and pay, for every time he or they shall be present as aforesaid, five pounds.

(March, 1750.)

Mr. [Joseph] Harper supposing, as we have already observed, that his performances would escape the letter of the Law by being entitled 'Moral Lectures,' proceeded in his theatrical career in defiance of many temporary and, in some instances, vexatious disturbances. One interruption in particular we recollect, which took place during the representation of the *School for Scandal* [5 Dec. 1792]. Some begotted zealots who, it appears, happened to have more Law than reason on their side, obtained of the Governour authority to arrest, under sanction of the Act which we have given above, our thespian delinquents. A warrant was accordingly issued, and during the performance of the above mentioned Comedy, Sheriff Allen actually arrested Mr. Harper while, in the character of 'Charles Surface,' he was knocking down to 'Mr. Premium' the portraits of his ancestors. In this dilemma Mr. Harper saw no other remedy but that of making an immediate appeal to the spectators of this outrage, and he accordingly addressed himself to the audience, which was large and highly respectable, and requested their advice concerning the course of conduct which in such a vexatious situation, it was becoming in him to pursue.

Though the audience were justly indignant at such an unexpected interruption of an innocent as well as rational amusement, several gentlemen in the boxes advised Mr. Harper to close the performances and accompany the Officer, remarking at the same time that from whatever motive such an unreasonable step had been taken, it was the duty of the manager to submit to the constituted authority. Mr. Harper accordingly announced that the entertainments were at an end and that the Box–Keeper would return the money which had been received for tickets. But, as it was the benefit night of Mr. Kenney, who had become a favorite from his indefatigable attentions to his profession, it was suggested, and the proposal unanimously applauded, that the deserving actor should retain the whole amount of receipts. This affair, so creditable to the generosity of our townsmen, being thus settled without opposition, the spectators were about retiring, when a young gentleman adventurously leaped from the second row of boxes—indignantly stripped the *Arms of the Commonwealth* from the pannel of the stage box and stamped them under foot; and the audience expressed their sympathy in the indignation of the youth by a burst of enthusiastic applause. We record this anecdote for the purpose of showing the temper of the times and the confirmed attachment which even at this early period, (1792) all classes of our townsmen exhibited for the drama; an attachment which continued rapidly to strengthen and extend itself, until the period when the present managers commenced their mismanagement of the Theatre; since which ever-to-be regretted era it has been the fate of Bostonians to learn with silent indignation the important lesson—how the noblest of institutions may be degraded by the government of those whose taste operates only in their Kitchens, and whose principle is found only in the Bank.

[66] [Circumventing Boston's Anti-Theatre Law]
The Boston Weekly Magazine [1816]

We omitted to observe, that the first performances at the theatre in Board Alley, did not bear that regular dramatic form, which our theatricals have since assumed. Indeed the children of Thespis made their first appearance among us in scarcely a more matured state, than when their progenitor amused the good citizens of Athens with his motley exhibitions. Theatrical performances were not, at that time, so generally popular as they have since become, and the most efficient patrons of the theatre were found among that class of citizens, with whom any *novelty* was amusement, and who received their first ideas of the drama from such mutilated representations of it, as Mr. Harper found it convenient and profitable to give his audience. We find accordingly that on the 15th August, 1792, the theatre, which was then denominated the *New Exhibition Room*, was opened with an irregular medley of entertainments, such as tight and slack rope dancing, songs and recitations from approved plays; but in September following, when the company were reinforced by the performers already mentioned, the exhibitions were extended to *Ballettes* and some amusing French pantomimes, in the performance of which, the persons already mentioned were so admirable, as to give interest to a species of amusement, that never ranked high among the lovers of the drama, though far preferable, from the professional skill of the performers, to much of the mummery and machinery that has since been obtruded upon us. The performances, soon after the accession of Mr. and Mrs. Morris, who had now joined the company, began to assume a more regular dramatic character, and several tragedies and comedies were for the first time, performed entire. The performances continued to progress in this improved form until the 5th December, when the house was closed by public authority, through the influence and interference of the enemies of the theatre, and under circumstances which have been already related, and continued shut until the middle of January, 1793, when it was reopened [. . .].

In the month of March following, the law prohibiting theatrical exhibitions was repealed, and a resolution adopted permitting theatres to be opened four months in each year. This event was considered at that time as a signal triumph for the friends of the drama, who were indebted to the eloquent and manly exertions of several members of the General Court [. . .] for a measure which reflected much credit upon the liberality of our legislature.

From this period until the establishment of the Federal Street Theatre [opened 3 Feb. 1794], the town was amused with occasional exhibitions at the Board Alley "Exhibition Room," and at Concert Hall. [. . .]

[67] [A Project for Moral Criticism of the Boston Stage]
The Boston Weekly Magazine [1817]

[. . .] The general design of our future observations will be to prove that the Stage is not confined to the mere negative quality of doing no injury, but that, according to the opinions of the best and wisest of mankind, it is not only capable of affording an elegant and rational amusement, and of being converted into a school of rhetoric and gentility, but that it may be made a powerful auxiliary in the cause of virtue. In comparing our own Stage with this elevated standard, we shall find that its pretensions not only vanish into air, but that it has not even the negative merit of doing no harm; and that the philanthropist, in taking a comprehensive view of the mediate causes of general licentiousness, will be justified in considering it the hot-house in which the germs of incipient vice are quickened into life, and prepared to luxuriate in the vilest haunts of debauchery.

To produce this conviction in the minds of those who are not already convinced, we shall pursue that method which a consideration of the subject naturally suggests. In considering successively the subordinate subjects that form the component parts of this general aggregate of delinquency, we shall at our leisure animadvert,—

FIRST, On the peculiar disadvantages under which we labour in depending on an alien taste to cater for us; and in our acquiescence in that intellectual imbecility which receives with asinine stupidity all the modish trash of Covent Garden and Drury Lane. Under this head we shall shew the absurdity of making the success of the most worthless productions on the London Stage, (where they receive a factitious aid in the peculiar talents of actors for whom parts are expressly written,) a criterion of that merit which should recommend them to an American public.

SECONDLY. We shall consider the general character of our dramatic corps, for some years past, and this will necessarily involve the duty of making an impartial estimate of the merits and defects of the present company. We presume that this examination will terminate in a concurrence with the general opinion,—that they are totally inadequate to sustain the dignity and usefulness of the Drama, in the metropolis of New-England.

THIRDLY. As one of the advantages of a well conducted stage, is to describe to youth the customs of past ages and distant countries;—and as one of the means by which the Poet effects his purposes, is a strict adherence to the fiction of the scene, we shall consider how far this two-fold duty, of pleasure and instruction, is attended to, on the Boston Stage, and shall adduce instances, not only of partial negligence, but of a total heedlessness in this department of the internal economy of the Theatre.

FOURTHLY. As all impropriety of conduct in performers, while in the immediate presence of their audience, may be justly considered as an insult of the blackest hue, (of ingratitude and impudence united,) to those from whom they receive their support,—we shall consider how far they concur with Managers in rendering the Stage a nuisance, instead of a benefit to the community. We shall view this subject under the heads of *Obscenity, Profanity,* and palpable *Intoxication*; and, instead of using the cant of puritanism as the test by which to try this question, we shall only require that the countenances of the female part of the audience shall be made the standard, to determine the license and the inroads to be allowed indecency. [. . .]

[Here the author proceeds with his moral criticism of the Boston stage.]

[68] [Plea for an End to American "servility" to English Dramatic Taste]
The Portico [1817]

[. . .] England is the Mirror that we look to. We adopt her practices, imitate her corruptions, and play nothing but her pieces; if her Stage is prostituted to the puerilities of Spectacle, ours will also share the same deformity. If a *Mr. Maturin* produces a mongrel monster of German incongruities and horrours, and it is exhibited with applause on the London Stage; it is certain of being performed with applause in America, whether it merits praise, or proscription. Such is the servility of fashion; the absurdities of prejudice; the ridiculous inconsistency of surrendering judgment to opinion. It is quite time, that we should strike from our minds these fetters of intellect and taste. The English have banished Massinger, Jonson, Shakspeare, Otway, Congreve, and Young; let us afford them a sumptuous asylum, in the American theatres; and while we dissent from them in taste and judgment, let us at the same time convince them by such a conduct, that it is not through envy, or ill-will, through ignorance, or prejudice.

To this suggestion, I already see the critic impatiently expressing his dissent: *That it is impossible, we have no good players, to fill the parts in standard Comedy, and legitimate Tragedies.* If this be true, and I am rather willing to allow it, the evil is the growth of your own indiscretion; and want of management. Bad plays never give birth to good actors. [. . .] To produce great players, there must be strong allurements of ambition, as well as gain. [. . .] Here then lies the chief evil of our Stage; the radical errour, that requires removal, previous to excellence being attained. If we enact good pieces, good players will spring up, and our English friends instead of sending us a cargo of *Stage acting Horses*, will speedily furnish us with a company of rational buskin-heroes; and in place of gaping in idle wonder, that a horse should ape the menial actions of the hind, we may gaze with the noblest pleasure, at the perfect delineations of a Caesar's, a Cato's, or a Mahomet's passions.

[72] [Historical Accuracy of Scenery—a "duty of the stage"]
The Boston Weekly Magazine [1817]

[. . .] We can safely affirm then, in confirmation of what we have already asserted, that there has been scarcely a performance within our remembrance during the present management, particularly in tragedy, in which there has not occurred some gross anachronism or impropriety to break in upon the fiction, and excite either the laughter or indignation of the spectator. [. . .]

We have no doubt, that, were Brutus to blow Caesar's brains but with a *pistol*, or Alexander to slay Clytus with an *air-gun*, we should all exclaim against actor and manager for such a disregard of the poet's directions; yet we excuse absurdities as glaring as either of the above, when they relate only to the scenery, and sin merely against the testimony of history. Thus the self-same scene, which, on one night, is used indifferently for the "*hall at Eastcheap*," the "*fireside*" of Job Thornberry, or the drawing-room of Sir Peter Teazle, is, perhaps, the succeeding evening, absurdly enough palmed upon us for the domestic retirements of Caesar and Coriolanus, or the "*closet of the Queen of Denmark*;" and it is by no means an uncommon sight to behold the sumptuous palace of a Roman conqueror *decorated* with ricketty *Windsor chairs* and homely *Dutch looking-glasses*, with the same wings and drop scene, which, before the performances are over, may be used for the humble dwelling of an English farmer.

During the "banquet scene" in the tragedy of *Macbeth*, we have frequently seen the "ghost of Banquo" make himself perfectly easy in a very ordinary new fashioned chair of Boston manufactory, without shewing the least symptoms of surprise at such a transformation of the accustomed seat of his ancestors, or wondering with the spectator "*how the devil it got there.*" [. . .]

We would not be understood to imply by these observations, that it is the duty of the managers to adapt *all* their scenes, beyond the reach of the antiquary's criticism, to every variation of time, or all the topographical niceties of place. This would be impracticable. We merely desire them to follow the example set them by others, of having some *correct* as well as pleasing representations of places notorious to every school-boy, to be appropriated to those standard plays, which are always performing and will always be admired. That this adaptation of the character of the scene to that of the play, gives additional interest to the exhibition, and richly repays the manager for any trifling expense, was amply evinced during that portion of the history of our theatre already alluded to as its golden age. We may refer too to the New York Theatre, which is not the more superiour to ours in the excellence of its company, than it is allowed to be in the vigilent attention paid to the embellishment and conduct of its stage decorations.

It is then certainly inexcusable in one of the first theatres on the continent, to be destitute of any decent representation of a *single spot* of ancient Rome, in which our dramatic writers have laid the scenes of their most popular productions. This neglect is still the more reprehensible, as that noble city contains, in the commanding beauty and simple grandeur of its famous structures, the most desirable subject for the exercise of the painter's art. To disregard these things, is a pointed neglect of one of the most useful as well as pleasing duties of the stage—that of giving a correct picture of ancient times and distant countries:—and in the performance of this duty both the shewy and useful may be united—the eye may be delighted, while the understanding is informed.

We possess, it is true, but little knowledge of the domestic accommodations and domestic architecture of ancient Rome; yet this need not be regretted while there remains, for the purposes alluded to, many a splendid monument of her architectural glory. Let us then have something that will at least *approximate* our conceptions to those heroic ages on which the imagination loves to dwell. The splendours of the *Roman Forum* no longer remain a wonder to the traveller, or a model for the artist; but we have still left many a grand and venerable ruin of the scenes in which the favorite heroes of antiquity acted their parts. And surely it can be scarcely necessary for us to observe what an incalculable interest would be given to the representation of a favourite play, or how much more completely the feelings and the imagination of the spectator would become identified with those of the poet, could the former be aided in his conceptions by some delineation of those Roman scenes where Romans acted. [. . .]

There are likewise, some favourite pieces, the plots of which are carried on at Venice, though our theatre does not, that we remember, possess any thing like a representation of that celebrated city, which also affords many beautiful subjects for scenic effect. [. . .]

[73] [The Common Dramatic Heritage of England and America]
The National Register [1817]

[...] the American Drama is essentially, in language, scenery, and decorations, that of Great Britain. With few exceptions, our plays are all English; and our players, more or less, natives of one or the other of the United Kingdoms.

This imitation affords no just ground of reproach to the character of the American understanding. The morals, the manners, the habits, the prejudices, and passions, of the citizens of the United States and the subjects of Great Britain, are radically the same. Theatrical laws and regulations were ready formed to our hands and to our taste; and the genius and wit of the mother country had furnished appropriate productions in abundance: we pursue a course in this case similar to that which we follow in another, and we import, and perhaps with more wisdom, our dramatic entertainments from London as we do a great portion of our hardware and clothing from Birmingham, Sheffield, and Manchester. The intellect of Great Britain and Ireland is our lawful inheritance. What superior claim has an Englishman over that of an American, to the works of Shakespeare, Ben Jonson, Otway, Young, Sheridan, and many others? In our turn we shall add to the capital stock; and of these additions the British public will have an equal right to partake.

Society must reach a certain height of perfection before the excellent writers of poetry or plays can appear in any nation. [...]

[...] we are improving in this respect; and the principal evidence of it is to be found in the diminution of those mountebanks, rope-dancers, and slight-of-hand-men, who formerly so much infested our cities. A better taste is cultivated; and an American audience is no longer satisfied if the very best productions which are brought forward in the London Theatres are not introduced upon our own. Another proof is, that whenever the least portion of dramatic merit is shown by a citizen, it is warmly and fondly cherished. Farther than this we do not desire to see our countrymen go. In that department of literature, as in others, we are not in the least disposed to encourage nonsense because it is native. [...]

[76] [*George Barnwell* Reconciles the Critics of the Theatre]
New England Galaxy [1817]

Dec. 24. An uncommonly numerous audience were assembled at an early hour to witness the representation of *George Barnwell*, for the second time this season. It has been said, and probably with truth, that no tragedy has so uniformly met the approbation of the moralist, as this. The supposition that its incidents were real facts, and the moral lesson which is calculated to impress on the mind of youth, have removed the objections of many to scenic representations, and extorted approbation from fanaticism itself. In every theatre where the English language is spoken, it is customary to bring it forward about the season of Christmas; when children and youth are allowed a little extra indulgence in amusement [. . .].

[78] [The Defeat of "the good old plays"]
The American Monthly Magazine and Critical Review [1818]

From the manner in which the [Park] Theatre was attended, during the last engagement of Mr. Cooper, compared with the thronged boxes during the exhibitions of [the British vocalists] Mr. [Charles] Incledon and [T.] Phillips, we should infer that singing and songs are in much higher esteem in New-York than the most just and striking personification of the passions—the most bold and accurate delineation of character—the most pathetic bursts of feeling, or the fullest flow of eloquence. If the theatre is deserted when such talents as Mr. Cooper's are employed to give interest to the scene, who can hope for encouragement? And if age, wealth, fashion, youth, and beauty hurry to the play-house to drink in, with thirsty ears, the voice of the songster, no matter of how melodious and "sweet stop" his pipe may be, while the finest moral lessons, enforced in the most impressive and engaging manner, can scarcely gain a listener, where is the just taste of the city? [. . .]

But now, the good old plays, replete with thought and observation, and hung round, like the galleries of the old baronial castles, with full-length portraits of real life, where each gazer of the human family may trace some lines of likeness, and where he may learn, as he compares himself with his ancestors, how new prejudices and new opinions, which are but the costume of character, vary the general appearance and expression of what are in fact the same features—these good old plays—these transcripts of life, and true exemplars of human character are compelled to give place to caricatures of nature; to dramatic performances which, instead of being the mirrors of life, exhibit a medley of reflecting surfaces—convex and concave—in which nothing is seen but distortion. If the legitimate occupants of the stage are thus compelled to surrender to melo-dramatic romances, horse-playing, and jugglers, Tragedy cannot too soon drain her own bowl, nor Comedy too soon give place to satire. [. . .]

[79] ["Perplexities" in Modern Tragedies]
The Boston Weekly Magazine [1818]

Thursday, Feb. 19—APOSTATE. Our modish writers of tragedy appear to be extravagantly fond of Aristotle's maxim, that 'the marvellous is always delightful.' Accordingly, a plot in their hands is made up of a very ingenious snarl of perplexities, the unravelling of which constitutes the great interest of the piece. These dramatic story-tellers lead their readers into paths well 'puzzled with mazes,' and the *argument* consists in extricating their heroes and heroines from what, in real life, would be unpoetically considered as inextricable difficulties. Their fable is a labyrinth of delightful perplexities; and if they succeed,—by the imminent dangers of their situations, and the dexterity of their 'very nick of time' escapes,—in raising the reader's curiosity to such a pitch of intensity as to prevent any scrutinizing attention to the utter barrenness of the road over which they hurry him,—the design is answered; a charmingly interesting play is the result; curiosity is excited to be gratified, and the new production is thrown aside and forgotten. The agents concerned in these plots are equally 'marvellous,' and pathos is produced (according to the modern recipe) by making the characters so diabolically wicked as to render their deaths a relief to the harrassed feelings of the reader; and they fall, despised for their vices instead of being—as they should be—pitied for their human weakness. [. . .]

[80] [The "impropriety" of Soliloquies]
The Boston Weekly Magazine [1818]

[. . .] We have already hinted at the inattention paid to the business of soliloquy, and now take the occasion to observe more fully, that there is no instance in which the practice of the stage departs farther from nature, than in the usual manner of delivering these monologues,—which the actor commonly performs by looking the audience very intelligibly in the face, and talking with them, instead of communicating with himself; and this too, with much of the spirit and fluency of ordinary conversation. We take this impropriety to be one of the causes that have induced judicious critics [. . .] to regard the soliloquy as an unnatural appendage to the dramatic art and altogether improper. We are very far, however, from concurring in the opinion that thus condemns the most beautiful, and, indeed, the most natural portions of Shakspeare's dramas. There are *postulata* far more unnatural that must be admitted, before any kind of dramatic fiction can be supported in the representation;—such as a public assembly being privy to actions which every member of it knows were performed in secret. If we are thus gratuitously admitted into the closets of the *dramatis personae*, why not into their thoughts—the utterance of which by soliloquy, is countenanced by the facts of ordinary life? Old men frequently express their cogitations audibly; and even men in the prime of life, when moved by strong passions, and a lively sensibility, do the same.—Upon this foundation has the dramatist built the practice that some would censure as unnatural. It only remains, then, that he make this peculiar species of dramatic composition characteristical of those extemporary bursts of an agitated mind of which a good soliloquy is the symbol. [. . .]

[81] [Disorder in the Pit]
The Boston Weekly Magazine [1818]

[. . .] The audience at the theatre is occasionally subjected to a very disgraceful annoyance that might be effectually removed by the sacrifice of a few dollars. In almost every instance of a crowded house, the entrances of the pit present a scene of disorder, which, both as to tumult and appearance bears a strong resemblance to the ocean in a storm. The uproar necessarily occasioned by the elements of such a crowd struggling for preeminence of noise, as well as of place, operates, to those in the side boxes in particular, as a complete interruption to the performances. There are evidently more seats disposed of than the pit can accommodate in the manner in which they are always occupied. The question then is,—have the managers a greater regard for a ten dollar bill, than the comfort of a large portion of their audience? In times past, the *Cash* side of the question would have inevitably been taken,—it yet remains to be seen whether the old spirit still lags behind, and requires exorcising.

The shameful outcries of the followers of *Ale*, in the third row, might likewise be put a stop to at the expense of a dollar or two an evening, for a peace officer. We are at a loss to determine why the theatre should be made a scene of assignation for the celebration of such Bacchanalian orgies. [. . .]

[82] [Virtuous and Vicious Members of the Audience and the "present mode of acting"]
The National Register [1819]

[. . .] One great objection to theatrical exhibitions has been, that they occasion dissipation. In this allegation we do not concur. That the dissipated resort to theatres cannot be disputed. But the steady part of the audience are a great restraint upon them; and it may be a question well worthy of consideration by the enemies of these establishments, whether the contrast between the respectable and vicious portion of the visitors of the play-houses is not, itself, a corrective of considerable influence, outweighing all minor objections, and tending to reform profligates, whose habits had been previously and elsewhere formed, and who would otherwise indulge their propensities in a more solitary and sequestered manner. The church, in the earlier ages, did not disdain to resort to the instrumentality of the stage for the advancement of virtue; and the "Sacred Drama" was once as much in vogue, in the priestly style, as the play is now with laymen. [. . .]

[. . .] The outline of the present mode of acting may be decribed by three rules in tragedy—they are, 1st. The stride and stamp; one foot about half a yard from the other, and a brisk stamp, to signify a sudden, violent emotion. 2d. A slap upon the forehead with the open right hand, to signify grief and distraction: 3d. A deep sepulchral tone, fixed eyes, and a holding in of the breath, to represent agony of mind and horror. In this last case, both arms are extended straight forwards, with the hands and fingers in a vertical position. As to comedy and farce, the usual acting is any thing you please: a simper, a twirl of a bamboo cane, and a sort of shilly-shally, shambling motion, make the fine gentleman; whilst in farce, the more wry faces that are made, the more in point the acting is generally viewed by the ordinary personages who tread our boards. [. . .]

[83] [Reasons for the "discontinuance of theatrical criticism"]
New England Galaxy [1820]

[. . .] If it be necessary to assign a reason for the discontinuance of theatrical criticism in this paper, there are several at hand, any one of which is sufficient for our justification. In the first place, readers remote from Boston feel no interest in such essays—they know but little about the theatre, and they care less. In the next place, the subject has become tiresome and disgusting to ourselves. To write, weekly, a column or two of remarks upon performances which are remarkable for nothing but ignorance and stupidity, or wilful violations of common sense and propriety, is a task rather too low and humiliating for our ambition. Thirdly, theatrical criticism is unprofitable to the subjects of it, and consequently useless to the public; for actors, who are qualified by nature and education for their profession seldom need a monitor; and those who are not so qualified, will never listen to admonition, though Aristotle, Horace, Addison, Johnson, and all the other criticks of ancient or modern times, should unite to censure, and attempt a reformation. [. . .]

[Nevertheless, the *New England Galaxy* continued to publish theatrical reviews occasionally, but only for a short time and only half-hearted ones.]

[84] "A Tragedy More Interesting Than a Prayer–Meeting."
Boston Recorder [1823]

From the *Evangelical Monitor.*

Mr. Editor,—I lately spent a night in a considerable village in Vermont, where I learned the following facts. In that village, a weekly prayer-meeting had been attended for several years by a few, who mourned over the desolation of Zion, for the particular object of imploring the effusions of the Spirit upon that church and people. On the appointed evening, a gentle snow was falling, in consequence of which, only one person appeared at the house, where the prayer-meeting was appointed; and probably, the usual attendants thought the storm furnished them a sufficient excuse for their neglect. On the same evening, and in the same village, was an exhibition of a tragedy, where the terms of admittance were twenty-five cents, and notwithstanding the tax and badness of the weather, the spacious hall, where they assembled, was full of spectators. [. . .]

[A lamentation about the "deplorable . . . state of religious feeling" follows.]

[89] [*George Barnwell*: Its Moral Usefulness Doubtful]
The Boston Weekly Magazine [1824]

It has long been the custom for masters to send their apprentices to see this play represented, under the impression that it had a good moral tendency. Whether a youth was ever diverted from the path of vice and dissipation, by witnessing the performance of this antiquated piece is very doubtful. Possibly the perusal of the history of Barnwell, on which the play is founded, might have a good effect, but not so the dramatic representation. It is often asserted that a theatre is a school of morality, but it might more properly be called, a "School for Scandal," or rather a scandalous school. It is true that moral sentiments may be uttered from the stage, so they may be any where else, but in listening to these sentiments, can we divest ourselves of the fascination of the place? Can we forget that we are after all in a mere place of public amusement, and are rather there for the purpose of killing time than improving it? Admitting that a youth goes to see the performance of Barnwell once in twelve months, and that the representation makes a solemn impression on his feelings; still does it not lead him to desire to see other plays of quite an opposite character, plays exactly calculated to make him forget the scenes of woe and misery, set forth in the latter part of that dismal tragedy. Is not the youth instructed in acts of villainy which he never before conceived? Is he not taught by the manner in which Barnwell supplies himself with money to lavish on the infamous Millwood, with what facility he might resort to the same means, should his principles ever become so vitiated as to prompt him to it? A youth naturally virtuous, and possessed of a good degree of native genius and integrity, needs no lessons from the dissipated inmates of the green room to strengthen his principles. [. . .]

[91] [Theatre Performances on National Holidays?]
The Boston Weekly Magazine [1824]

We agree with a writer in the *Palladium* of yesterday, that our Theatre ought to be closed on Thanksgiving evening. This writer very justly remarks that the Boston Company, being mostly composed of foreigners, respect the usages of the Church of England, so far as to refrain from performing during Christmas week, while no respect is paid to that day on which the people of New-England, offer their homage for blessings received during the year. We hope that for the future, the theatre may be closed by order of the proper authorities on that evening, which is rendered sacred by the usages of our forefathers.
[For a ban on performances on Saturday evenings, see [123].]

[96] [Different Standards of English and American Theatre]
The New York Literary Gazette and American Athenaeum [1826]

[. . .] We have been present at the representation of two acts of the equestrian melodrama, entitled, *The Invasion of Russia, or the Conflagration of Moscow*, and the impression it created was decidedly unfavourable to the merits of this *grand* and *splendid* piece. The bills inform us that it was performed for 100 successive evenings at Astley's, in London; and well calculated is it, both by the construction of the plot, if it can be allowed to have any, and by the general tone of its politics, for the atmosphere of the British capital, and for the taste of an English audience at an equestrian show. But in an American theatre, devoted to the purposes of the legitimate drama, such European popularity seeking melo-drama, is entirely out of its native element. Entertaining this general opinion of the inaptitude of this piece for an American theatre, we do not deem it necessary to descend to a formal criticism upon its utter want of claims to any merit, either in incident, plot, language, or in a delineation, even tolerable, of the august personages so hardily introduced upon the stage. To see Napoleon—the hero of the Pyramids and of Simplon, of Austerlitz and of Jena, and of Lodi, the prisoner of combined Europe mimicked on the stage—it was asking too much of human forbearance. [. . .]

[97] [The Theatre—a "wide-spreading pestilence"]
Boston Recorder and Religious Telegraph [1826]

THE THEATRE,

In this city, was opened for the season on the Monday evening of last week. We do not mention this fact to give *information*; for all the devotees of pleasure among us are already apprized of it, and have given the event more attention than they would to authentic accounts of a hundred revivals. We mention the fact, to excite Christians to pray against the wide-spreading pestilence; to exhort Christian parents to keep their children from the vortex of destruction; to sound an alarm among all ranks of society, where a relic of virtue or morality remains, and beseech them to feel and tremble while they feel, that "the hour of temptation is come." [. . .]

[98] [*The Stranger*—a "revolting" Specimen of the "German School"]
The New York Literary Gazette and American Athenaeum [1826]

The Stranger.—This play [by August von Kotzebue, adapted by William Dunlap] is more frequently acted on our boards than any other of the German school, excepting perhaps that of *Pizarro*. We admire the [. . .] metaphysical genius of German philosophy, the wild creations of German romance, and the mystical grandeur and shadowy beauty of German poetry. But the *Stranger* is not at all to our taste. It has too much sickly and morbid sensibility, and we are generally disposed with Sir Peter Teazle, to "d—n all sentiment." Because a man's wife runs away, is he to foreswear the world, renounce his rank in life, neglect his duties to society, and forego the activity and the energy of soul which alone keep existence from stagnation? There is neither common nor uncommon sense in this. Macduff, who *disputes* his misfortunes "like a *man*," as well as "*feels* them as a man," is worth a hundred of these moping and sentimental recluses. The play is revolting too in its termination. The Stranger, to be in character, ought to take his coffee at sunset, gaze on the declining orb as he bathes with his glory the arc of the horizon, load his pistols with the best canister powder and leaden *pills*, deliver a speech extempore to Francis, and then blow what brains he has in "tenues auras". Then let Mrs. Haller come in and faint, after giving a hearty shriek, and to wind up, let old Solomon enter and swear that his correspondent at Constantinople had not acquainted him with the Stranger's intentions to commit suicide. To reconcile a man of delicacy, spirit and honor (as the Stranger is represented to be) to Mrs. Haller, after the eternally-dissevering cause of their estrangement, is equally inconsistent with the principle and the pride which belong to a high-blooded and high-minded man. They should be made to go through the circle of life upon its diverging radii, and each step should widen the distance between them. [. . .]

[99] [National Plays Do Not "admit of any criticism"]
The Albion [1827]

On Monday, the anniversary of the battle of New Orleans, a "national drama" called *The Battle of New Orleans* [by William Dunlap], was performed for the first time [at the Bowery Theatre, New York]. These things neither require nor admit of any criticisms. They are offerings on the altar of national pride. He must be a cold-hearted individual who can stop to criticise such appeals to his patriotism. The victory of the 8th of January was honourable and glorious to the American army. The story of that victory written up for dramatic effect could scarcely fail to be received with enthusiasm. The "national drama" of Monday was quite as good as the general run of such pieces. Of course there was no attempt at character. [. . .]

[100] [Shakespeare's Plays Unfit for the Stage]
The Albion [1827]

The Park.—On Monday *Romeo and Juliet*. This tragedy, although one of the most beautiful and pathetic of Shakspeare, has, we know not wherefore, lost much of its attractive power. It is written upon a subject which is familiar to all readers, and wrought up with a truth, skill, and melancholy pathos, which makes it affecting to all hearts. It is an intense story of youthful and untoward passion, told in the sweetest verse that human genius ever penned. It is one long hymn of love. Yet its interest is for the closet, where the heart communes with itself, and not for the open stage where the exquisite delicacy of the poetry is too often marred by the incapable grossness of the personation, and purity of the sentiment debased by the trickery and gaudy "appliances" of the scene. Poetry like that of *Romeo and Juliet* cannot easily or adequately be declaimed. The rich and sparkling conceits—the epithets full of imagination, and the delicious versification of this play are matters not to be made very impressive by any theatrical skill. Nor does any lover that we have yet seen, come up to the vision of youth and beauty which plays before our fancy as *Romeo*.—The heroines of the stage are not of that gentle, sylph-like, heavenly mould which belongs to the *Juliet* of our mind's eye. Even the wit, waggery, and conceit of *Mercutio* are of too artificial texture to be seen through at a glance. It is not at all paradoxical to repeat the assertion, that the love-stories of Shakspeare are wholly *unactable* (if we make such a word.) His historical dramas are of a more representable character, but even these must first undergo a revising process. They must be clipped, trimmed, and embowelled before they are fit for the public eye.—They must first be cut down by some literary tailor to the measure of the stage. [. . .]

[101] [A "well regulated" Theatre—a "school for morality and virtue"]
The Correspondent [1827]

[. . .] That the stage has been often licentious, and its managers eccentric, is beyond all doubt; but this is no argument against its usefulness, or any just cause for its suppression. The theatre, under due encouragement, and proper management, should be regarded a school for morality and virtue. Here we learn, and learn in the most lively and affecting manner, the tendency and force of our affections and passions, and the great use of reason in their conduct and regulation. We see the mischiefs and horrors which result from vice; and the happiness and blessings that crown a regular course of virtue. The sight of a hero, bleeding in the cause of his country, inspires us with courage; and, what is more, the misfortunes of the brave, the virtuous, and the innocent, teach us to feel and to weep; and to society it is of no small consequence to humanize the mind of man, and render the heart tender and susceptible of these impressions; since it would be a curb to wild ambition and lawless power, and prevent the effusion of much human blood.

Nor are these all the advantages that might result from a well regulated drama; for in the theatre our youth could learn an elegant taste, a just and graceful deportment and behaviour, and a proper and forcible elocution and pronunciation, which are no where so well cultivated as on the stage. To fill youth with the love and virtue, to infuse into them noble sentiments, and lead them on in the road to honor and happiness, proper examples should not only be set before them, but these examples should be enforced by proper persons. A lecture on charity by a miser, on economy from an extravagant, on virtue from a debauchee, or on chastity from a prostitute, however well enforced by elocution and pronunciation, is not sufficiently felt, because we perceive the deception. If an orator would affect his audience, (says Cicero,) he must really be affected himself; a rule which concerns the player as well as the orator, and points out the reason why, in some cases, we are so little moved by the most masterly imitators. Propriety of character is, therefore, of infinite consequence on the stage. He who would teach men to live well, should learn to live well himself; for there is no other way to recommend virtue forcibly and effectually.

We go to the theatre to be diverted, and we return instructed. In tragedy, we weep at the misfortunes of others; we perceive by what means those misfortunes arose; and by this example are taught to guard against them. In comedy, when we see our own vices, or foibles ridiculed in others, though we laugh we are stung, and go home and endeavor to correct and conceal them, lest we should be pointed out as the objects of that ridicule. Thus the dramatic

poet, whether serious or gay, makes our pleasures conduce to our profit; awakens the heart to a sense of its duty, and gives us lessons that are permanent and lasting. [. . .]
[Continued in [102]; see also [103].]

[104] J. K. Paulding. [The Situation of the American Drama and Theatre]
The American Quarterly Review [1827]

It might, perhaps, be a question with some, whether it be more indicative of a want of genius in the dramatic writers, or a want of taste in the readers, of these United States, that a large portion of the latter have, we believe, remained to this day ignorant of the very existence of the former. To the frequenters of the theatre, it is known, that some such strange monsters did once, and perhaps do still inhabit this barren wilderness of literature, unless perchance they have been starved to death, or become extinct like the mammoth and various other animals, whose remains sometimes rise up in judgment against them. But to a vast proportion of our readers, they are as if they had never been—not forgotten, for that would be something—but never known.

For this reason, it will no doubt surprise the reader, to learn that we have actually in our possession, nearly sixty American dramas, consisting of tragedies, comedies, operas, serious and comic, melo-dramas and farces, besides others that baffle all our attempts at "codification." [. . .]

To those who have had occasion to observe, and to regret the prevalence of a certain colonial spirit, which equally affects our legal and literary tribunals, and, by a natural consequence, the opinions of the public, it will probably occur, that this total oblivion of our dramatic productions, is entirely owing to the accident of their not being worth remembering, or even meriting a passing notice. A perusal of the plays in our possession, has, however, satisfied us, that this is not altogether the fact. Unless we are greatly mistaken, there are some among them, not entirely unworthy of being read, and which, if represented on our stage, with the advantage of good scenery and good acting, would, or at least ought to be successful. They are, we really think, to say the least of them, quite equal to the productions of the present race of London playwrights, which are regularly brought out at our theatres, and to which the certificate of having been performed a hundred nights, with unbounded applause, gives all the efficacy of a quack medicine.

[. . .] Of all popular amusements ever devised, dramatic exhibitions are, when properly conducted, the most elegant and instructive. They address themselves both to the understanding and the senses, and carry with them the force of precept and example. In witnessing them, we are excited by the passions of others instead of our own, as is the case in the real transactions of life; and that stimulus, which may be pronounced to be one of the actual wants of our nature, is thus afforded to us, without any of the evil consequences resulting from an indulgence of the passions in our own proper persons.

It is by this mode of giving play and excitement to the mind, by mimic representations, that the force of the operations of the passions in real life is unquestionably tempered and restrained; and hence it has always been held with justice, that the stage, in its legitimate and proper state, is a most powerful agent in humanizing and refining mankind. It operates also in other ways in bringing about this salutary result. It allures the people from an attendance upon barbarous and brutifying spectacles—from brawls, boxing-matches, and bull-baitings;—it accustoms them, in a certain degree, to intellectual enjoyments and rational recreations; and substitutes innocent amusement, if not actual instruction, in the place of those which afford neither one nor the other. A theatre, where the price of admittance is within the means of the ordinary classes of the people, is a substitute, and a most salutary one, for tavern brawls and low debauchery. Those whose faculties are too obtuse to relish or comprehend the intrinsic excellence of a plot, the lofty morality or classic ease of the dialogue, are still instructed and amused through the medium of their eyes, and actually see before them examples to imitate or avoid. If it be said, that these examples are too far removed from the ordinary sphere of those who witness them, to be of any use, still it may be replied, that chastity, fortitude, patriotism, and magnanimity, are virtues of all classes of mankind, and that all can feel and comprehend them, though they may be exercised in circumstances and situations in which they never expect to be placed. That the Drama may be, has been, and actually now is, in some degree diverted from its proper and most important purposes, will hardly be denied by those who have the misfortune to like a good play [. . .].

It is generally, we believe, considered a sufficient apology in behalf of the persons who preside over this most delightful of all intellectual banquets, that the degradation of the stage originated in the necessity of administering to a taste already vitiated. The public must be pleased, that the manager may live. If the people require the attractions of a menagerie and a puppet-show combined, and will relish nothing living, but horses, dogs, dromedaries, and elephants, prancing in the midst of pasteboard pageantry, conflagrations, bombardments, springing of mines, blowing up of castles, and such like accumulations of awful nursery horrors, it is alleged that there is no help for it. This taste must be gratified, like the appetites of other animals that chance to prefer raw meat, and offals, to the highest delicacies of the table. This may be true to a certain extent; but we are, notwithstanding, satisfied in our own judgment, that it is very materially in the power of the managers of theatres, to give a better direction to the public taste; and that it would eventually lead to the most profitable results, were they to take equal pains and incur equal expense, to cater for a good taste, that they do to pamper a bad one.

[. . .] If one-half of the sums laid out on pasteboard, tinsel, and trumpery, were offered as a premium for good actors, a first-rate company might be collected, permanently, and fully adequate to give effect to the finest efforts of the dramatist. There would then be no necessity to depend upon perpetual novelty, which supplies the place of good acting; and perpetual shows substituted for the beautiful creations of genius. [. . .]

We are therefore of opinion, that no small portion of this bad taste which we deplore, in relation to the stage, may be fairly laid to the charge of the managers, who, if we mistake not, have been at least accomplices in producing that very state of things which they now offer as an apology for persevering in the same course by which it was brought about. [. . .]

There certainly was a time, when a sterling play, in the hands of sterling actors, was a sufficient attraction to ensure a good house. The public neither required the excitement of wild beasts, nor the allurements of pasteboard mimicry of what nature every day presented to view, in all the attractions of her own inimitable grace and beauty. Can it be pretended that it would not be so now, if the same motives were held out to the public? [. . .]

The perpetual exhibition of shows, possessing no other merit but that of imitating or rather caricaturing nature most vilely, has by degrees rendered the more refined classes of society quite indifferent to the stage, which has of consequence fallen, in a great measure, into the occupation of those who relish *Tom and Jerry* better than Shakspeare or Sheridan. The fashionable people have, for this reason, decided the theatre to be unfashionable [. . .]. One of the first results of this abandonment or indifference to the stage, is the deterioration of both plays and actors. There is no use in writing a good play to please people who have neither taste nor capacity to admire it; and no occasion for first-rate actors, to please an audience whose keenest relish is for dogs, horses, and opera dancers.

The standard plays of a better era will, therefore, remain without any reinforcement from the contributions of later bards; and if any attempt is occasionally made by a manager to bring forward a legitimate drama, for the purpose of exhibiting a *star*, it is taken from a class of productions, excellent indeed, but so destitute of novelty as to be almost indifferent. We have seen it so often, that its very beauties have become stale, and we are fain to follow the universal instinct, which prefers indifferent novelty to worn-out excellence. For this reason it is, that a succession of new plays of merit is indispensable to maintain the stage upon a proper basis. We ourselves are free to confess, that we have so often witnessed the performance of *Hamlet, Macbeth, Othello,* and *Venice Preserved*, as to require the concomitants of new actors and new acting to give them a proper relish. [. . .] The expectation of rewards from those who have the means of rewarding, and the hope of being praised and admired by those whose notice is the height of our ambition, are often the indispensable stimulants by which the morbid sensibilities, and proud indolence of bards, are quickened and inflamed into action. The effort of inspiration, so necessary to all poetical excellence, and which communicates such a glow to every thought, and such a rich redundancy of ideas, is very often but the wish and the hope of being admired by the world. An indifference to any one species of literature, with a decided preference for another, on the part of the public, is the almost certain precursor of decay in the one, and improvement in the other. Hence it has happened, that the talent which, under different circumstances, would have developed itself in dramatic excellence, has, of late, expended itself in novels; simply because all the world reads novels, and but a very small portion of it goes to the theatre.

Another reason, probably, why so few writers attempt the stage of late, is the utter hopelessness of seeing justice done to their productions by the actors. Large as are our modern theatres, they can accommodate but one good performer at a time. [. . .] If it should, therefore, unfortunately happen, that the author has developed more than one character in his piece, which requires something beyond the ordinary talent of a candle-snuffer to personate, it will almost inevitably happen that the piece is condemned. The really good actors belonging to the company, are kept in reserve, while the *star* is exhibiting its splendours; or if brought forward at all, are condemned to toil through their parts neglected and unapplauded, while the course of the *star*, however wayward and eccentric, is hailed with shouts of admiration. In such situations, actors have no motive for exertion, and consequently no exertions will be made. Hence it has become supremely important for a dramatic writer to have but one real character in his piece. The rest must be walking ladies and gentlemen, mere necessary implements, or speaking automata, to afford the *catch-word*, and answer as foils to set off the glories of the *star*.

These stars, or as they may justly be denominated, malignant planets of the stage, it will be noticed, are generally very confined in their excellence. They are, for the most part, incapable of performing more than half a dozen characters, with any extraordinary degree of talent; after which they shoot to some other sphere, and coruscate there awhile, until their lustre is extinguished. If, therefore, an author wishes to produce a successful piece, he must devote it exclusively to the bringing out and exhibiting the peculiar excellencies of the star. If the illustrious itinerant Roscius excels in starts, shrugs, and grimaces, the author must devote his talents to the production of opportunities for the unceasing display of this prominent excellence. If Roscius is great at the single rapier, he must be kept fighting his way through the whole dramatis personae. If he is great at enacting the beast, let him be drunk the whole evening. If inimitable at cold sarcasm, our author must be most bitterly sarcastic. If dignified hauteur be his forte, the play must be stiff as buckram. If his voice happens to be peculiarly loud and sonorous, our author must give him scope and occasion, and "restrain and aggravate" his muse, till she roars throughout like honest Nic Bottom's lion: if, on the contrary, it is especially touching, your play must dissolve in perpetual dews of lachrymal tenderness. In short, the piece must accommodate itself to the actor, not the actor to the piece; and the genius of the author becomes the mere slave of the peculiarities, perhaps the very defects, of the performer. This is assuredly reversing the natural order. The genius that creates, ought to take precedence of the genius which merely exhibits beauties.

The custom of *starring*, as it is now technically called, is, without doubt, highly injurious to the best interests of the stage, the public, and even the managers. From having been at first the privilege only of such as stood decidedly at the head of their profession, and who merely took advantage of the temporary closing of the theatre to which they were attached, to make a summer excursion through the provincial towns, it has become the ordinary privilege of every actor who can attempt one or two of Shakspeare's heroes. They come upon us from all points of the compass—glimmering for a few moments—attracting perhaps one or two full houses, and staying till the imposture is detected; and then pass on to delude some other simple community, which naturally believes they must be great performers, because they travel from place to place, and make such a figure in the play-bills, where their names are always put in great capitals. [. . .]

Really, and seriously, it is quite provoking, to witness the exhibition of not a few of these *starring* performers, who, if the truth must be told, are, for the most part, utterly inadequate to sustain the ordinary characters of a respectable drama, with any tolerable degree of propriety. We are informed, it has become almost impossible to engage the permanent services of a tolerable actor, even by the most liberal offers. By the prevalence of this absurd vanity on the part of the actors, and the equally absurd credulity of the public, our theatres are deprived of any permanent attractions other than those of gorgeous spectacles, prodigious dancers, and prodigious wild beasts. It is beneath the dignity of the theatrical stars to shine in constellations; and the lovers of the true drama, are, consequently, condemned to behold a noble production of genius marred and murdered by negligent or incapable actors, who, if they were ever so capable, have no heart to exert themselves, from a consciousness that their best efforts will receive little attention from an audience so accustomed to the glories of the *stars*, that taper luminaries offer no attraction. The best, if not the only remedy for this evil, would be for the managers to enter into an association not to engage any performers but those unquestionably at the head of the profession, for less than a season. This mode would secure to the principal cities of the United States, the services of respectable actors, since it is in these alone that the public patronage is sufficient for a permanent support, which will remunerate the managers for the expense of retaining a good company. By being thus stationary for a certain period, and to a certain degree dependent on the support of a single community, every actor would then feel the necessity of exertion and improvement, to supply the place of mere novelty, and those who were capable of it would improve accordingly. On the contrary, under the present system of *starring*, a performer goes from place to place, affording no opportunity for a comparison of one effort with another, careless of improvement from a consciousness that novelty and puffing will afford all that is necessary to a temporary success; and that he will be gone before the audience has had time to study his defects. Every other part of the theatre is impoverished to pamper the illustrious itinerant—the orchestra is a desert—the stationary performers are put upon the shortest possible allowance—poor *John* is stript of his livery—and the very play-bills are stinted in their customary allowance of paper. All this is to enable the manager to conciliate the benign influence of a *star*; fill his house some half dozen nights, and make it a desert for the rest of the season. [. . .]

There are many other causes which have, without doubt, co-operated with the preceding, to bring down the stage to its present dead level of degradation. Our limits will not permit us to enumerate them; and having thus far confined ourselves to those which equally apply to this country and England, we will now revert to such as peculiarly belong to the former.

The want of a National Drama, is the first thing that strikes us in this inquiry. By a national drama, we mean, not merely a class of dramatic productions written by Americans, but one appealing directly to the national feelings; founded upon domestic incidents—illustrating or satirizing domestic manners—and, above all, displaying a generous chivalry in the maintenance and vindication of those great and illustrious peculiarities of situation and character, by which we are distinguished from all other nations. We do not hesitate to say, that next to the interests of eternal truth, there is no object more worthy the exercise of the highest attributes of the mind, than that of administering to the just pride of national character, inspiring a feeling for the national glory, and inculcating a love of country. It is this which we would call a national literature; and, unless we greatly err, it is these characteristics which must, eventually, constitute the principal materials of one. We have no peculiar language to create an identity of our own; and it must, in a great measure, be in its apt and peculiar application to ourselves, our situation, character, government and institutions, that our literature would seem destined to become national.

We do not wish to be understood as making an appeal to the national feeling, an indispensable requisite in all American productions; but we do mean to say, that such appeals, when introduced with genuine sentiment and without affectation, are proper and praiseworthy. They are equally advantageous to the author and his readers. They give to the productions of the former, all that peculiar and decisive interest, derived from an association of the efforts of the mind, with manners, incidents, and local affections; and they instil into the latter a more powerful feeling of patriotism. Every man contemplates his country with a greater degree of affection and pride, when he sees its happiness, virtues, or glories, commemorated by genius in a manner, which evinces that he who thus celebrates them, is himself worthy of admiration. There are so few writers of powerful creative imagination, that it savours of a base desertion, to withdraw their genius from the service of their country, and devote those powers which were bestowed by Providence for higher purposes, to themes and exploits having no connexion with her situation or history. The best and most permanent foundation for fame, is our native soil; and a man who is admired or beloved by his own countrymen, may almost dispense with the praises of the rest of the world.

[. . .] For many years subsequent to the establishment of our independence, an American writer laboured under the worst species of discouragement to an aspiring mind. There were comparatively but few general readers, and those were so accustomed to the productions of the mother country, that they viewed the appearance of an American work pretty much in the light a Parisian coterie would the intrusion of a half-civilized Indian. A gentleman of that day would as soon have thought of wearing a homespun coat, as of reading a book of home manufacture. [. . .]

But times have changed, and are daily changing for the better. Abroad, the public curiosity is excited towards the new world; and at home, there is a growing taste for historical truths, and romantic fictions, connected or associated with the progress of this nation. The public mind and taste have been, and now are, in a state to encourage and reward the successful efforts of genius employed on domestic subjects; and although it must be confessed, that some considerable leaven of the old colonial vassalage still remains, to embarrass and discourage, yet still, it may be fairly asserted, that no native writer can now justly plead the fact of the discouragements to which we have just alluded, in extenuation of his indolence, or in explanation of his ill success. By a proper choice of his subjects, and a tolerably happy mode of treating them, he may reasonably calculate upon a moderate success. [. . .]

The remarks we made in relation generally to American literature, may, we think, be specially applied to the drama, which appeals most strongly to popular feelings. Were it not for the obstacles and discouragements we have previously noticed, among which are conspicuous, a want of taste in the audience, and a want of proper management in the conductors of theatres, we think there is little doubt that successful efforts could and would be made, in this branch of literature. This land is full of materials—such as novelty of incident, character, and situation. Like the forests of our country which have never been cut down, those materials remain unemployed and unexhausted—fresh and novel, with all the bold features of primeval strength and vigour. It only requires a brave, original intellect, to convert them into the materials of excellence. It has been often imagined as one of the obstacles which stand in the way of a national drama, that we lack variety in our national character. No idea, we think, can possibly be more erroneous than this. There is, probably, no country in the world, which affords more numerous and distinct characters than the United States. Our cities are full of bipeds from every quarter of the old world, bringing with them all their peculiarities, to be exhibited in a new sphere. From the city on the sea-side, to the frontier settler—from him to the white hunter, more than half savage—to the savage himself—there are continual gradations in the characters and situation of mankind; and every state in the Union is a little world by itself, exhibiting almost the same degrees of difference that we observe in the English, the Scotch, and the Irish. Their manners, habits, occupations, prejudices, and opinions, are equally various and dissimilar. For these reasons, we believe that there is no want of sufficient varieties of character in the United States, to afford ample materials for a diversified drama. We rather fear the obstacle has hitherto arisen from the habit of imitation we have noticed. The author perhaps did not catch any original characters, because he did not think of looking for them; and complained in consequence of the scarcity of what he never took the pains to find. But even conceding, for one moment only, that complaints of a want of variety of character are just; still no one will deny, that there is an abundant field for novelty of situation; and novelty of situation is the best possible substitute for novelty of character, if it does not in reality create it.

The American dramatic productions which we have been able to collect, are many of them, indeed, founded on incidents connected with our past history; but, with few exceptions, they want certain characteristics of locality, as the mineralogists say, and are not properly naturalized. In some of the serious pieces, there is the same lofty, noisy, measured and sonorous dialogue, which constitutes what is called a cold tragedy, and betokens the bad taste of the author, if not his utter incapacity to feel a passion, or communicate it to his readers. [. . .] [Here the author gives examples of faults in language or style from several American plays.]

[. . .] We cannot but confess [. . .] that a majority of the pieces in our collection may be consigned over to oblivion, without any material loss either to the present or future generations. They are marvellously defective in plot, sentiment, and dialogue; and do not even come up to the present standard of a London audience. They would hardly run a hundred nights in that great emporium of commerce and taste, without the aid of an elephant, a rhinoceros, or a *star* at least: they are the efforts of writers destitute of almost every requisite for dramatic composition; and who ought never to have obtruded them upon the public eye. Others, on the contrary, indicate talents which only require the discipline of study, reflection, practice, and encouragement, to attain at least a respectable eminence. [. . .] The first requisite for producing a National Drama, is national encouragement. We do not mean pensions and premiums—but liberal praise and rewards to success—and a liberal allowance for failures. The second, is a little more taste and liberality in the managers of our theatres; and the third, is the presence of competent performers, collected in companies of sufficient strength to give effectual support to a new piece, and sufficient talent to personate an original character, without resorting to some hacknied model, which has descended from generation to generation, and like all copies, lost something of the original in the hands of each succeeding imitator. [. . .]

[110] [The Virtue of the Drama vs. the "pest-house" of the Theatre]
Boston Recorder and Religious Telegraph [1827]

[. . .] The Theatre hath had its enemies and its hired defenders; the good and ill effects of the drama have been often pointed out, oftentimes cried out unto the heedless world, who care not, in the search for enjoyment, whether the grasp is good or evil: suffice it to say on the one point, no man of reason can be an enemy to the drama—I mean the written works of genius—the perusal—the honest enaction of some of which, if it were withheld from the world, would be a loss to virtue, of lessons more powerful, more impressive, than a thousand homilies from the lips of paid preachers; but it is the mimics, the charlatans, the performers, and the fashion of the enaction, that every moral man should condemn; in these consist the danger, and the causes for which the Theatre should be shunned, even as a pest-house, where disease and death is to be received. What is the life of an actor? drunkenness, debauchery, harlotry and dissipation of every kind. Who are those men? vagabond strollers at first, characters of the most desperate description, who have had but one choice, the highway or the stage. [. . .] And then there is a drinking-house about the purlieus of the town (Theatre?) where there is more riotous revelry, or more encouragement, open and unbridled by law, for youth to be led astray. [. . .] The very nature of an actress' life is such, that she must be a woman of little honor:—for what modest female would expose herself before the sight, the rude and daring eyes of thousands, and bear the remarks, and the examination, of the sensualist and the debauchee; for their amusement assume dresses, habits unbecoming her sex, and even common modesty. [. . .] Ought, then, such a place to be encouraged as a resort? The brothel of infamy should be perferred to the stage, which is alone prostituted to show off bawds, drunkards, and gambling sharpers. And do not those who encourage impurity by resorting to the home of charlatry, soon feel the ill effects:—it is the rock whereon youth is wrecked oftener than any other that can be shown; it leads to drunkenness, gaming, and every other wickedness. There have been formed Societies to suppress vice; they will persecute the poor wretch who steals for his bread, and yet the very root of crime is maintained, the abode of sharpers, dissipation and ruin; for there is an enchantment about the Theatre—beauty that is to be bought, and riot that can be pursued; the apprentice will rob his master, the child his parent; the husband hath taken the labor of the day to gain him admission, while at home his family is wanting food; a few years beholds the first an inmate of a prison; the second a poor lost wretch, discarded from his home, and begging for money to obtain liquor, that all reflection may be drowned in its overwhelming influence; the last the pander of some brothel, while the sod covers the broken heart of his wife, and his innocent and unfortunate offspring are scattered on the bosom of the cold and pitiless world.

[112] [Causes for the Decline of the Drama and Suggestions for Remedies]
The Albion [1828]

[. . .] There are several causes existing for the general decline of the drama during the present age, but it will be sufficient for our purpose to point out the following.—Dearth of talent, both male and female—the practice of authors making plays for actors, instead of compelling the actors to conform themselves to the plays as heretofore—the system of *starring*—the inordinate introduction of showy pieces—the increased quantity of fashionable reading in novels, magazines, reviews, &c.—and the improved state of society in private parties and *soirees*. The last, however, is one of the principal, for while the state of private society has been advancing, the state of the stage has been retrograding; so much so that during one half, perhaps, three fourths of the season an intellectual man has far more inducements to pass his evenings at a party, than to go to the theatre. Finding their houses deserted, the managers, instead of applying a remedy to the proper place, resorted to *stars, spectacles*, and other novelties, which soon disgusted the man of real taste, and in the end produced a diseased appetite in the public mind, which required to be fed with increased quantities of extravagance and bad taste, until the unnatural stimulus lost its effect altogether. [. . .] If it be asked, why do not the managers bring forward in due rotation the fine old comedies and tragedies which delighted our fathers? the answer is obvious—there are no persons living, with one or two exceptions, to take the first parts. Our Garricks, and Kembles, and Siddons's, and O'Neils are gone, and the managers having spent all their money upon *stars* and *spectacles*, have been obliged, or have allowed the good second rate actors to fall into neglect;—or the latter, seeing the rage for *starring*, have attempted to become stars themselves, and have thereby either perished in the attempt, or rendered themselves unfit for any thing. [. . .] Under such a state of things, what inducement has an author to write? He must condescend to write a play for a particular actor, and render his genius subservient to the notions and peculiarities—perhaps mortal deformities—of a blockhead, or his piece is *damn'd*. And even if an author does thus condescend to prostitute his talent, and is successful in his *measure*, the character (for among other absurdities of the modern school there is only one hero in the play) will not fit any other person, and therefore becomes temporary and ephemeral, adding nothing to the general stock of literature, but soon passing away to make room for another equally fleeting, worthless, and evanescent.

Having shown that the present system is replete with mischief to the true interests of the Drama, and sufficient to account for its present degraded state, we shall say a few words upon the subject, of reforming these abuses. The grand remedy, in our opinion, is, to form good stationary companies, and to get up the old classic plays in a style which their merits entitle them to. Let no play be attempted, unless it can be well performed in all its principal parts—let the public know, that when a performance is advertised, it will be *well done*—and thus remove the general impression, that it will be badly done. It is, in fact, now taken for granted, that, unless one shining *star* is present, every piece attempted at a theatre will be regularly *murdered*, as the phrase is. [. . .] We will suppose, then, that the manager of the Park, or the Bowery, or any other Theatre, engages as strong a company as the country will afford, in tragedy, comedy, opera, melo-drama, and farce, and brings out all the pieces he attempts in a complete and perfect manner,—will not the public reward him accordingly? We say, decidedly, they will, even if he doubles his salary list. A good and efficient company being organized, a list of the best comedies and tragedies should be made out and published, specifying when each would come in turn to be acted; nights also should be set apart for the different kinds of entertainment; thus, on Monday a tragedy may be performed; on Tuesday, an Opera; on Wednesday, a Comedy; on Thursday, a Melo Drama; on Friday and Saturday, a repetition of Melo Drama and Opera, or a Benefit, as may be necessary and advisable. This plan would enable the public to make their choice, not only of the kind [of] play, but the play itself, and the night which they shall devote to dramatic amusement,—an arrangement of great convenience, and would prevent the collision of private parties with favourite nights at the Theatre. [. . .]

[113] [Call for a National Drama]
The Critic [1828]

[. . .] The stage, under proper regulations and supervision, is the most—or, at all events, one of the most—powerful means that can be made use of for the dissemination of correct principles of taste, for the inculcation of heroism and virtue, and a fixed detestation of vice. When genius creates, and wisdom revises, and eloquence pronounces, and painting adorns, and music accompanies, the productions there exhibited, the heart of the spectator must be callous indeed, if it thrill not in responsive acknowledgment of the potency of the combination. It is then that "illusion's perfect triumph comes," and the mind is vanquished by the united power of precept and example. The dead are evoked from their graves, not to teach, but *live* the lessons of the sage, and the sentiments which they utter receive a forceful commentary from their actions.

As an instrument for the formation of national character, the stage might be made to work a very important influence on society; and with those who view the subject in a proper light, the deficiency of our dramatic literature is considered a matter of serious regret.

The materials for a national tragic drama amongst us are not very abundant. The heroic achievements of our fathers, during the dark hours of the revolutionary struggle—that starless moral night, the horrours of which tried men's souls—are still too recent to be moulded to the purposes of the tragic muse. The mind would turn with disgust from any portion of fiction, intermingled with scenes, with every feature of which, all are familiar; and the unities necessary for scenic effect could not be preserved, without, in some instances a slight, and in others, a material departure from historic truth. The wars of the early settlers with the fierce and unrelenting savages, are not liable to the same objection; and in reading the accounts of these one would naturally suppose that characters, situations, and incidents, might be drawn from them, which, woven into tragedy, could not fail to delight an audience. At all events, it is to be hoped that some of those who have given such indubitable proofs of poetic genius in lyric compositions, may attempt a loftier strain, animated by the praiseworthy desire of presenting, in a proper light, the peculiarities of our national character, of warming the public breast with the ennobling sentiment of national love, and kindling a laudable pride on account of our national glory.

To the muse of comedy more abundant materials lie open. The kind of incidents proper for this branch of the drama are of every day occurrence; and we wonder that no vigorous writer has not hitherto seized hold of some of them, for the purpose of introducing to an American audience portraits of themselves, in which their peculiarities both commendable and blameworthy, both of an exalted character, and ludicrous, should be happily hit off. For the life of us we cannot see why New-York, or Philadelphia, or Boston, or Charleston, or any other of our numerous cities, would not be as good a location for the fable of a comedy, as London; why an American gentleman would not make as good a hero as an Englishman; why one of our dandies might not be brought in as his foil; why the distinct and strongly marked stateisms (to make another word) might not be placed in amusing contrast; why our pretty city belles would not be good heroines, and lastly, why our lawyers (for there must generally be one of that class to make up the *dramatis personae*) could not supply as facetious knaves, as transatlantic writers have found or feigned in London.

Perhaps the apparent dearth of dramatic talent among American authors may rather result from a want of proper and sufficient encouragement, than from any real deficiency of ability. He who only glances at the subject can hardly believe, that of all the attempts by native writers, in this department of literature, not one was meritorious; and should he have curiosity enough to enter into an examination, he will be convinced that such is not the case. For ourself, we have perused several productions, which, after lingering a few nights before thin houses, that damned with faint praise, were soon crowded from the stage, by pieces of less genuine merit, but more pleasing—(why? because they had received the stamp of a London audience, and, of course, must be current gold!) we say we have perused several of these, and do not hesitate to pronounce them, in most respects, far superiour to half the successful trash that is every season imported from abroad. The truth is, the reason why an American is forced to blush, when he speaks of American dramatic literature, may be found in the clogs and hindrances which American prejudice has thrown in the dramatic author's path. We are distrustful of our own judgment, and afraid to condemn or applaud, when not directed in our decision, by the previous decision of English critics. It is but a very short time since we released ourselves from British leading-strings, in relation to the other walks of letters, compelled to do so by the genius of an [Washington] Irving, a [James F.] Cooper, a [William Cullen] Bryant, a [Fitz-Greene] Halleck, and the like; and until some great dramatic writer shall arise amongst us, to tell pale-hearted fear it lies, to force us to depend upon ourselves, and judge for ourselves, to draw, by the magic power of his genius, the tribute of applause from our hearts, while they tremble at their own temerity—till then (and there has hitherto been but one Shakspeare) we shall be afraid to encourage native dramatic bards as they ought to be encouraged, and shall be obliged to depend on England for our plays, as, till very recently, we did for our players and managers.

The mention of managers, reminds us of another, though subordinate cause of the deficiency of indigenous dramas. These men have a much greater share than is generally supposed, in debauching the public taste, particularly in this community, which, of all communities on earth, is the most gullible. In the language of Dr. Johnson, they exclaim,

> Ah, let not censure term our fate our choice,
> The stage but echoes back the public voice;

but this, though it sounds very well in poetry, is not exactly so in point of fact. It is too often the case that managers foist entertainments upon the public, for which the natural appetite never would have asked; and like the foolish mother, after having suffered her infant offspring to taste of deleterious sweets, they affect to wonder that a gust should be created for the noxious banquet. When was it the case that sterling tragedies, and comedies, and farces, well supported, did not prove attractive? And if never, how can managers have the unblushing effrontery to declare that the public voice required horses and dogs, and lascivious dancers? Let us be fairly understood. We say the legitimate drama, properly sustained, never yet proved unattractive. But in this assertion it is not meant to deny, that this community, or any community, though twenty times as numerous as this, may become tired with the repeated exhibitions of a single individual, who has but one style, and plays but a limited number of characters. Because the play bills announce one actor, or even two, engaged at an enormous sum, in the principal part, or parts, of a tragedy, it does not follow of course that the benches of the theatre will be crowded; for unless the minor parts are also well supported, there can be no illusion, and that is an essential deficiency in the majority of those who patronise scenic representations. Let our managers abjure French dancers and flying Indians, elephants and horses, phantom ships and real ships, and all the rest of the nonsensical trash, with which they have surfeited the public; let them, also, for the speaking parts, engage men who know how to read and write; let the parts of gentlemen, noblemen, &c. be personated by those who have some semblance of gentility in their manners and appearance; and let them remand to the stall and workboard the animated blocks that have heretofore destroyed the entertainment of an audience, by their execrable caricatures, and we shall be sadly mistaken if they do not find their advantage in the reformation. [. . .]

[115] [Proofs of the Immorality of the Theatre]
Hopkinsian Magazine [1829]

[. . .] The Theatre has been recommended as a school of morals, until the company of those who have been ruined by it has become too large to be passed by unnoticed. Clothed in rags, they stand at the corners of the streets and linger around the bar-rooms. They prey upon the community, they throng our prisons and work-houses, and cast a blight over every green thing. These *dead* are *living* witnesses against the Theatre, for there they began their downward course. But still there are a few men, and but a few, who persist in calling the Theatre a school of morals. And if you press them for proofs, they will always tell you of the man who was brought to reflect upon his wicked ways, and to forsake them, by witnessing the performance of George Barnwell. This is the only instance we ever heard mentioned of a man's becoming better by going to the Theatre. This man, *they say*, became a good man, an eminent Christian, a minister of the gospel; and he received his first impressions at the Theatre! It may be so. And there are other bad places in which men have become alarmed at the sight of their own wickedness. Doubtless, this man advised all his hearers to visit, without delay, this place so favourable to piety! But where are the men whose morals have been bettered by constant attendance on theatrical amusements? [. . .] we will [. . .] attend to a few arguments, which have satisfied our minds upon this subject.

In the *first* place, *That* cannot be an innocent amusement which tends to intemperance. Within the walls of the Theatre, bar-rooms are kept, which bring great gain to the proprietors. They reason thus: A large proportion of those who visit the Theatre, are accustomed to the daily use of ardent spirits; and if we do not offer them facilities to the gratification of this habit, they will not patronise our establishment. Our business is to please the public. If there were no bar-rooms in the Theatre, and no grog-shops in its neighbourhood, the cry would be, "*Rum or no play! Brandy or no play!*" The managers are perfectly aware of this, and have concluded to give their patrons what they like best, regardless of consequences. In this way the Theatre has become a manufactury of drunkards.

In the *second* place, *That* amusement cannot be innocent, which tends to extravagance in dress. If the mirror and the toilet could testify, they would tell of hours and days spent in preparing to shine at the play. And then the expense. If it had been given to the poor and the sick, it would have rejoiced the widow's heart, and restored the flush of health to the faded cheek.

Thirdly, The Theatre is a place, where nature is overacted—where false notions are instilled into the mind—where vice is held up to applause, and virtue degraded—where religion is ridiculed—where vile and immodest inuendoes are thrown out, in order to please the most worthless portion of the community. Think, too, of *the waste of time*. What if religious meetings were held *five evenings* in a week, until 11 o'clock at night, and after breaking up, the company formed themselves into smaller circles, in different neighbourhoods, and then read and prayed, and sung and conversed on religious subjects, until two or three in the morning—How would the cry of *extravagance* and *fanaticism* ring throughout the country? The papers of the day would be loaded with complaints; the husband and wife would be separated; *the peace of families would be broken up*. What if the anxiety to attend a meeting for religious purposes, were as great as the anxiety to hear a favourite performer upon a benefit-night? What if the anxious should throng around the doors of our churches, as some do around the ticket-office, and should cry, "what shall we do," with a feeling as deep as theirs? Surely *the world would be turned upside down*.

Finally, *That* amusement cannot be innocent, which tends to *lasciviousness*. It is a fact, not to be concealed, that the company of lewd women is expected and desired, at the Theatre. A place is assigned them, so prominent, that every body can see it. It has been said, and it is undoubtedly a fact, that tickets of admission, free of all expense, are sometimes sent by the managers to these abandoned wretches. The *freedom of the Theatre* has been conferred upon them, in consideration of their important and highly acceptable services!—Others must pay for the privilege of witnessing the performance; but the abandoned go for nothing. And how is this? Are harlots so necessary to this *innocent* amusement? Are they a part of the corps theatrical? Doubtless they contribute their full share of interest. Enough, however, has been said, respecting the innocence of that amusement which calls into exercise the worst passions of our nature. [. . .]

[116] [The Theatre As "public instructor"]
The Philadelphia Monthly Magazine [1829]

[. . .] The principal object contemplated in the ensuing observations, is, to enumerate and expose the corruptions which have been so long prevalent in the construction and display of dramatic productions. [. . .] It will not, however, be considered irrelative to the main subject of the present article, to advert to some of the reasons which may be adduced in support of dramatic exhibitions, in reference to the capacity which they possess of promoting the improvement of society, by inculcating precepts of morality. [. . .]

[. . .] that a well regulated drama might be not only inoffensive, but of positive advantage to the interests of morality, may be learned from the past history and the actual condition of every country in which theatrical representations have been and are properly encouraged. Compared with other countries, where the efforts of dramatic writers and performers have been either feebly supported or entirely prohibited, those in which they have received their just commendation and recompense exhibit in the character of their inhabitants unexceptionable moral purity. England, France, the United States, and some parts of Germany, where genius is permitted and even encouraged to devote itself to the cause of the drama, are infinitely superior in the morality of their population to any other portions of the world, in which the stage is suffered to languish or exposed to persecution. Who admires or applauds the moral excellence of Italy, of Spain, or of Portugal? In these countries the theatre, if it can with truth be said to have ever flourished, has been for centuries degenerating, and can now hardly be considered as having an existence. It is not intended to assert of the drama, that had it been properly supported in these debased and licentious countries, they would, by its influence, have been preserved from the moral ruin by which they have been visited. But if any argument against theatrical exhibitions is to be founded on the effect which they may have upon the moral condition of society, it is perfectly just to infer from the comparison of countries in which they are known and liberally encouraged, with others in which they are neglected or forbidden, that they do exercise a favorable influence over moral principles and conduct. [. . .]

[. . .] The stage may exert a powerful control over opinions and manners, when its precepts are deduced, not from speculative or romantic sources, but from actual nature and experience; when they are devised with wisdom, and delivered, not as arbitrary dictations, but as kind admonitions; when the examples by which it illustrates their propriety and the catastrophes that it develops conform to reason and probability, and enforce the justice or impropriety of human actions, by exhibiting the guilty as suffering the just punishment of their offences, and the innocent and virtuous as receiving their merited recompense. If the moral lessons which it is designed to impart are to be considered as unavailing; if it has in reality no control over opinions and manners, all the reasoning of moral writers, most of the examples which are held up to view in real life, even the sacred admonitions and expostulations delivered from the pulpit, may be considered as equally ineffectual. For if the morality of the drama be correct and practical; if it be dispensed by those who are worthy of being its teachers; if the causes to which the dramatic writer refers the triumph of innocence and the punishment of crime, be natural and rational, and if he maintain a proper consistency between them and their results, his influence upon the consciences and conduct of men must be both powerful and beneficial. [. . .]

[. . .] Yet it will not be denied, that some of the great men who have devoted themselves to the practical exercise of the dramatic profession, have been as eminent for the accuracy and dignity of their diction, as for the genius which they displayed as representatives of the characters that they assumed. Among them are to be found those who have united with the practice of their avowed profession, a severe and philosophical research into the principles of language; whose elevated and correct conception of it was acknowledged and admired; whose proper modulation of voice, distinct and pure enunciation, and exact conformity to the best rules of philological literature have imparted to their reputation a lustre which others, equal to themselves in personating human character, have not acquired. The improvement which they attempted or effected in language may be thought of minor importance, when compared with the power which their art exercises over taste; and it certainly is so. That such a power is possessed by the drama, and has an effective operation, may be demonstrated by the foregoing reference to countries in which it has attained to the greatest degree of perfection, and contrasting their refinement with the rudeness which is apparent in other countries, where the stage has never been known, or is in a state of decay. Without seeking examples in the ages of antiquity, or the classical cities of Athens and Rome, we may find in modern Europe and in our own country, sufficient evidence of the happy effect which is produced upon general taste by a theatre judiciously constituted and directed. London, Paris, Vienna, Berlin, and other capital cities of Europe, have undoubtedly derived from the spirit which the dramatic Muses have aroused and maintain within them, a refinement in taste which is not visible in other places, where that spirit does not prevail. In the large cities of the United States, where the theatre is properly organized and supported, a similar result is perceived. If their inhabitants are not all, or nearly all, superior to those of other cities for the correctness of their language and the courtesy of their manners, there may be observed among them a general character of refinement, which is not so discernible elsewhere. If they are not so distinguished for the critical precision and elegance of their expression, as the people of Attica are reputed to have been, there is apparent in their language, as well as in their habits and taste, a propriety, which is not observed where the drama does not exist or is not favored.

If the theatre be acknowledged to exercise important influence in forming and preserving correct principles of taste, the expediency of observing a scrupulous vigilance over it will be conceded. All innovations upon rules which have been devised by men of genius, for its government, ought to be opposed. Dramatic writers and actors should be held responsible to the community, to whose pleasure and improvement they profess to contribute, for the false and corrupt taste which they endeavor to inculcate. If they are recognised as public teachers of polite manners and refined taste, they are the more reprehensible, for abusing the great trust which is confided to them, by perverting the principles of which they avow themselves to be the advocates. And have they not frequently violated—are they not now violating these principles? [. . .] Instead of the substantial productions which so many men of genius have offered in the two great departments of the drama, we are surfeited with the wild absurdities of those who write, not to benefit society, or gain high and lasting reputation for themselves, but to gratify the ear with pompous declamation, and excite puerile curiosity, by calling to their aid the magnificence of decoration, which is considered necessary to supply the want of sense and consistency in plot and dialogue and catastrophe. The eye, rather than the mind, is appealed to for the success of these fantastical exhibitions. The scene painter, the property man, and the mechanist are the actors, to whom the performances are intrusted, and on whose exertions they depend for their favorable reception. [. . .] Splendid illusions are presented, as substitutes for the representatives of men and things which, although we survey them as only copies of realities, we do not consider as altogether ideal, or as having no originals in existence. The imagination is bewildered, by the supernatural achievements and creatures that the ingenuity of the great show-makers has contrived. The sight is dazzled with the unearthly splendor of the palaces and thrones that spring up before it, at the touch of some magician's wand, the glorious charms of princesses, who occupy the regal edifices, and the magnificent state of the fairy kings who are placed upon these imperial seats. Pantomime and melo-drama, burletta, extravaganza and opera are rapidly acquiring—they have already acquired precedence of regular and rational dramatic pieces. Harlequin and Columbine, and all the buffooneries of the Italian stage will soon expel from the lawful dominion of the Muses, the proper representatives of men and faithful portraitures of human character and manners. These are deemed too tame, too insipid and uninteresting to merit the study of actors and admiration of spectators. Every thing connected with the stage must now be grand, imposing and extraordinary. [. . .] Grand military spectacles are indeed becoming so fashionable, that there is great danger to be apprehended to the amicable civic spirit which should bear rule among christian men. We may well fear that there will soon be substituted for it the warlike propensity, which shall convert all our ambitious youth into blood-letting, fire-eating heroes, as Schiller's Charles de Moor is reported to have transformed so many mild striplings of Germany into ferocious highway-men. All is glitter, pomp, noise and smoke; and if the ears and eyes of those who frequent the theatre can retain the full possession of their senses, under the incessant assaults which are made upon them, there must be more optical and auditory power of nerve in the world than has yet been known to philosophy. [. . .]

[120] [The Stage—a "copy of human life"]
The New-York Mirror [1829]

[. . .] Now, the stage is much better than the world. It is there that the *spirit* of the real drama of life is given, separated from the wide field of dry detail, and the ocean of commonplace. Wit and humour have there exhibited the faults and foibles, the whims and oddities of mankind in their richest and happiest lights. Genius has pored over the deep and mysterious volume of nature—has soared into the boundless regions of imagination—dwelt upon the records of history—listened to the wild traditionary legends of other years,—and the pictures which have thence arisen in his mind, he has clothed in all the gorgeous glory and everlasting beauty of poetry; and from the stage, they make their appeal to the hearts and souls of men;—that is, when the players are good for any thing—otherwise, the aforesaid goes for nothing; for a "poor player" (poor in the worst sense of the word) is a greater transmutator of metals than any alchymist that ever studied the golden science—he can make Sheridan heavy and Shakspeare bombastic, and his dulness is more omnipotent than the humour of Colman or the wit of Congreve.

The stage! It is an abridged copy of human life—a selection of its most prominent points—the few grains of wheat separated from the many bushels of chaff, and which, unlike Gratiano's reasons, are well worth the having. It is here that pleasure is real and pain fictitious, for sorrow ceases with the fifth act, while the gibes and jokes—the merry thoughts and happy conceits, become the property of the audience. A tragedy is the best illustration of the "luxury of wo," and the harrowing feelings that might be left upon the mind by the representation of Othello's jealousy and Desdemona's sorrows are mellowed by the recollection that the "wronged Othello" is probably, after death, swallowing his wine, and the "gentle Desdemona" discussing her supper. And however the stage may have been profaned by blockheads, or denounced by worthy well-meaning gentlemen who did not know exactly what they were talking about, and who ran full tilt at its abuses, altogether overlooking its uses, it will ever continue the favorite amusement of a moral and sensible people. In semi-barbarous nations, like Austria—in deplorably ignorant ones, like Spain and Portugal—or in those totally debauched and degraded, like Italy, the drama is in very slight request; but wherever taste, intelligence and prosperity prevail, it has been, is, and will be, held in deserved estimation. [. . .]

[121] [The Overabundance of Spectacles on the Stage]
The New–York Mirror [1829]

[. . .] There are [. . .] some things occasionally exhibited which there is no getting over, to wit, dogs, horses, elephants, and the brute creation in general—real fire and real water, wonderful ascensions from the stage to the gallery, impressive ceremonies of shooting deserters, jugglers, rope-dancers, and little children—these are unalloyed, unmitigated evils.

But though gauds and show, and spectacles and melo-dramas are pleasant enough occasionally and in their place, it is the interest and duty of every one who values sound rational dramatic representations to raise his voice against them when they are too frequently introduced, and assume an undue importance in the evening's entertainment. They are well enough as a dessert after more solid and substantial aliment, but if furnished as the principal intellectual food for the theatre-going public, the inevitable consequence will be depravity of taste and attenuation of intellect. Let a good tragedy or comedy, which in itself contains enough poetry and passion, wit and sense for any reasonable man for one evening, be first enacted, and then let whatever popular nonsense most in vogue occasionally follow, by which arrangement all parties will be satisfied. Though the public cannot justly be charged with indifference in respect to Shakspeare, yet it is to be regretted that they certainly do display an apathy towards the genuine old comedies (ah! they know not the treasures that they pass unheeded by) yet this, in a great measure, arises from their not being familiar with their merits. The Park theatre has now a stock company capable of, to say the least, acting respectably almost any comedy in the English language, and the managers ought to endeavour to *create* a taste for the more correct appreciation of the genuine excellencies of the old dramatic authors. Let them not be discouraged by a few indifferent houses, but persevere. If they were to set apart a particular night in each week for the production of a sterling comedy, this would amount to between forty and fifty pieces of real merit in the course of the season—an immense acquisition. And if the newspapers and literary journals were to make a point of especially noticing and commenting on that evening's performance, there is little doubt that in a short time it would not only be creditable and profitable to the managers but creditable and profitable to the public.

[124] J. K. Paulding. [Literary Independence Expected]
The American Quarterly Review [1830]

[. . .] As yet [. . .] it must be confessed, our feelings of independence seem altogether of the physical and political kind, and we are content to be enslaved in mind, so long as our political institutions and actions are free. We have lost sight of the noble maxim, that dominion over our own minds is the noblest species of freedom; and that of those who have not the manliness to think for themselves, it is of little consequence whether or not they possess the power of regulating their own actions.

[. . .] The truth is, that all nations in their progress to maturity have enriched their literature, in the first instance, by borrowing. This has been the foundation of their national literature, which adapting what it borrowed to their peculiar habits, manners, language and opinions, at length by degrees infused into it the national spirit and genius. [. . .] We begin by imitating, and end in setting up for ourselves as originals.

We think it is high time for the Americans, we mean the people of the United States, to begin to aspire to the latter distinction. We do not mean by departing from the good old sound rules and examples, derived from the authority of past ages, but by adapting those rules, and applying those examples, to the delineation of those peculiarities, which may be called national, and of which every country presents more or less to an observing eye. It is not necessary to be always writing on national subjects, or illustrating our own history and manners. But we do think, that the literature of a new country, new in its existence, its institutions, and situations, ought to have a special reference to these circumstances. It is this reference which alone can give it originality, and maintain its claims to a national character.

[. . .] Let us continue to yield due attention to the cultivation and patronage of our own genius, and there is not the least fear, but that in due time, we too shall produce our masterpieces in every department of the arts, sciences and literature. The genius of liberty has never yet allied itself to ignorance; and the people of the United States are certainly not destined to afford the first example.

Influenced by these ideas, and animated with this honest confidence, we are at all times happy to see and willing to encourage the attempts of our young writers, whenever we can do it without misleading the public taste and belying our own sentiments. In a new country every thing is to be created, while in an old country every thing is going to decay. The progress of the first to maturity is slow but sure; and, while the other may throw out an occasional spark of its ancient fires, or exhibit a few convulsive throes of expiring strength, the calm reflecting observer, who applies the experience and history of the past to the solemn, significant warnings of the present, cannot but see that it is gradually sliding from that high eminence on which others will perhaps ere long be its successors.

The number of attempts at dramatic productions lately made in this country, encourage us to hope, that the time is not far distant, when we shall see the American stage, sometimes at least, occupied with American performances. We do not mean that the masterpieces of the English drama will be superseded, but that we shall be no longer obliged to borrow the wretched offals of English play-wrights, which are every night exhibited on our theatres, to the utter corruption of the public taste, and the total debasement of a polite and elegant source of rational amusement. [. . .]

[American Drama Should Represent American Democratic Values]
[A comment on David Paul Brown's *Sertorius; Or, The Roman Patriot* (1830):]
[. . .] No one can doubt but that it is perfectly in character for Sertorius to speak contemptuously of the people; but it may, we think, be doubted, whether it be equally in character for an American writer and citizen, to select a subject, in which it is proper to introduce such sentiments. It was very natural and proper for Shakspeare, the subject of a haughty mistress, addressing himself to a proud aristocracy, and dependent on it for patronage, to take every opportunity of throwing contempt and ridicule on every interference of the people in the affairs of government. But is it natural and proper, that a writer, claiming the high honour of being the citizen of a free country, where all power emanates and is acknowledged to emanate from the people, should follow in the same beaten path, and commit disloyalty to *his* sovereign? On the contrary, it seems to us, that we should take a different course; and if we chose to introduce the people at all on the stage, it should not be as the writers under a despotic government have done, to represent them as beasts of burthen, having no voice in the state, and no business to interfere with it, even when they are crushed to the earth by oppression. It should, we think, be one characteristic of an American writer to speak respectfully of the people; to treat them as rational beings, and to incite them to noble feelings and actions, by raising instead of depressing them in the scale of being, rather than indulge ourselves in imitating those in whom such things are perfectly natural. This would be one step towards a national literature. At present, while all our political writers are paying abject homage to the people, those of every other species are combined, it would seem, with the advocates of despotism, in making them appear as degraded and contemptible as possible. It would be better for all parties to unite to instil into them true principles of government and morals, and to impress them with a just sense of their real consequence in the state.

[American Drama Should Exhibit American Heroism]
[A comment on Richard Penn Smith's *The Eighth of January* (1829):]
[. . .] We cannot forbear cautioning the writer, however, when next he may attempt a patriotic piece, for the illustration of an American act of heroism, not

to leave it doubtful where an American audience is to bestow its admiration. In the present instance, the stern integrity and sturdy patriotism of honest John Bull, the English miller, present a most formidable offset to the daring gallantry and disinterested heroism of the saviour of New-Orleans [Andrew Jackson]. Let us do full justice to our enemies; but it ever has, and ever will be found impracticable, to please both sides. We should be content to let the English praise themselves, and we may rest assured they will never want praise. Propriety, as well as poetical justice, required that there should be but one incontestable hero of the piece, and that he should be our countryman. But our author can plead precedent. There is an American drama, written by a very worthy, amiable, and clever American [William Dunlap's *André*, 1798], on the subject of the capture of Andre, which is performed in New–York almost every 4th of July, and in which the whole interest centres exclusively in the spy. [. . .]

[125] [Incompetence and Dishonesty of Theatrical Critics]
The Euterpeiad [1830]

On entering upon our new career, we are extremely happy to find that much trouble is taken off our hands, and that theatrical criticism is a thing of so easy attainment, as to be within any Tyro's reach, even if from the lowest form of the lowest class. To explain ourselves briefly: it is reduced to the following simple formula:—Take a sheet of writing paper. If you have not previously resolved in your mind whether you will praise a *manager, establishment,* or *performer,* or d—n him, or it, this must be determined. Then take up any modern popular print, extract therefrom all the strongest epithets, which float upon the surface of the column, devoted to any given theatrical aspirant, or interest. If these are too evanescent to stay upon the paper while it finds its way to the printer, then have recourse to a file of old newspapers, and see if, by throwing into your ink a resinous drug, called *tickling gum,* you cannot make your *characters* permanent. Then look into the works of [British satirist Charles] Churchill. Afterwards introduce some choice old magazine scraps, which may answer your purpose, translated verbatim. And sometimes you may, if you have time, copy out passages from contemporaries, if you are an adept at disguising what you borrow, never forgetting those honeyed phrases, and jessamine and woodbine turns of compliment, of which lady performers are so fond, and which call up almost tears of joy into those bright orbs, which do so much mischief from the foot-lamps. To all this add something of your own, at least enough to swear by; but be sure to make your plaisters stick—lose not a ship for a ha'penny worth of—you know the rest; in homely phrase, lay it on thick; cause the dew of Hermon to descend, and the flakes of manna to fall. The following are some of the best approved exemplars, which we have seen in the fashionable prints:

"We are happy to find by letter, that our noble favourite, *****, who is at present playing to suffocated houses in *****, lately caused such a rush, that two men were instantly killed, three had the *os coccygis* dislocated, five were taken away with *rib* fractures, and eleven ladies swooned, and did not recover until the following morning, notwithstanding the apparatus of the humane society, which was promptly applied."

"Our talented correspondent, *, has favoured us with the maiden perusal of a melo dramatic opera, called the mouse-trap, which we are told will shortly make its public debut. The soliloquy of the mouse, in an addagio movement, on first smelling the 'curdled bait,' opens the piece; and his lament on being 'taken in,' exceeds in melancholy pathos, any thing we have before seen or heard. His dying chaunt, before being immersed in a bucket of water, is full of the softest and most plaintive passages. It will add most materially to the reputation of the composer and immortal author."

"That blooming Hebe, the symbol of eternal youth, and rose-bud of charms, Miss *.*. appeared last evening: the thunder of the gods, the pit, and the upper boxes at her entrée, was heard at Hoboken, as per the accounts of the milkmen the next morning. Her attractions seem to be like the miraculous fountain, which fed the prophet's camels in the Desert—that is, they come just when they are wanted. Meet her in Broadway at 12 M. and she is simple as a country girl—but in the evening at the Park! Ye gods! her beautiful-speaking countenance—emotion chasing emotion upon her damask cheek! The brain turns with the intoxication of ecstacy—our pen drops from the hand that guides it—we shall go mad—oh dear! oh dear!"

On the contra column, and when a slashing operation is to be performed, if you find out a sore place—bare it to the bone—establish a *raw* spare not—your victim will only writhe a little—solace your conscience by the reflection, that if the party did not deserve it that time, meaning the performance which you criticized, he *would* probably at some other. In a word, work up your commodity so elaborately, that it shall serve the purpose of *aqua fortis* in one case, and *soft soap* in the other. Candour, equity, fairness, are only words—words—and mean—*interest*. If Johnson (the scrap engraver we mean) sent a man to the lunatic asylum for returning a borrowed umbrella, how much sooner should one be sent thither for writing a *fair* critique? And for this simple reason, because he would *please nobody*. Who that has a heart is impervious to the frowns of managers, the scowl, and the *omitted recognition*? Who has nerve enough to encounter the offended dignity of emperors, kings, queens, princes, generals, chiefs, senators, and divers other elevated personages, whose levees he nightly attends? [. . .]

[132] [Absurdities on the Stage]
New England Magazine [1834]

It will be admitted that there are only two grand ends to be aimed at in dramatic representations. The first is the production of great noise and bustle; the second, the introduction of some incident, little short of a miracle, that will have a most startling effect upon an audience. For the first purpose, guns, trumpets, horns, thunder-storms, and earthquakes are in great repute; and if your plot happen to be laid before the invention of gunpowder, the use of it will be so much the more wonderful. For the latter purpose you can use trap-doors, ghosts, sudden and mysterious assassinations; and the occasional resurrection of a person supposed to be dead will be hailed with the most rapturous approbation. [...]

[133] [Characteristics of a Good Play]
The New-York Mirror [1834]

[...] We have endeavoured to be as brief in our account of the plot [of Robert Montgomery Bird's *The Broker of Bogota*, 1834] as a clear narration would permit; and we feel sure that the reader will be struck with admiration at the number of incidents the author has introduced, all of them having a direct and obvious connexion with the denouement. This it is that redeems the story from the fault of complexity, since there is no separation of interests, or distinctness of action, to speak technically, among the different characters; no incidents run in parallel lines, making separate under-plots, but all are intertwined in one ever-varying yet consistent whole.

We are happy to point out another feature in the *Broker of Bogota*, which places it far above the other dramatic productions of Dr. Bird. We refer to the more general distribution of the interest among the several characters, of which there are three that may be called prominent—the Broker, Cabarero, and Ramon. We are the more pleased to notice this, as it is the harbinger of better times for our native drama, and indicates a departure from the system of starring, which has been the means of spoiling many good old plays, and giving birth to many bad ones, whose greatest defect has been the undue importance and prominence of one character, to the entire overshadowing of all the others. It is true that, by dividing the interest, a greater burden is thrown upon the author, but this has been borne full lightly by Dr. Bird, and he has composed a tragedy in which, as in the natural world, each one, from the viceroy to the alguazil, performs a part suited to his station, unawed by any stage-sweeping and monopolizing hero.

In another important point, this tragedy is without fault. The interest does not reach its climax, as in some plays we could mention, at the close of the second or the third act, leaving us to wade through a wearisome succession of scenes we have already anticipated, to a close we have long felt assured of, but is sustained and increased till the last scene of the last act, nor in any part of the play can the imagination predict the probable course of the events narrated, for a single scene in advance. This shows in the author an ingenious and masterly arrangement of the incidents of the plot, which, as far as we know, and we are familiar with the English and French drama, is entirely original in conception and execution. [. . .]

[134] "Directions How to Make a Tragedy"
The New–York Mirror [1834]

Select any period of history, ancient or modern, the more obscure the better, because uncertainty helps the imagination, and you will have no disagreeable facts to stare you in the face, and paralyze your invention; then cut out a space of time, not less than fifty years, that you may be sure of elbow-room and have a field wide enough for any number of dramatic personages you may bring upon the tapis.

Next, pick out from the moving mass of humanity in your brain the requisite number of heroes—never less than three—let them differ from each other in character, disposition, &c., just three hair's breadths; however, you must take especial care to enlighten the public as to this, for fear that they, in their ignorance, should not perceive it; therefore, you must get somebody to say in their newspaper, magazine, etc., that the first is an open villain, the second a close villain, and the third, a villain compounded of the other two [. . .]. This difference of character will be greatly increased by a difference of dress, which will prevent the audience from mistaking one for the other, if they keep their eyes open as well as their ears, and trust more to the former than to the latter.

Next, take a dozen plots, and mix them well together, so that none can tell where one ends and another begins. This will be an exercise for the ingenuity of the critics, who will infallibly be at fault, and instead of belabouring your piece, as they do every thing they understand, will pass it by, as a hound does a curled-up hedgehog, through mere inability to seize it. However, as a proof of their good-will, if they had an opportunity, they will drop a gentle hint about "complexity of plot," "hurried incidents," "striking scenes," "spirited action," "attention always awake," etc. There is another obvious advantage in a multiplicity of plots—if any one fails, you have several others to fill up the void as a "corps de reserve" [. . .]. Besides this, whatever the public do not comprehend, they will take upon trust, provided it is seasoned with any thing rampaging, uproarious and unexpected. Thus, when you have brought ten of your plots so near to an end, that there is some prospect of a conclusion, (for the simple reason that your play is advanced in the fourth act, and the bills inform the audience you have but five,) surprise them all by some unforeseen explosion, and throw back the action to the exact spot where it commenced; thus you will have an opportunity of condensing your play over again in the fifth act. Besides, you will excite a "breathless interest" in the audience, who, being deceived in their former calculation, will be too wise to hazard another, and will await the result with open-mouthed admiration. Thus you will get great praise for ingenuity, originality, vigour of conception, and a thousand other qualities, which are always attributed to an author who is like nobody else, and who evinces a supreme contempt for established rules.

Let the action be unceasing, and "without hope of end"—crowded with divers incidents as thick as a pudding with plums, and succeeding one another with tremendous rapidity like the reports of a regiment firing in platoons. This will be of infinite utility, as the audience, in striving to keep in mind the train of circumstances, will have no time to attend to the composition or style of the play as a literary production; and should you imprudently have a soliloquy or address of more than ten lines in the body of the play, let it be spoken with the most violent gesticulation and startling tones, accompanied with furious strides from right hand entrance to left hand ditto, and vice versa; thus you will prevent the play from flagging, and will succeed in masking the feeble part by what military men call a "diversion;" it being a known fact that actors dread poetry rather more than country managers do "stars."

The necessary adjuncts of scenery and clap-traps must on no account be forgotten. Thus you may mix up a profusion of gold, paint and tallow-candles, and call it the temple of the sun, or paste up a quantity of bits of tin and broken looking-glass, and denominate it the palace of the stars, or make a round hole in a board, and it straight becomes the moon. This last luminary is a most appropriate presiding deity, and will not fail to inspire those acting under her influence with humours "changeable and infinite," and sufficient to account for any complexity of plot, however indeterminate and endless [. . .].

Lastly, if there is in the people an ounce of what is termed "nationality," make it weigh down your side of the balance. Say that your play is American, talk of the "new school," "native talent," "patriotic attachments," "intelligent people," etc., and deprecate any criticism as cruel, and having a tendency to crush the "rising drama of America," as if salutary criticism could "harm desert," any more than pruning excrescences and superfluities injures a thrifty tree: and as if the earlier dramatic productions of ancient days, as well as those of England, do not equal if not surpass those of a later date.

If any distinguished actors, who have the misfortune to be foreigners, should, by the course of events, be brought in collision with you and your interests, make a bold use of the above arguments, and your play may float sublime upon puffs through all the theatres in the Union, and prolong its existence for the space of one dramatic year; at the end of which time you can afford to let it drop into oblivion, having in the interim fabricated another

"Amphytrion," with half a dozen "Sosias" to take the place of their departed brethren.

A parting advice, and I have done. Let no considerations induce you to swerve so far from decorum as to permit your play to be printed. Never forget this maxim—let no wheedling flatterers, or insidious praises, lead you to commit this *faux pas*, to pass this rubicon—to throw off this invisible coat, which, like Jack's in the fairy tale, invests you with tenfold power and influence. "O! that mine enemy would write a book!" was the pathetic exclamation of Job; but this enemy was wise, and meddled not with writing, and Job disquieted himself in vain; therefore keep dark, and—*Cetera desunt.*

[135] "Decline of the Modern Drama"
New England Magazine [1835]

One of the principal, if not the principal cause of the degradation of the dramatic literature of the present day, appears to us to be the prevailing practice of writing exclusively for popular actors, or 'Stars.' The popularity of the Star will carry a bad piece through, or he pays for it; and, in either case, the author does not lose his labor. It is rather humiliating to the pride of literature, to be obliged to advert to the hope of gain, as one of the main-springs of literary exertion; but so it is. [. . .] For a Star, therefore, an author must write, if he would gain anything by his labor, and if he would not see his piece damned, on its first appearance. [. . .]

The consequence is, that the piece is conceived and written, not with a view to the faithful delineation of human nature and passion, but for the sole, and almost the avowed, purpose of exhibiting the peculiar powers of an individual. The minor characters of the play are all contemptible; the unities are violated; and common sense and probability are set at defiance. The piece must abound in clap-traps. If the Star have a stentorian voice, he must be provided with an opportunity to rant, rave, and bellow. If he have a stalwart arm and leg, he must have an opportunity to fight in single combat, and kill his antagonist upon the stage—an exhibition as gratifying to the mob as it is repugnant to good taste. [. . .] There is a [. . .] pregnant example of the pernicious influence of starring, upon this department of literature.

Edwin Forrest offered a reward of five hundred dollars for the best play, that should be written, within a given time, for his especial use. Though five thousand dollars would be too small a sum for a really good tragedy, yet a considerable number of writers put into the lottery for this paltry pittance. The prize was awarded to a piece entitled *Metamora*, called, by courtesy, a tragedy; and so, in some sense, it was. Common sense, historical truth, human nature, and the king's English, were alike butchered without remorse. But it had abundance of stage effect. It was successful beyond all example, and continued so to be, until the Star went to Europe; though it is a mere thing of shreds and patches, altered by half a dozen hands, to suit half a dozen tastes, and all of them bad ones. In a word, the thing, as a literary composition, was beneath criticism, and even contempt.

Yet it ran, night after night; and the author and the actor reaped a golden harvest from its popularity. [. . .]

[138] [The Utility of the Drama]
The Knickerbocker [1836]

[. . .] Having thus rapidly sketched the rise and progress of the drama, and endeavoured to establish the position that its *intellectual* influence on society has been extensive, we shall now attempt to analyze the causes which produce this influence, and shall also hazard a proof of its *moral* tendency.

The chief excellence of dramatic composition consists in its portraying, with truth and propriety, the manners and passions of mankind. No other composition, (we speak of the acted drama,) can raise those strong emotions, which are elicited by this 'mirror of nature,' faithfully depicting the human passions—their gradual development, and their direful effects, when suffered to become preponderant. No other means so distinctly convey to us *ideas* and *things*, as dramatic representations. We behold *ourselves*, as it were, embodied in the mimic scene before us, and find our thoughts and actions—nay, the very springs of thought and action—brought palpably to our sight. For the cultivation of taste, the acted drama presents facilities of no ordinary character. The sister arts are generally so harmoniously blended in these representations, that we have in them at one grasp the very essence of the arts.

Music, adapted to, or assisting *poetry* of the highest order, spreads its glowing and soul-subduing influence over our best feelings and affections, while *painting* illustrates and realizes the vivid conceptions which her magic sisters have created. 'Who,' it may here be asked, 'can listen to the powerful language—the discriminative excellence—the inimitable personification of character—and the poetical beauties, contained in our best dramatic authors, and not feel a growing expansion of intellect—a progressive improvement in knowledge?'

Its *power* over society is so extensive, that all governments of a despotic character have dreaded its influence, unless rendered by them the engine to propagate their doctrines, or perpetuate their power. We need but refer to the rigid supervision which surrounds the acted drama, in all monarchical countries, at present, to establish the fact of its importance.

Its *utility* in civilized society, may also be advocated, on political grounds. In all populous cities, where commerce and industry are furnishing the means of obtaining wealth and consequent indulgence in luxury, the minds of the rich may become too absorbed in their wealth and enjoyments, and the laboring portion of community may grow dissatisfied at viewing their relative position in society, or revel in gross dissipation. What means can more effectually correct the laxity of one class, or calm the angry feelings of the other, than dramatic representations? [. . .]

Of the *moral* influence of the drama, and its reverse tendency, much has been written. We may safely hazard the assertion, that its moral influence is tenable, when it is under judicious regulation.

[. . .] In our rapid historical sketch of the drama, we have seen it the scourge of vice, folly, and profligacy,—the inciter to, and rewarder of, patriotism, courage, and virtue,—and such might still be the influence of a well-governed stage.

The best specimens of dramatic composition invariably represent virtue in favorable colors,—enriched with every beauty which sentiment and feeling can bestow. Vice is portrayed in all the hideous aspects which it is its peculiar characteristic to assume. We have exhibited before us the latent springs which prompt the wretched slave of passion and malignity to barter his eternal hopes for horror and despair. We view the gradual development of crime,—we shudder at the final close of the guilty career,—we rejoice at the triumph of virtue: and all the kindly feelings of our nature are aroused to a renewed energy of action by the glowing scenes we have beheld.

If satire be the object of the drama, how powerfully can it wield the pointed shaft! Embodying the follies it aims to correct, they are reflected with such unerring accuracy, that the most obtuse mind cannot fail to recognise the picture. In accomplishing these varied powers of drama, the whole range of created matter was within its grasp. The boundless beauties of nature have been seized upon to aid its decoration, and increase its effects,—the highest efforts of poetic talent have upheld its glory, and enriched its stores, by their splendid genius, and their laurel'd fame.

These we conceive to be the broad grounds upon which the moral and intellectual influence of the drama may be advocated. Its perversion to unworthy ends we are not champion enough to defend; but we do conscientiously believe with Chesterfield, that 'a well-governed stage is an ornament to society,—an encourager of wit and learning,—and a school of virtue and refinement.'

[139] [The Success of Dramatized Novels]
The New–York Mirror [1836]

Every novel is sure to be adapted to the stage, if once the publick voice is unequivocally expressed in its favour—and in this species of indulging the prevalent appetite for excitement, this theatre [Bowery Theatre] has taken the lead. There is both reason and precedent for this course. In the first place, it is a very profitable, and a very easy way of attracting audiences, and as the works of fiction of the present day must be necessarily filled with startling incident, vivid sentiment, and warmly-drawn characters, the popular feeling is pretty sure to be enlisted in favour of those exaggerations and caricatures of humanity with which the vulgar of every country are always captivated. In the next place, the dramatizing [of] Sir Walter Scott's novels made the fortune of one of the London theatres [Covent Garden], while poor [Daniel] Terry was alive. This scholar and player made it a point, as each novel appeared, to reduce it to the purposes of the stage, which the author called *Terry*fying his works. *Rob Roy, The Antiquary, Lady of the Lake, Guy Mannering, The Maid of Judah*, from *Ivanhoe*, etc. still keep their place on the stage as melodrames or operas, and as the plan has succeeded in England, we have appropriated the process here, and there is reason to expect that every novel published by the Harpers, will be given to the publick by the rival establishment at the Bowery, and almost simultaneously, if we are to judge by the recent specimens of diligence afforded by the playwright of this establishment. In fact, a quick and capable playwright is now an essential property to a theatre, as the publick appetite is voracious for novelty, and must and will be satisfied. People, after reading a novel in their closet, always like to see it afterward in action, and this is the secret of the great success of these dramatized novels. In reading a work of fiction people generally select some personage in whose fortunes they are interested, and whom they follow through the many-coloured page with a personal identification of feelings; and they bring to the representation the same sentiments by which they were influenced in the perusal. They are acquainted beforehand with the incidents, feel an interest in the scene, and fill up the gaps in the unity of the story rendered necessary by the mutilations it must receive in its adaption to the stage. Mr. Bulwer's novels dramatize effectively—witness the impression produced by the *Last Days of Pompeii*, by the writer who is now employed upon *Rienzi* [Louisa H. Medina]. This system of appropriating novels and romances for the stage, immediately on their appearance, is of no little service to the original writer, as those who have only seen the play, naturally wish to ascertain how far, and in what manner, the conception of the novel has been preserved, and how the playwright has succeeded in what is a thing of no ordinary difficulty—to wit, compressing a novel of two volumes, and in some thirty chapters, into a three act drama, at the same time preserving the continuity of the events, and the congruity of the characters, into the narrow limits of a few scenes. This, however, has been most admirably done during the present administration of the Bowery theatre, and, what is more to the purpose, most advantageously to its finances.

[141] [Dramatic Servitude and the Degradation of the Theatre]
The American Monthly Magazine [1837]

Almost every civilized nation on the face of the globe has a drama of its own, more or less remarkable for national peculiarities. England can produce a long and brilliant list of dramatic authors, with the "world-renowned" bard of Avon at their head; France can boast her Racine, Corneille, Molière, and Voltaire; Germany her Goethe and her Schiller; there is even a man they call the Danish Skakspeare; but where is the national drama of America? One of the first things about which a traveller of taste and curiosity inquires, is the theatre. "Have you a theatre?" he will ask of some plain, intelligent American. "Oh! yes," replies our countryman. "We have plenty of play-houses. Yonder is one."

"What! that building, with a Grecian front and Gothic windows?"

"Yes—that's it; and a very pretty piece of architecture it is too, uniting in harmony the four antique orders with Gothic ornaments."

"And pray what do they act there?"

"Oh! every thing. The manager is very liberal and enterprizing, and always gives us novelties; in fact, if he didn't, we shouldn't patronise him. We have tragedy, comedy, farce, opera, rope-dancing, men-monkeys, figurantes, and a man that spins a dinner-plate upon his nose. Every thing, in short."

And so we have; almost every thing—which a pure taste condemns. Perhaps the traveller enters "the drama's home," to borrow a phrase from the men who write the prize addresses, and beholds an interior tastefully decorated, and better adapted to the purposes of seeing and hearing than the mammoth theatres of London, the great Babel itself. To be sure there are hats and boots in the dress circle, and people lounging across two or three benches at a time; but these things are excusable in a free country, where people like to show their independence and contempt of the aristocratic laws of etiquette. On the whole, the inside of the play-house is much like an European one. The curtain rises, and our traveller perceives a yet more striking resemblance. He hears the very same jests which delighted the pits of Covent Garden, the Olympic, or, perhaps (*horribile dictu!*) the Pavilion theatre, uttered in the same farces; and although the local allusions invariably fail of effect, still the *double entendres* and open obscenities are rapturously applauded. The stranger leaves the house, admiring the patience with which the good people listen to details of scenes and peculiarities with which they are unfamiliar, and in many of which they can take no interest.

But as farces were only written to make us laugh, not reason, it is of very little matter whence they are imported; they are trifles to send us smiling away after a heavy tragedy, a light dessert following a substantial dinner. It is, however, a matter of regret that we should be so entirely dependent on a foreign market, not only for the dessert but for the first and second courses; and that our caterers should so exactly model themselves upon "liberal and enterprising" managers of the London stage. No sooner does a famous plate-spinner, or an inimitable man-monkey appear, than a mammoth bill informs us that "the manager, ever anxious to gratify a discerning public, is happy to inform them that he has succeeded in effecting an engagement with Signor Viviani, the celebrated European Plate-spinning Saltator, who has performed at Naples, Paris, and London with unbounded applause. In consequence of the ENORMOUS EXPENSES which the manager incurs, the box tickets will be sold at auction." Simultaneously with this announcement, sundry editorial puffs appear in the newspapers. Expectation is represented as being on tiptoe, the excitement in the fashionable (?) world prodigious, and Signor Viviani the tenth wonder of the world. In consequence of these reports the Signor becomes very popular, his audiences are very large, and when every body has seen him spin his plates, the manager announces his appearance "for the last time." Every body rushes to the theatre, and the Signor takes a formal farewell. But lo! the next night the Signor appears "*positively* for the last time, as his engagements at the South do not permit a longer stay." If he still continues "to draw," the manager "effects a re-engagement for nine nights." Thus,

> With more 'last words' they linger o'er us,
> And, like a tom-cat, die by inches.
> *Croaker and Co.*

To merit the "liberal patronage" of the public, how very "enterprising" these managers do become! It is "out of their power" to bring out original plays, or raise the salaries of stock actors; but they can afford to give Signora Rumblante Quiverante a guinea a crotchet for her ear-splitting bravuras, and allow Mademoiselle Entrechat three hundred dollars a night for her pigeon-wings, and pay her in specie. As for rope-dancers, learned dogs, and live snakes,* their services are invaluable.

I am no enemy of "horse and hound," but I think that the stage of a theatre should be something better than an arena whereon the arts of the *menage* and the training of the kennel should be exhibited. I own I have lost the ardour of my youth, and if any thing can prejudice me against a play, it is the promise of the entire stud of beautiful Turkish horses, with one Bactrian camel, one Syrian dromedary, and an elephant. We shall soon have birds as well as beasts. Somebody will dramatise Audubon's Ornithology, and then we shall have "First Night of the Ring-Tailed Golden Eagle, who will make his appearance in

---

* Two very aspiring reptiles have been going the rounds of the theatres, performing in a piece written expressly for them—entitled, *The Children of Chittagong, or the Anacondas of Ceylon*. What will the lovers of the legitimate drama do when these poor snakes have shuffled off this mortal *coil*?

a play written expressly for this bird." To return to horses. When a poor devil of a manager can procure a stud of nags, he is much in the predicament of a "beggar on horseback." An equestrian mania carries him away. Whenever a dilemma occurs in a piece, it is ever with him as with the king in the fine old ballad of Hardyknute—

Bring me my steed Madge, dapple-gray!

He mounts his heroes and heroines. They talk, kiss, and fight in the saddle. We once beheld (upon the stage) a whole troop of horses in a coronation hall. We believe they had no better precedent for their appearance than the entrance of the champion of England in a similar scene riding a gallant barb.

Next to an equestrian spectacle, I detest a *horrible* play—stage horrors are so laughable. There was *Der Freischütz*. There was a fine old German story spoiled when they brought that on the English stage; Carl Maria Von Weber would have shuddered at it. The story was one of the very best of its kind. We have taken a fearful pleasure in reading it, for it was really a ghost story, not wound off with a tissue of explanations that laughed in the face of your credulity [...]. As a drama, *Der Freischütz* is not eminently successful, because the stage horrors are so palpably artificial, so totally at variance with the images created by the strange melodies of the composer. There is a mighty "flare up" of red and blue lights, a great flapping and flourishing of canvass bats and owls, a strutting about of real flesh-and-blood skeletons, and a profuse expenditure of India fire-crackers; but it is not the thing after all. The smoke does invade our lungs and make us cough, and the skeleton supernumeraries do make us laugh; and we cannot realize much horror after reading in the play-bills, "the incantation properties by Mr. Such-a-One, the monsters by Mr. Somebody Something."

I know that the task of finding faults is not difficult. I know that it is easier to abuse the stage as it is, than to suggest some practical amelioration. In the first place we must create a national dramatic literature. It is in vain for managers to say that the public will not pay for native literature, the experiment has not been fairly tried. There was a time when publishers would not look at the manuscripts of American novelists; but a few American novels that were smuggled into the world succeeded, others followed, and now the production of a tale or romance on this side of the water is no longer regarded as a miracle. Let the managers of theatres afford facilities to our authors, encouraging them to write and offer plays, allowing them a liberal share of the profits of those which succeed, and we shall soon see whether the same talent which can produce interesting novels is adequate to the composition of interesting dramas. There is no reason for our servile dependence upon England for the amusements of our evenings. Her dramatic star has set; but must we, because she has few dramatists of note, because her stage is degraded, and her modern drama a name; must we conclude that we are doomed to a similar inferiority, copy her dulness, and echo her inanities? Our enterprize forbids this. I confess that I am among those who hope for the regeneration of the drama on the western shores of the Atlantic. I hope to see our theatres, freed from every pollution, the resort of the intelligent, the cultivated, the wealthy and the lovely of our land; I hope to hear their walls echo only the loftiest sentiments, such as Shakspeare or Schiller would not have blushed to own.

[144] [Call for a National Drama]
The New–York Mirror [1837]

It is a matter of much surprise to us that we have no national drama in this country. With plenty of material to work upon, and plenty of talent to do the work, there is scarcely a single play on our theatrical lists that can with propriety be called American. We have one or two Indian plays, with Indian heroes, whose originals never existed save in the author's brain. We have Yankee plays, with Yankee heroes, that, in their own persons, have performed every 'cute trick ever told of a Yankee pedlar; and western plays, with western heroes, whose deeds of wonder would cause Colonel Crockett himself to hide his diminished head. But a genuine drama, with characters such as you meet with every day, we have not—at least, it has not been our good fortune to see any such.

Now, the system is radically wrong which keeps constantly before our eyes, whether in fireside novels, or theatrical representations, the characters and manners of foreigners, to the exclusion of our own. The stage can never be to us a School of Reform, until the mirror be held up to ourselves, until we see our own follies reflected. While we laugh at the blunders of Mrs. Malaprop, and the stolidity of Bob Acres [in R. B. Sheridan's *The Rivals*, 1775], we forget that there are thousands of absurdities among our own countrymen, equally ludicrous, which pass unnoticed. And, on the other hand, there are as many virtues, peculiarly American, which, if literature would make them fashionable, might be more frequently practised. [. . .]

[146] "Theatrical Puffs"
The New–York Mirror [1838]

The folly of puffing actors and actresses, and making them *"ne plus ultras"* on every occasion, is finely hit off in the following criticism upon Miss Tree's acting in St. Louis. It is written by a Hoosier, and comes much nearer to the truth than one-half the senseless jargon that is met with, almost every day, in many of our papers:—"I'll tell you an almighty strange thing of how that gal (Ellen Tree) works the feelings of critters. When she was acting Julia in our parts, the door-keepers came away in, for it was tarnation cold, and no one took no notice of the doors, cos no more could get in; when an old bear sniffed his way into the town, and finding no one astir, for they were all at the play, what does the critter do, but shifts his way there too, and crawls up behind the boxes. I guess he meant to sup off some of us chaps; but, however, he listened, and listened, till he got *quite affected*, and so mollified, that he vowed he would never go man-eating any more; next night he came again and brought his wife; and the thing was only discovered on the third night, that he was seen coming down to the box-office with an alligator."

[151] [A "recommendation of the theatre"]
The Knickerbocker [1840]

[. . .] As another preventive to dissipation and vice, I would recommend young men to visit the theatre; not to see French dancers and Italian buffoons; not to hear mock heroic melo-dramas and vulgar farces, which, after the Restoration, the vitiated taste of Charles introduced from France; but to see comedy and tragedy, the productions of the great poets of the Elizabethan age, and those who have since emulated them. I may be told that the stage is immoral, indecent, obscene. Grant it, if you please. Who made it so? The people. It is in the people to restore the theatre to its primitive purity and decorum. Managers, to make money, must cater for the public taste; just as merchants change the style and pattern of their merchandise, to suit the fashion of their customers, or to attract by novelty. If full boxes applauded the productions of the purest comic and tragic muse, and if empty benches stared at fustian melo-dramas, and silly farces, managers would soon discover where their interest lay, and reform it altogether. If objections be made to some gross expressions and incidents in the plays of the old dramatists, we answer, the fault was not theirs; it was that of the age in which they lived. We may easily prune them, if necessary, though by doing so, we emasculate their noble lines. In olden days, they were plainer of speech than we are, but not less virtuous in heart. In fact, we have just reversed things; they talked, we sin. Why should the *innocent* be offended with mere expressions? It is *knowledge* that raises objections.

Again, a portion of the theatre is appropriated to a class of people whom we shall not name, and another is used to sell intoxicating draughts. This, I willingly confess, is a serious evil, which ought to be corrected. Let the public frown upon managers who permit such things within their walls; make it an object to them to remove the cause of this complaint: and we shall soon see it done. The people are sovereign, and must be obeyed.

[...] I ask that all who differ from me in my recommendation of the theatre—and opposition arises almost invariably from religious feeling—should inquire seriously into the origin of the drama; should consider of the virtue it has inculcated, the patriotism it has enkindled, and the spirit of liberty it has animated; and then he may not deem our approval so very monstrous. [...]

All extremes are tyrannies. He who would bar the doors of the theatre, or tear the building down, would do as manifest a wrong as the infidel, were he to shut up or demolish the churches. The one act would just be as unlawful as the other. [...]

[156] W. A. Jones. ["The low state of our theatrical criticism"]
Arcturus [1841]

A remarkable neglect is visible, on the part of our periodical writers, in the department of theatrical criticism. Whether this neglect arises from the low state of the Drama in this country, from the puritanical abhorrence in which the entertainments of the Theatre are held, or from the deficiency of critical acumen in the attendants on those performances, we will not pretend to decide. We merely advert to the fact. We have no dramatic critics, worth the name. The newspaper notices of plays and actors, are just the counterpart of the judgments given, in the same places, on new books and authors: so general as to fit either side of the question; so extravagant, both in censure and praise, as to amount to nothing at all. With those who are acquainted with these matters, such notices produce the negative effect of exciting contempt of their writers; and with the ignorant, they serve to bewilder and confuse.

They manage this better in England. There, theatrical criticism takes rank as a seperate department of Art, and forms a prominent branch of periodical writing. A good dramatic critic is there well paid, and occupies an honorable position. In this country, notices of the Theatre are, generally, prepared by different hands; friends, or persons connected with the paper or magazine. This leads to a variety and distraction of opinion, and breaks up all unity and order:—they undertake to judge of the art of acting, who have yet to learn the art of criticism. To paint an animated portrait, disentangle the meshes of a plot, or trace the incidents of a drama, require a knowledge of both of these arts—the one furnishing the material: the other, the instrument.

Occasionally, papers strictly theatrical, devoted entirely to the stage, have been started: but tenth-rate merit could not prolong a very short existence. They gradually fell off. In some of our weekly journals, too, sensible remarks enough, have appeared on certain Stars: nothing, however, like nicely balanced and thoroughly digested criticism. A neat theatrical paper, in the *London Examiner*, is worth (we had almost said it) a month's notices in all our journals. [. . .]

Probably the separate causes we assigned for the low state of our theatrical criticism, all concur in producing it. We are without good actors; public opinion has set in, with all the force of ignorant prejudice, against the profession of an actor and theatrical entertainments; and, we have not as yet the right race of critics.

The comedians have left us: tragedy is extinct. Opera and burlesque, the melo-drama and the ballet, have literally swallowed up the legitimate drama, (a cant phrase we employ in default of a better). Then, we are not a theatrical people; decidedly the reverse. The best reason is, we want critics—clever critics would make something out of the very defect of ordinary matter. They would make us laugh, at all events. They would create entertainment of some sort. [. . .]

The tendency of judicious theatrical criticism is most beneficial, both to the actor and to the public. To both, it presents, as it were, the comparative anatomy of the stage. It paints individuals, as well as groups. To the public, it is useful, inasmuch as it educates their tastes: to the actor, it furnishes the aid of just applause and well-directed censure. It is his best guide. It is his surest support. Without it, there will be much indifferent acting, even in good actors. Where the standard is low, performance will not be likely to rise to a high pitch. Actors rarely lead the way: the critic must often point out the true path.

Successive critics write connectedly the history of the stage, each from his own point of view, with fresh feeling, and amid all the peculiar interests of his time. Future actors ought to study the lives and characters of their great masters, for imitation and as beacons—endeavoring to rival their splendid qualities, and to avoid their captivating errors.

[160] "Prospects of the American Stage"
Arcturus [1841]

Notwithstanding the difficulties that oppose the present advancement of theatrical property in America, and the incidental discouragements are numberless, we yet believe there never has been a period in which the real interests of the drama may be more favorably cultivated than this. Circumstances enough exist to depress the stage, but it must be remembered the general character of the stage and its performances is one of painful mediocrity; and it is better that mediocrity be so destroyed at once. The prevalent discontent with the stage is itself a sign, though it may be a distant one, of reform and improvement. Destroyed the stage cannot be, for it is the index of certain indestructible faculties of the mind; an acted drama is as universal a means of delight and benefit as a written literature. The formation of a theatre, or something equivalent to it, is the first impulse of savage life, and the chief graces of civilization have flourished with the best labors of the stage. [...] The historical fact of the permanent existence of the stage, as a part of social manners, may put to rest the arguments of those who think it can ever be superseded. Books cannot perish, neither can the acted drama. With this faith in the vitality of the theatre, we dismiss all regret at the present feeble support of the stage. The public have rightly tired of the poor conventionalisms of acting and authorship palmed off upon the boards; the audiences have fairly abandoned the theatre. Nothing, it would apparently seem, can restore the stage. But there has been one thing left untried, of sovereign virtue and efficacy in the restoration of the arts, the only panacea for a worn out literature or drama; and that untried remedy is, originality. A new order has grown up in the intellectual and social habits of the times; modes of thinking are altered; changes of manners more rapid and variable have occured; and the theatre, "the abstract and brief chronicle of the time," has said nothing of the new revelations of thought and experience. In this we see the secret of all the complaints of the decline of the stage. Accidental circumstances, not immediately connected with this, have not been wanting; there have been defects of stage management, revolutions in the currency that have affected the demand for popular amusements (though this in a less degree than has been generally supposed), the starring system has destroyed the discipline of the boards; but these are all incidental evils, that would be controlled if the first principle of the stage were correct. The theatre has not been true to its own law; it has abandoned its legitimate position for mean expedients; it has sought mediocrity, and deserved its fate. Particularly is this true of the stage in the United States.

What is the first essential of the drama? It is nationality. The drama is the immediate growth of the age and country. Taste or fashion may reign in literature, and withdraw the studies of the learned to distant periods of time and foreign habits of thinking; we may read as antiquarians, as mystics, as egotists, and preserve our unsocial individual manners; there are many interests represented in books, there is but one of the drama. It is addressed to the people immediately, and lives or dies on the breath of the moment. The public must believe in it, with an ardent sympathy, or it is nothing. [...]

When we speak of nationality in the drama, we do not mean the inculcation of mere patriotism. There are higher habits of thought in a commonwealth than this national self-love. The love of country may yet be merged in the love of the world, when war—the antagonism of patriotism, and necessary to its life—shall cease; but then nationality will continue to exist. It springs directly from the individual, and government is but one of the many influences that go to its formation. The thought uttered on the stage will be in unison with the best possible form of politics, and agree with the best spirit of the deeds of the revolution, though there may be not a single flag, cannon or hurrah in the whole play. Patriotism, as commonly employed, is a low source of emotion; it appeals to externals, it reaches the heart through the memory, it is a kind of upbraiding with the deeds of others. Let us act our own.

One characteristic of a new dramatic literature in this country we may venture to predict: the democratic spirit by which it will be informed. Hitherto, poetry has been on the side of power, for the world has been governed by the authority of power; it has drawn its chief images of greatness from the old aristocratic ideas of sovereignty, war, military glory. Its language has been of courts and camps. Its splendid phraseology has echoed the sound of the trumpet, the roll of the drum; has reflected the imperial purple. The Muse of Tragedy has rested on the throne. Wolsey, high in power, Lear, a king, Hamlet, Lady Constance, all belong to royalty. But kings have lost their dignity with their despotism, and are fast vanishing from the earth; revolutions have deposed some and unromantic constitutions have robbed others. Modern kings are no longer heroes by divine right. Is tragedy therefore to be extinct? Not while the heart throbs in a single human frame. There is a tragedy in every man's death, and perhaps a sadder one while he was still alive. The revolutions in the heart for a single day may be unwritten scenes of more pathos than those in Agamemnon or Orestes. The dignity of life does not need the outward aid of power or station.

With the emotions of private life, with domestic tragedy on the stage, will be blended the heroic ideas of the age. The present is full of hope, benevolence and philanthropy. It has courage and manly action for the present and faith in the future. We should look for this sentiment reflected at the theatre in living characters drawn from the times. Why may not a modern enthusiast, with his schemes of reform and dreams of earthly happiness, have the same or greater eloquence on the stage than a faded old alchymist whose visions were mostly material? Why have we not a tragedy of Luther rather than of Henry VIII? The clergyman is a character endowed with sufficient importance in Protestantism; yet we do not remember a single exhibition of this character in any tragedy we ever read. The audience would be surprised to hear a school-master on the stage talking as he might of his art; yet the school-master is one of the modern heroes. We want a theatre that shall be foremost in guiding the public taste to the loftiest habits of thinking; that catching the earliest developments of the popular mind, shall carry them out nobly. The country at present is more or less agitated by the topic of war, and newspapers everywhere are exhibiting sketches of its horrors and reading lessons of peace. Why do we hear nothing of this on the stage? There are memorable lessons in history and great arguments in the future that might be there taught. But the drama is silent. We attended the theatre the other night, and found an actor reciting out of an old play a tribute to the glorious campaigns of Marlborough? "What's Hecuba to him or he to Hecuba that he should prate thus?" This is our present drama.

But though we know of no modern productions in English that worthily represent the new era of ideas, we may yet discover in recent attempts, both in this country and abroad, the beginning of a characteristic drama. Though the plays are founded on old models and have a sufficient share of Italian princes and heroes, the sentiments are generally liberal, and they contain passages for modern ears, which, however, thrown in for effect, are evidences of a desire to meet the wants of the day. We need a new race of writers in the drama, with a new class of subjects. Let an author of real dramatic power once seize the materials which now lie waiting such a one and the properties of the stage will soon follow. Actors will spring up, the theatre under a fresh popular impulse will be respected and draw together all the talent in its administration that is required. If we had a Shakespeare, or the tenth part of one, to write tragedies for us, there would soon be no complaints of the low state of the drama.

At present the theatre has no resources in itself capable of its revival. Its best efforts, those to restore the legitimate drama, are feeble; the revival as a work of art of old plays, the restoration of ancient costume, the recollection of old theatrical scenes, deserve always to hold a place in the performances of a cultivated theatre, but the interest in them is too remote to excite any great popular enthusiasm. The truest evidence of the real decline of the drama is at present exhibited in the gradual loss of actors, the decline of talent on the boards. [. . .]

What then is to be done? We have pointed out as it appears to us the direction that a new dramatist must take in the walk of tragedy. A wider field yet remains in comedy and farce. There is no country in the world in which a greater store of materials is laid up for a humorous writer. A system of life that brings into collision masses of men and individuals, with greater variety and frequency than in any other nation, must be the most favorable to the exhibition of character. Where there is the greatest activity there is the best opportunity for observation. In the bustle of men, among the thronging hopes and fears, out of the designs and disappointments, the schemes and failures of active life, the dramatist seizes his incidents and dialogue. The fitness of American life for the purposes of the drama is simply this, that it is the most dramatic off the stage in itself. No one with an eye to see or heart to feel, (for there must be some sympathy before he can see), doubts of the earnestness, the force, the picturesqueness of the every-day scenes passing around us. There is needed only the artist to place these scenes for us by his genius in a proper point of view for all to see and appreciate them.

It has been thought that a certain repose of manners, a fixed scale and gradation of society, was necessary to the ends of comedy. In such a state the effect of long custom and traditional usage offers, in truth, great facility to the comic painter. He is but to transcribe the unwritten comedy around him, and paint not merely what is laughable, but what the people have long been in the habit of laughing at. There is a series of traditional pictures, in English comedy and fiction of this kind, of parish beadles, old country squires, Yorkshire farmers, sure to come up in the writings of every successive humorist, though of late the social changes have rather outgrown them, even in England. In this country there are no such aids to laughter. Literature growing out of national life has been too little cultivated to make the popular humors thus familiar. The resources of the writer exist only in the raw material. But this very necessity of originality is to prove the greatest advantage. We are fortunately placed in a position, so far as this portion of our literature is concerned, in which imitation is impossible. The comic writer must be original or be nothing. [...]

[162] [The Stage—No "vehicle for politics"]
The Ladies' Companion [1841]

At this theatre [Bowery Theatre, New York] Mr. Forrest has performed a round of his peculiar characters, among which the most prominent was Jack Cade [in R. T. Conrad's *Jack Cade*, 1835]. [...] there is a redundancy of matter which could be most advantageously dispensed with, and as to patriotism, enough to spare to concoct a dozen more such dramas. It was however, even in its present crude state, most admirably suited to the audiences assembled on the nights of Mr. Forrest's engagement, who failed not to receive every sentiment and expression with the most "enthusiastic delight and approbation." While witnessing the performance of this "national drama" we could not help thinking, that could the ruffian, Jack Cade, have again "revisited the glimpses" of the moon and avowed his intention of invading the Canadian territory, he could not have found a riper or a fitter race of *patriots* to have accompanied him "to desperate ventures and assured destruction." We honor the genius of Judge Conrad, but denounce the principles of his drama. They are calculated to do no good, but much evil. Throughout the whole play there is scarcely a sentiment uttered but which is directed to the *ad captandum vulgum*. It contains not the language of poetical inspiration, not the spontaneous breathings of nature, free and fervent, but the destructive and demoralizing doctrines of a political clique, which are a violation of all law, truth, and justice. We should like to have a "national drama," but such a production as this will never lay its foundation. "A poet's soul should own a richer fruitage," not pander to the feelings of any sect. Were our columns a vehicle for politics we would show and descant upon the bad taste which has directed this composition. As a writer we regard the author an ornament to his country, and even in the present case, he has evinced high capability for dramatic composition, but we regret that he should have been so deluded as to sacrifice his genius at the shrine of party. [...]
[See also [157].]

[173] [Realism Inappropriate on the Stage]
Spirit of the Times [1842]

The new comedy of *Such As It Is*, written by J. M. Field, was produced at the Park [. . .]. The comedy is the author's first serious effort as a dramatist, and contains much that is ingenious in plot, and impressive and beautiful in language; there are some palpable hits at the follies of the times, and occasional flashes of wit which tell well. But it is written too much like real life to meet with much success upon the stage, where every thing must be extravagant, vivid, and broad, to produce interest and effect. Had the author employed more time in maturely digesting and strengthening his plot, and condensing his language, he would have much improved it. We trust he will not be discouraged from making another effort, for many worse productions have been played night after night, and called successful.

[174] [Causes and Effects of the Decline of the Drama]
The Knickerbocker [1843]

It is indeed a painful contemplation, to the true admirer of the legitimate drama, to observe the contrast presented by the 'drama as it was,' and the 'drama as it is,' especially when that contemplation is enforced by reminiscences of the 'palmy days' of the drama, as it flourished some thirty years ago. [. . .]

In suggesting to managers the course imperatively demanded of them by the present depressed state of the stage, we cannot omit calling their attention to that destructive species of the modern drama, known as the *Burlesque*, which we conscientiously believe has accelerated the decline of a healthy theatrical taste to a greater extent than many are willing to acknowledge. This degrading excrescence of the stage has not only exposed the secrets of the '*Bona Dea*,' but has actually introduced the public 'behind the scenes,' and has familiarized the uninitiated with all the trick and mechanism of the theatre, showing how 'the thunder is made,' and consequently destroying all the illusion before so sedulously concealed by the folds of the 'magic curtain;' '*Necessitas non habet leges*' we know is the plea for all this; but are not managers, like the man in the fable, cutting open their golden goose, the sooner to obtain the eggs?—And may not their experiment end in a similar disappointment? We appeal to the most determined admirer of the burlesque, whether the genuine wit and humor of a sterling comedy or farce have not afforded them more real satisfaction than the best of these extravagant and ludicrous productions? [. . .]

[. . .] With this decline in the patronage of theatres has grown up an entire change in the character of dramatic representations. Melo-drama, first intended as a more exciting species of tragedy, has now become the vehicle for presenting the grossest absurdities, and the coarsest kinds of profligacy, combining with it horrors that 'out-herod Herod.' As our leading novelists now select the felons of the Newgate Calendar for their heroes, and consecrate, or rather desecrate their genius, to dress up the crimes and follies of these worthies, as fit dishes for the public taste; so also our dramatists, who follow assiduously in their wake; and no sooner has the public appetite gorged upon the delectable treat through the pages of the favorite novelist, but forthwith they are called upon to repeat the enticing banquet in the dramatic representation, aided by all the accessories which painting, music and costume can now so well bestow on this degraded species of the modern drama. The voluptuous ballet and the entrancing opera, guiltless of all approach to nature, and divested of all literary pretension, complete this picture of the 'drama as it is,' which, contrasted with the sterling worth of the 'drama as it was,' is 'Hyperion to a Satyr.'

From this sweeping denunciation of the modern drama, however, we are bound in justice to exempt an interesting and effective species of entertainment, termed the 'domestic drama,' and many of the eccentric farces and interludes of the present day, which abound either in natural portraitures of character, or in palpable hits at the extravagance of the age, and which, in the absence of a continuous series of sterling tragedies and comedies, serve to keep alive in the minds of the public a taste for the legitimate objects of the stage. We readily confess also, that occasionally a beaming of the 'light of other days' flashes over the theatrical horizon, and a tragedy or a comedy appears that seems to indicate the returning glory of the drama. Yet even these are too often marred in their effect, from the paucity of histrionic talent, and from being written to fit the peculiarities of an individual actor, being either void of due interest in scenes where the hero or heroine are not engaged, or only effective when personated by the particular artist for whom they were created. In any notice of the 'drama as it is,' it would be unjust not to acknowledge the perfection of scenic representation, the beauty of appointments, and the correctness and magnificence of costume, which now decorate the stage. These are points in which the 'drama as it is' may justly claim a proud superiority over former periods. Indeed the scene-painter and the machinist, the property-man and the costumer, are your veritable Shakspores, Sheridans, Otways and Farquhars of the modern stage. We have only to add, that *'decline and fall'* seems stamped upon the 'drama as it is,' and our picture would be complete.

Now whence has all this deterioration arisen? Numerous causes have been assigned by those who still cling to the drama, as to 'an early love,' as well as by those who are exulting over its downfall. The general intelligence of the age, which unfits men's minds for representations of the fictitious and the ideal; the perversion of the drama; the growing sense of the drama's immorality, and its objectionable associations with the hardness of the times, etc.; all are urged by partisans to these separately-assigned causes for the decline of public taste for theatrical amusements. That each and all of these causes may combine to produce the present depression of the drama, we will not deny; yet still we maintain that the taste for dramatic amusements is not extinguished; nay we boldly assert that in our own country at least the taste is not even *on the decline*. We have watched with interest every indication exhibited by the public on this subject: we have lately seen audiences delighted, nay enthusiastic, when any thing really sterling in its character was presented for their approbation. Managers should study these symptoms of the public pulse; they should keep with the age; not drag their unwilling energies after the public taste, but *lead* it. Let managers husband the resources yet left them in catering for their patrons. The increased intelligence and refinement of the age require that representations (at our principal theatres, at least,) should be in accordance with the taste of the audiences. Less will not suffice; a *uniform* fitness and propriety must be observable in the production of every piece; a stock company must be collected which can present, in the *aggregate*, respectable talent, so as not to offend the proprieties of the scene, even in a solitary particular. Managers are too often blindly obstinate on this point. Their conventional prejudices will not allow them to see how destructive it is to the interests of a theatre to have a few ignorant and incompetent underlings nightly destroying the effect of the really good actors in an establishment. A mediocre company, where the business of the stage is conducted with propriety; all perfect, the appointments, etc., in good keeping, and a general attention manifested in the minutiæ of the scene; will convey a more lasting satisfaction to an audience than even the highest efforts of an overwhelming 'star,' supported and surrounded by the drawbacks we have described. And to all this attention and energy on the part of managers they must add a disposition to meet *cheerfully* the 'exigences of the times,' by continuing the reduction of prices they have already begun; by not relaxing their efforts in consequence of this reduction, but affording entertainments equal if not superior to those given at their former rates. Their profits may not be as rapid, but they are certain to be more secure. Actors too must coalesce with managers, for their interests are one and indivisible. They must not allow a ridiculous vanity to prevent them from giving their support in characters which they may please to think below their dignity. There are few fallacies connected with the theatrical profession more erroneous than this. Actors of merit never lose their *caste* with the public by occasionally taking an inferior part. The public experience a delight in seeing their favorites, and are often more ready to acknowledge the merit of an actor in an inferior character than in one of acknowledged excellence. In the former, they trace the actor's genius, creating beauties which the author never contemplated. By a steady attention to such a course, improved upon and modified as circumstances may suggest, managers and actors may yet render the 'drama as it is' as successful as the 'drama as it was.'

[177] [Star Actors Responsible for the Decline of the Drama]
Brother Jonathan [1843]

For several years past, there has been a continued complaint of "the decline of the Drama," and certainly facts of the most stubborn kind have proved that it has indeed been seriously affected with this complaint. [. . .]

Among the nine hundred and ninety-nine causes assigned for this decline, we think the right one has not yet been forthcoming. The fault is not with the public—they always have and always will go to the Theatre, when there is really an ordinary attraction—and when there is an extraordinary one, they will go in a rush. But the taste as to theatrical matters is as peculiar as it is uncertain, and requires more tact, more nice discrimination, more careful watchfulness, to mark and follow its variations, than almost any other; and to the neglect of this on the part of managers and actors, may be partly attributed "the decline of the drama." They became careless in their business—their efforts were characterized first, by inattention to little matters—'inconsiderate trifles' in the abstract, perhaps, but of vast importance in the aggregate estimate of excellence. The wants of the public were disregarded—things with which they had been already surfeited were attempted to be thrust down their throats, and a nausea was the consequence. Men of ordinary talent, too, became suddenly affected with a strange idea of their own importance, and having mounted the stilts of pride and vanity, considered they were hiding their 'light under a bushel,' by remaining members of a stock company, and so started on a *starring* expedition, in the vain hope that they might be mistaken for some of the 'lost pleiades.' Stock companies, of course degenerated—their strength was distributed, and their effectiveness in a great measure destroyed; the expenses of managers increased so much, that they were unable to offer a fair remuneration to a talented actor, and consequently it has been a common thing to witness at a respectable theatre, *one star*, and the rest of the company the veriest sticks that ever 'strutted their hour on the stage,' behind two farthing rush-lights in a country barn. And this is the curse of the stage now—men—aye, and women too, are continually thrust into business to which they have no pretension—the fitness to represent a character is judged by the figure, and not by the mind—to study and understand it thoroughly in all its phases—to know the meaning of the words you utter, is out of the question altogether—so long as you can walk the stage with some degree of confidence, and with the smallest particle of grace,—and repeat the words as a schoolboy repeats his lesson—it is sufficient—you are an *actor*! How many do we nightly see who offend decency with their vulgarisms, and outrage common sense by their gross ignorance of the first principles of orthography?

But let us refer to another cause of this decline—it may be traced to a still different effect of the same self-importance of actors, which leads *them* to reject parts *they* consider beneath their talents,—and not only so, but actually refuse to appear on the stage with an actor who would be likely to throw them into the shade—and this, we believe, has actually occured at the Park Theatre, since the engagement of Mr. Macready. Is this to be tolerated by managers? Or are men fit to have the management of a theatre who make their engagements in such a loose way as to render themselves liable to such conduct from a few self-sufficient actors, who in their best efforts are merely endured by the audience. [. . .]

[179] [Elements of a Successful Play]
The Albion [1844]

The grand national spectacle of *Putnam! or, The Iron Son of '76* [by N. H. Bannister], was produced on Monday evening [5 Aug. 1844, at the Bowery Theatre, New York], to one of the most crowded Houses of the season, and met with complete success. It has been repeated every night during the week, to literally overflowing Houses. We consider this piece to be one of the best original productions [Thomas S.] Hamblin [the manager of the theatre] has produced, during the present season. Many of the leading incidents of Putnam's life, as well as other stirring events connected with his history, have been skillfully interwoven into the action of the Drama, and produce, with the aid of the usual Melo-Dramatic accompaniments, an effective and very graphic picture of the times. [. . .]

[. . .] Too much praise cannot be awarded to the getting up of this piece. The scenery is correct and appropriate—the famous leap of Putnam down the rocky steps of Horse Neck, is a graphic specimen of scenic effect, for which this house is proverbially famous—the descent is literally from the top of the Theatre, 150 feet in height, and is really a beautiful effort of the scene painter and the machinist combined.

[180] [Toward a More Natural Style of Acting]
The Albion [1844]

[. . .] The most casual observer of Theatricals must be satisfied that the time is past for the pompous mechanical style; even Tragedy is no longer tolerated on stilts, except at the minor Theatres—and even there, extravagant melo-drama is preferred. In Comedy, the revulsion in public taste is more apparent, all must be pit-pat, rapid and brilliant; all sentimentality is pronounced mawkish, and the short sparkling vaudeville, the petite comedy, abounding in equivoque, and presenting a running fire of puns and witticisms, are the only entertainments really in favour with an audience. Shakspeare's Tragedies are voted a bore, except when an artist of uncommon merit is the

Hero; and the old five act comedies must be cut down to three (as they are doing in London) to command even the decent toleration of a modern audience. Actors, too, who expect to win the approbation of the public, must fall in with this march-of-mind spirit-of-the-age. They must reform their style altogether (which, it must be confessed, is very much needed). They must go back to NATURE. The mouthing, spouting, sing-song declamation of the old school is entirely out of keeping with the age. Actors have only to cast their eyes around the House when they are inflicting their nightly doses of elaborated artificialities upon their audiences, and witness the apathy, almost amounting to disgust, which follows their efforts, and then to notice the hearty bursts of approbation which reward some genuine stroke of nature, and we should have a total reform of the present artificial style of playing. The manager, who could achieve this change in his company, would realize a fortune, even in these degenerate days of the Drama.

[185] [*Fashion*—a Drama of "sterling excellence"]
The Albion [1845]

On Monday next [24 Mar. 1845], Mrs. [Anna C. O.] Mowatt's Comedy of *Fashion* [*Or Life in New York*] is to be produced [at the Park Theatre, New York], with every accessory, which a strong cast, and lavish expenditure on scenery, upholstery and decoration can effect. The management has spared neither pains nor expense in putting this Native Comedy upon the stage, in a style worthy the sterling excellence of the piece, and we confidently expect that the Public will amply sustain Mr. Simpson's judgment and liberality.

We believe *Fashion* will satisfactorily solve the query, "Are there materials in American society, for constructing a successful comedy?—and is there a writer capable of adapting these materials?"—Mrs. Mowatt has brought to her task, a familiar intercourse with the best society; travel has improved her naturally keen powers of observation; a refined taste and a close and critical acquaintance with the stage, has quickened her perception of dramatic effects, and she has thus been able to achieve a production, that we think will astonish her countrymen, by its vigour and fidelity of execution. Having read the manuscript, we think it but justice to the fair author to state, that the comedy is entirely devoid of personalities—specimens of classes, are presented with bold and graphic skill, but not *individuals* of those classes. The piece is caustic in the extreme on modern follies, but the sanctity of private life has not been invaded to afford specimens for this Dramatic castigation. Mrs. Mowatt has a severe ordeal to pass through on Monday night; it is but just that she should appear, only as censor of general follies—not the caricaturist of personal foibles. [. . .]

[186] [*Fashion*: "the best American comedy in existence"]
The Albion [1845]

It is with no ordinary feelings of satisfaction that we record the triumphant verdict of the public, in favour of Mrs. Mowatt's Comedy of *Fashion* fully sustaining the predictions we ventured to make previous to its representation. It has created a sensation, unexampled in theatricals,—and has decisively established the fact, that the time has arrived when a strictly American Drama can be called into existence. Mrs. Mowatt herself, has but presented us with the "Waverly" of her series.

The satire on modern views and follies, conveyed through the medium of importations from the London stage, fail in their application in this country, from their local character. The "Mirror of Nature" reflects only *English Manners*, and peculiarities—the satire is consequently pointless here,—but change this stage reflector, to New York, Boston, Philadelphia, and other large cities, let it faithfully exhibit the "manners living as they rise" in American society, and the drama then assumes its legitimate mission, and we believe it will also regain its original ascendancy.

It is contrary to the uniform system pursued in the pages of the *Albion*, to enter into the discussions of the peculiarities of American habits and manners,—we must therefore confine our strictures to the Comedy, as a work of art, leaving it to our contemporaries to decide the fidelity of the picture it presents of American follies and eccentricities.

A very brief sketch of the plot will serve to illustrate the few remarks we shall venture to make as to its merits.

[. . .] It will be observed that every character may be taken as a specimen of a class; and not the least of the merits of this comedy is, that it is only classes that are depicted—*individuals* have not sat for the portraits; it would be doing Mrs. Mowatt great injustice to suppose that she would serve up particular persons for public laughter or derision; we believe her incapable of the act—and we hear that she unequivocally denies the charge.—That several persons have been named as models, is tolerably conclusive evidence that the application of the satire is a general one.

To the composition, in a literary point of view, we shall confine our remarks. The language throughout is natural and colloquial, terse and pointed—hence its great charm. Two acts are actually nothing but conversation—the action of the play does not progress—and yet the interest of the audience is sustained without flagging. There is not, perhaps, much brilliancy in the dialogue, but the absence of this is sufficiently compensated by the point and solid truths conveyed throughout. The language of Trueman, in particular, is energetic and pointed in the extreme; he is the moralist of the comedy, but he never poses.

Mrs. Tiffany is a modern Mrs. Malaprop [in R. B. Sheridan's *The Rivals*,

1775] in the French tongue, with a dash of Lady Duberly [in George Colman's *Heir at Law*, 1797], and the duality is skilfully managed.

The dramatic incident or action exhibits, perhaps, the unpractised hand; the characters talk too much, for modern comedy. We have felt, at times, like the critic on the first representation of the *School for Scandal*, who exclaimed—"why do not those people leave off talking, and let the play go on!" This defect has been materially obviated since the first night, by judicious curtailments in the dialogue—yet still, more action is desirable.—Upon the whole, Mrs. Mowatt may lay claim to having produced the best American comedy in existence, and one that sufficiently indicates her capabilities to write one that shall rank among the first of the age.

[188] [*Fashion*: A Drama of "inferior quality"]
Spirit of the Times [1845]

Mrs. Mowatt's comedy, *Fashion*, was represented for the first time, on Monday [24 Mar. 1845], to a very crowded and indulgent audience. The friends of the fair authoress did her injustice by previously disseminating opinions in praise of her comedy—its nature and nationality. By thus exciting curiosity the well wishers of the lady overstepped the mark of propriety, and the people, who were allured to the house by these prejudged opinions, were naturally disappointed from the inferior quality of the composition. Mrs. Mowatt possesses few qualifications for dramatic writing, as she lacks the essentials—vigor and ingenuity. Every one, who has seen a play represented, immediately considers himself able to produce a like work, little reflecting on the difficulty of the task, and here we have a solution for the many failures in dramatic composition. The language of comedy is not the ordinary slip shod conversational stringing together of words, employed in every day life, and the story of a play cannot be a mere recital of occasional occurrences. Comic writing should be terse, epigrammatic and nervous, and the plot should comprise a narration of real events, intermixed with others of a decidedly artificial nature, and above all, the action should never be stayed in the course of the piece. On the contrary to these results, the dialogue of *Fashion* is unpolished, spiritless, and disjointed, the satire is dealt out in unconnected items, much after the manner of Newspaper squibs, the plot is entirely too light for the dialogue, and the action, although not encumbered by an under plot, is cut up by unnecessary deviations. The first act has no earthly connection with the piece, and the third and fourth were perfect superfluities. [. . .] We will not attempt to analyse the plot, because we could not find it, and neither will we attempt to detect the sources of the characters, who, by the way, are most all the property of earlier dramatists. [. . .] To conclude, we may say that the piece, taken as a comedy, is a dreadful failure, and viewed as an exaggerated farce, may be tolerated until the arrival of the steamer. The satire, which bears little connection with the dialogue, is a mere collection of newspaper truisms, and is, we judge, as applicable to Scinde as to New York, while the humor is of a low school unsuited for a dramatic composition of the pretensions of *Fashion*. We would willingly undertake to assist our contemporaries in maintaining the dignity of 'Old Drury' [Park Theatre] and patronize a female writer, but at the same time we have strong conscientious objections against the inflictions of an indifferent comedy on the public, even if it be for a laudable purpose.

[191] [*Fashion*: The Beginning of American Drama]
The Albion [1845]

Fashion has continued to draw crowded and fashionable audiences during the week, and such is the increased popularity conferred on it, by the stamp of public favour, that Mr. [Edmund] Simpson [manager of the Park Theatre] might continue its successful run, were he not prevented by his previous arrangements [. . .].

We cannot refrain from expressing our sincere congratulations to all concerned in the production of this successful American Comedy. To the manager it has proved a mine, and at a period when such a "windfall" was invaluable. On the fair authoress, it has conferred a name, that we believe she will render still more conspicuous in the Dramatic Literature of her country. But we hail the production of *Fashion* on higher grounds than mere personal considerations. We believe the foundation stone is laid, by this comedy, for a superstructure that shall prove an enduring monument of the American drama, not merely local in its character, nor entirely dependant on home incidents or peculiarities for its construction. There are active and intelligent minds which have received an impetus from the success of their fair countrywoman; the "key-note" has been struck and we have no doubt of the results.

It is rather singular, when taken into consideration with the triumphant career Miss C. Cushman is running in London, that the American drama should, at this moment, be indebted for its highest character to *woman*! [. . .]

[192] [*Fashion*: A Failure As to Its Moral Principles]
The Anglo American [1845]

The new comedy of *Fashion* has been performed nightly from the time it was first brought out. Concerning its literary merits we have not been able on farther reflection to change the opinion we first expressed; and shall therefore now look a little into the *morale* of the work. There is this difference between a play and a novel; the former ought necessarily to bestow poetical justice on the characters, whilst it is not necessary for the latter actually to exhibit either punishment or reward. The novel writer, whilst displaying the human actions can enter into the recesses of the heart, decribe its workings, and bring to light the hidden feelings; or if not, he can by judicious reflection point out the nothingness of a life of successful vice or crime, though unreproved to the end. There needs not a poetical justice in the novel, because it may be inculcated in the mental philosophy of the writer, and the characters may remain exactly as we find them in real life. But the Drama must give an Epitome of life, action, and consequences; therefore moral evil whether consisting of vices or mere follies must have their attendant results exhibited.

Let us apply this to the play of *Fashion*. The cold-hearted and impudent scoundrel Count Jolimaitre is detected, it is true, but he is neither disgraced nor brought to reformation; the low scoundrel Snobson is overreached by the superior information of the Cattaraugus farmer, but the rascal escapes with impunity to carry on his rascalities elsewhere; the dishonest merchant is tormented with fears for his own personal safety, but even his detection and exposure do not work any change in his heart. The narrow escape of Seraphina from a low impostor, does not impress her with any sense of the follies in which she has been so long immersed; she does but regret that she was so nearly being a prey, and feel mortification that she cannot be a Countess; and the selfishness and meanness of the mother convey no other lesson than contempt for the individual character. But in all this, what application can by possibility be made to "Fashion,"—or can this be indeed "Fashion" in New York? We do not say that the dramatic morals should stand prominently in view like the Jewish Phylacteries of old, but they should be made manifest for they convey a feeling of approbation and of instruction—in short a lesson in ethics. [. . .]

[194] [Protest against a New Theatre on Broadway]
Broadway Journal [1845]

[. . .] we should regret exceedingly to see a theatre erected in Broadway [as the manager of the Bowery Theatre, Thomas Hamblin, planned] [. . .]. Considering the effect which theatres invariably have in the neighborhood where they have been built, we should expect that the owners of property in Broadway would protest against the erection of one in that noble thoroughfare. The little Olympic [on Broadway near Grand Street] is probably the best conducted theatre in the city; but we see it surrounded by dram shops, billiard rooms, and other equivocal resorts for the profligate and idle. We see no necessity of making a theatre a drinking house, a gambling house, and a something else house, as well as a play house, but there seems to be the real unities of the drama, and pea-nuts and punch are as essential concomitants to the acting drama as tin foil and rouge. It is one of the strangest things in life, that every institution has been modified by time excepting the theatre. It is just as dissolute now as it was in the days of Charles the Second. Though governed by no laws, and its professors reckoned as vagrants, it is one of the most conservative institutions among us. Quakers and Jews change, but the theatre holds to its old usages. Mr. Simpson [manager of the Park Theatre] is the only man in New York who has remained unchanged during the past twenty years, and his theatre is the only building in the city which has not been renovated. All the churches have been remodeled; preachers have changed their style, their theology, and their habits; society has suffered a dozen revolutions; the whole order of living has been reversed; we have altered our food, drink, habits, and even our speech; cotillions have gone out, and the Polka has come in; finger glasses and silver forks have become common in hotels; drunkenness has grown unfashionable; the national name has been changed; new streets have been built; Texas has been annexed; cheap books have been invented; hanging is almost abolished; the Croton river runs through the streets;—but Mr. Simpson and the Park remain the same, as unchangeable as the eternal sphinx of the desert. He looks as gloomy and saturnine as he used to look when he played Charles Surface [in R. B. Sheridan, *The School for Scandal*, 1777] in a claret colored coat and straw colored shorts; and his theatre is as dingy, as English, and as expensive as ever. The filthy saloons, with their red moreen curtains and yellow refreshment sellers remain unchanged, and probably will remain so for the next century; and the same plays are presented on the stage that were witnessed by our grandmothers and our grandmothers' grandmothers. There is no church in christendom half so conservative as the theatre: there are isms in every thing but the drama, which has never known a schism. Mr. [William] Dinneford, to be sure, got up a Greek tragedy the other day, which was stepping backward a thousand years or two, instead of moving forward, as any one must do who would produce a sensation in the drama; and it appears that he lost twenty-five hundred dollars by his devotion to the classics, which should be a caution to other managers to let the classics alone [Dinneford had opened Palmo's Opera House on Chambers Street on 7 April 1845 with Sophocles' *Antigone*].

We have no reason to believe that Mr. Hamblin would break adrift from the legitimate drama, or that he would do any better in Broadway than he has heretofore done in the Bowery; and therefore we would rather see him fail than succeed in his present undertaking: not that we wish him any ill as an individual, but as a manager he cannot but do harm in the community. He has had a large theatre under his control for many years, but he has done nothing to elevate the drama or correct the corrupt tastes of his audiences. If Mr. Hamblin must have a theatre, let him by all means stick to the Bowery. He would be a fish out of water in Broadway, and his theatre would mar the beauty of our magnificent thoroughfare. [. . .]

[195] [The Moral Lesson of *Fashion*]
Arthur's Ladies Magazine [1845]

[. . .] We are among those who believe that the stage, properly conducted, would be a powerful auxiliary in the cause of virtue, and tend in a high degree to improve our morals and refine our tastes. Unfortunately, instead of holding the mirror up to nature, and showing us vice and virtue in their true colors, the stage has, for many years, presented mere caricatures of real life. Melodramatic performances of the wildest kind, or other representations in which overstrained and unnatural sensibilities are exhibited, are the too common characteristics of the ordinary drama.

In the play of *Fashion* few of these faults are visible. Its moral is palpable and undeviating, and the characters, as conceived by the author at least, with some exceptions, natural and life-like. These, combined with its evident honesty, purity of intention, and truly national sympathies, make us wish that such representations were more frequently given on the American stage.

For good or evil, dramatic representations make strong impressions. All minds, and especially youthful ones, are naturally more open to practical illustrations of the deformities of vice and beauties of virtue, than to mere didactic instruction. The stage, therefore, while exhibiting an epitome of life, should also go beneath the surface, and show how true happiness, and true nobility, depend upon the inner man, not upon the mere external,—how the poorest and humblest may be noble, while the rich and aristocratic may be contemptible; in short, how nature's gentleman is the only true gentleman. This lesson is inculcated in the play of *Fashion*. [. . .]

We sincerely trust that more of such plays will be produced upon our stage, that gradually our dramatic taste may be purified from every thing wishy-washy, and enervating, and that the time is not far distant when the stage will exercise a healthy and beneficial effect, inciting virtuous thoughts and actions in the minds of its patrons. [. . .]

Although we by no means consider *Fashion* as equal to many of the sterling old English comedies, our approval of it is cordial, because it is American, and, inspires a love of country; and because we see in the hearty reception that it has met, an earnest that new laborers are about to come into the field of dramatic literature, and give to it a newer and a better life. It would be easy to point out many faults both in the play itself, and in the cast of characters as it was produced here. But this would be of no use at present.

[196] [The Stereotyped National Drama]
The Albion [1845]

[...] On Tuesday a new National Drama, called *The Black Rangers, or The Battle of Germantown*, was produced, with all the stage effect this Theatre [Bowery] has ever been famous for exhibiting. The piece, as might be expected from the subject, has been completely successful. It is of the Putnam school, but not equal to that excellent Drama. It is a pity the authors of these National Dramas do not strike out some novelty, in the construction of their pieces. The incidents and characters of these Dramas have become almost stereotyped, and the acting of the performers is nearly similar. The National History of America is a fertile field, capable of more variety than has hitherto been exhibited in Dramatic adaptations. Authors should strike a new vein.

[198] [America "on the eve of a great dramatic Revolution"]
Broadway Journal [1845]

[...] a new spirit is abroad in the Drama. The advent of this better feeling we predicted long since. Among its earliest indications was the reception of the new comedy *Fashion* (to which we cannot altogether give our critical approval, but which, as from the hand of a well-liked woman, was a fortunate pioneer,) and of its authoress as a performer on the same boards where her play had been successfully produced. To these, are to be added, the interest excited in Mr. Hudson's admirable Lectures, appealing to the higher standards; the general attention called to the peculiar reception of Mr. Forrest, and Miss Cushman, an American actor and actress in England. Accumulating in the same direction we have another comedy, from the pen of Mr. Epes Sargent, the offer of a handsome (but inadequate) sum for a new play of American Life and Manners, by Mr. Manager Burton; a small offer for a shorter piece of a similar complexion, by Marble, the Comedian—and, to crown all, the appearance of an American actor upon the stage, in the person of Mr. Murdoch, who at a bound has passed his English rivals who were making a handsome figure in the country, or are on their way to do so, and satisfied the American Public once for all, that if they will be at the pains to look at home when they are in want of actors, they may possibly find them. [...] In our notices of the Theatre, we shall always have an eye to its reform and elevation. We are, in this respect, on the eve of a great dramatic Revolution.
[See also [197].]

[199] [Shakespeare Improved but Mutilated]
The Anglo American [1846]

We have a truly grateful task upon our hands; that of recording the most complete and triumphant success of the most magnificent representation ever given in America. The historical play of *Richard III* was produced here [at the Park Theatre, New York] on Wednesday evening in a manner which, to the eye at least, defied criticism's censure, however fastidious the critic. There were not fewer than five-and-twenty new scenes, painted expressly for this purpose, and every one of which was a carefully executed one of the places and circumstances so given, at the time in which the action of the piece is placed. The principle of these are The White (or Rufus') Tower and grounds; The apartment of King Henry VI. in the Tower, with its magnificent window of stained glass; The Traitor's Gate (as it is now called); The Cloisters of Old St. Paul's, with the Cathedral itself in the back ground; Crosby House (Richard's residence) with a view of the river, and St. Paul's in the distance; The interior principal apartment of the same with all the escutcheons, arms, bearings, and devices peculiar to the period, such as the Arms of the Nevilles, the Bear and Ragged Staff, and Gloster's own cognisance of the Boar; The Presence Chamber of Edward; The Coronation of Richard; The City Gates, London Bridge, and River Thames; various scenes in rapid succession in the neighborhood of Tamworth, Bosworth, &c., where the last fight between "The Roses" took place; The Encampment of Richard; The Tent and the Watchfires; various views of the Battle-field in the course of the action, &c. &c. all of which were done with the most artistic skill and the most special regard for fidelity. As each scene was successively placed before the audience the most unbounded applause was bestowed upon it—which was indeed strictly due to the artists. With respect to the costumes there was not one, from King Richard himself down to the most insignificant messenger or menial, which was in the slightest degree out of keeping. Great pains had been taken to ascertain the costumes of all ranks at the period, the blazoning of the shields, the style of the arms, the dresses of the soldiery, the draperies of the female characters,—everything, in short, calculated to restore that *particular past* to the *present* was minutely attended to. [. . .]

We have always been impatient at the unwarrantable liberties taken from time to time, by interpolators, particularly with the work of those in whom their country prides herself. This has been done to a most immoderate and shameful degree in the case of the Bard of Avon, and most frequently by those who fancied they understood the taste of their day, but whose abuses have been retained after the day and the taste have gone by. Of such abuses we have to complain in the acted *Tempest*, of such we had eminently to complain in the acted *Lear*, until Macready purified and restored much of the original; and of such we have bitterly to complain in the case before us. As the text now stands

it is a downright insult to the understanding of every lover of Shakspeare to call it by his name. It is Cibber's *Richard* with the plot and sundry passages stolen from the Shakspeare plays; with passages turned over from one character to another, the lamentations of Northumberland in *Henry IV, Part II.* put into the mouth of Henry VI., a character not in *Richard III* at all; with the moral remark of the latter Henry in one play on conscience transferred to Richmond in another; in short with so much juggling and transferring, mixing, altering, and adulterating, that the original play would not even be recognisable except by its plot. Cibber seems to have thought that the Shakspeare Richard was too much of a prince and too little of a ruffian, he has therefore degraded him into a vulgar, brutal, butcher. The real Richard of history was doubtless ambitious and not overnice in gaining the point of his ambition, but it is well known that even Shakspeare over-blackened the picture in order to please the house of Tudor, a descendant of which house was on the English throne. More than half the acted text is not Shakspeare's *at all*, yet a contemporary congratulates the public on its fidelity to "the original!" Can he have been in the theatre during the performance,—and, if so, does he *know* the original? [. . .]
[See also [205].]

[200] [Shakespeare Adapted to 19th–Century Taste]
The Albion [1846]

Among the *cants* of the day may be classed the continual cry for the unmutilated text of Shakspeare—and this demand comes occasionally from men whose critical experience should teach them better. Why, there is not a single play of Shakspeare's that would be tolerated by modern audiences as written by the author. We do not allude to the passages which have led to the foolish "expurgated editions," but it is the change in the dramatic taste of the time, which prevents the use of Shakspeare's original text on the stage. The circumlocution and quibbling in which the great bard indulged, and which was in accordance with the taste of his age, when euphuism was the current, fashionable phraseology, and nothing was considered tedious in dramatic composition, when clothed in vigorous or harmonious language—has rendered a revision of his acting plays necessary, previous to their representation in more modern times. [. . .]

[211] [American Plays Should Be Local]
The Albion [1847]

[. . .] Mrs. Ellett's play [*Wissmuth & Co., or the Merchant and the Noble*] is founded on a drama by Franz Dingelstadt, a German author. We understand that the play as written, or rather as adapted by Mrs. Ellett, differs materially from the original work. New characters have been introduced; the play has been re-constructed; and the language of the German play is entirely remodelled so as to constitute a claim to the authorship, as valid as might be assumed by other dramatists of standard excellence, who have availed themselves of the labours of their predecessors and contemporaries for reconstructing Dramas on which their fame has been based.

We somewhat regret that Mrs. Ellett should have adopted this at all times equivocal expedient, and particularly is it impolitic in a native writer, at this peculiar crisis of American Dramatic literature. There is a strong desire in this country at the present moment, to foster native dramatic and histrionic talent; and writers for the stage should present pieces in accordance with this feeling. These dramas should be strictly national in their character, drawn from national sources, and should be made to illustrate periods and events in American History, or they should present the features of national peculiarities, habits and manners. We believe that the young American drama must be *local* in its character, in this, its infant state, to insure the entire sympathies of its supporters.

Among the other causes which have led to the partial failure of *Wissmuth & Co.*, is the absence of local interest. The audience went prepared to admire a new play by an American authoress; they were disposed to give it all their support from the laudable pride of National feeling. They witness its representation, and find a vigorously written production; a strikingly original plot, and a series of high wrought dramatic incidents, but there is nothing to stamp it as *American*. The whole piece is German, essentially German in its construction. There is nothing to satisfy that want which the play-going American public now demand.

[212] ["Historical accuracy" and "the tastes of the multitude"]
The Albion [1847]

[. . .] On Monday Judge [Robert T.] Conrad's tragic play, called *Aylmere*, was revived under its original title of *Jack Cade*. [. . .] [The original version of the play failed in 1836; Conrad revised it for Forrest, who produced it with great success in 1841 and made it part of his repertoire.]

The facts of history are distorted to suit the author's design. The converting of Jack Cade into a highly educated man, even making him the representative of royalty, is so gross a violation of historical accuracy, that even the allowable latitude of poetical license cannot cover it. [. . .]

The play is, however, well calculated to catch the tastes of the multitude; it abounds with striking clap-traps on the community of rights and property, which lose nothing of their force in Mr. Forrest's powerful delivery. Indeed, bating the anachronisms of the author's design, he has given a faithful exposition of the "spirit of the times" as it was embodied in the following verse, which was the common watchword of that period:—

When Adam delv'd, and Eve span,
Where was then the *gentleman*?

A play designed as an exposition of principles so popular, plentifully garnished as it is with murders and melo-dramatic effects, and supported with all the physical capabilities Mr. Forrest brings to his task as the hero, and that hero the sole point of prominence in the piece, it will keep its place on the stage in defiance of objection based on the ordinary rules which govern dramatic criticism.

[214] [Cornelius Mathews's *Jacob Leisler*]
The Albion [1848]

[. . .] We have attended two representations of the new play, produced at this theatre [Bowery] by Mr. Murdoch, from a desire to render full and impartial justice to its merits, and we regret to be compelled to say, that however meritorious *Jacob Leisler* may be, in parts, taken as a literary production, yet judged by the standard which constitutes an effective acting drama, it comparatively fails, and precisely, we think, from its lack of those necessary constituents of a good play, concentrated interest and connected action. [. . .]

The public press has so fully and extensively given the plot of this piece that we may be spared the task of repeating it in detail. The principal events in the brief public life of Leisler are embodied in the play, and a fictitious love plot is called in to aid in the interest of the drama. [. . .]

Out of these varied materials, it would appear that a very effective, active play might be constructed, especially with the high poetical talent already exhibited by the author in his tragedy of *Witchcraft*. We have before stated where he has failed. The interest is so diffused as to lose all concentrated point; the scenes are disconnected, and do not gradually lead to a development of the main plot with an increased force of interest. [. . .] The other great disadvantage we consider is, that like many modern plays, the chief character absorbs nearly the whole attention. [. . .]

The language of this drama breathes the very spirit of Republicanism, and so far it is truly what an American drama should be. The author has availed himself of all the lights that an age of progress has developed, and a somewhat anomalous cast is given to the expressions of the leading characters, who are made to talk in the stereotyped phraseology of our times; they seem, indeed, to have been gifted with prescience, and feel and speak two hundred years in advance of their age. This perhaps is all allowable, but it destroys the verisimilitude of history, as does the intellectual, lofty, and pure tone given to the Hero falsify the positive facts recorded of Leisler's character and mental qualifications. Antirentism is forcibly advocated in connection with other ultra liberal views, but to balance these equivocal doctrines, the author has made Leisler hesitate to commit any overt act of rebellion, until he learns the abdication of James 2nd, when he considers himself absolved from his allegiance. It is a noble trait in the character of Leisler, and a well directed compliment to the supremacy of the law.

We cannot close our necessarily brief strictures on this new play, without expressing our strong objections to two radically defective points in its constructure. The introduction of the supernatural machinery, and the final catastrophe.

The author incurred a heavy responsibility in attempting to imitate the accessories which give such effect to Shakspeare's *Macbeth*, whose Witches with their unearthly language created for the occasion, their sublime and mystic accompaniments, aided as they are on the stage by music almost as immortal as the language they are embodied in, present such an unapproachable sublimity of excellence, as to render the task of successful imitation hopeless. Loopwinge, the Indian Prophetess, speaks only the paraphrased language of Cooper's novels. The supernatural visitations in the incantation scene, where Leisler seeks to learn the fate of his proposed enterprise, provoked comparisons with the similar scene in *Macbeth*. This the author should have avoided.

The final catastrophe of the piece should be changed. It is a violation of all the rules of good taste and correct feeling. Conceive the horror of such a scene, in this age of refinement:—Leisler is actually beheaded in sight of the audience!—the axe is seen to descend—we hear the blow—the headless trunk is partially exposed, and Derrick Leisler rushes to the scaffold, dips his handkerchief in the blood of his father, tears the reeking trophy, and gives a portion to Vermilyea, and waving the bloody symbol on high with vociferous shouts, the curtain falls! Such an accumulation of horrors is a perversion of the drama's legitimate purpose. It is calculated to brutalize audiences who should be refined and sublimated by dramatic exhibitions. [. . .]

[215] [Pruning Old Plays for Modern Audiences]
The Albion [1848]

[. . .] Beaumont and Fletcher, with many of our other elder dramatists, may have been the delight and admiration of their own times in all their prurient and uncurtailed originality, when women of quality were compelled to visit the theatre in masks to preserve even the appearance of modesty.

But when these plays are prepared for modern audiences, they should undergo a thorough pruning to render them innoxious and inoffensive. The modern acted drama requires purifying in these particulars, and we trust that *Romeo and Juliet*, which we see announced as being in preparation at this house, from the *original text* of Shakspeare, will be carefully revised before it is submitted for representation. [. . .]

[216] [Forrest's Acting and the National Character]
The Albion [1848]

[. . .] This pre-eminence of Mr. Forrest over his gifted contemporaries, has been with us the subject of interesting ethical disquisition, coupled as it is with the fact that this great actor has also been subjected to severe criticism by those who profess to judge him by the usual canons applied to the histrionic art. We are inclined to believe that Mr. Forrest is not to be judged by the ordinary canonical standards of criticism, at least on his native soil. He has created a school in his art, strictly American, and he stands forth as the very embodiment, as it were, of *the masses* of American character. Hence his peculiarities. Hence his amazing success. And further, Mr. Forrest in his acting is not merely the embodiment of a national character, but he is the beau ideal of a peculiar phase of that character—its *democratic idiosyncrasy*. Of this, both physically and in his artistical execution, he is a complete living illustration.

All this was perhaps more palpable in his acting some years ago, than it is at present, when study and experience have subdued much of his original impetuosity and disregard of the conventional rules of his art. But there is still enough left of his original leaven to characterize his performances as being distinct and peculiar. His Shakspearean characters are all stamped with the same intense energy of expression, and overwhelming displays of physical force. The imbecile Lear, and the melancholy Dane, are in his hands frequently like enraged Titans, both in look and manner. Macbeth is the ferocious chief of a barbarous tribe—and his Othello, with all its many beauties, becomes in his hands truly the ferocious and "bloody Moor." We mean in all this to say, that the courtly guise, the old world conventionalisms, which "hedge in the divinity of kings," and the polished graces that surround the great and high born—are not held by Mr. Forrest as the imperative auxiliaries of his acting. His graces and his dignity have been founded on other models—the free aboriginal of his country, erect and fearless in the freedom with which nature has endowed him, has afforded to this great actor lessons in the histrionic art, which the finished artists of Europe take only from the Court or the *Salons*. And in striking out this originality, Mr. Forrest has touched the hearts, and jumped with the tastes of a majority of his countrymen. [. . .]

[220] "Dramatic Copyright"
Spirit of the Times [1849]

[. . .] It may not be known to our readers, and most especially those who are inclined to support that most chimerical of phantasmagoras—the National Drama—that there is in our country no copyright whatever for dramatic productions—no protection against the stealing and reproduction of any piece which may emanate from a native brain. It may with justice be said, that as yet we have no dramatic authors, or at least but few, who have made any sensation, or coined money in the theatrical world. We are sorry to add, that this is most true; that, with the trifling exception of Mr. Howard Payne, no American has up to this time composed a piece which has maintained possession of the stage, and as long as the present state of things continues, we shall present the singular spectacle of a nation reputed among the best educated in the world, destitute of a dramatic literature. The meanest community of ancient or modern times has this advantage of us; even the Sandwich Islanders. Undoubtedly we have some MSS. plays, which have flourished on our stage, wherein a bay horse, a red shirt, or a six-barrelled pistol, has attracted local or temporary notice, but these pieces have been generally vile concoctions, whose paternity would be repudiated by a respectable boot-black, who had any pretensions to scholastic acquirements. Another, and a more assuming class of dramatists, have manufactured some five-act affairs—*Fashion* [by Anna C. O. Mowatt, 1845], *Spartacus* [original title: *The Gladiator*, by Robert M. Bird, 1831], *Jack Cade* [by R. T. Conrad, 1835]—still, these are the property of individuals, who, fearing to lose their possession, most properly deprive the printer's devil of the right to soil their dainty pages; for the very instant a play comes off the press, or is even transcribed, any actor or manager who may have the good fortune to buy, beg, or steal, a copy, can appropriate it to his own use. The great reputation of a dramatic author, in common with all other writers depends upon the dissemination of his compositions—any law, or want of legislation, which deprives him of the right to publish, unless with detriment to his pocket, is an unjustifiable injury to national literature. The other day Mr. Forrest purchased for the sum of $1000 a five act, full bloom, tragedy, which he will most assuredly produce at some theatre for his own individual benefit—a perfectly proper proceeding on his part, as he has paid what, in his opinion, is the marketable value of the article; still, at the same time, the guarantee of his right deprives the public and the author of the pleasure of having it presented to them in good clear type, instead of from the mouth of the great tragedian. Many prefer to escape the infliction too often submitted to by good natured audiences by perusing a play in the cabinet; and others, who are opposed to stage representations, or are too poor in worldly wealth to lend their constant support to theatres, yet, being admirers of dramatic works, would willingly purchase a copy.

Now that the legislature of our State have incorporated an institution—long since advocated in the columns of the *Spirit*—whereby decayed Roscii and broken down Garricks, can be comfortably provided for, now that the "Dramatic Association" [American Dramatic Fund Association, founded in 1848] is in successful operation, let the next move be towards the ensuring of Authors' and Actors' rights in dramatic compositions by a fair and liberal copyright. Let every one who may be inclined to fee the clerk of the Southern District [. . .] have a fair chance for immortality, both on and off the stage. Do not deprive those managers and performers who are inclined to foster dramatic talent, (and we are happy to say there are many such) of their right to secure pieces suited to their theatres or personal capabilities, yet, at the same time, permit aspiring genii to appeal from managerial or artistical caprice by means of the book store. Such a law, based on the French copyright act, which can be further improved by some international arrangements, can be productive of no injury, and may result in great benefits, if not to authors, at least to trunk makers.

We well know the brains of a great number of our community are considered of very little value, and still less use, yet we trust there are legislators who may be inclined to allow some poor devils to attempt to set a value on those despised organs, and enroll themselves with us under the broad banner—"Protection to American Intellect." [. . .]

[221] [Native American Drama]
The Albion [1849]

[. . .] The avidity with which the theatre-going public flocked to support Mrs. Mowatt's comedy of *Fashion*, a few seasons since, satisfied us that the period had arrived when a *native dramatic literature* was demanded, and would be supported by the American people. Whatever difference of opinion may exist as to the merits of that work, the fact is certain, it gave an impetus to the movement of fostering and upholding a distinctive American drama, and that too of precisely the peculiar cast in which native talent at present is most certain of achieving success.

To reflect the manners, habits, and distinctive idiosyncrasies of American character, either by the pungent satire which forms one of the essential elements of comedy, or by embodying works of American history familiar to the masses, or in the construction of domestic dramas, which shall graphically illustrate the stirring incidents so constantly occurring in newly settled districts of the country—these seem to be the legitimate grounds upon which the early American drama is to base its claim for distinctive originality, and consequent success.

Taking the results of Mr. Forrest's efforts to procure an American tragedy as data on which to predicate an opinion, we should judge that the cast of American dramatic genius has not yet been moulded into the peculiar conformation necessary for producing a great tragic composition; although we cannot but reiterate a formerly expressed opinion, and say, that we do not think the highest order of American talent will submit to enter into an indiscriminate scramble of competition for the rewards annexed to a prize tragedy! Writers of real eminence in this country can employ their time and talents more advantageously than by devoting themselves to this uncertain, and at best, unsatisfactory employment [. . .].

Tragedy draws its inspiration from the lowest depths of passion; it seeks for its materials in the records of human crimes and human sorrows. It associates itself with the past, rather than with the present; it clings to the memory of bygone ages consecrated by antiquity, and lingers on the customs, habits, and characteristics of the periods of romantic interest, with all their time-worn and now exploded peculiarities, instead of the matter of fact, utilitarian movements of our own progressive times. The energy, enterprise, and unceasing perseverance of the American character is prospective, not retrospective in its movement; time must mellow down its exuberances, and the avenues to rapid and certain wealth must become less numerous than they at present are, before men of genius will sober down into the calm reflection and abstractions necessary to complete the formation of the true tragic writer.

There is, however, ample range for the exercise of native and home-made dramatic literature in the walks we have designated, and in the adaptation of works of fiction from popular authors. The latter department is positively becoming quite a thriving trade. [. . .]

[222] [American Drama Must Be Patriotic]
The Albion [1849]

The new drama, *Kate Woodhull, or the Price of Liberty*, by C. Edwards Lester, Esq., author of the *Glory and Shame of England*, was produced on Wednesday evening to a crowded house [Broadway Theatre].

The audience were evidently most favourably disposed to receive with enthusiasm a drama founded on American history, and written by a native author; and yet with all these advantages, so influential in deciding the fate of a first representation, Mr. Lester obtained but a very equivocal verdict of success. There were but few bursts of genuine applause throughout the performance, and the curtain fell with scarcely any demonstration of approval.

Mr. Lester is either unfortunate in the subject he has chosen for dramatic illustration, or he has treated that subject in an unartistic and false style. We fear he has erred in both points. American audiences have not been accustomed to witness the incidents of the "War of Independence" represented on the stage otherwise than by appeal made directly to the patriotic feelings arising from the glory and success achieved by the American arms. And we hold this mode of treatment, so naturally and so nationally adopted by American dramatists to be wise and laudable. Mr. Lester has struck out an original course. He has taken up one of the most gloomy periods in the eventful history of the war of the Revolution, and through five acts he presents the American cause under the repulsive aspects of defeat and suffering. To add to the difficulties of such an unpopular theme, he has written as if his drama were intended for the meridian of London, rather than that of New York, and as if the suffrages of his London critical friends were the point of approbation he was aiming at. [. . .]

The patriotic sentiments strewn liberally throughout the piece, are but the usual clap-traps, and these neither hearty nor healthy. They did not come home with a thrill and a tingle, as such indispensable hits should do—and half the time the effect they might have produced was altogether impaired by high-flown eulogiums on English chivalry and British greatness. The audience were kept in a perfect whirl of bewilderment by the singular display of ultra liberality—one moment applauding a well known bit of patriotic clap-trap—the next, actually frightened out of their propriety by elaborated praise, or deprecatory excuses on behalf of England—when the action of the piece demanded the entirely opposite feeling.

[. . .] the American dramatist, who fails to give a strong, healthy, hearty, patriotic tone to dramas founded on incidents which have occurred in his country's history, does not justly estimate the feelings of his countrymen; nor has he learned the true element of success so far as a native drama is concerned.

[. . .] Mr. Lester must reconstruct his drama before it can possibly succeed; and should he make the attempt, we would venture to suggest a searching revision of portions of the language employed. [. . .] His plain matter-of-fact men talk heroics, deal out their classical allusions, and cite the examples of the heroes of antiquity with a profusion that would do honour to the orations of a Sophomore on an exhibition day. It was amusing to hear my Lords Howe and Percy, in powdered perukes, straight cut coats and military boots, spouting sentiment in blank verse: nor was it much less amusing to see Colonel Burr and honest-hearted Gen. Woodhull transformed into similar parodies of the antique Grecian or Roman orators. We would also advise—if the drama be worth improvement, which is doubtful—an excision of some at least of the most familiar poetical epithets. [. . .]

[223] [Social Standing of Actors Improved]
The Albion [1849]

Watching, as we do, every indication of public feeling that promises the restoration of the drama to its once pure and elevated character, we cannot but congratulate the officers of "The Dramatic Fund Association" upon the truly elegant and satisfactory festival given in honour of their first anniversary, the particulars of which will be found above.

It was not alone the excellence of the cheer provided at the Astor House, nor was it the varied mental entertainment provided by the stewards, which gave weight and tone to this interesting occasion—it was the fact that, for the first time, the members of the theatrical profession were assembled together on this continent in a corporate capacity, recognised by law, and taking their stand among their fellow citizens as a body legally authorized to maintain their privileges upon equal terms with other benevolent institutions of the land. And to give additional weight to this important step in the future elevation of the histrionic profession, the meeting was graced by the presence of many private citizens, whose position and influence enable them to shed respectability and dignity upon any cause that they cordially espouse. [. . .] It afforded a satisfactory proof that the profession of an Actor is not incompatible with the attainment of the high-toned character of a *gentleman*, although fanatics and exclusives may deny the fact.

Barron, the great French actor of the last century, was accustomed to assert in a very pardonable spirit of egotism, growing out of a consciousness of the dignity of his art, "That actors should be nursed in the laps of Princes." There is much philosophy in the remark, for high art can only be attained by high culture. The American stage, and the American drama, demand the fostering hand of the pre-eminent in mind, the dignified in station, and the powerful by wealth—these are the princes of America, and can control, not only the personal characters of actors, but they might give to the drama its true and all-influential tone as a conservator of taste and sound morality.

[229] [The Astor Place Riot]
The Independent [1849]

Terrible Riot in the City.—Mob dispersed by the Military.—Twenty Men Slain.

[. . .] The occasion arose from a protracted quarrel between two actors—Forrest of New York, and Macready of London—Forrest complaining of some indignity done by Macready in England to hinder his success or injure his reputation, and appealing to the American spirit to stand by him. Macready being engaged to appear for several nights last week at the Astor-Place Opera

House, a party opposed to him determined to silence him by mob violence. They succeeded on Monday evening in stopping the play, the police not interfering, and no arrests following the riot. Macready thereupon abandoned his engagement. But a large number of leading gentlemen of the city, headed by Washington Irving, addressed him a note, urging the fulfillment of his original plan, and assuring him that the good sense and respect for order prevailing in this community would sustain him. This request was acceded to and Thursday night appointed for the performance.

Unfortunately, the publication of the correspondence was regarded as an open challenge to the other party; placards were circulated that the crew of the English steamer America were resolved to sustain their countryman with arms; and the calling out of the military by the Mayor on Thursday afternoon, as a measure of precaution, added fuel to the flame.

When the time arrived, the police force stationed inside secured and removed every disturber, and the play went on to the end. Outside, an attack was made on the building with stones, which soon demolished the glass of the windows. The mob growing furious with their own noise, increased in violence, until the military were ordered to come on the ground. The troops were assailed with stones, and many injured, and at length the order was given to fire, and about 20 persons were killed, or have since died of their wounds, many of them mere lookers-on, and some transient passers-by. [. . .]

[For the controversy between Macready and Forrest, see [218]; for a detailed account of the riots, see [225] and [226].]

[243] "The Modern American Drama"
The American Whig Review [1852]

However strange it may sound to divide into *two* parts what many deny we possess, we deliberately write the *Modern American Drama*, to distinguish it from those national pieces so prevalent some few years ago.

We conceive that much vagueness exists in the public mind as to what constitutes a national drama: many accept the limited definition, which excludes all subjects drawn from a foreign source: in this point of view universality is at once negatived, and the drama merely becomes the history of a nation flattered and falsified, or at all events condensed, colored, and emphasized: this definition substitutes a practical *romance* for what should be the picture of *life*, without reference to any particular locality. The human heart, with all its lofty and cosmopolitan aspirations, is limited to the *cordon sanitaire* of a parish;

The soul's uneasy, and confined at home;

the far-searching intellect is put into the village stocks; the philanthropist has to narrow his sympathy to his own parish; the glorious gift of charity is a mere legal poor's rate; and Olympian Jove, by this bigotry, is dethroned to make way for the beadle. If the universal can be narrowed into the national, what is to prohibit the latter from becoming the parochial? [. . .] The motto of the *great dramatist* is,

Homo sum, et nihil me alienum puto.

Measured, however, by the other rule, the Drama is but a very "little bit of man indeed," scarcely a finger. Our Drama, therefore, (in our opinion,) does not depend upon our writer's choosing American subjects, but in the excellence of their treatment of the subject itself. Judged by the former standard, how few of Shakspeare's plays are national! His comedies are limited to the *Merry Wives of Windsor*, and his tragedies to his histories. The greatest triumphs of his genius are excluded from the English Drama by this absurd definition. *Hamlet* belongs to Denmark; *Timon of Athens* to Greece; *Troilus and Cressida* to Troy; *Othello, Romeo and Juliet, Merchant of Venice*, and a host of others, are part and parcel of the Italian stage; for a mere glance will show how few of his subjects are national. In our times the rule holds good; Bulwer, Knowles, Talfourd, Browning, Horne, Stephens, and Heraud, avail themselves of the history of the human heart, without thinking of geography, which is more useful to the hack-driver than the poet. Faith and morals may depend somewhat upon latitude and longitude; but poetry, which has man for its subject, claims him wherever she finds him. Indeed, it may be taken as proof of *want* of genius, when an author confines himself to his own nation and times; this is evident in the plays of Jerrold, Bell, Marston, and Boursicault, which are very flimsy things. This class are rather reporters than poets; mere observers, not creators; and their works consist of conventional dialogues, turning more upon manners than man. Boker's *Calaynos* [1848] belongs as truly to the American mind, and is as genuine a specimen of our Drama, as the *Witchcraft* [1846] of Mathews, although the scene of one is laid in Spain, and the other in Salem.

This brings us at once to the consideration of the cynical complaint we occasionally hear, "that we have no national literature;" forgetting that to a certain extent we have no *distinctive* existence as a people; the constituent parts of all that constitutes nationality, or rather the elements of them, being identical with those of England. We are the brighter noon of her dawning day; a young giant endowed with her idiosyncrasy; we possess her memory, and every faculty that is used in either political or literary thought; in sitting down to write, we think in English; our judges decide on English principles; our moral and religious prejudices have their root on the other side of the Atlantic; we inherit her history, manners, and customs, modified certainly by locality and circumstances. Notwithstanding the vast interfusion of foreign blood, it has never dethroned the predominant idea; had it done that, it would have changed our language. Language is the symbol of sovereignty; this has remained untouched, not because the absolute majority are of the original English stock, but because they are, more than any other, a constituent part of the population; this will account for our identity remaining untouched. We are improved, not changed; a new edition, "amended and corrected," certainly, by a superior commentator, but not another work; a fuller, grander, deeper development of England. We have thrown aside the *formulae*, and purified our creed. We have outgrown the superstitions of the old religion; our genius moves no longer in the ancient fetters of the feudal past; in a word, we are free! [. . .]

The hereditary leprosy of the feudal age was outgrown to a great extent, our relations with the mother country becoming a convenience on our part, and a sympathy on hers: possibly there was more of habit in it than either necessity or reflection. Although we were weaned from a churlish breast, established in our own home, we remained a part of the same family. We are consequently precluded, by our very origin, from the possession of a distinct or original literature, which is, like ourselves, a continuation of England; and until a current of foreign blood is poured into our veins sufficiently large to change our language, it must of necessity remain so. Our feelings and opinions will progress, but our spirit will be intact: this occurs in individuals constantly. [. . .] The foundation of the future is the past; and what is true of a man is true of a nation, for the simple reason, as Wordsworth writes,

Have we not all of us *one* human heart?

And the greatest of poets says,

One touch of *Nature* makes the whole world *kin*!

In like manner, although our external policy became independent at the Revolution, our nature was substantially untouched. Americans pored over history with the same feelings as they did before, when they were nominally colonists. Washington, Jefferson, Franklin, even Old Hickory himself, as well as their present descendants, never read the wars of York and Lancaster with the same emotions as either a Frenchman, a German, or a Pole; and this will be the case with *our* descendants, to the last "syllable of recorded time."

As the poet says,

Our blood was first the cause; since then, our tongue.

Indeed, what blood is to the body, language is to the mind: language may be called the sap; and we may as reasonably expect oranges and lemons to grow upon an apple tree, simply because it is transplanted from England to Spain: at the same time, grafting and transplanting may improve its fruit, endowing it with a superior bloom, size, and flavor; but it will bear apples only as long as it grows. [...]

Every year diffuses education among the masses; we have not, perhaps, so many *millionaires* of knowledge, but intellectual wealth is more equally distributed. The human race is growing more and more republican every day; knowledge, like power, is becoming common property; no longer hoarded in the groves of Academus, the caves of Pythagoras, the cloisters or the palace, it is now all-pervading, like the air. Men must and will have it, or perish in obtaining it. This will account for the fact, that it is in the Drama alone that the moderns have gained upon the ancients, and this merely in the *scientific* part, construction. Compare the Greek stage with the modern, and the stride is immense; but, we repeat, only in the more *mechanical* part, the stage carpentry. We question if our modern poets knew *more* of the *human heart* than Euripides, Sophocles, Menander, Aristophanes, Terence and Plautus. We exclude Shakspeare from this comparison, as he is rather an exception than a rule; otherwise, in pure intellect, our dramatists have not advanced. Great allowance must likewise be made for the changing manners of the times; even in Shakspeare's day, the patience of an audience was almost antediluvian. What spectators, but an audience of Methuselahs, could afford to sit out tragedies as long as *Hamlet*, with its four thousand five hundred lines? Now the orthodox length of a play is thirteen hundred, and it requires almost a murder in every scene to make it endurable at that. In the days of Elizabeth, the dramatist was the instructor, as well as the amuser; and his works, however prolix, came upon the parched souls of the people, as rain upon a thirsty soil; now every thing is intensed. Electric telegraphs have made the human soul impatient; we demand sensation, not instruction; stimulant, not food; excitement, not repose. We brace our system by over-doses of passion; to borrow an illustration from Lamb, "like the tailor, we *rest* ourselves by *standing!*" [...]

At the risk of being considered national, we openly avow that we regard the position we have gained, whether in the arts and sciences, comprehending painting, poetry, sculpture, and mechanics, even taking all in their widest range, as one of which the most dispassionate judge has ample reason to be proud.

The nature of our present inquiry of course confines us to merely *one* branch, but no candid mind need fear applying the severest test to all; indeed, considering the many difficulties thrown into the way of our authors, their comparative progress is greater than that of any other nation. When it is remembered that they have to encounter the competition of laborers who work gratuitously—we mean the British authors who are impressed and kidnapped by our present infamous practice of literary piracy, which converts our mental commerce into a vast system of legalized smuggling, driving the native artisan out of the field, or else making him a mere literary beggar, dependent upon the precarious alms of a publisher—we marvel they have accomplished so much. What would become of our commerce and manufactures, if a band of smugglers and pirates inundated the market with the proceeds of plundered foreign stores, the prime cost of which was merely the iniquity of the robber, and the life-blood of the rightful possessor?

The present system deprives our authors of the greatest incentive to intellectual exertion; the battle is to be fought, forsooth, against the most desperate odds, and yet the palm of victory—the prize for which all fight—is to be withheld: scorn, if we fail; neglect, if we triumph. Genius requires sunshine for its development more than any other human faculty. What *vacuum* is to physical life, neglect is to the mind. Genius cannot breathe in silence, indifference, and obscurity. [. . .]

When these circumstances are taken into account, we repeat, the wonder is that we have done so much and so well. The last few years have produced as dramatists, Willis, Boker, Mathews, Pray, Ware, and Mrs. Mowatt, all of whom have written successful acting plays, some of a very high merit. Had there been "a clear stage," the list must necessarily have been far more brilliant. It is also another of the enemy's tactics to appeal to this apparent poverty of literary triumphs, and adduce it as a proof of our mental inferiority, thus justifying their own conduct in perpetuating the evil, by withholding the encouragement necessary to remedy it. Another class adopts the hollow cant of saying, that we have no time to waste upon poetry and literary pursuits; we must build our towns, grow our cotton, extend our territories, construct our railways, and sail our ships. Pray, do not the English perform these necessary works? Are they an idle people? They have colonies in every quarter of the globe, and yet they have the first literature in the world! [. . .]

We do not, however, in this particular, blame either managers or publishers. It is not natural to pay large sums for what they can obtain a bountiful supply of from England for twenty-five cents. Managers and publishers are merely tradesmen; one keeping his theatre, and the other his "Temple of Knowledge" open for the express purpose of making money; their motto is the same as that of the peddler or *free-trader*, "To buy in the cheapest, and sell in the dearest market."

The real culprits are the Nation, indirectly, and the Legislature, *directly*, who refuse to throw the protecting mantle of law over the highest order of work. It is a gross anomaly, that the noblest, most intelligent and disinterested class of laborers should be left without any security for their property, as though they were outlaws! This is the worst kind of Socialism. This subject is, however, one of too great magnitude to be dismissed in a few words; we shall therefore consider it more fully in a future number, merely remarking that the wrong done to the native author is the least of the evils inflicted by such a monstrous system of injustice. We entirely leave out of view the rights of

British writers. We think, however, we perceive a growing disposition in the public mind to rectify this singular injustice, which has become the more glaring, since, by a recent treaty between England and France, a copyright has been recognized even for the protection of original works against translators. Surely this ought to shame our Congress into an act of tardy justice, for, to a certain extent, a translator acquires a kind of *half title* to the work he transfers from a foreign language into his own. It implies labor, and enables the mass who are ignorant of the original to become acquainted with productions otherwise sealed to them. [. . .]
[The author's ideas on "what we conceive a drama to be" follow.]

[245] "The American Drama"
The American Whig Review [1852]

Referring our readers to the preliminary paper in our last number, in which a discussion of the general principles of the Drama was attempted, we now proceed to a more definite consideration of the merits and defects of our American dramatists.

Mr. [Nathaniel Parker] Willis has tried his hand several times at the drama; but the very excellences which have given him *prestige* in the lighter departments of literature have been fatal to his success in its loftiest regions, although his great tact has preserved him from an actual defeat. [. . .]

In accordance with his idiosyncracy, Mr. Willis is eminently artificial; there is nothing truthful from beginning to end; all is meretricious, conventional, unsound; we know that it is a thing of shreds and patches inside, notwithstanding the fine veneer of polished language over the entire work; there is no soul within [. . .].

His heroes and heroines are a race of imaginative centaurs, produced by his invention upon his memory; his *Bianca Visconti* [1837] is a strange compound, like the animal Horace advises painters not to paint. We admit that it is perfectly proper to exhibit good and evil qualities in the same character; we observe this constantly: almost every human being, even that monster of perfection, oneself, combines *inconsistencies*, but not *incongruities*. There are certain qualities perfectly incompatible; a sort of moral black and white, never found in one person; the Passions cannot be tamed into a Happy Family, dwelling together in the same breasts, as cats, dogs, mice, and antagonistal creatures do in one cage at the Museum: Nature is not a Barnum. [. . .]

Tortesa, the Usurer [1839], is, we think, the best of his dramas; for, although the plot is not sufficiently simple, it is ingeniously worked out, and we are not met with such startling monstrosities as Bianca. Still, there is nothing natural, nothing healthy in it; it is redolent of Willis. He makes Zippa, the semi-heroine, love two gentlemen at once, and palms a daughter off upon her own father, as *her portait ready framed and glazed!* It may be stated in his defence, that a dramatist, whose name is so frequently quoted by us all, that we are positively ashamed to write it, has a somewhat similar device in *The Winter's Tale*; but it is much nearer probability to place a lady on a pedestal so artistically, with regard to light and shade, as, at a proper distance, to pass it off as the statue of a long-deceased wife, than the feat of Angelo in Mr. Willis' play.

There are also one or two graver errors of taste, such as Tomaso placing the resuscitated heroine, with her grave-clothes on, in the very bed of his master, her lover. The author, also, indulges in *asides* to a most ludicrous extent. These are only occasionally allowable, to elucidate the character, not to be a running commentary on the whole text, a sort of supplementary dialogue. [. . .]

Mr. [George Henry] Boker's productions are of a very different order, and he is undoubtedly the most promising of our dramatists; but he must surpass his present efforts, if he hopes to place his fame on an enduring basis.

His chief excellence, now, is the poetical beauty of his dialogue; some of his speeches being admirable for their justness of thought and felicity of expression. This, however, goes but a small way towards equipping a dramatist for the field of action; but we observe in the author of *Calaynos* [1848] greater qualifications than mere language, and he only requires opportunity to produce dramas infinitely superior to those of his English contemporaries, which are now placed by the managers before the American public simply because they can get them for twenty-five cents! Strange that actors cheerfully pay a thousand dollars for a suit of tinseled cloth to strut in, and managers expend fortunes upon *blue fire*, while they withhold every encouragement from a native author! [. . .]

Mr. Boker's first effort, *Calaynos*, had the "singular honor" of being played in London previous to its performance here; it was not very successful, and was considered by the best English critics as more of a *poem* than a *drama*. [. . .]

In the *Betrothal* [1850] we saw but little improvement in the essential requisites of a drama, while the plot was even more commonplace; it wanted depth, earnestness, and force, terrible deficiencies in a serious drama: it was certainly elegant, poetical, and frequently pointed; but these merits, great as they are, were possessed, even in a superior degree, by his *Anna Boleyn* [1850], which we think has the honor of being the finest play hitherto published by an American. Its chiefest defect is a want of distinct characterization; his persons have no peculiar individuality, talking so much alike, that were the printer to omit the names, we should be puzzled to know who was really speaking. Added to this, Mr. Boker has no geniality or humor; in his *Betrothal* there is an occasional dry sarcasm, hard joking, or perhaps it comes nearer solemn banter than any thing else; but, whatever it may be called, there is a total absence of that *unctuousness* without which the bones of comedy will not move naturally. Our comic dramas seem to labor under a severe rheumatism in all the joints and limbs, not even excepting the tongue, so that their jokes do not flow, but are jerked from the lips as though, like sugar-plums, they had been purposely placed there, and were not the original production of the mouth.

It strikes us as a singular trait in our dramatists, that, notwithstanding the humor very perceptible in our people, they either do not recognize it, or else consider it beneath their dignity to become its exponent. [. . .]

Mr. [Henry Wadsworth] Longfellow's *Spanish Student* [1843] has no claim to be considered any thing beyond a drawing-room drama, fitted for a company of parlor amateurs. It is a story, narrated in graceful dialogue, not a plot naturally evolved by circumstances acting upon characters properly developed. There is no stage effect, no dramatic situation; the story progresses by being carried by the author, not walking by itself [. . .].

Mr. [Cornelius] Mathews is of a very different class to those we have enumerated, being singularly deficient in all the graces of composition of which they are such masters, while in rough vigor and blind conceptions he infinitely surpasses them.

Of his three plays, two—*Jacob Leisler* [1848] and *Witchcraft* [1846]—have undergone the "fiery ordeal" of representation, and are consequently familiar to the public. [. . .]

It must at the same time be admitted that he has great defects. He has no passion, no poetry, no pathos; he can therefore neither warm nor rouse his audience. [. . .] In addition to these inherent short-comings, he made some practical mistakes. He miscalculated the effect his subject would have upon his audience; he forgot he was in America. He expected that his story, being national, would carry favor with the public; on the contrary, we should say, his choice of plots was against him; he should have laid the scene in Italy, England, France, or even Timbuctoo. As a nation, we are singularly deficient in self-confidence. We are a quick, vain, sensitive people, not a proud one. We pay more respect to what foreigners say of us, than what we think of ourselves. This amiable weakness affects, as a matter of course, our literary tastes, and justifies our asserting that the public have yet to be convinced there has been any thing heroic done in our native country, so far as tragic interest is concerned. [. . .]

Mr. Ware, the author of some minor melodramas, and the comedy of *Extremes*, merely claims a passing recognition on account of the latter professing to represent American manners; it is, however, too artificial throughout to merit a serious consideration. It is put out of court by the playbill itself, for the *dramatis personae* are quite sufficient to convince all of its utter worthlessness. It is a mere flimsy sketch of old stagers pushed into an *outre* position by the mere force of a distorted contrast. It is easy to write upon this plan; it is placing oneself in a go-cart! Mr. Jones, an *extreme* fool; Mr. Smith, an *extreme* politician; Miss Ball, an *extreme* flirt; and so on throughout the whole *gamut* of human absurdity. There is no truth in this; it is a mere outrageous *caricature*. Let Mr. Ware study man, imitate nature, and write simply, and he may yet produce a good play.

Mrs. [Elizabeth] Oakes Smith has chosen Jacob Leisler for the hero of a tragedy, which is still in manuscript, and is likely to remain so, as publication would hand it over to the tender mercies of the managers. [The play was published as *Old New York, or Democracy in 1689*, New York, 1853]. Generally speaking, women are not fitted for dramatists. They are deprived, by their constitution and the usage of society, of either ability or opportunity to gather a knowledge of human character requisite to form a group of human beings giving play to their passions. They excel in a nice discrimination of characters, more particularly feminine, or some nondescript knight, half hero, half milliner, fighting with kid gloves instead of gauntlets. [...][1]

Mrs. [Anna C. O.] Mowatt has written a pleasant, lively comedy, called *Fashion* [1845], and a very pretty tragedy, *The Peer and the Peasant* [*Armand; Or, The Peer and the Peasant*, 1847]. These display lady-like ability; but they lack the bone and sinew necessary for the wear and tear of a mixed audience; they are calculated rather to interest her personal friends than to hold the attention of an audience. She is, notwithstanding, a most accomplished woman, combining the *three* antipodes of a beauty, an actress, and a poetess; she has, however, not a dramatic mind. [...]

In conclusion we reiterate that America has no just cause to be ashamed of her literature, considering the obstacles systematically placed in the path of its professors; and that the chance of our becoming as eminent in our mental as we are now in our physical achievements depends upon our legislature affording to it that protection which they dare not withhold from a bale of cotton or a pair of shoes.

Till this justice is rendered, we may as reasonably expect our mechanics to continue, blindly and starvingly, to manufacture an article, which, however valuable and necessary, is unsaleable, simply because it is one which it is lawful for any person to steal, or else one whose market is glutted by the smuggler. [...]

---

1. Even sixty years later, this attitude had not changed: "Why is it that there are so few women playwrights? And why is it that the infrequent plays produced by women playwrights rarely attain high rank? The explanation is to be found in two facts: first, the fact that women are likely to have only a definitely limited knowledge of life, and, second, the fact that they are likely also to be more or less deficient in the faculty of construction." Brander Matthews, *A Book About the Theater* (New York: Scribner's, 1916), 124–25.

[246] "Reform in Theatres"
Spirit of the Times [1852]

Harper's Magazine ["Editor's Table." *Harper's New Monthly Magazine* 27, 5 (Aug. 1852): 406–411] revives the old discussion respecting the utility and propriety of dramatic performances. The editor objects to them because life is a very serious affair, and men may find better employment than playing fictitious parts. Perhaps it is *because* life is serious, and because our ordinary pursuits are so absorbing, that theatrical diversions are so agreeable, and, we may add, so proper. We have no intention, however, of pursuing this over-wrought topic. Theatres are fixed facts. People like them, and cannot be argued out of their liking. The taste for the drama is as old as the race of men. [. . .]

There is a tendency, now-a-days, to rush to the most irrational extremes. If, for example, an institution is not altogether what it should be, the cry is, not to improve, but to *abolish* it; if the holder of official station is not faultless, "turn him out," is thought the only resource; as though there were no conceivable punishment but—decapitation. If the editor of *Harper's Magazine* had devoted his attention to pointing out feasible improvements in our theatres, if he had demonstrated that excellence will "pay" better than trash—as he might—he would have performed a very creditable action. We say he *might*, for the thing is demonstrable. But what he has done will only have the effect—if it have any effect at all—of upholding those utterly frivolous, and, we may truly say, demoralizing entertainments, which have sprung into existence and attained their present importance only because of the odium which has been cast upon their dramatic rivals. We need not name those entertainments—they are but too well known.

But the theatre, at present, is grievously at fault—we cannot deny it. It does not fulfil, or attempt to fulfil, its proper destiny of being the powerful ally of all that is beautiful and good. As two or three dramatic enterprises are on foot, at present, in New York, and will soon be ready to march, perhaps we may venture to propose a pet reform or two of our own, for the consideration of parties concerned. Our first recommendation is, *to do away with after-pieces.* Exhibit one play in the best possible manner, and then drop the curtain for the night. It is the main piece of the evening that "draws" the audience, and not the after-piece, which persons of sense seldom stay to see. Send the audience home at an early hour, not fatigued and disgusted, but inspirited and in good appetite for more. We are persuaded that this reform would save expense and labor, without materially diminishing receipts, and that it would remove one good reason for the repugnance to the theatre which is now cherished by a great many excellent, though we think, inconsiderate persons. Another piece of advice which we would offer is—adopt as the motto of the management the words of Hamlet, "*The play's the thing*"—not the actor, or the scene-painter, or the property-man, but the play. [. . .]

[247] "Places of Public Amusement. Theatres and Concert Rooms"
Putnam's Monthly Magazine [1854]

[. . .] In this happy country of ours, where all the natural instincts are allowed their utmost expansion, it is very remarkable that the amusements of the people are the only affairs that are hampered by statutory restrictions. One may follow any business he likes, embrace any religion, join any party, or engage in any enterprise; but the law fixes the boundary of his amusements and forbids his recreating himself in certain ways. In the State of Connecticut, the law prohibits all amusements and recreations of a theatrical or dramatic nature; Shakespeare may be read in the parlor, or from the pulpit; but to present Shakespeare's plays in the way they were intended by their author to be represented, is unlawful and would subject those guilty of so wrong an act to fine and imprisonment. Horse jockeying is an indigenous trade in Connecticut, but riding horses for the amusement of others is there an interdicted employment. In the State of Massachussetts, the laws are less rigorous, and Shakespeare's plays may be represented according to their author's intentions, by the payment of a fee and under a special license, on any night of the week but Saturday and Sunday. On those two evenings Shakespeare is interdicted as an amusement in the good Old Bay State. In this city, a man may establish a dozen whisky distilleries, or manufacture firearms, or quack medicines with perfect freedom, without fee or license; but no one can establish a place for theatrical amusements without a special license and paying for the privilege. Every theatre, and opera house, and circus in New-York has to pay a yearly fee which is appropriated to the use of some public charity.

[. . .] Not only for the purposes of amusement, but of mental culture, dramatic show is a natural and efficient means. Regardless or thoughtless of this, good men have let it decline to base uses and then blamed the evil which in some measure at least, they might have prevented. Were every delicious taste or art abandoned on the same ground as the drama, our life would be bereft of the benefit and solace of the whole of them. [. . .]

It is a strange circumstance that while music, painting, poetry, elocution, and dancing, are not only considered as harmless, but as elevating and beneficial arts, in themselves, yet, when they are all combined in the production of a drama they are regarded as fit only to be anathematized. The church, too, combines in its ceremonials all these arts but the last, and, in all Catholic countries eclipses the feeble attempts of the stage, in their combination to dazzle the senses and thrill the imagination. Of course there can be no comparison between the theatre and the Church, because it is the province of the one to amuse, and the other to instruct the believer in the solemn mysteries of eternal salvation. The stage, too, professes to be moral, and the punishment of vice is the inevitable end of all dramas. There is no such *lusus* as an immoral drama. It is the delight of the coarsest natures to see poetical justice dealt out to the wicked, and the sufferings of the virtuous form the great staple of all tragedies. There is nothing that so certainly commands the tears of an audience, as the undeserved calamities of the innocent. [. . .]

[. . .] the theatre [. . .] was never before in so thriving a condition as at present. Players are no longer vagabonds by act of parliament, nor are they exposed to any legal indignities here on the ground of their profession. [. . .] Some of our actors are men of large fortune, and our actresses make themselves independent and retire to private life while they are yet young; and our managers become millionaires, and men of social standing. It is said that the stage pays well as a profession to those who are tolerably well qualified for it, and men of capital are not averse to investing their money in theatrical property. There are many pains-taking, well-intentioned men who have gone upon the stage, as coolly and deliberately as other men have gone to the bar or the pulpit, as a business pursuit, and have maintained themselves and families respectably by enacting the parts of "heavy fathers," and filling the posts of "utility men." It must be a sorry business, to be sure, but hardly worse than being a drudge in any other profession. The vagabondage of the theatrical profession, which is generally supposed to be the necessary condition of all its members, is rather imaginary than real. Actors are, generally, when off the stage, the most matter of fact and serious people to be seen; many of them have other callings, they engage in trade, or manufacturing, and perform the parts of good citizens with as much success as those of the stage villains and heroes whom they personate for a living. [. . .]

The theatrical business in New-York has, until within a short time, been almost entirely in the hands of Englishmen, and even the majority of the players are still foreigners, and it is doubtless owing in a great degree to this fact, that the stage has continued to lag in the rear of all other institutions on this side of the Atlantic; it has not appealed to the sympathies and tastes of the people; the actors have been aliens, and the pieces they performed have all been foreign; to go inside of our theatres was like stepping out of New-York into London, where the scene of nearly all the comedies presented is laid. English lords and ladies, English squires, clodhoppers, and Cockneys; English rogues, English heroes, and English humors form the staple of nearly all the plays put upon our stage. The actors and actresses speak with a foreign accent, and all their allusions and asides are foreign. The only places of amusement where the entertainments are indigenous are the African Opera Houses, where native American vocalists, with blackened faces, sing national songs, and utter none but native witticisms. These native theatricals [. . .] are among the best frequented and most profitable places of amusement in New-York. While every attempt to establish an Italian Opera here, though originating with the wealthiest and best educated classes, has resulted in bankruptcy, the Ethiopian Opera has flourished like a green bay tree, and some of the conductors of these establishments have become millionaires. It was recently proved that one of the

"Bone soloists" attached to a company of Ethiopian minstrels, had spent twenty-seven thousand dollars of his income within two years. It is surprising that the managers of our theatres do not take a hint from the success of the Ethiopian Opera, and adapt their performances to the public tastes and sympathies. The manager of the National Theatre [A. H. Purdy], one of the least attractive of all the places of public amusement, has made a fortune by putting Mrs. Stowe's *Uncle Tom* upon his stage [the original version by Charles W. Taylor, produced in Aug. 1852, was a failure; it was George L. Aiken's version, produced at Purdy's National Theatre, 18 July 1853, that started its triumphant stage history]. *Uncle Tom*, as a drama, has hardly any merit, it is rudely constructed, without any splendors of scenery and costume, or the fascinations of music; the dialogue is religious, and the Bible furnishes its chief illustrations; but it is American in tone, all the allusions have a local significance, and the sympathies of the people are directly appealed to. The result is an unheard-of success, such as has never before been accorded to any theatrical performance in the New World. The manager of the National Theatre is himself an American, and nearly all his corps of actors are also natives, and though he only aims at the tastes of the lowest classes of the people, yet his theatre has been daily and nightly filled with the élite of our society, who are willing to endure all the inconveniences which a visit to the place imposes for the sake of enjoying an emotion such as neither the preaching of their clergy, nor the singing of Italian artists could create. [. . .]

[. . .] The regular drama is as foreign now to the wants of the theatre, as the Greek tragedy, or the medieval mysteries. The theatre survives for other purposes than the representation of the drama; its presentations are merely sensuous, and not intellectual; Shakespeare is only endured for the sake of the star actor who impersonates the one character suited to his physical powers. The pieces which attract audiences and fill the treasury are as un-Shakespearian as possible. Tableaux, burlesques, thrilling melo-dramas, ballets, spectacles, horses, dwarfs, giants, rope-dancers, any thing that is monstrous and wonderful, form now the great attractions of the theatres, and any thing is considered as "legitimate" by the public, which affords amusement, and as proper, by the manager, which fills his house.

[. . .] The theatre has always been, and still is, the principal place of public amusement, and, though its character has greatly changed, and its frequenters are no longer of the class who once gave it its chief support, it occupies too prominent a place in the social organization of our great towns to be overlooked by professed moralists and religious teachers. Its existence, and the fact of its being frequented by immense numbers of people whose morals need looking after, should be sufficiently strong reasons for the clergy, and all others who are by virtue of their office public teachers, to exert themselves to render it as little harmful as possible. To stand outside and denounce the theatre without knowing any thing of its interior, is not the true way to improve it. The representation of moral and even religious plays has been found not only very effective upon the audiences who attend upon them, but profitable to the manager who brings them out.

As religious novels form a very considerable part of the popular books of the day, we see no reason why religious dramas should not also form an important part of theatrical entertainments. The fact that such a drama as *Uncle Tom's Cabin* [in Aiken's version] can be represented two hundred nights in succession, at one of the lowest theatres in New-York [National Theatre], converting the place into a kind of conventicle, and banishing from it the degraded class, whose presence has been one of the strongest objections to the theatre which has been made by moralists, is sufficient to show that religious plays, like religious novels, may be pressed into the service of education with powerful effect. [. . .]

[Characterizations of New York theatres and other places of public amusement follow.]

[248] "New Theatre and Opera House"
Gleason's Pictorial Drawing-Room Companion [1854]

[. . .] The new theatre will be opened under fortunate auspices. [The Boston Theatre opened under the management of Thomas Barry on 11 Sept. 1854.] The old prejudices against theatrical entertainments have been swept away by the enlightened spirit of the age, and there is no longer a doubt of their moral tendency, among persons of sound judgment. The fanaticism that denounced the stage as an active element of moral corruption, is obliterated, or hushed, and theatres, well conducted, now find universal favor. Throughout the country, theatrical establishments are signally flourishing, and their managers are making money. The grand step to this order of things, was the resolute extirpation of all incitements to vice in the material arrangements of the theatres. Another element of success was the admission of ladies to all parts of the house; another, the establishment of one price, and that a moderate one, for admission. Whatever may be averred to the contrary, the spirit of equality is thoroughly ingrained in our people.

In places of amusement, it is indispensable that all should stand upon an equal footing. Lines of demarcation, established by a gradation of prices, will never do for a country like ours. People do not like to confess that they cannot afford to pay as much as their neighbors, nor do they like to see them enjoying better places simply because their purses are better filled. One price of admission, and the principle of "first come first served," exactly suits our notion. Moreover, ever since Franklin's story of the boy who paid too dear for his whistle, our people have had a rooted aversion to dear amusements. [. . .]

[. . .] A growing taste has of late manifested itself for the production of domestic pieces, portraying to the audiences familiar themes and such characters as they meet in everyday life. This is well. American life and American history are teeming with an unworked mine of dramatic wealth, that would richly repay the talent expended in producing therefrom theatrical and striking pictures, suitable for stage delineations.

A celebrated English general confessed that his acquaintance with English history was derived from Shakespeare's plays. Why may not the stirring events of our own history be so presented as to interest and instruct our people? Hitherto, American historical dramas have been got up in wretched style, prepared by second rate scribblers. Why not employ men of talent to present the great phases of our story in a manner worthy of the theme? Our managers would find it pays much better in the end than to invest an English shilling in a trashy London piece, though the original play would cost them some hundreds.

[252] "Shakspeare Darkeyized"
Spirit of the Times [1855]

In a street of this city, not more than four miles from the City Hall, in humble imitation of the magnificent temples of the Drama erected by ambitious managers in more pretentious portions of the town, the sable portion of our population have also built an appropriate mansion wherein is supposed to reside the dingy Genius of Ebony Theatricals.

A portrait of some sable Garrick adorns the drop curtain; a thick-lipped lady of dark complexion on one side of the proscenium represents the Goddess of Tragedy; and on the other a woolly-headed brunette in short skirts is supposed to stand for the Goddess of Comedy.

What though the portrait of the African Roscius in the drop centre, instead of Classic Roman robes, is attired in a swallow-tailed coat, with brass buttons and a red velvet collar? And what if the ladies before mentioned are resplendent in sky-blue dresses and yellow turbans? Perhaps their unusual garb is quite as appropriate to the atmosphere of the place, as the more elaborate, more classic, more costly, but considerably less gaudy wardrobe allotted to corresponding divinities in more fashionable Theatres.

The appointments generally at this place might not be considered very tasteful by the "white trash," who get their ideas of propriety from Wallack's or Burton's; but any impartial observer will admit that the scenery is more creditable than the dirty green and brick-red abomination of the Metropolitan, or the paint and canvas hash with Dutch metal seasoning, which has been for years a standing dish at the Broadway, and which is still served up nightly to a surfeited audience.

The female visitors who attend the delectable performances of the talented corps of this colored establishment, do not make themselves quite so ridiculous with their dress as their white competitors, but it is only because they have not the money to be as fashionable; the desire is probably full as strong, but the cash don't hold out.

And, as the white folks, in the construction of their pieces for dramatic representation, sometimes represent in a peculiar light the warmer blooded passions of their "dark complected" neighbors, in retaliation the colored dramatists reverse the order and make the white men in their drama wait upon the colored heroes, black their boots, groom their imaginary horses, brush their coats, and perform all the varied round of servile duties which in representatives of the same plays by white men are assigned to them.

The play of *Othello* is the single exception—they make the Venetian warrior a white man in a red roundabout, who makes fierce love to Desdemona, who is the molasses-colored child of a respectable darkey white-washer.

Lorgnettes, Opera-hoods, and white kids are not exhibited here in such profusion as in some other places of amusement; on the contrary, green spectacles, sun-bonnets, and calico dresses are rather in ascendant.

As a phase of city life which does not often turn its side to the public, and as a place to enjoy an unlimited amount of fun for a little money, the Church Street Colored Theatre is well worth visiting.

A grand Shakspearean festival was lately announced to come off here, on which occasion the tragedy of *Macbeth* was to be performed with "all the original music, new and gorgeous scenery, rich and elegant costumes, magnificent scenic appointments, &c.," according to the time-honored "gag" in such case made and provided.

The novelty of seeing a black Macbeth with the entire tragedy done in colors by the best artists, promised to be almost as good a burlesque as the bearded Indian exhibition made by the great American Tragedian at the Broadway; and so with a varied assortment of friends I started to witness the unusual spectacle of a Bowery darkey representing a Scotch king.

Paid the entrance fee all in dimes, as the door-keeper couldn't read the Counterfeit Detector, and wouldn't take bills for fear he would get stuck with bad money.

Orchestra consisted of a bass-drum, one violin, and a cornet-a-piston. Seats, new benches with coffee-sacks spread over those constituting the Dress Circle.

Orchestra essayed the Prima Donna Waltz, which gradually degenerated into "Wait for the Wagon," and concluded in "Few Days."

Great deal of whispering and shuffling about behind the scenes, a great deal of emphatic ordering about from the unseen prompter, who was trying as nearly as I could judge, to have Macduff take his chew of tobacco out of his mouth, and at last the curtain rolled up.

Macbeth was a fat gentleman of jetty hue who might have been headcook at Delmonico's for twenty years, and who would, had he been subjected to a melting process, have furnished soap and candles enough for a small chandlery business.

Whether he *intended* to give the tragedy a gastronomical interpretation or not is uncertain, but it is a veritable fact that he dressed the character in a cook's apron, had a paper cap with a long turkey feather in it on his head, his steel by his side, a butcher-knife in his hand, and the cover of the soup-pot for a shield.

Macduff was attired more like a Lake Superior Indian than anything else, with a superfluity of red flannel fringe, and silver rings in his ears and nose.

Lady Macbeth rejoiced in a tin crown with seven points, each one with a crescent on top, brass-heeled gaiters, a dress with a purple waist, and a green baize train, two cameo bracelets, and lemon-colored kid gloves.

Old King Duncan was a young man who seemed to labor under the impression that to support his royal dignity it was only necessary to grin incessantly, and turn his toes in when he walked; his royal highness had on a high hat with a red feather, plaid pantaloons (being the only symptom of Scotch costume visible during the evening), and an embroidered vest, through which, as he wore no coat, the sleeves of his blue shirt appeared in agreeable contrast; he sported a silver watch, four seal rings, an opera glass, and a gold-headed cane.

All the other characters were dressed with equal regard to propriety and elegance of costume, and with equal *dis*regard to expense.

The warlike paraphernalia were on the same appropriate scale; instead of Scottish claymores and basket-hilted swords, muskets were introduced which had probably seen service in some target company, until too battered and damaged for further use; shields were dispensed with except in the single case of Macduff,—instead of daggers, many were provided with horse-pistols, and one aspiring individual had a sword-cane and a slung-shot.

Several of the "supes" were painted like Indians, and carried banners made of horse-blankets, nailed to barrel staves—the three witches had each a hoe and a stable-fork, and Hecate was equipped with a straw-hat and a pair of linen drawers put on hindside foremost.

The play commenced, and everything proceeded in the greatest harmony until the caldron scene, when the apparitions, instead of rising through the trap into the caldron, deliberately crawled from the ring on hands and knees, and stuck their heads through a hole in a board which was painted in admirable imitation of a dinnerpot, and delivered their prophetic speeches in a huge whisper to the anxious Thane.

The apparition of a "child's head crowned," as the stage direction reads, was done by a piccaninny, who was drawn on screaming and kicking in a willow basket by a hidden rope, and the speech was read by the prompter, who squatted down behind the basket, and held his hand over the baby's mouth in a vain effort to stop his noise.

During this scene Macbeth, who was too obese to stand for so long a time comfortably, seated himself composedly on a three-legged stool which did duty afterwards as a throne,—and in fact, whenever during the performance he found himself incommoded by the warmth, he would sit flat down on the most convenient resting-place.

His rendering of the dagger scene was peculiarly original—he took his butcher-knife, tied it by a tow string to a pitch-fork, which he stuck in the middle of the stage, sat flat down on the floor before it, and proceeded to deliver the speech with great force and emotion; pausing occasionally to mop his forehead with a yellow bandana handkerchief, and refresh himself by long sips from a pewter mug of beer which he had bestowed in his original shield.

The rest of the company got along very well, managing the removal of Birnam wood in rather a unique manner—when the soldier spoke of a "moving wood" a back scene opened and discovered four darkies carrying pine kindling wood from a wagon with a jackass team, down cellar into a coal-hole.

Whenever an actor forgot his part the prompter would rush out from his hiding place, put the offending artist in the proper position, read his lines for him, and suddenly disappear, until some fresh delinquency called for another shirt-sleeve advent.

Matters progressed towards the close of the piece—Lady Macbeth had played the lighted candle scene (using a bed-lamp, a candle not being forthcoming) had made her last exit, leaving the green baize train, which had come untied in the middle of the stage, a sad memorial of her fate—the soldiers had met in a pitched battle (every "Supe" had insisted on dying a death of his own, in order to display his tragic genius), and had expired in various uncomfortable positions; one sitting up against the flat, with his leg through a trap-door, and his mouth open, and another with his head through a bushel basket which he had brought on to use as a shield—all the minor business of the piece was got along with, and it only remained for Macduff and the rotund Macbeth to have their fight, say their say, die their die, and finish the play.

They entered arm in arm, being evidently determined, like prize-fighters, to do their "bloody business" amicably, and as old friends ought.

Macduff remarked to the audience that they were going to "settle that quarrel"—they then proceeded to strip for the contest.

Macduff retired to one corner and pulled off his boots and spectacles, Macbeth went to another and laid down his jacket and shield—then they met in the middle, shook hands—one flourished a long toasting-fork—the other wielded a rolling-pin—Macbeth made the last speech as follows—

"Come on!!! Macduff be damned!!!" both pitched in—first round, toasting-fork ahead, rolling-pin in the corner with his nose bloody—second round, toasting-fork knocks rolling-pin through a parlor scene and falls back exhausted—third round, both come to time with difficulty, toaster hits roller in the stomach, roller shies his weapon at toaster's head, toaster spears at roller's toes, and breaks his fork.

All their munitions of war being exhausted, they close in an expiring wrestle, and Macbeth eventually dies, having first in the terrible struggle suffered amputation of the pantaloons immediately above both knees.

Macduff recovers his rolling-pin, and stands over the conquered Macbeth in a grand saw-buck attitude of victory and triumph.

[264] "The American Drama"
Emerson's Magazine and Putnam's Monthly [1858]

That the Drama is in a state most deplorably low at the present time, few will take upon themselves to deny. The cause of its degradation lies with the actors, we boldly assert, more than with the authors. Material enough, and that of a high and ennobling quality, may be found with the latter, which the former, either from laziness or mental incapacity, will not, or cannot, present properly to the public. [. . .]

We preserve the type of the absorbing passions almost exclusively by means of the Drama. The commercial life of our people, the intrigues of the demagogue, the poorness of our social aspect, made up of fashion, folly and boarding-houses, (that miserable substitute for a home,) present us with little that is ennobling, and we should half forget that such things as generosity, magnanimity, and disinterestedness were legitimate human traits, did we not sometimes behold their exhibition amid the conceptions of Art. Such is the deplorable dwarfing down of the character of our men, that even women are assuming the stronger shades of our nationality, and are very likely to be the more positive of the two sexes. Were it not for Shakespeare they would lose sight of the deeper passions, or they would be confounded in their minds with the low ruffianism of the robber, the pirate, and the rascals in general, who fill the prisoner's box in our courts of law. [. . .]

Still we contend some good has been achieved in the Drama even now; better things have been written than our own people realize, and better than the actors are able to present. The latter, for the most part, are the veriest machines in creation, who follow the old stereotyped modes of the stage, the manner of presenting a character which has come down by tradition, or otherwise, without the remotest idea of anything better, and woe to the child of genius who attempts any innovation. If he have not a sturdy self-reliance he will be overwhelmed and crushed by the sneers of his contemporaries and the yelpings of the press. In this way the few who have been able to achieve celebrity have come up through a perfect storm of ridicule and reproach.

Every person of taste and discrimination knows that nothing is more dreary and common-place than ordinary stock company acting. Few such attend the theatres except when the attraction of a star is presented. We sometimes hear the uninitiated regret that these persons of genius are not better sustained in the subordinate characters. To ourselves this is of little consequence. A Drama worth representation is always first a study in the closet, and we go, not to see how this or that small actor presents his part, but to witness the reading of the man or woman of genius.

When Booth, for instance, played *Richard III*, all the rest of the play might have been given in dumb show so far as we were concerned. We saw nothing, heard nothing but the wonderful little man, whom genius transfigured to a giant. We forgot we were in a theatre, and lived on the broad acres of old England, amidst the intrigues of courts and the stir of the battle field. It was not Booth but the veritable Richard who turned his back upon the audience, and now glared with his sardonic smile, and now glozed with his serpent tongue, till even we, (disregarding the interpolations of Cibber,) saw how those oily accents were likely to seduce the heart of the shallow Lady Anne.

We hope the time will come when the scenery of the stage will be dispensed with. It is only needful to children, and those of a larger growth. Mere spectacle soon wearies, and Shakespeare in the hands of mediocrity is a desecration. [. . .]

We believe if some manager of forecast and culture would prepare a small theatre to be opened only three nights in the week, with little or no expense for scenery, the portion to be introduced, being of the most appropriate quality, and the plays introduced only of the highest character, he would secure to himself not only reputation, but money also.

We believe that New York holds within herself a community of intelligence, taste and culture, amply sufficient to sustain such a place of superior amusement, not to say instruction.

When the Rev. Mr. Bellows declared himself in favor of the theatre, it is not to be supposed that he would bring the weight of religious influence to sustain the theatre as it now exists. [Bellows spoke before the American Dramatic Fund Association, 29 Apr. 1857; for the contents of his speech, see *[265]*.] He had in his mind's eye an idea such as we propose. In a theatre established upon such a basis, artists of the higher order of histrionic ability would find expression for the highest thought and action attributable to their profession, and the public mind would eventually reject the grosser shapes of the drama. The factitious and demoralizing dramas of the French school would be entirely excluded. The public taste under such a school would be immeasurably advanced. The clergy might attend without scandal to their calling. Parents might carry their families without the hazard of contamination, whereas we, and we speak advisedly, know of nothing more demoralizing than the theatre as it now exists. [. . .]

The managers of nearly all our theatres are foreigners, who have no sympathy with the institutions of the country, and care little for moral questions provided their own purses are filled; hence their boards represent the grossest French novels; hence their literature is foreign, not native. If we except Forrest, and the few dramas of native growth which he has made public, and whose literature is so mediocre in character, that these productions must die with him, the drama of our own country is not at all represented. Charlotte Cushman, with her commanding genius, we believe has done nothing for native authors. Is it, because we, as a people, have produced nothing worthy of public favor? We think not, though we have not as yet done what we have a right to do. [. . .]

No American author, without miraculous courage and great individual genius can write an American drama upon an American subject. No drama can be complete in which the element of the gentler sex does not largely enter. There is ambition, and many of the stormier passions to be introduced, but without woman there is little opportunity for tragic pathos. The great commanding stir of the human heart lies in the relation of sex. [. . .] Comedy (and comedy is never ennobling,) may exist in our literature under the present aspect of women in our country, but there can be no tragedy. The moment we attempt to introduce her in this aspect, the attempt becomes something only fit for the courts of law, or for a police report.

Women have no acknowledged sphere out of the domestic relation in this country. In Europe she is part of the stirring events of the period. She is a crowned queen—she is imperial upon ancient thrones, holding the baton of command; she divides scepters and harangues multitudes; opens parliaments with her own sweet voice, and dispenses wisdom in learned halls; she is crowned the Queen of Beauty and the Empress of Song; she is the goddess of the saloon to which crowd poets and philosophers, statesmen and courtiers. If she have genius, she may lead a charmed life, sure of the approval of the generous and the aspiring. If a devotee, her voice commands in the midst of a sisterhood, and her influence and vote sway even the See of Rome.

How is it with us? She is utterly dethroned. Except the indirect influence which she exercises in the household; she is powerless, and the folly, not to say profligacy, of our idle, fashionable women, who live only to eat, drink and die, is the comment. The whole tone of society is lowered by her helplessness. Aspiration dies out; and luxuriousness prevails; pettiness and discontent, to the death of all that is heroic in our men, and noble in our women. Yet men talk as if nothing was required—as if this vanity and imbecility of the sex were both lovely and desirable. We thank God that our sense of manhood implies more, and our reverence for womanhood is not to be content with their short comings, else we should shame the noble woman whom we called mother.

These are the reasons why the American drama remains at so low an ebb. Woman is not a queen, but a chattel, in public estimation. She is not a person, but an appendage; she is not an equal, but accounted inferior; she has no office but such as she holds not by the grace of God, but the tolerance, necessities or luxuries of man. Where is the author to look for his models? how feed his fancy? If an American woman exhibits superiority, ten to one she is maligned by one sex, and lampooned by the other. Malice will be busy with her fame, and envy out of its own slimy chambers concoct the venom which is to drag her down to its own level.

Again we say there can be no great drama accepted till our people have advanced much farther in ideas—till woman is reïnstated, not into old and outworn dignities, but into those which spring naturally from human progress and republican methods of thought.

Let our readers examine the drama of our country, and they will find, if at all capable of analysis, that its feebleness is to be imputed to this cause alone. Our authors have been compelled to choose foreign subjects. When they have done otherwise, their women are either viragoes or imbeciles, of no more interest than the heroines of Cooper's novels. We might name an exception which is of no moment to the general question in hand. [. . .]

[265] [The Church and the Theatre]
The United States Democratic Review [1858]

[. . .] In short, until one or both the steps we have briefly alluded to be taken; until managers adopt the practice of employing really good and efficient stock companies, to the total exclusion of presumptuous aspirants calling themselves stars; until they consign to the waste box ninety-nine out of every hundred of the abortions in these days represented as, and honored by the name of plays, and substitute therefor productions of a superior order; until clergymen and the better classes of citizens generally, consent to lend their countenance and their presence to theatres, all hope for a resuscitation of the Drama must prove altogether futile.

Having given, in the foregoing pages, a brief outline of our views with respect to the Drama, especially with respect to its present condition and the immediate causes we believe to have been most instrumental in bringing about such a condition, we now propose to refer to the famous address (the only one of its character ever known to have emanated from the lips of a divine) of the Rev. Dr. Bellows, before the American Dramatic Fund Association, April 29th, 1857, as presenting, in all probability, the soundest argument for and against the subject in question, that can readily be adduced.

Dr. Bellows begins his address by setting forth the claims of the Drama upon all classes of society. He says:—

"There is nothing essentially wrong in the stage, or in the player's vocation; nothing which should necessarily place the theatre under the ban of the Church, or the dramatic profession aside from other honest callings; or which demands their suppression as radically injurious and unchristian.

"In saying thus much, I say what thousands of serious and thoughtful Christians, both teachers and disciples—in short, what the class I particularly address—will utterly repudiate. The stage, with them, is the most essentially wrong of all institutions, because it is the most attractive, dazzling, and complete of public amusements; and all public amusements—not to say amusement in general—fall under their sincere and earnest suspicion and Christian jealousy. How much, then, of the theatre?

"It is, then, with the defence of amusement as the principle, that the defence of the stage must begin, if the class I am arguing with is to be reached. [. . .]

"[. . .] Instead, therefore, of interfering with business, duty, sobriety, piety—with scholarship, economy, virtue, and reverence—amusement, viewed merely as a principle, advances and supports them all. [. . .]

"[. . .] amusement is a serious, practical interest and concern of society, and not a mere indulgence and weakness, to be excused and apologized for. Society is the better, the safer, the more moral and religious, for amusement. It is as good a friend to the Church as it is to the Theatre; to sound morals and unsuperstitious piety, as it is to health and happiness. [. . .]

"I am not here to deny or conceal the exposure to excess, and actual lapse of the young into excess, in the love and pursuit of pleasure. The moment that it becomes anything more than a relaxation from toil—the unbending of a bow kept ordinarily at its strain, the exception and not the rule, the leisure of the busy, the fun of the serious, the play of the worker, the self-forgetfulness of the thoughtful, the recreation of the weary and exhausted—it is in excess. But things are not to be abandoned because their use requires judgment and self-control. The best things are most open to abuse; and amusement, like food, love, power, money, requires to have the dangers of its pursuit pointed out, but not its lawfulness or its innocency, in its place and degree, denied or concealed. [. . .]

"I suppose it would not for a moment be denied, that, if the theatre were compatible with Christian sobriety, it would be the most complete and interesting of all amusements. Nothing but scruples of conscience, and a fear of countenancing a seducive pleasure, keep even the most sober portions of the community from an occasional visit to the play-house. I must except, of course, those who by disuse of their sensibility to pleasure have lost the power of being amused, and those whose original temperament is constitutionally averse to pleasure. But those, few or many, must not mistake their defects for advantages. [. . .] The stage is the most winning of amusements, because the combination and aggregate of all others. [. . .] The Drama condenses what is most intensely interesting or affecting in real life, or what, from the constitution of our nature, genius knows might be real life, into a compact, rounded, and finished story; omitting what is common-place, irrelevant, or simply painful, and by careful adherence to the great rule of art, which never forgets that its end is pleasure, extracting from crime, or vice, or passion, whatever in their actual occurrence it would shock us to behold, leaves what moves our passions and affections with pleasing though tearful sensibility.

[. . .] Supposing it to be innocent, I perceive no element wanting to render it theoretically a perfect pleasure. It appeals to the intellect, the imagination, the heart, the senses. [. . .] Poetry, invention, story, mimetic talent, elocution, personation, spectacle, beauty, passion, architecture, painting, music, society, light, all combine in the theatre to make it the most brilliant, complete, and untiring of public amusements. [. . .]

I believe from my very soul—and to what other conclusion has the whole evidence tended? that the Church and the so-called gravity, and moral worth of society, are really, though indirectly and unintentionally, the authors and propagators of the malignant disorders and perilous influences of the theatres, leaving both the dramatic profession and the public at large comparatively blameless, and answerable only for its more venal sins. . . . The vices of the theatre have uniformly been those of the time, no more, no worse. The theatre has no serious vices of its own, like trade, with its fraud and perjury; like the Church, with hypocrisy and arrogance. The mirror of bad times, it has reflected the vices that passed before it, not those it originated. Drunkenness has carried its victims, and licentiousness its votaries into its precincts. Profanity and coarseness from the pit and boxes have required profanity and coarseness from the stage, while vulgarity and ignorance have demanded rant and fustian. What is the theatre, that we should expect it to be wise, and moral, and pure, and reverential, to an audience that, by the theory of the class I address, cares little for these qualities, and when it has no character to lose by any pandering it may practise to the degraded tastes of the rabble and reckless? Were the Church itself frequented only by the ignorant and the wicked, how long do you imagine the pastors would be pure and the doctrine sound? No interest, no class, can bear the withdrawal of the virtuous portion of society. [. . .]

"The levity, excess, association with vice, and general lack of moderation in the theatre, its opposition to, or defiance of religion; its lax morals and bad taste, be they more or less, are due mainly, in my judgement, to the unhappy separation between the Church and the World—the guides and examples in morals and virtue, and the public at large; and to the special emphasis which this separation has had in the case of the theatre. What are we to look for, in general, when the young and the old no longer mingle in the same society; when the grave and the gay keep themselves systematically apart, and society is divided into those who partake and enjoy amusement and those who abstain from and decry it? Will it not necessarily occur that one class will ruin itself by excess in pleasures, while the other is seriously injured and narrowed by the lack of them? [. . .]

"I charge, then, the vices and follies of the theatre, as of our other amusements, and of our general society, to the withdrawal, the self-separation, of the moral and religious portion of the community as a class, from the pleasure-loving resorts of the people. I believe that all the specified classes of evils connected with the theatre would disappear to as great an extent as they ever disappear, even in respectable society, if, after having recognised the essential innocency and necessity of public amusement in general, and the stage in particular, the sober and virtuous people of this and every city would go in moderation to the theatres. [. . .]"

[267] [Theatre Advertisements]
The Albion [1859]

To tell the truth of the theatres in these days is to shame not Satan exactly, but the stage-managers. For it is perfectly out of the question for one pair of human eyes to see, or for one pair of human ears to hear, or for one human heart to conceive the half of the wonderful things that daily enter into the promises of the playbills, and the newspaper posters, of these ingenious and imaginative gentlemen. [. . .]

[. . .] There is nothing so trivial or so poor, that we do not find enriched and expanded in the columns of our daily journals, into rhetorical proportions little short of colossal. The eloquence of the peripatetic showman has become stereotyped in our metropolitan managers: and while we are perpetually lamenting the degeneracy of the drama, we are as perpetually confirming that degeneracy, and deepening it into degradation by the atmosphere of vulgar absurdity and flagrant charlatanism with which we insist upon surrounding the stage.

I take up, for instance, the first morning paper that comes to hand, and run my eye over the advertising column of the theatres. Am I really reading the play-bills of those familiar houses I have known so long?

I wish, we will suppose, to know whether Miss Keene has opened her theatre. I look in vain for any information to that effect. Here is the name of Laura Keene certainly, gleaming like the N. of a French Imperial illumination, through a perfect bouquet of pyrotechnics: but the dazzling metaphors with which it is encircled leave one rather bewildered than enlightened.

TRIUMPHANT INAUGURATION!
CROWDED TO OVERFLOWING!!
BEAUTIFUL DRAMA!!!
MAGNIFICENT CAST!!!!

Clearly this must be the programme of some little Circus, or strolling company which chooses to baptize itself by the name of Laura Keene, just as the hose-companies give themselves the high-sounding titles of Lafayette or Washington. Let us than turn in search of Wallack's.

UNIVERSALLY PRONOUNCED
THE QUEEN OF TRAGEDY!!
UNEQUALLED SUCCESS!!!
CROWDED HOUSES!
CROWDED HOUSES!!

No hope here! [. . .]

[268] [The "passion for localization"]
The Albion [1859]

[. . .] The evil I protest against then, is what may be termed the "passion for localization," now burning like a consuming fire in the hearts of all our playwrights. The best comedy that can possibly be imported from England or France cannot now be put upon the stage without an attempt to Gothamize or at least to Americanize all the incidents of the plot, and all the personages of the play. So far have the ravages of this new and singular disease extended, that I shall not be surprised to see *Othello* placarded, one of these days, as *Fred Douglass, or the Moor of Syracuse*, or *Romeo and Juliet* enacted under the name of the *Diamond Wedding*. The thing has really gone beyond endurance, and, that it has done so, the public, I am happy to say, have already begun to show. Two pieces have virtually perished within the past ten days at two theatres, mainly because the managers who borrowed them were not content to take them in their natural "form and pressure," but must needs array them in fabrics of Yankee manufacture. The death of Scribe's drollery, *The Bear and the Pasha*, under the depressing influence of an Arkansas Break-Down and a Virginia Reel, I last week chronicled. The like fate impends over Tom Taylor's comedy of *The Election*, which Miss Laura Keene has thought fit to disguise with [. . .] devices of Tammany Hall. In both of these instances, the plays so travestied were quite capable of "travelling" on their own merits. Scribe's extravaganza, if it must be produced at all, might perfectly well have been produced as the author wrote it, the very slightest flavour of local allusion pervading a composition essentially grotesque and fantastical, and therefore essentially cosmopolitan in character. Tom Taylor's comedy, considered as a picture of English political life, had points and a plot of sufficient pregnancy to interest an American audience, merely as a glimpse into the ways and manners of another people. The axis on which the whole story turns is essentially English, for no respectable American audience can now be induced to acquiesce in the representation of a wife urging her husband into Congress; while nothing can be more natural than that an ambitious English woman should wish to see her lord and master buy or work his way into Parliament. All the machinery of English politics too differs so essentially from the machinery by which the unterrified control the state on this side of the Atlantic, that neither in its darker nor in its lighter aspects can the photograph of an English return for the county or the borough fail to appear a senseless caricature when inscribed with the name of a New York election.

Nevertheless "the piece must be localized." And the stage-carpenter goes to work accordingly, claps me a Genin's hat upon the bluff poll of the British boor, thrusts a quid of tobacco into his cheek, gives him a black satin waistcoat, and a whittling-knife, and lo! a confessed Republican of the newest pattern. Delicate allusion, pointed satire, the natural movement of incident, and the natural contrasts of character all vanish. The Comedy becomes a caricature, and the audience, without reflecting on the critical secrets of its dissatisfaction, goes away vexed or but half amused, convinced that there must have been a "screw loose somewhere," or that the whole play was a botch from the beginning. I do not dwell on the downright injustice done a dramatic author, in taking such wanton liberties with his work. The dramatic author is a kind of Pariah, having no rights which a manager is bound to respect. [. . .]

[269] *"The Octoroon.* A Disgrace to the North, a Libel on the South" *Spirit of the Times* [1859]

It is a significant fact, that while at one end of the La Farge House a few gentlemen were discussing the propriety of getting up a meeting in this city to prove that the North was not entirely abolitionized, the other end of the same building was occupied by the rehearsal of a five-act play, the effect of which is to misrepresent and villify the South; and it is also a significant fact, that while the object discussed by the "conservatives" has been treated by the public with singular indifference, a gross libel upon the social relations of the South has been hailed, by a part of the press, and a gaping multitude, with "an unparalleled enthusiasm."

"The Winter Garden"—a very appropriate name for this dreary theatre, for there has never been a really green spot in its history—has been struggling, under the management of Dion Bourcicault, all the season to sustain itself by the representation of Cockney plays. The legitimate attractions of the house, it seems, finally proved abortive, and as a last resource, Bourcicault has taken advantage of the existing anti-Southern excitement, for it is no longer aimed at the slave, but at the citizens of the South, to bring out a play, which, for all practical purposes is more pernicious than anything which has heretofore been conceived in the spirit of sectional hate. *Uncle Tom's Cabin* aspired to no higher aim than to represent that plausible thing, *a heavenly old negro!* and an impossibly bad white man. The hero of the play, however, was "a darkie," the legitimate representative of the American slave; but Bourcicault is not content with this, his Exeter Hall training has carried him further; he has been made familiar with white slaves in his own country, so he dares to represent them in this. As false as the incidents of the play are in fact and in sentiment, as a literary composition it is wretchedly bad, judged even by the low standard applied to all the modern trash of the Bourcicault school, the materials that were worth attending to being miserably managed, the plot and the dramatic effect implying a total want of ingenuity; all the author has evidently relied upon being the *excitement and inflammatory* effect that its representations would produce, rather than any really theatrical merit. The scene, says the elaborate play-bill advertised in the daily papers, "is laid in the Delta of the Mississippi, on the plantation of Terrebonne;" the name of the planter is "Peyton," the place itself is "Sunnyside." All Louisiana names certainly, which would naturally be made familiar with Bourcicault, while acting as a New Orleans theatrical manager, the recipient of Southern hospitality and a witness of Southern city life, but with the names, all correctness and truthful localisation ceases. The natural representations are always false, and the characters are, with one exception, libellous. In the first scene, an alluvial plantation, which is as free from pebbles even as a cup-custard, is faced in the foreground with huge piles of rocks that would be formidable even in New England, while a tall palm waves over them, which is as unknown in Louisiana as in Labrador.

To give our readers a slight idea of the gross exaggeration, we will notice that the play opens with Jacob McClosky, "half owner of the Terrebonne estate," say worth a hundred thousand dollars; with Salem Scudder, the overseer of Terrebonne estate; and George Peyton, a Southern young man, "educated in Europe, and just returned home," all in love with Zoe, the octoroon, and all severally making love to her, *and offering their hand in marriage!* In rude language, in the first act, three white men, two of independent fortune, and one with character enough to be an overseer on a large estate, seriously propose to "marry a nigger." This is Bourcicault's idea of Southern institutions, and this idea is the English and the Wendell Phillips idea, to endeavor, by false sympathy, to break down caste, and elevate the negro to the same level with the whites.

To accomplish this object, Miss Agnes Robertson, who is a pretty Scotch woman of a singularly pure complexion, dressed in snowy muslin, and overflowing with sentiment and sensitiveness, is the octoroon. To render the thing still more offensive, her parentage is freely discussed by the ladies of the household, her free papers talked about, while, meantime, instead of acting the part of a servant, this Bourcicault heroine is receiving, as we have already intimated, serious proposals of marriage from the gentlemen, and being enveloped in the arms of Mrs. Judge Peyton, who is familiar with her origin and her mixed blood. Dora Sunnyside is held up as a Southern belle, and here Mrs. Allen, a very handsome delicate beauty, comes on the stage, slatternly dressed, and so inanimate, so overcome by lassitude, that she can scarcely keep from "dissolving away." This caricature upon Southern young ladies thus moves along, only to be awakened from her lethargy to *make love* to George Peyton, who had previously sworn to sacrifice fortune and all for love of the octoroon! and who frankly tells the "Southern belle" that his heart is already engaged by what seems to us to be "the yaller gal." If offensive caricature of the South, and of the most sacred ties of life can go further than this, we do not recollect the example. Among the male characters we have prominently "Jules Thibodeaux, a young Creole planter," bearing one of the most honored names among the old French population, answering to our Livingstons and Lees, of the North; this "young planter" is personated by Miss H. Secor, who has the manners of a "Dead Rabbit," and is in the meanwhile persistently smoking an execrable segar, the offensive odor of which sickens the audience located in the remotest parts of the house.

Wah-no-tee is an Indian "of the Lepan tribe," an aborigine, as far as dress is concerned, such as you see in lady book illustrations. Now the Lepans were a terrible flat-headed tribe originated in Grub-street, London; the natives natural to the vicinity of Terrebonne, La., have been exterminated at least one hundred and fifty years, and were known as the Houmas and the Attakapas. Wah-no-tee, however, is a wonderful creation, written expressly to display the acting dramatic power of Bourcicault, who has nothing to do but drink whiskey and flourish a large club; not understanding English, he despairs of conversation, and naturally confines himself to guttural sounds, a large "whew!" such as a bear makes when suddenly come upon by a pack of dogs, is all he has to say, but his head-dress and tail-feathers are immense.

Salem Scudder is a Yankee from Massachusetts, and holds the position of an overseer, whose slang about "civilization" and "human rights," joined with his nasal twang, would cause him to be run out of any decent community in Louisiana as a disagreeable associate for Southern gentlemen, and an exemplar of bad manners before the negroes.

Now the above is a fair representation of the prominent persons in this play, announced as representing "American character, American scenes, and *Southern homes!*" the minor parts being filled up with vulgarisms of all sorts, miserable white men, women, and children, blackened up to represent field hands and house servants.

The dialogue of the play opens with McClosky, a fine example of a Baltimore "Blood Tub," announcing his intention to "degrade the pride of the first families," a sentiment thoroughly sympathised in by the Yankee, who has his fling at "the chivalry." McClosky, in the course of the piece, meets with Zoe, announces the ruin of the Southern family, makes love to her, and being despised by that interesting creature, very naturally decides "he will buy her at the sale." By a series of ridiculous and puerile "actions and plots," he manages to bring the estate to the hammer, thereby introducing the "negro sale," which our city papers, even those which try to be very fair to the South, with one or two honorable exceptions, pronounce "wonderfully life-like." Here is a chance for broad misrepresentation. White women, men, and children, are artfully dressed to produce effective groups—husbands are sold, and there spring up discussions among the buyers about separating them from their wives and children; the auctioneer diversifying "the bids" with asking for tobacco and "brandy smashes;" quarrels ensue, and bowies and pistols are most awkwardly drawn, the Yankee flourishing a big jack-knife and "cavorting about," until it seemed to us strange that the beings who were enacting this outrage upon a section of the Union, had not thrown the fellow out of the window in sheer and seriously felt disgust. Finally comes the climax; Miss Agnes Robertson, for it was her the audience saw, was put on the block for sale. That such an exhibition was offensive, there cannot be a doubt, but that it should be for a moment taken as a representation of Southern life is disgusting, and those who desire it should be so understood are guilty of the worst kind of treason.

The ignorant and degraded beings who are trafficked in by the South have none of the sentiments and feelings accorded to Zoe; in that country, if such a being as Zoe ever existed in person, her mind and the taint of her blood would create a gulf between her and the whites that would be wider than the poles asunder, and all the sympathy and sentiment the incendiary author of this piece creates, is founded upon the false idea, that there is an equality in the races, an idea that is preposterous, unnatural, and profane.

Starting from the theatre after the sale of Miss Robertson, and reflecting upon the fact, how miserably cheap the crowded audience was also "sold," as exhibited by their expressions of sympathy, we ran against a multitude of the poor victims of Northern society, who were driven by the lash of necessity along the gas-lighted streets [. . .].

These victims of oppression, of bad laws, and of "the inhumanity of man to man," were pure-blooded whites, and in their veins coursed the purest fountains of blood. Their fathers and mothers are free, and in many instances, possibly, people of consideration and estate. These wretched Zoes of the North have no negro taint; they are often full of womanly tenderness, of refined natures, have been in many instances nursed as the pets of the Christian family circle, have read and appreciated Milton and Shakspeare, have hung with rapture over the productions of the inspired pencil—are, in fact, *white women* doomed to inevitable servitude and degradation, compared with which the sufferings of the Southern Zoe, even of the worst possible estate, would be heavenly in comparison. And yet these Northern slaves, to say nothing of the thousands of children of infirm women, of aged men, who fill our almshouses, and crowd our walks, have not a tear dropped on their condition, every one of whom would be happy, could they enjoy the daily comforts which are at the command of the least favored of the Southern slaves. Nay, worse than this, white women, without protest or sympathy, are not only heartlessly and openly sold in the streets of our Northern towns, but whole families of high respectability are bid off at prices which would hardly pay in Charleston or New Orleans for a likely-looking coachman, three thousand dollars being deemed by a Boston jury quite enough for a seducer to pay for the crushed hopes and honest affections of a kind husband, the disgrace of innocent children, and a mother's blasted fame, the whole family circle, according to Bourcicault's play, going for thirty-seven thousand dollars less than the single physically and mentally degraded Octoroon bought at a Southern auction mart.

We have no disposition to pursue this disgusting subject further; the fact is patent that the play is nightly greeted by a crowded audience, and the basest attack that has yet been made upon the South is likely not only to do its damaging work in poisoning the minds of our people, but will possess the additional sin of putting money in the pockets of the base creatures who have clubbed together their mercenary brains to produce this outrage.

For this the press is much to blame; the criticisms which have been written on this play, even in the best quarters, have been characterized by a secret desire to sustain it, or have been the result of wilful and besotted ignorance. As an abstract dramatic representation, it would not live a second night, but when the papers applaud, or, feebly denouncing, always add, it is a true picture of the South, they give it the only endorsement that carries weight and makes it "draw." So entirely reprehensible, and so consistent is this hypocritical course, that the *Times* of Tuesday last, although it had several editorials denouncing the fanatics of the North, and deploring sectional agitation, and seemingly ambitious to be very fair and conservative, yet in its notice, in another column, of the *Octoroon*, it is careful to say, that the play is a "MODERATE *and truthful picture of Southern life*," thus, in a line, showing its real sentiments of the South and Southern people.

We pronounce again the whole play a libel; it is more false than if a Southern theatrical manager should bring out at New Orleans, or Charleston, a play in which the degraded men and women, and the associations of the vilest stews of New York city, were produced, and called a "moderate and truthful picture of the best Northern life." This representation would be true, at least, of much Northern life, but the *Octoroon* has not a glimpse, if we except old Uncle "Pete," that can with truth be termed characteristic of Southern life and Southern homes. [. . .]

[270] [Mrs. Boucicault Withdraws from *The Octoroon*]
Spirit of the Times [1859]

[. . .] We gave last week at length our ideas of the *Octoroon*. Since the publication of that article we find the following letter addressed to the public through the press:

To the Editor of the Herald—Sir—I have withdrawn from the Winter Garden: but my reasons for doing so have been incorrectly stated in your journal of this morning. Yesterday I wrote the management as follows:—

To W. Stuart, Esq:—Sir—I decline to appear any more in the *Octoroon*. I regret to find that the piece has given offence to a portion of the public, and my part in it especially. I receive continually letters threatening me with violence, and when I go on the stage I do so in fear of some outrage to myself or to my husband. Therefore, I beg to withdraw the play.

Yours truly, Agnes Robertson Bourcicault.

The press had pointed out the political tendency of the *Octoroon*, and your journal especially had blamed its production at this unhappy crisis. Oppressed by the sense that many of the public regarded the play as you did; that I was the object of just censure, having received letters from many families in this city urging the withdrawal or alteration of the play; intimidated by letters threatening us with violence, as a woman, I could not hold the position which the management desired to compel me to endure. I felt that I was unconsciously made the instrument to wound the feelings of one part of the public to gratify the other. In every sense my position was a painful one. I will not permit my name (or my husband's, if I can help it), to be associated with any scheme to make money out of a political excitement—especially on any such a subject as slavery and at such a moment as this. The *Octoroon* was not intended to succeed on such merits. In your notice this morning you state that it has produced me over thirteen hundred dollars for six performances. It is true; but I cannot consent to sell my own self-esteem and the good opinion of my friends at that or any price.

Agnes Robertson Bourcicault.

[272] M. D. Conway. "The Citizen and the Drama"
The Dial [1860]

[. . .] The friends of the theatre have every reason to be thankful that, since the early divorce of the Stage from the Church, the alliance has not been renewed.

It can never be an Institution worthy of the admiration of the citizen if it sets itself to build up religions, any more than if it sets itself to build up politics or the mercantile interest. The Church is sectarian; Politics are partizan; the Theatre, thank God, is neither; and the citizen, pledged to all that elevates man, and not any section of him, can not be sectarian. [. . .]

[. . .] The Church might wink at a little dancing here, or a frolic there; but to have all the gayeties and Arts concentred into one rival Institution, requires a concession that the Church is scarcely up to. But it is quite complementary to the Theatre: were it not attractive, it would not need to be denounced.

Having thus made our peace with the moral sentiment, if not with the Church, our subject comes fairly before the citizen, and makes its case.

And, first of all, it is to be represented that the Theatre gives substantial, regular, and material encouragement to every variety of trade, mechanic art, and fine art in a community. It is probable that the public little understands the extent of employment furnished by our Theatres. I have found, by personal investigation, that every Theatre gives regular and well-paid occupation to from one hundred to one hundred and twenty-five persons; that is, persons who live almost entirely by the Theatre. In the city of Cincinnati the Theatres furnish an entire livelihood to about four hundred persons, each year.

The Theatres of this city expend among machinists, mechanics, and for glues, paints, ropes, gas, coal, lumber, dry-goods, more money than goes into trade from all the Churches and Schools combined. The Drama in this city, with four Theatres, purchases its right to live with the handsome annual sum of $150,000.

At this point the manager, or lessee, or owner of the Theatre has a right to inquire of the citizen if there is a response coordinate with this immense outlay? It does pain me to see men of unwearied industry laboring year in and year out to amuse, instruct and elevate mankind; perhaps building for us, as one honored man, worthy of the high name of Citizen, has done, a Palace of Art; employing every species of toil during the day, and blessing it with beauty at night; making our city attractive to the stranger and sojourner of a night, who otherwise would not stop here, but who does stop here and put money into the pockets which never gave a dollar for the Theatre; paying the highest rents and the highest insurances, to amuse us; and after doing all this, never feeling sure of their audiences, always certain that the best citizens will not be in them. I wonder that there is not more recklessness, carelessness, bombast and nonsense on the Stage; and more spleen against the self-righteous classes which abandon this Institution, that shields them from paupers, and animates every vein and artery of the trade by which they live.

In the next place, it is to be regarded that the Theatre is the only form in which Poetry and Art become democratic. Shakspere comes down from the scholar's shelf, and through the interpretation of Booth or Cushman, comes as near to the flatboatman as to Messrs. Knight and Collyer. So do the great composers; I heard a news-boy, the other day, whistling on the street a theme from the overture of *Der Freischütz*. I know that it is supposed by those who do not attend the Theatre, that the Arts represented there are of a very low degree: if this were so, the sufficient answer would be, Help then to make them better,—since, good or bad, the people have no other. But it is decidedly not so. [. . .] As to the costumes, there is, perhaps, more popular misapprehension than about anything else connected with the Theatre. It is supposed that the wardrobe of a Theatre abounds in gaudy, flimsy trappings, dependent on the illusions of the place for their elegance. But there is no more illusion here than in real life; the stage-silks and velvets are generally of even a superior quality, and many a costume, supposed to be tinsel, has cost one or two hundred dollars. [. . .]

And this brings us to remind our citizen that the stage is an important means of the remedial force (*vis medicatrix*) which exists in the characters of men as in their bodies. Let me not be misunderstood in what I am about to say. I do not believe that the theatre ever can exist for the purposes of moral or religious or reformatory influence; nor do I desire it. The sentimental, moral or anti-slavery or temperance plays fall from grace as soon as they touch the stage. But it is inevitable that some effect must be produced upon the minds of men by holding up in other forms their follies and vices. [. . .] It is a good way toward the cure of any deformity when a man finds a mirror which shows him to himself as he is seen by other people. This suggests to us, also, the reason why, from its very nature, the Drama saves itself from doing any positive harm: it depends for its very existence upon holding the mirror up to what already exists, without adding thereto. It can not create the evils which it is its mission to illustrate [. . .]. The Theatre succeeds only so far as it gives a true exposé of what already exists. [. . .]

And here let me remind the Citizen, as an offset to the charge of impurity, that it is in the Theatre alone that full justice is done to woman, to both her labor and her intellectual dignity. In the State woman has no existence in her own right; she can not hold property seperately, nor vote, nor hold office. In the Church she is a cipher, whilst she is spending her time making ministerial slippers and ottomans. I know of only two places where it is clearly understood that women have souls, to-wit, the Quaker meeting and the Theatre. The most distinguished preachers among the Quakers are women. But it is on the Stage alone that every land may acknowledge a Queen. The most cultivated Englishmen maintain that the most radical blunder that America has made is in following the Salic Law, which excludes women from participation in public affairs, and point to feminine sovereignty as the soul of England's strength. It *is* rather shabby that if Americans wish to pray for a Queen, they have to pray for England's Queen. But in the Drama she has no such restriction; through it lies woman's clearest path into all her rights; there the Muses and the Graces are weaving her coronet; in her quiet step on the stage I hear the shaking of nations. [. . .]

The Theatre not only honors woman, and emancipates her intellect, but it does something more sacred yet by her: it pays her full and solid wages. Our Schools and Colleges, without exception, stint woman in her wages; in them the stupidest man gets more than the brightest woman for the same offices; but in the Theatre, if there is any difference in rates, it is in favor of woman.

Let us take a lesson just here, gentlemen, of the difference between the real and the seeming. The respectabilities and the sternly virtuous accuse the Theatre as the corrupter of feminine purity. So says the pious merchant who gives a woman sixty cents for a shirt which he sells for three dollars; so says the preacher who denounces all efforts at opening new employments for woman as woman's-rights-ism. The Theatre, oh, shocking! Just here the Theatre comes in and actually saves woman from her most terrible temptation by paying her enough money to support herself. Such wages can be found nowhere else. Also, a high intellectual employment is given that secures her from that idle mind which is the "devil's work-shop." Thus the Theatre doesn't talk about woman's virtue: it saves woman. Even the ballet-girls, whose business it is to stand on the stage in those short dresses which so distress the sanctified, thereby get four or five dollars a week, and are left the whole daytime in which to get wages for other work. [. . .]

[279] "The Drama in Richmond"
The Magnolia Weekly [1864]

In times of national calamities—when the desolations of War combine to depress the hearts of men, and cause them to turn to other influences for surcease from the griefs that surround them—all those means of healthy amusement that tend to the forgetfulness, for the time, of those abnormal evils, are not only proper in themselves, but should be sustained. The drama, when properly represented, stands the chief among these amusements. But the drama should never be the echo of the prevailing evil.

If War be that evil, the mind should find refuge, in the theatre, in the portrayal of scenes diametrically opposed to what weighs upon the popular mind. Comedy should drive from the stage the Phantom of strife, and, in the witnessing of the humorous antics of the jester, or in listening to the artistic stupidities of the low comedian, we should be made to laugh into oblivion, for a happy hour, the troublous recollections of battle and its miseries.

What interest can we take in the fortunes of those painted and tinseled chieftains who, in these days of bloody reality, strut the stage in a ghastly counterfeit of fight? Do not the recollections of the bitter truth make the sham a weary farce?

Our theatrical managers would do well, then, to reproduce upon their boards those lighter plays wherein Life, as seperated from blood and terror, is delineated. The higher order of comedy, the roaring farce, the drama divested of the unconscionable horrors of the *Lucretia Borgia* [by F. Haynes and J. Rees, produced at the New Orleans Theatre, 4 May 1836], and the *Tour de Nesle* school, should usurp the Gorgon Muse of Tragedy [*The Tower of Nesle*, George Farren's adaptation of J. Haynes's translation of Victor Hugo's play, produced at the American Theatre, New Orleans, 7 May 1833]. Let Macbeth, sleep-murdering and King-slaying thane, rest in his robes of usurped royalty. Let Richard, parricidal duke, dream in peace of the sun that shall rise on Bosworthfield. Let the terrible row of black coffins upon the staring poster—that mysterious necessity to a proper understanding of *Lucretia Borgia*—affront the popular eye no more. If the stoney eye of the spectator give no token of feeling when brought to the feast of dramatic horrors, flank him by a roaring farce and let him forget the dull, blank time in an honest laugh.

There has been too much of this morbid feature of late in our theatres. The repertory of the tragedian and the actor in melo-drama has been exhausted in the search for those old dramatic heirlooms that have their ending in but one *finale*—Death. The grizzly Terror, as if in a ghastly competition with the battle-fields of the country, has been paraded in the tawdry appanage of the stage, and, under a marvellous scenic effect, has made his apotheosis before the eyes of a wondering audience. [. . .]

[280] "The New Richmond Theatre"
The Magnolia Weekly [1864]

[. . .] We hear an *on dit* in theatrical circles that looks to a possible exemption (or detailing) of certain persons as actors at this establishment. If this should be deemed advisable by the Executive, no one, we are sure, would feel more satisfied at his decision than the soldier. The theatre is the great resort of the soldier, and an amusement so easily secured for him should, in our opinion, be maintained, if for this reason alone, that, often void of acquaintances in the great city, and transiently abiding in it, the gallant son of Mars is sometimes too prone to rehearse, in the streets, hours of conflict and deeds of reckless valor. But when he knows that he can be amused, he is apt, on the contrary, to seek the source whence that amusement springs; and so we find him thronging the theatre nightly. In the Crimean war, before Sebastopol, soldiers were regularly detailed as actors for the amusement of others. This kept up the spirits of brigades and divisions, and redounded vastly more to the good of the army than if they had been engaged in the performance of their regular military duty.

The comparatively small number of men so exempted from military duty would scarcely affect the efficiency of the army, but, on the contrary, would, whilst assisting to relieve something of the gloom of the hour, afford many a hearty laugh and pleasant moment of innocent amusement to those who, casting aside for a little while the harness of war, seek the portals of the theatre as a relief to the ghastly memories that surround them.

[282] ["Pernicious practices in the matter of criticism"]
The Albion [1865]

[. . .] By established custom critics of the drama, who represent the Press, have free admission to the theatres. This arrangement, although prompted by motives of courtesy and by considerations of convenience, is not the best that could be made. If all men were intelligent, were men of culture and of liberal ideas, it would be well enough. Even as things are, it works well in some cases. But, in common with other influences, it promotes false ideas. Thus, for instance, we find that many managers of theatres, in awarding to the representative of the press the facility of free admission, imagine that they are conferring a great privilege, a precious boon, which ought in effect to lay him under everlasting obligation, to flood his very soul with gratitude, and to make him an inexhaustible puffer of themselves and their various enterprises. This notion is of course, foolish and ludicrous. It is a false idea. Left to itself, it would bear no fruit. But, unhappily, there are journalists sufficiently narrow-minded to sympathise with it, to believe in it, and to act upon it. The consequence is that managers are fortified in their error, and that newspapers print senseless eulogium instead of criticism of the drama, thereby winning what is called "advertising patronage"—and the contempt of all judicious readers.

Another consequence, still more lamentable, is that the popular standard of taste in theatrical matters is kept down, and that the drama is depraved. The theatrical profession, properly considered, stands, in fact, upon a level with other learned professions. The theatre itself is an educational institution. This is the right view of the subject, and, therefore, the view that ought to be taken by every critic. Yet, in the general practice, we see that dramatic criticism (as it is called), is written with cautious deference to the prospects of the advertising columns; that the theatre is regarded, and very often described, as "a mere place of amusement;" that bad plays are tolerated and even admired; that persons of little real talent, or none at all, are elevated to distinction; and thus that the drama is kept for the most part in a barren condition. All this, I say, results from the prevalence of false ideas, and pernicious practices in the matter of criticism—and mainly from the latter. [. . .]

The responsibility, then, rests with critical thinkers. If the drama is to be rescued from the jackals of speculation, the rescue must be effected by just, liberal, independent criticism [. . .]. We have simply to tell the truth as to plays and players, as to the principles of dramatic art and the fruits of dramatic labour. By thus disseminating true ideas, we shall continually affect and gradually elevate the standard of popular taste, until at last that taste, which is now content with merely vulgar force and gaudy commonplace, shall suddenly find itself disgusted with these trivial matters, and shall utterly repudiate the "treadmills," and dismiss them for ever.

This kind of critical labour, I say, may not be easy, and may not be agreeable. It will not secure a great deal of "advertising patronage." It will not open many bottles of claret, nor will it win the approbation of empty-headed actors and actresses. A certain kind of unpopularity, indeed, always attaches itself to one who speaks the truth. [. . .]

[285] [Vulgar Language on the Stage]
The Albion [1866]

[. . .] I believe it is not an exaggeration to say that there is scarcely a theatre in the land which a gentleman or a lady can enter, without risk of encountering, in some form or another, the taint of vulgarity. Swearing, upon the stage, has long been the rule. Nobody appears to think there is anything distasteful in that. "Damn it" and "you be damned" are but faint specimens of the choice phraseology which may be heard at the theatre. Indeed, to deprive the dear public of their "damns" would be, as appearances imply, to deny them a very great gratification. Damns are always laughed at, and sometimes are whistled at. It is difficult, not to say impossible, to understand the latent humour which seems to reside in stage profanity; but the public sees it, and the players are content. Against swearing, therefore, protest, perhaps, is vain. But there is a still worse form of stage vulgarity, which, if men, who take their mothers, wives, daughters, or sweethearts to the theatre, have not the spirit to resent and put down, ought to be dealt with by the law. That form is—indecency. Within the theatrical season which is now slowly waning, this nuisance has attained a surprising growth. Within the last few weeks, at more than one theatre on Broadway, such language has been uttered upon the stage, as, spoken in any gentleman's house, would cause the speaker—and very properly too—to be kicked into the street. I do not care to specify instances, although it would be perfectly easy to do so. The subject is not one upon which it is pleasant to linger. Perhaps, indeed, protest against this loathsome feature of local theatricals is also vain. But, if such abuse of a noble and useful institution is permitted to go on, the consequence, which is not at all doubtful, cannot long be deferred. That consequence is, that decent people, not to speak of the cultivated classes, will abandon the theatre altogether, and let it drop to the level of cellar brothels, and dance-halls. Already the evil has wrought great mischief. There are few dramatic exhibitions which are habitually attended by refined and cultivated people. [. . .]

[286] [Call for Realism on the Stage]
The Nation [1866]

[. . .] If anything distinguishes the epoch we live in, it is a decided tendency towards realism, or, as some call it, naturalism—a disposition to be severely true to nature. This character is stamped on all the genuine products of the time. The artist paints nature; the poet draws his inspiration and takes his theme from the sentiments of ordinary existence, and tries to set common humanity to music; prose composition in every kind is direct and simple; the best literary style is the most unaffected style. [. . .] The stage alone betrays an unconsciousness of the change that has come over the tastes of the people. The theatres are smaller, as if intended for the exhibition of the quiet social way of our age instead of the grand heroic life which the drama of the last century loved to display: the stage itself is narrower, as if for lowered voices and more familiar action among the players, but otherwise the new order of things is not recognized. The actors hitch and strut after the old manner; mouth and drawl and rant, do everything with their voices but use them as gentlemen and ladies do; make horrible grimaces and saw the air with their hands in a most unnatural manner; they neither enter a room, nor leave it, nor walk across it; they neither sit nor stand, neither salute nor converse, as ordinary men and women do those things. The stage appointments are bad. There is no skill in arranging parlors to look like the rooms people live in. The plays are poor, not born of the social experiences nor representing the manners of the time. If they have merit, they were written by the authors of the last generation, and cannot be acted naturally; if they can be acted naturally they have no merit, because they present unattractive or low phases of social life. Few of the good plays are modern—little of the acting, therefore, is modern. But it will not do for the playwright to live in one century and the play-actor in another. [. . .]

Here we are persuaded is the secret of the failure, and failure here involves failure elsewhere, every kind of failure. For to make amends for this radical defect, which they will not or cannot cure, the managers of theatres appeal to the love of amusement in its cheapest, gaudiest form, and try to catch the interest of the people without engaging their minds. The eye is dazzled by tawdry spectacles. Every kind of fancy is brought in to make the show novel. Comedy, burlesque, extravaganza, absurdity, caricature, dumb-show burlesque and picturesque are overworked. Ideas are excluded or so covered up with affectations and drolleries that the people shall not be reminded of real life or aught thereto pertaining. Their risibles, not their intellects, are addressed. We are not taking any high position or claiming any elevated mission for the stage, as if it should undertake to instruct or edify the public. We are willing to concede that its great function is to amuse. This has always been its function in modern society. [. . .] But is it necessary that, in order to amuse us, the theatre should treat us as if we were children, who could be entertained with nothing but the gaudiest spectacle or the broadest farce? Is there no amusement without fanciful tricks or side-shaking laughter? Is the comical, the grotesque, or the impossible a necessary element in entertainment? Grant that the uneducated part of the people desire this and will welcome nothing better, is the theatre designed for the uneducated part of the people only, and is it satisfied when it can reach them at their lowest point of unrefinement and can give them just what they desire and no more? [. . .] Why not have plays that will interest the better portion of the middle, even of the working classes, and playing that will have sufficient vitality and grace to charm them? There is no reason why not, except that theatrical managers choose to make money in the easiest way, and if they can fill their houses with decently-behaved audiences, give little care or thought to the perfection of their art or the extension of their influence among the better class.

[. . .] The theatre, perhaps, can never be expected to do more than reflect the moral sentiment, and catch the moral tone, of the society it belongs to. It is not its business to preach; it is not a censor or a judge. Its duty, let it be conceded, is merely to hold the mirror up to nature. But then its mirror should not be cracked, or clouded with film, or covered with dust. And it should be held up so as to reflect "good" nature, as the artists call it. It should show the actual morals of real life, be they what they must be. [. . .] The old way of scourging vice on the stage proceeded on the assumption not only that vice was a thing to be scourged, but that virtue was powerful enough to scourge it, and that men and women were virtuous enough to bear the scourging and be thankful. The new way of scourging vice on the stage seems to proceed on the assumption that all are vicious: that, if the truth were told, none are virtuous, and the glee occasioned by the whipping is simply the glee which one set of rogues takes from seeing another set of rogues get their deserts. The stage portrays the vices and the virtues of the most vicious and the least vicious classes in society. It would escape from such a falsification of truth if it would undertake to represent comprehensively human life in all its phases as it goes on about us, at home and abroad. People are no less virtuous now than they have been formerly; on the contrary, we believe they are much more so, and nothing more would be required to elevate the moral character of the stage than a faithful delineation of the actual character of refined social existence.

[. . .] No one could guess from our theatres what our world was like; and the world does quite right in letting them severely alone. Our dramas are not even American in the most distant sense. With one or two exceptions, they are English and English adaptations from the French. They portray, therefore, English life and French life, as it was their duty and purpose to do. Whether they do that well or ill is a matter that concerns English and French critics more than it does us. English and French life are very different in almost all respects from American life. All the forms of society are different. Institutions and customs, morals and manners, dress and carriage, are wholly unlike. The transplanting of the theatre is as illegitimate as the transplanting of the journal, the bar, or the platform. The French stage pleases not because it is French, but because it is finished in art. An American stage equally excellent would please so much the more. The theatre will not be real till it is grown on our soil. When it is born of American life, it will represent American society, and cultivated people will be its hearty patrons.

[287] [Musical Accompaniment]
The Albion [1866]

[. . .] Nothing of any moment is now done upon the stage, without a corresponding sensation among the fiddles. The approach of an important incident stirs the brass drum to its most hollow and resounding depths. The entrance of an important character imparts a sudden blast to the vivifying trumpet. A catastrophe gives voice to the melancholy trombone. A triumph of virtue over vice is sure of sympathy from the indignant fife. Almost any pretext serves to set the bugles blowing. In short, while the old custom of musical accompaniment was restricted to dying to slow music, the new custom enjoins that dramatis personae shall live and breathe and have their being, to music of all sorts. [. . .]

[288] [A Polyglot Performance of *Othello*]
The Albion [1867]

The polyglot performance of *Othello* at [the] Winter Garden on Saturday evening, drew together one of the largest audiences of the season—an audience in which the Teutonic element largely predominated. The presence of the Germans in such force in an English-speaking theatre, was due to the fact that their favourite actor, Mr. Bogumil Dawison, was to interpret the part of Othello in his mother tongue, while Mr. Edwin Booth played that of Iago in English, and Mme. Scheller, a German lady, acted Desdemona in both languages. So far as the "confusion of tongues" was concerned, the experiment proved a success; the three principal actors displaying a keen scent for "cues," amid the distractions of a strange dialect, that was quite remarkable. We only noticed one or two instances in which an actor proceeded with his part, before his predecessor had given the word. [. . .]

[297] [A Strike at Wallack's Theatre]
The Albion [1869]

The patrons of Wallack's theatre have been entertained during the present week by a real strike, in addition to the melodrama, *A Long Strike*, which was produced by the Boston Combination, on Monday evening. All went smoothly until the end of the second act, when, so imbued with the spirit of the piece had the actors become, that they refused, in a body, to proceed with their parts, unless certain arrearages of salary, which they asserted were owing to them by their Boston manager, who accompanied the troupe to this city, were paid. To escape the inconvenience of the situation and induce the unfaithful Bostonians to complete the performance, a temporary arrangement was made, but the next morning found the members of the Boston Company without engagements, and the following evening witnessed a very fair performance by the "stock" of the theatre. Whatever may have been the grievances of the Bostonians, their method of seeking redress was certainly reprehensible. They sought to punish an innocent public for the alleged shortcomings of a manager, who was not even responsible for their engagement. The prompt manner in which Mr. Moss discharged persons who could resort to so contemptible a trick, is deserving the warm acknowledgments of the public. [. . .]

[300] [*Hamlet*—"the play as an historical study"]
Appletons's Journal [1870]

Hamlet has been produced at Booth's Theatre with a perfection of scenery and accessories unsurpassed, if not unequalled, by any thing in the history of dramatic "revivals." The pictorial splendor of its setting has been accompanied by a scrutinizing care in all the details of its production. There has been an attempt to present a complete historical picture of the period—the tenth century having been accepted as the probable time—and the result is a marvellously vivid and picturesque portraiture of the rude, semi-barbaric splendor of an early European court. The costumes have been constructed in accordance with the most trustworthy authorities; all the armor, the weapons, the furniture, and other accessories, have been modelled from antique patterns—and hence, the play seems thoroughly pervaded with the atmosphere of the period it designs to represent. It is rare, indeed, that a theatrical audience can find itself so thoroughly transplanted into another period. Ordinarily an historical play is acted with too many anachronisms to make us fully realize a distinct age from our own. The familiar look of the actors themselves is often sufficient to dispel the illusion. But in *Hamlet* the actors seem to put on the aspects, the tone, the conditions of another period. They are so carefully made up in their visages, as well as in their costumes—their beards and hair being as well considered as their cloaks and hose—that one is impressed with the antique remoteness of the entire picture. Usually actors give us modern heads set above antique dresses; the drapery may be old, but the features are as familiar as our own. In *Hamlet*, at Booth's, this incongruity is avoided. Each actor looks from top to toe a very ancient, bearded, stalwart Dane, such as might have followed Canute to his wars. Hence the historical unity is complete. Even the small matter of giving the woman-part, in the band of players, to a boy—female actors being unknown at the time—adds notably to the harmony of the play as an historical study. No doubt there are errors and anachronisms, but these are not obvious to ordinary observation, and, to whatever extent they may exist, they do not invalidate the impressions of historic remoteness. And, what is surprising, the thoroughness of these details, instead of, as is so often the case, rendering conspicuous the faults of the actors, seems to compensate for or to remove the customary defects. The actors in their long, blond hair and red beards seem so suggestive of by-gone manners, that one feels disposed to accredit whatever awkwardness or deficiency they exhibit to the characters themselves—as defects entirely consistent with the period, and the individuality of the persons. [. . .]

[303] [*Saratoga*: Wrong Conception of Comedy]
Appletons's Journal [1871]

It is often surprising with what persistence the burnt child will return to the fire. As many times as critics and theatre-goers have experienced the incoherent absurdities of what is called "American comedy," we still find them returning with patience and ever-recurring hope to each new dramatic attempt of this character. It was almost certain before the curtain went up on the new comedy of *Saratoga* [by Bronson Howard, 1870], at Mr. Daly's theatre, what sort of extravagant nonsense would be served up as comedy, and yet there were many hopeful people gathered at the theatre, on its first representation, with the vague hope that something was at last to be done in the way of true American comedy. But the title of the play ought to have been a sufficient warning. Who writes of Saratoga, or Long Branch, or Newport, without at once assuming that the manners of that place are fast; that slang, pretension, vulgarity, parvenuism, intrigue, and imbecility, are the sole characteristics of American pleasure-seekers? And what comedy-writer of the slightest originality would venture upon the old, wearisome, and long-since detestable ground? One experienced in American comedies had only to read the play-bill of *Saratoga* to forecast the whole performance. How remarkable it is that men can essay to write comedies without apparently the slightest knowledge of what comedy means! A comedy, according to traditional notions, is a picture of manners and a reflex of society. But a comedy, according to the ideas of American dramatists, is a burlesque of manners and a *mélange* of farcical incident. That a comedy as a work of art should have a sane and coherent story, and humorous, of course, but probable and pertinent incidents, seems never to enter the ideal of our native stage-writers. That it should contain real people, and not purely eccentric inventions, and, while justly attempting the satire of social follies, should depict and not imagine the objects of its wit, are also theories that are entertained apparently by everybody but dramatists. *Saratoga* has the merit of not being dull. Its succession of absurd and impossible incidents serve to amuse undiscriminating audiences, and so the manager's purpose is in one way answered. But, in the name of art, do let the man who next attempts to write an American play have some sort of conception of his task. Don't let him imagine that a jumble of incidents, a collection of men and women, and a profusion of slang, make a comedy.

Pertinent to this matter of American comedy, arises the question, whether satire, if a legitimate, is the best expression of dramatic art. "Shooting folly as it flies" has at all times been the occupation of the dramatists, but we imagine that ordinarily the effect of this is to make us like the sport rather than hate the game. The manners of a people are more likely to be improved by good than by quizzical examples. [. . .] Instead of American comedy-writers ceaselessly holding up for the example of our young people pictures of fast girls, with slang upon their lips, rouge upon their cheeks, and boldness in their faces and manner, why not try the delineation of some pure and true types of American womanhood? Let our dramatists select for once the best and most agreeable phases of our native life for dramatic delineation. This need not exclude wit nor piquancy; it would require a little invention perhaps, and a little art, and a little knowledge; but, if the dramatist has not these things, let him stop writing altogether. The artistic presentation of our happier domestic life would excite surprise, for it is quite unknown to the drama, awaken not a few pleasurable emotions in the hearts of those who believe that culture, and dignity, and "simple faith," are as often found in American life as elsewhere, and, in supplying right examples of life and character, serve to elevate the public taste. [See also [321]: *Saratoga* is "preposterous nonsense."]

[304] [The Rage of Realism]
Appletons's Journal [1871]

[. . .] The fondness of the modern theatre-goer for the realistic has become proverbial. Mr. Crummles's "real tub" and "real water," absurd as they may seem in the pages of Dickens [in *Nicholas Nickleby*], are just what every manager is nowadays attempting to realize. We recollect that Wallack once introduced a real pump on the stage, and, when a young woman entered, hung a pail on the spout, and, proceeding to operate the handle, caused a stream of real water to flow into the vessel, a hearty burst of applause rewarded the brilliant stroke of histrionic genius. In the same scene the stage-manager attempted to give additional reality to the scene, by tying a number of live pigeons on a frame covered with a painted rose-vine. No one appeared to notice or care for the incongruity, and the audience enjoyed the flutterings of the pigeons with vast relish. Real fountains, real cascades, real trout-streams, are not uncommon in our stage-furniture. In Chicago a play has recently been acting in which a man is really hanged—on one occasion nearly fatally so. It is only in keeping with the latest ideas of dramatic art that Tom Taylor should give to his audiences real fagots and real fire for the Joan of Arc catastrophe; the critics may mourn, but the enlightened managers claim to understand what best pleases the enlightened public.

[305] [Daly's *Divorce*]
The Albion [1871]

[. . .] Mr. Augustin Daly ventures out with a new play from his own pen [*Divorce*]. It does not seem to be imported from French soil, but has an American flavor peculiarly new. He has, in fact, accomplished the remarkable feat, for the first time on record, of writing an American comedy. The scene is American, the motive is American, the characters performed are American. The facetious servant from the Emerald Isle was missing, if we except one of the subordinate characters, quite well done too; no rich German accent was permitted to please the lovers of low comedy, but the African was, as usual, present. *Divorce* was the title of the drama, and divorce was its motive. Two couples, becoming dissatisfied with each other, use the machinery of the law to free themselves. There are plots and counterplots, not of a very elaborate nature, but sufficiently so to enable the actors to give fair scope to their genius. [. . .]

[309] ["Common place realism"]
Scribner's Monthly [1872]

[. . .] At the Fifth Avenue Theater, under the same management, the usual cataclysm of expensive clothes and cheap small-talk (by the title of *Diamonds* [by Bronson Howard, 1872], and not *Saratoga* this time) has set in with an autumnal rustle of silk and hail-storm of would-be brilliant repartee. It ought to be an encouragement to the creation of a school of genuine realism to see how eagerly the public accepts anything, however trashy, which claims that character. It is astonishing what pleasure it brings to the average appreciation, in novel, picture, or drama, to see the every-day life of average men and women carefully and minutely depicted with whatever degree of artistic skill and truth to nature the fates may permit. Nothing but this widespread enjoyment of common place realism—not even the fine clothes—will explain the interest with which apparently intelligent audiences will sit, night after night, absorbing the thin and tasteless, if not nauseous water-gruel of so-called "society" small-talk, and absorbed in the pinchbeck loves and sorrows of the irretrievable snobs or vulgarians who figure in the average Fifth Avenue drama. [. . .] The indirect tendency of such pictures of life and manners as *Diamonds* and *Saratoga*, is to pull down all high standards and pure ideals in social or artistic life. The intellectual level of the pseudo ladies and gentlemen who figure in their tedious scenes is one from which the gradation is direct and easy to the more outspoken vulgarity or corruption of opera bouffe, or the worst of French sensationalism. [. . .]

[310] ["Mania for mechanism"]
The Galaxy [1873]

By way of birthday treat we took, the other night, our little guests, Jack and Ethel, to the play of *Acquitted*, for which the lad had conceived a prodigious fancy through reading in a poster that the drama "presented One Unbroken Coruscation of Magnificent Effects, Startling Situations, and *Thrilling Battle Pictures*, sustained by 160 Artists and Auxiliaries, and witnessed with Cheers, Tears, and Peals of Laughter by Spell-bound Thousands." We had chosen seats in the parterre, near the stage, so that the children might hear everything. The first acts passed with grateful tameness; but in the third, the eight-score Artists and Auxiliaries began a pandemoniac battle, some furiously drumming or blowing the brass, some clashing swords (with the old stroke, three up and down), some charging bayonets, and the rest firing guns; while, behind the scenes, every spare hand was banging, gonging, and booming upon sheet iron, to signify the roar of artillery and other military sounds. Ever and anon, cotton bombs, artfully made to fizz without wholly burning, hurtled through the air; and there was even a small field-piece (frightening Ethel till we explained it to be only a Quaker weapon), whose gunners were successively shot away by the enemy while in the very act of touching it off. At length, when the bombs had been thrown, the cartridge-boxes emptied, and the young women personating the British Army had overcome the young men personating Sepoys, the welcome curtain fell upon a half-stunned audience, all coughing and gasping and gagging and phewing—for the playhouse was full of powder smoke; and then, at last, Portia tranquilly uncorked her ears, that prudent woman having plugged them tight at the beginning of the act, with wads prepared for the purpose the day before, when Jack had disclosed to her the probable nature of the treat in store for us.

As we had bargained for a battle that night, we of course should have felt swindled had the play failed to choke and deafen us. But in general the powder business ought, I think, to be reserved for military dramas. On any save these supreme occasions such a treat should be withheld, lest its magic be marred by familiarity. [. . .]

This musketry business, with its full service loads, is only one triumph of the vaunted "realism" of our modern stage. I don't take up the cry of "legitimate drama," when it merely means attack against all living playwrights, and preference of what is ancient and musty, no matter how dull; but when the machinist eclipses the dramatist, when Mr. Sawdust becomes a more important functionary than Mr. Shakespeare, the mania for mechanism is surely going too far. The "Parnassus," which began this season by a "grand Shakespearian revival," quickly dropped to a revival of William Dunlap's *Niagara Falls*, with (in capitals) "AN ENTIRE STUD OF TRAINED HORSES." Such dramas are played because they "pay"; whereas, artistically, the manager perhaps deplores their squandering of energy and misdirection of ingenuity. [. . .] There is puerility in such struggles towards "realism." Nothing can make "Bosworth Field" a complete illusion to the spectator; or, at any rate, one spark of genius in *Richard III* is a more potent spell than a ton of the carpenter's machinery. Sometimes devices for deception even irritate, like wax figures, the more pretentiously they claim to delude; the offence is in "imitating abominably." Nevertheless, money and minds of managers, authors, actors, are bent on compassing "spectacular grandeurs" and "realistic scenes," to take the place of those simple adjuncts of histrionic skill once satisfactory to scenic art.

[. . .] What did actors do in days when theatres were mere scaffolds, the costumes but goat-skins? In due time mechanism came to the Greek and Roman stage—scenery and scene-shifting apparatus; steps for the ghosts to ascend from Acheron, as we have trapdoors for demons; brazen vessels containing stones, for manufacturing thunder; devices for floating their gods and goddesses through the air, as we hoist our fairies and ballet-girls amidst crimson clouds to the pyrotechnic Realm of Happiness. But a luckless Roscius or Aesopus had no blue lights, real cataracts, real fire-engines, live pigs and poultry, live Indians secured at fabulous expense, leaps from genuine precipices, locomotive explosions, or tumblings of *bona fide* brick houses, to eke out his effects. He would stare at the devices of our matter-of-fact melodrama, his modest "realism" being confined to the study of character and emotion in real life, and to a care in their delineation which did not suffer a gesture to be made in public that had not been chosen and tried at home. The modern aim is to dramatize the freshest society sensation, so that the newspapery virtues of the subject may atone for any commonplace writing and acting.

The ancients, too, thought it enough to distinguish the youth, old man, slave, cook, priestess, heiress, mother, maiden, by well-known varieties of mask, of color in tunic and mantle, and by what was held in the hand, as the peasant's cudgel, or the parasite's comb and box; but what begets success for a modern society play? The toilets of the actresses. Journalists, heralding its rehearsals, recite not its gems of expression, but the palpitating rumor that Miss Harlotte's gown in the comedy of *Croquet* is to cost $1000; that Mrs. Modiste's laces are exquisite in the bewitching play of *Flirting*; that Ida Leggett will exhibit another new set of pearls in *Crinoline, or What a Bustle!*; that in *Men and Millinery*, the graceful Putty changes costumes eight times, each garb eclipsing the last. Is not the decorative carrying it with a high hand over the dramatic art? [. . .]

The current drama seems to develop agreeably in two directions—first, into the millinery plays, and secondly, into the railroad smash-up plays. Its danger in both directions is, that in seeking what is "real" and avoiding what is ridiculous, it may descend to the trivial and commonplace. A great writer once said that plays full of action, without true delineation of character, though they delight, remain at the threshold of the scenic art. "The rude man is content if he sees something going on; the man of more refinement must be made to feel; the man entirely refined desires to reflect." A little heavier dash of intellectuality, of endeavor to portray character and emotion, would add interest and value to a style of drama now overloaded with mechanism and given to achieving "situations," without fully depicting the effect of such situations on human conduct.

[314] [The Failure of the American Playwright]
Appletons's Journal [1875]

[. . .] It is, we know, no new thing to deplore the infertility of American dramatists, and to speculate upon the cause; but annual periods like this may excuse a return to the subject; and especially now when new theatres spring up so rapidly, and when foreign plays are achieving unprecedented success, it is peculiarly pertinent to inquire why the American comedy still fails to respond to our hopes.

There is, we think, a peculiar difficulty in dealing with American life—a certain lack of mellowness and perspective which is apt to render local places and topics raw and crude when transplanted into art. It needs a sensitive, artistic temperament to deal with this difficulty successfully; but, so far from our dramatists attempting to grapple with it, they surrender themselves to it. They seize upon it as a feature, and as a national quality not only amenable to art, but desirable for the artist's purpose. It has become a canon of dramatic writers that only the detestable crudities of our civilization are suitable for dramatic purposes. There has been no attempts to portray the pure, and fine, and true phases of our life; on the contrary, parvenuism and vulgar show are continually assumed to be the only aspects of our social problem that our people care to see in dramatic form. That our public delights in the best of the old English comedies; that the pure and delicate productions of the modern London stage are appreciated here as thoroughly as there; that in no single instance has the vulgar type of American comedy met with more than the most ephemeral success; that all the facts show that we do *not* want pictures of vulgar life, but ask for a just reflex of our better conditions—seem to be nothing to our dramatists. They adhere to certain traditions with a blind faith which failure and discomfiture never seem to shake. They began with underrating public taste, and they have gone on producing far below it. They have assumed that slovenly haste, crudity, and vulgarity, are what the theatre-goer demands; and, although slovenliness, crudity, and vulgarity, have invariably been rewarded with empty benches, there is still no enlightenment, still no perception of the real conditions of the problem. It may be said truthfully that the American public has never had an opportunity to condemn or neglect a really good American comedy. Native plays have been acted with certain good points; but no dramatist has yet fairly tested the intellectual capacity of our audiences. Whenever a play shall be written that unites a good and interesting story with artistic construction; that assembles a well-contrasted and well-delineated group of characters; that affords felicitous pictures of life; that, in brief, unites just and acute observation with artistic quality—then we shall know, and not until then, whether there is a public that can understand and will support it. For our part, we are confident there is.

[315] [The Pattern of "Original" Comedies]
Appletons's Journal [1875]

A new comedy, entitled *Women of the Day* [by Charles Morton], which first saw light on the American stage at Philadelphia, was produced last week [20 Jan. 1875] at Daly's Theatre. It is a society comedy; and, like all comedies of this character, is made up largely of brilliant dresses and fine scandal. It is called an American comedy because a few local names familiar to us are used, and the greater part of the action is supposed to take place at Saratoga; and no doubt it bears almost as much resemblance to social life here as anywhere else, its likeness to any thing human off the stage being as distant as its likeness is close to many phases of life the stage has hitherto depicted. The plot is too slight, and the characters too sketchy, to give the play much tenacity of life, although the language is bright, and some of the characterizations are amusing. In one scene it degenerates into farce, but the scene elicits roars of laughter from the multitude; and the actors will here be tolerably sure to heed this applause rather than listen to the censure of the few. The story is of love and jealousy—of course; a young lady is betrothed, flirts with a notorious lady-killer during her *fiancé*'s absence; is compromised; but all is cleared up by a duel—that inevitable and truthful feature of fashionable comedy.

This comedy purports to be an original one, but there are some indications that it is of foreign extraction. Unfortunately, the bad example of the dramatists leaves one ever in doubt whether a play is original or not, inasmuch as commonly the claim of originality is not supported by the facts. No author would dare claim a book to be his that he had only translated or adapted; no one, in science or art, is permitted to appropriate any thing he did not originate. Why is it, then, that a different code of morals exists in regard to plays? It is time, we think, the public and the critics should endeavor to change all this, and to insist that dramatic writers are as bound as other writers are to acknowledge the source of their performances.

[316] B. Matthews. "The Decline of the Drama"
The Galaxy [1875]

[. . .] [After arguing extensively against the opinion that the drama has declined:] Even in that peculiar production, the local drama, there is improvement; *Kit* [the frontiersman type in such plays as T. B. De Walden's *Kit, the Arkansas Traveller*, 1870] is better than *Mose* [the type of the New York fireboy in such plays as B. A. Baker's *A Glance at New York*, 1848]. [J. M. McClosky's] *Across the Continent* [1871], [Bronson Howard's] *Saratoga* [1870], and [Augustin Daly's] *Divorce* [1871], differing greatly in merit, alike show a reaching after national facts—after national characteristics. And there is more hope now for native and naturalized dramatists than there was years ago, when Dunlap had to give out that his own adaptations from German plays and English novels were the work of English playwrights, and had already seen the light of the lamps in the English capital. To-day there is a distinct demand for dramas on local subjects, containing American characters and reflecting American characteristics. But hitherto most of the many attempts to supply this demand have been made by men who could only see the outside of American life. They have given us the husks and the chaff—not the winnowed wheat. Their plays, externally dramas, are really hollow shams, without heart or soul, or even body—but only a mechanical skeleton. The cry for American art, an American literature, an American drama is natural, but illogical. Art is not local—it is universal. We need American artists—not an American art. Art is alike everywhere. The matter may change, but the manner will be substantially the same. The form will only differ from foreign art as it is influenced by the fact. The subject may be—in most cases must be—even national and local; the style is universal and individual. Few writers have treated subjects more characteristically American than Mr. Bret Harte, but his style seems to be distinctly modelled upon Dickens and Thackeray. But American literature and American pictorial art are artistically in advance of the American drama. Most of the native productions of our stage are written by artisans and not by artists; by playwrights, not by dramatists; by men more or less expert in building pieces, but entirely incapable of creating a play. There is no decline, however; the prospects of the drama in America are better than ever before. It is but little more than ten years ago since the satirical paper *Vanity Fair* printed a cut of a critic ordering an extra cup of coffee, and saying, "Make it strong, for I'm going to see an American comedy, and I must keep awake somehow!" [. . .]

[324] [Defense of the Stage]
Appletons's Journal [1877]

[. . .] It seems to us that many of the arguments against the theatre are rendered effective by the erroneous attitude of its defenders. Is it not obvious that dramatic entertainments cannot be explained nor excused on the ground or within the domain of morals? If the purpose of the theatre is to inculcate ethics, then, as one writer cogently says, it is far too expensive and cumbersome a device for the end in view. The church, the Sunday-school, the printing-press, the lecture-platform, can each accomplish much more in the direction of morals with far less expenditure of force. The mission of the theatre seems to us to be of another nature altogether. It is an art the influences of which are limited to the sphere of aesthetics, and its defenders might claim that there is no more reason why the drama should be expected to inculcate moral lessons than that painting, or sculpture, or poetry, or music, or decorative art, should be required to do so. Acting appeals almost exclusively to the imagination and the sensibilities: it embodies painting, sculpture, poetry, music, and epic action, and it may be affirmed that it has no mission to transcend as a whole that which any of its parts were created to fulfill. [. . .] The drama, in justice, should stand or fall with all the other arts. If it is wrong in the theatre to captivate the senses with splendor of color and beauty of form, if it is hurtful there to stir the emotions and thrill the imagination, then it is wrong and hurtful to do these things in the passionate lines of the poet, the glowing colors of the painter, or the glorious forms of the sculptor. It would really seem as if the only consistent people on this question are the Quakers, who exclude music and color from their places of worship and their domiciles, studiously resisting everything that charms or allures the senses. Their ground is the only tenable ground. If it is conceded at all that imaginative art in any form has a right to exist—if, in this world of temptation, sin, and human frailty, it is right to indulge the imagination with pictures of beauty and ideals of life—then assuredly the drama has every justification for its being that each of its sister arts has.

But it has been said that the stage is peculiarly pernicious, that no other art is so gross and harmful in its influences. The friends of the theatre must admit that the stage is sometimes evil, but can justly affirm that the drama is the only outcome of imaginative genius that is persistently judged by its worst rather than by its best achievements and influences. No one thinks of denouncing poetry because there have been licentious poets. Painting has never been condemned because it has given the world many sensuous and pagan productions. It is not usual to put music under ban because of Bacchanalian songs and Offenbach airs. If literature were judged solely by the number of vile and wicked books that have been produced, public sentiment might well demand the breaking up of the printing-press, and the consignment of letters to a place among the lost arts. Now, it is only just to ask that the theatre be judged with the fairness and discretion shown toward other human performances. [. . .] How is it that, in everything else but the theatre, people select the best for enjoyment and praise, and consign the bad to neglect? Good romances are read by scrupulous people, who cautiously select those that are pure in tone. As these people do not banish from their houses the entire world of fiction because of some bad examples, nor deny themselves the pleasure of reading Tennyson because Swinburne is improper, they have no moral right to subject the theatre to a test to which nothing else of the kind is brought, and which nothing else of the kind could successfully stand.

There is much that is strange in the history of the stage. Bitterly as it has been condemned, evil as it is supposed to be, it has yet given to the world some of the highest and most exquisite creations known to art—the most perfect ideals of womanhood, the noblest portraitures of men, the sweetest idyls of love, the best types of heroism. [. . .] the stage in this particular is unique: the most persistently condemned and deplored of every imaginative art, it has taken a foremost place in the creation of beauty, and has given to mankind a group of men and women that the world could almost less afford to lose than anything else art or imagination has endowed it with.

[325] D. Boucicault. "The Decline of the Drama"
The North American Review [1877]

[. . .] It is comforting to reflect that the fine arts, together with every form of literature,—in truth, all the staple products of the brain,—have suffered a decline during the last half-century. There is a certain satisfaction in reflecting that the drama has been steadily declining for two thousand years, since Caesar, deploring the falling off in the Roman stage of his time, when compared with the Greek, stigmatized Terence as a half-bred (*demidiatus*) Menander. We, dramatists of this age, can therefore hope there is a still lower depth in years to come, when we shall be regarded as men of stature by a pygmy posterity.

The *Spectator*, writing in the time of Queen Anne, deplores the degradation of the stage of that period. [. . .]

Goldsmith, writing fifty years later, mourned over the departed greatness of the drama of 1770 as compared with the grandeur of the previous age of Addison.

It may be that these critics failed to reflect that the drama is the necessary product of the age in which it lives, and of which it is the moral, social, and physical expression. It is divided into two classes. The first may be called the *contemporaneous* or *realistic* drama, which is a reflex of the features of the period, where the personages are life-size, the language partakes of their reality, and the incidents are natural. The object of this drama is to produce in the mind of the spectator sympathy with human suffering by effecting a perfect illusion that he is witnessing a destiny towards which the *dramatis personae* are progressing. The other is the *transcendental* or *unreal* drama, where the personages are larger than life-size, their ideas and language more exalted than human conversation, and the incidents more important than we meet with in ordinary life. The object of this drama is to lift the spectator into a high atmosphere, and to expand his moral stature by association with *dramatis personae* of gigantic proportions. In this region the drama cannot produce perfectly the theatrical illusion, because we cannot sympathize with beings more noble than ourselves. The contemporaneous drama possesses an archaeological value. It is the only faithful record of its age. In it the features, expression, manners, thoughts, and passions of its period are reflected and retained. In the plays of this kind written during the sixteenth century by Marlowe, Ford, Shakespeare, Decker, Jonson, Beaumont, Fletcher, and Massinger we are enabled to live and move amongst the society of the period. They recall to life the romantic characters, stately manners, and robust thought of the Elizabethan age. [. . .] The prose comedies of Wycherley and Congreve faithfully reflect the dissolute scenes and worthless characters of these times when sharpness of wit was preferred to breadth or depth of thought. [. . .]

During the last hundred years the mind of mankind has been eagerly devoted to the application of scientific discoveries to useful purposes, and particularly to the unification of political and commercial interests. Information has become a drug; investigation has set bounds to romance and rendered fancy ridiculous. The whole world is plotted out and turned into real estate. [. . .] Such is the positive generation that calls its drama into existence, requiring the mind of the dramatist to be practical, utilitarian, to be in sympathetic accord with the minds of the people. He must not consider anything too deeply; his audience cannot follow him. He must not soar; their prosaic minds, heavy with facts, cannot rise. He cannot roam; their exact information turns him back at every step. I earnestly believe the human mind always maintains the same average level. There is always a Homer, a Virgil, a Dante, and a Shakespeare in existence, but mankind is pleased not to call them forth. [. . .] If we have no such poets, painters, sculptors, or philosophers now, it is simply because the mind of the nineteenth century has other aspirations. [. . .] Great intellect, no longer meditative, is active. It has been diverted by command of the world to other objects and has accepted other functions.

[. . .] If it [the drama] has descended below the level at which it ought to have rested, it owes its further decline to the destructive influence of the newspaper press.

This literary machine was invented about a century ago. [. . .] At first its object was simply to circulate news. Then it began to manufacture opinion. As mankind became more and more busy in commercial affairs they had less time for meditation, and it was very convenient to buy opinions ready made, and to have their minds made up for them without the trouble of consideration. So this machine soon came into universal use, and the slow craftsman of literature, the old-fashioned thinker, the weaver of sound, strong argument, finding no market for his laboriously fashioned brain-produce, became a press man. The inexorable machine now calls upon him for so much composition, not for thought. [. . .] This daily milking of his brain, this eternal diarrhoea of thought, has debilitated his mental system. He is under instructions to write for commonplace intellects,—that is, to treat his subjects in a shallow or showy manner, as "the impression" is only intended to live for one day. He is appreciated not for the truth of what he writes (that is a secondary matter), he is urged to be racy, and so learns to cover with pertness of style his baldness of treatment, and to put a satin face upon a shoddy argument. [. . .]

As the newspaper press has prospered, so in proportion have the poet, the novelist, and the dramatist disappeared. [. . .] Have you ever examined meditatively the counter of a bookseller? Have you not found nine out of ten new works of fiction, displayed there for sale, to be the product of female brains? Why do women almost monopolize this branch of literature? The answer is that men are recruited for the ranks of the press. [. . .]

In the drama the mischievous influence of the press is still more fatal in its effects. It has superseded and displaced the band of critics that used to stand upon guard over the production of a new play or the appearance of a new actor. This self-elected troop of exercised and experienced folk, priding itself in its power and its office, was cheerfully recognized by the rest of the public as a leader in taste. It was the body-guard of the drama. Its functions have been of late years usurped by the newspaper press, and the old critical band has been dissolved. Unfortunately the newspaper critic is, and always has been, incapable of discharging these functions. [. . .]

The editor of a newspaper regards the drama as a popular and trivial resort, and issues directions to his subordinate who "does the theatre" to be kind and say everything pleasant. This kindness is fatal to the best interests of the drama. The critic "must be cruel only to be kind." Again, the theatres occupy a large space in the advertising columns of the press, and the newspaper is a commercial, not a literary enterprise. So the proprietor must take care of his customers, and the hired scribe writes as he is bid.

As a low state of health is liable to let in a score of maladies, so a low state of the drama has developed the *commercial manager*. This person in most instances received his education in a bar-room, possibly on the far side of the counter. The more respectable may have been gamblers. Few of them could compose a bill of the play where the spelling and grammar would not disgrace an urchin under ten years of age. These men have obtained possession of first-class theatres, and assume to exercise the artistic and literary functions required to select the actors, to read and determine the merit of dramatic works, and preside generally over the highest and noblest efforts of the human mind. [. . .] To the commercial manager we owe the introduction of the burlesque, opera bouffe, and the reign of buffoonery. We owe him also the deluge of French plays that set in with 1842, and swamped the English drama of that period. [. . .]

But the most irreparable loss inflicted on the stage by this management was the loss of *tradition*. [. . .] The grouping of the actors on the stage, their relations to each other, their movements and gestures, all the product of the careful study of two or three centuries, formed this artistic treasure which we call tradition; and all this is utterly lost. The commercial manager having disbanded these leading companies of artists, all the wealth of the past has been dispersed. [. . .]

[326] [*Rip Van Winkle*: A Temperance Play?]
Appletons's Journal [1878]

[. . .] Mr. Jefferson has been called the "Sunday-school comedian," because he never says on the stage what he would not say in the family circle. [. . .] He recognizes the fact that nowadays a theatrical audience is made up mostly of girls and young men [. . .] and he considers it wrong that a young lady at a theatre should be compelled to listen to words which no gentleman would think of using in the drawing-room or in the public prints. "Just think of it!" I heard him exclaim one day; "what right has a man to say on the stage what he cannot put in the newspaper?"

The only objection on moral grounds that I have ever heard made to *Rip Van Winkle* is that at the end of the last act, when Rip has been recognized by his wife and daughter, and when the former tells him in the exuberance of her delight at finding him, "Rip, you can get tipsy as often as you like," he does not refuse the cup which she offers him. Everybody who has seen the play remembers how Rip accepts the cup, and repeats his old formula, "Well, I won't count dat one, den; here's your good health, and your family, and may you live long and proper;" and many persons, undoubtedly, are sorry that he does not refuse the cup, and assert his resolution to drink no more. Drink has been the cause of all his troubles. Now that his troubles seem to be past, and a new and better era to be beginning, why does he not bid farewell to his former habits, and determine never again to touch another drop? With such an ending the play would become a veritable temperance-lecture. Many a time have committees of ladies, and committees of gentlemen, delegations from benevolent societies, and delegations from reform societies, "waited upon" Mr. Jefferson, and urged him to make a change in that last act. "If," they have said, earnestly and imploringly—"if, Mr. Jefferson, you would only decline the cup that Gretchen offers, and announce your solemn purpose never to drink anymore!" To all these entreaties the actor has turned a deaf ear.

Why? Well, in the first place, he believes that, if the drama teaches at all, it must teach only as life teaches. It holds the mirror up to Nature; it is not a moral lyceum lecture. Its influence departs when it usurps the functions of the preacher or the moralist. In the next place, he thinks that it is unfair to transform the stage into a platform, and to change himself from an actor into a temperance-lecturer. The people who listen to him have paid a dollar and a half each to go to a play, they have not paid their money for the privilege of listening to a sermon. And in the last place, and chiefly, the unity of the impersonation requires that Rip should take the cup, and not that he should reject it. Rip is a drunkard, and his life is an awful warning. Even when he knows the sorrows that his vice has produced, he is unable to rid himself of it. The great joy of refinding his home and his daughter is not his savior. Like every other confirmed inebriate, he naturally falls back into his old habits. [. . .] The thralldom of the drunkard, that is what the play teaches, if it teaches anything in this respect.

[. . .] Could the loudest advocate of temperance find a more impressive illustration than such a spectacle? [. . .]

[329] [Moral Improvement of Theatres]
Scribner's Monthly [1881]

In an article published some years ago [4, 2 (Jun. 1872): 238–39], we recognized the drama as an institution that had come to stay as an important factor in the social and intellectual life of the people—as a source of much pleasure and a possible source of much culture. Since that day, the drama has had its place in this magazine. [. . .] It seems to us that theaters are improving, and that there is much less that is objectionable in their conduct and influence than formerly. We have been witnesses to the fact, right here in New York, that the cleanest and best plays have been the most successful. Plays without any equivocal situations in them—plays that leave no stain, and excite no unwholesome imaginations—have run for months, and made their managers rich.

[. . .] There is undoubtedly an increasing attendance upon the theater among refined and religious people, and we rejoice in the fact, for it is full of promise for the theater itself, and for the bodily and mental health of those who are attracted to it. [. . .]

The old and familiar claim that the theater is "a school of morals," so far as it was intended to declare it to be an educational institution, with morality for its object, was without any foundation whatever. The theater is never ahead of the people who patronize it. If it has any definite aim, it is to please—to reflect the tastes, the moralities, the opinions, and the enthusiasms of those who attend it. [. . .]

Public opinion and public taste are the master and mistress of the stage. It is but a short time since it was proposed to produce a Passion Play in New York. Now a play representing on the boards of a theater the Passion of our Lord could have no apology or justification save in the ignorant devotion of those producing it. No such apology or justification exists in New York, and public opinion rose against the project and vehemently protested. The manager who had it in hand bowed respectfully to the public voice and withdrew it. The incident is a good illustration of the power of public opinion over the theater. The truth is that the life of the theater depends on its power to please the public, and it is bound by every consideration of interest to reflect the moral sense and moral culture of those upon whom it depends for support. It is for this reason that we have no fears of a bad moral result of the theater upon the public. If an immoral actress wins a great success in New York, it is not because she has debauched New York, but because New York is tolerant of immorality. If a bad play succeeds in a New York theater, it is because there is not moral sense enough in those who witness it and in the public press to rebuke it and drive it from the boards. The better and purer the patronage of any theater may be, the better will that theater become, in every variety of influence which a theater can exert; and it is delightful to believe that the dramatic instinct which is the source of so much pleasure to so many good people can be gratified without danger of pollution.

[341] L. Hutton. ["The American play is yet to be written"]
Lippincott's Monthly Magazine [1886]

[. . .] During the single century of the American stage not twoscore plays of any description have appeared which have been truly American and which at the same time are of any value to dramatic literature or of any credit to the American name. By purely American play is meant the original production of an American writer, with American scenes and characters, which is thoroughly American in tone. In this category cannot be included dramas like Mr. Daly's *Pique* [1875] or *The Big Bonanza* [1875], for the one is from an English novel

[Florence Lean, *Her Lord and Master*, 1871] and the other from a German play [Gustav von Moser, *Ultimo*, 1874]; nor Mr. Boucicault's *Belle Lamar* [1874] or *The Octoroon* [1859], which are native here, but from the pen of an alien; nor plays like *Uncle Tom's Cabin* [1852], which are not original, but are drawn largely, if not wholly, from American novels; nor plays like *The Twelve Temptations* [a musical spectacle by Joseph C. Foster, 1870] or *The Black Crook* [a melodramatic musical spectacle by Charles M. Barras, 1866], which are not plays at all. [. . .]

The American drama, such as it is, may be divided into four classes: the Indian and the Revolutionary drama, which are generally identical and coincident; the society plays, of which Mrs. [Anna C. O.] Mowatt's *Fashion* [1845] and [Bronson] Howard's *Saratoga* [1870] are fair examples; the Yankee or character plays, like [Joseph Stevens Jones's] *Solon Shingle* [as *The People's Lawyer*, 1839] or [Benjamin E. Woolf's] *The Mighty Dollar* [1875]; and the plays of local low life, like *Mose* [the stereotype of the New York fireboy, first appearance in B. A. Baker's *A Glance at New York*, 1848] or [Edward Harrigan's] *Squatter Sovereignty* [1882]. [. . .]
[A historical survey of the American drama follows.]

[342] A. Daly. "The American Dramatist"
The North American Review [1886]

[. . .] Possibly our national drama, from a literary point of view, will reach its best period when native writers vie with each other in illustrating native character and contemporaneous fashions and follies. It does not seem easy to get our best playwriters to practice in this field of exertion. In selecting plots and characters they have a decided bias, acquired from reading the masterpieces of modern fiction—these being mostly foreign: [. . .] this must be given up, of course, when the native dramatist closes his wistful eyes upon the Old World and opens them upon the New. But why not give a picture of the new aping the old? Some attempts have been made to combine the old and the new in one picture—for instance, by placing the scene in a foreign country, among the very bluest-blooded grandees, and then precipitating a wild, whooping American girl upon them to amaze and bewilder the foolish foreigners. But is there any real necessity for laying such a scene in a foreign country? Any respectable New York, or Boston, or Philadelphia family, would be equally amazed and distressed by the behavior of such a girl. There is one sacrifice in giving up the old world and its works which our native dramatists find it hard to make—and that is the duel! The fascination and breathless interest that cling to the combat seem to be irresistible. The duel dies very hard out of the native drama. But, then, you may have an affair of honor without fighting, for that is quite customary among our best young bloods, I believe;

though it would require a master dramatist to excite serious interest with such an episode. Of course our stage is occupied with innumerable plays purporting to afford studies of native character—such as Solon Shingle [in Joseph Stevens Jones's *The People's Lawyer*, 1839], Davy Crockett [in Frank Hitchcock Murdoch's *Davy Crockett*, 1872], Colonel Sellers [in George Densmore and Mark Twain's *The Gilded Age*, 1874], [. . .] and so forth, but these are mere outlines of plays that might be written. They have no literary value and serve no purpose in the structure of the national drama, because they perish with the actor who has given them substance. There is no way to perpetuate the convulsive effects of the "gags," or impromptus of the comic star. The dramatist who is coming will undoubtedly do better. [. . .]

The future American dramatist [. . .] cannot altogether differ from all who have gone before him. What will be his work? Shall he embody, in a series of historical dramas, our national events, or satirize, in comedy, our native foibles, or work into dramatic shape the sensational narratives of our daily papers and call it a picture of American life? All this has been done. Perhaps the new man is to do it better. But our national drama will be established without restriction as to subject or plot. The coming dramatist will be indifferent on that score. His fancy will roam, at its own sweet will, for song or story to crystallize into dramatic form. Neither Shakspere nor any of his contemporaries, nor Corneille nor Racine, nor Schiller nor Goethe made the national drama of their native lands by the delineation of national character only. Originality of plot and incident seem, by the common consent of the highest dramatic censors in every age, to count for nothing in the estimate of literary pretensions. [. . .] We must not exact of American dramatists more than has been demanded of its dramatists by any country. They have been permitted to draw their themes and their characters from foreign sources; their praise was for doing their work well, and vindicating the claims of the national literature by their genius. [. . .] The present masterpieces of the stage, in every tongue, are pictures of the passions of mankind in general, rather than attempts at national portrait painting [. . .].

There is a cheering prospect for the American drama, as far as the actors and the theaters are concerned. The American stage to-day possesses native born or thoroughly naturalized artists, who have no superiors in their respective lines. The tragic, the comic, the eccentric, the delineator of the easy, well-bred man or woman of society and of every other grade of life, are now to the manner born. Not many years ago the companies that acted in our theaters were largely English. Here and there twinkled an American "star," but the firmament was studded with foreign constellations. The development of the histrionic talent in the United States augurs well for the future dramatic literature. So many clever men and women must not only produce but must inspire genius in that direction. [. . .]

But the brightest prospect of the American drama is found in the present position of the theater in this country, with reference to the social world. Our advance in that direction is almost incalculable. The best portion of the community has taken possession of the theater, as it ought to take possession of all public amusements, and has made it its own. The purification of the temple of the drama has been so thoroughly effected that the worthiest people find it worthy of their affectionate regard. From the topmost gallery down, respectability reigns. The "third tier" and the pit of thirty years ago, with their bars and their loungers, have disappeared. There is no attraction for the vicious. The constant patrons of the drama belong to the class of people who are strictest in the performance of every duty, moral and social. [. . .]

To sum up, I should say the prospects of our national drama are bright, because: 1st, our theaters, as places of resort, are wholesome, and are controlled by the best classes; 2d, the development of dramatic capability and power in the art of acting is marked and increasing in Americans; 3d, our native authors are numerous and industrious, wanting but the resolution and perseverance of American writers in other departments to systematically help the native drama and not leave its development too much to chance; 4th, the standard of the best management is high except where theaters are managed purely as commercial speculations. Even the latter would be well enough if the commercial instinct were present as in other business undertakings, and required the employment of a competent artistic head.

[344] J. Magnus. "The Condition of the American Stage"
The North American Review [1887]

[. . .] The causes which have mainly attributed to bring about the present unsatisfactory condition of the American stage are:

1. General mercantile depression.
2. The lack of particularly good English or French plays.
3. The want of encouragement of American authors.
4. The rise and growth of the acrobatic comedy.
5. The prevalence of the combination system.
6. The fact that management is so largely in the hands of mere speculators.
7. The flooding of the profession by novices from comic opera companies.

(1.) Strikes, labor troubles, the low price of agricultural produce, the dishonest management of railroads, and the nervousness of some capitalists at the transference of political power to the Democracy have combined to cause a stringency in money matters which, naturally, has resulted in a general economizing of expenditures. And the very first expenses which people curtail are those of their amusements. At one time it was contended that in periods of panic and business failure men would go to the theatre to divert their thoughts. Experience and observation have, however, shown this theory to be a fallacy. Nor is it the very rich and fashionable class, who are least affected by the condition of business, that are the best supporters of the theatre. They have so incessant a round of social amusement that, except when a play is so strong as to become a general topic of conversation, about which it is necessary to know something, they can rarely spare time for the drama. The most constant and liberal theatre-goers are those who may be most accurately defined by the Anglicism, "the upper middle-class." It is precisely these persons, whose incomes are largely dependent on the momentarily existing state of trade or the demand for professional services, who are the first to feel the necessity for economizing. [. . .]

(3.) Not having been able to secure good plays from abroad, have our managers endeavored to give American authors a chance to make their abilities known? Unfortunately only to a very limited extent! [. . .] Mr. Bronson Howard [. . .] is certainly the cleverest of American dramatists, and even he finds it desirable to live for the greater part of his time in England, where his pieces are fully appreciated and find ready hearing. In a recent article in *The North American Review [342]*, Mr. Daly pointed to a number of American dramatists who had done good work, and were certainly capable of doing more, but scarcely one of them succeeded in getting a play upon the boards during the season of 1885–6. A man who has a story to tell dramatically will only do his best work when writing for a stock-company, unfettered by the necessity of bringing a "star" or "stars" into prominence to the detriment of the natural development of his plot. Now when there are only in this vast country four permanently-established stock-companies, it is evident that the opportunities for the native dramatist, who aspires to something higher than "star-fitting"—the dramatic tailoring of writing—are very few. One of these four is almost permanently closed against him, for the fortunate manager, Mr. Daly, is able to adapt and arrange his own plays. To his credit, it must be said that he accomplishes his task in a masterly style, and probably no one else could so well fit his company or so thoroughly please his audiences. Then, too, he has settled on a class of light play, which excludes from his stage the writers who deal with the stronger emotions and passions. So the American dramatist's field is narrowed down to three theatres, the managers of which are bidding against each other for established foreign successes, and who, as a rule, will only deal with the native product when their favorite source of supply has temporarily run dry. The extremely uncertain chance of having a play adequately produced is so remote that it deters writers who are able to put their ideas into any other form of literature from attempting to write for the stage. It is absurd to state or suppose that the literary ability which Americans are constantly displaying, could not be profitably employed on the drama. The technical knowledge necessary can be gained by a close study of plays and the theatre, or may more easily be obtained by taking into collaboration an experienced stage-manager or a hack playwright.

(4.) [. . .] Such alleged plays, which may be termed "acrobatic comedies," appeal only to the eyes, and tickle the ear with "catchy" melodies; but they never give intellectual gratification, and never arouse any thought, except, perhaps, among those who look on them as a degradation of the drama. Now, a few of these theatrical hashes might not have done any harm, and would have been certainly enough to please the audiences who find it tiresome to follow the thread of a story, or to have their deeper feelings stirred. But, unhappily, the majority of American managers have no distinct policy. When one makes a "hit" with a special style of entertainment, the others all cry out "that is evidently what the public want," and immediately rush off to try and get as close an imitation as possible. The result has been that the country has been literally flooded with acrobatic comedies, each successive one endeavoring to be more outrageously absurd than its predecessor. Last season, what appears to be the climax was reached, in making one of these ollapodridas the medium for putting a circus upon the stage. It was not successful, though the acting people engaged did their best to work up interest for the horses and their riders. It scarcely seems possible that the putters-together of these farce-comedies can extend their field of operations much farther. They have tried moving trains, revolving houses, clowns, acrobats, performing animals, and very nude dressing until it seems that their efforts must fail from lack of novelty. Scarcely any actors are employed in these pieces, nearly all the performers being known as "specialty people," whose singing, dancing, or gymnastic accomplishments form nearly their whole claims to notice.

Audiences have become so used to this combination of burlesque with what is technically known as the "knock-down-and-drag-out" business, that they are in the position of a man whose palate has been so long tempted with "kickshaws" that he is unable to enjoy a wholesome diet of plain roast beef. [. . .]

(5.) The prevalence of the combination system, by which all theatres outside of New York and Boston are furnished with their entertainments by traveling organizations, has wrought almost incalculable damage to our dramatic art, in every one of its departments. Formerly, when actors and managers of taste and long experience, like McVicker in Chicago, De Bar in St. Louis, Albaugh and Ford in Baltimore, Miles in Cincinnati, Ellsler in Pittsburgh, and others too numerous to mention, controlled the chief theatres of the various States, they kept resident companies, produced new plays, and were, in the true sense of the word, managers. Now they are little more than janitors of their respective houses, having no control whatever over the entertainments given on their stages, beyond, in the first instance, the selection of them. The authors who used to get, in these theatres, an occasional chance for the production of their plays, are now effectually barred out. The actors who were able to make homes for at least a season, are now perpetually traveling—a life that destroys comfort and imperils health and the sanctity of domestic relations. Instead of playing a great number of parts each year, thereby gaining the ease and experience which are absolutely necessary to good acting, the actor represents one character for an entire season, and probably plays it far worse at the end than at the beginning of his engagement. His performance becomes mechanical and perfunctory; his audiences are always changing, and he cares comparatively little what they think of him, for they may not meet again for a long time. When the actor was in the "stock" he was ever striving to become a local favorite, knowing that the doing so would insure his reengagement for another season, possibly in a more advanced position, or secure a transferrence to a theatre of higher standing. There is, undoubtedly, more raw talent to-day in the ranks of actors and actresses than ever before, but the practical impossibility of securing proper artistic training leaves it, for the most part, imperfectly developed. Then, too, the accidental "hits" made by a few stars of no decided ability leads many players to have no ambition beyond "getting a piece" and inflicting themselves on the public in what they too frequently vainly believe to be their specialties. The desire to be a good leading stock actor is far more commendable, and more truly artistic, than that to be a star playing one rôle continually. But as with managers, so with actors, the desire for money-getting overrides devotion to art, and the followers of this greatest, because most absolutely realizing—fleeting though its form be—of all arts, come to regard it merely as a business.

(6.) How few managers of stock companies there are left, has been previously stated. With the exception of Mr. Daly, every one of them seems at times to be feeling his way and not to have a distinct policy. Each occasionally jumps from comedy to farce, from farce to melodrama, and from melodrama to domestic drama. Their companies are, naturally, not equally at home in all kinds of plays, and unsatisfactory performances often result from these violent alternations. The experience of older countries has shown the advisability of a manager restricting himself to one class of play. His company is then seen always at its best, for it is doing the work for which it is especially selected. His patrons, moreover, know what to expect, and learn to go to his theatre, without even particularly inquiring what the night's bill may be, for they are assured they will witness something good and of the kind they like. At one time Mr. Wallack had such a reputation for the presentation of high-class comedies of both the old and new schools; but his production of sensational melodramas, however remunerative temporarily, has, it is generally believed, driven away his old and, for a long time, faithful lovers of comedy.

The road-manager has very rarely been an actor. He is a business man, pure and simple, and is generally rather given to boast of the fact. He has no "weakness," as he would term it, for art; he is "in to make money," which he proceeds to do by beating down the salaries of actors till they reach such a low level that ambition is almost crushed. He makes his companies play nine, ten, and even, sometimes, twelve times a week, and is happiest when he reaches some Godless Western town where he can give two performances on Sunday. Whenever it is possible he makes an actor play two or three parts, and the best actor is very often to him the one who will accept the smallest salary. As for encouragement, sympathy, or consideration, an actor might quite as hopefully look to a calculating machine, and would, at least, have in that case an assurance that its figures were correct—a confidence he does not always feel when the manager exhibits a statement which shows the impossibility of paying salaries. These so-called managers are, moreover, constantly on the look-out for rich and ambitious amateurs, who, for the sake of exhibiting their supposed charms and gorgeous dresses, will forego the trifling consideration of salary. It is these people who too frequently take the bread out of the mouths of the well-trained professional; and it is these people, with whom the stage is only a means of gratifying vanity, who are responsible for by far the larger share of the immorality so freely, and often so baselessly, charged against actresses.

(7.) When *Pinafore* [W. S. Gilbert's *H.M.S. Pinafore; Or, The Lass That Loved a Sailor*, 1878] overran this country like a virulent epidemic, amateurs and church-choir members by the hundreds became, in their own opinions, professional actors and actresses. A few weeks' work in the chorus sufficed to render them so dissatisfied with their old means of earning a livelihood that they have never returned to it. Posing as actors and actresses they have been engaged by undiscriminating or unscrupulous managers at salaries so low that many old-time actors, rather than compete with such incompetence and inexperience, have retired from the profession. The writer has repeatedly met girls, who, after one season in the chorus of comic opera, have sought positions as leading ladies in dramatic companies, and, what is worse, have sometimes obtained them. The inefficient actors and actresses, of whom the public so often complain, come most frequently from this class. [. . .]

The public has grown weary of the romanticism of the novel. It is already wearying fast of that of the stage. It is beginning to demand truth and naturalness, and of such kinds as it daily meets and knows. To render these attractive, the skill of the able writer must be added to that of the technical playwright. When this shall have been done a few times, and managers have found courage to present such work, we shall hear no more of the "permanent divorce of literature from the stage." The parting will prove to have been, happily, only a temporary separation. [. . .]

[345] J. Magnus. "Wanted—A Representative Theatre"
The North American Review [1887]

[...] The great need of the American stage is a theatre, the policy of which shall not be guided solely by the desire of money-making; where the manager shall not be debarred from engaging a valuable actor, because he can not feel sure of his availability for every play; where the programme is frequently changed, a repertory gradually formed, and where alone, in the metropolis at least, its successes could be seen. [...] To this theatre should [...] be attached a training school, with the principal actors and actresses as instructors; and the most promising graduates should be absorbed, as rapidly as consistent with reasonable economy, into the regular company.

Several of our managers are frequently prevented from producing plays which their own tastes and inclinations prompt them to accept, because they fear that they are "over the heads" of the majority of their patrons. This dread has deprived us of adaptations of many of the best works of the contemporary foreign drama, and relegated us to more melodramatic and sensational plays. Yet the receptions accorded during the last two or three seasons to several high-class plays ought to be sufficient proof that our theatre-going public, in New York at least, is willing to accept the best, and not, as some pessimists have declared, averse to anything that will make it think.

In many respects no better basis could be chosen for the formation of a representative theatre than that of the *Comédie Française*. The selection of plays should rest with the manager, assisted by a limited number of the company. A financial interest should be given to certain members after a specified time of service, and retiring pensions should also be allotted. To gather a splendid company for a theatre so conducted would not be difficult. Many of our "stars," who are now compelled to travel, would gladly embrace the chance of once more having homes. [...]

The prospect of retiring pensions would be held by many actors to quite compensate for the possibly greater profits that might accrue from "starring." Positions in this theatre would be the prizes of the profession, and would give to all a much needed stimulus for study and self-improvement. And they who might gain entrance, would feel their futures assured, and thus the public and the profession might be spared the humiliation of seeing a really great actor having at the end of his career to appeal, through a benefit, for the means to support his last years.

That such a theatre would also help to develop the art of play-writing in this country, I firmly believe. To have their plays interpreted by so great a company would attract to dramatic work writers who, while in sympathy with the stage, do not consider that it offers "a fair field and no favor." One of the most eminent of our managers once said to me, "give me an American and a French play of equal merit and I will take the French one." So unpatriotic a decision would not, I hope, be often arrived at, if the manager were assisted in his selection by a council of American actors. I would not urge that plays written here should be produced in preference to superior foreign work, but all things being equal, in a representative American theatre American plays should have precedence.

[348] A. Daly et al. "American Playwrights on the American Drama"
Harper's Weekly [1889]

Mr. Augustin Daly's Views.

I do not consider that there is any such thing as an American school, or an American drama. The drama is one and the same thing wherever it is written. We do not vary from the form that has come down to us, and I do not see that we can. Of course there is tragedy, and there is comedy, and there are the other classes of plays, but I do not recognize different schools. Whether a play is written by an American or a Frenchman does not make the difference. It is merely a matter of the individuality of the author. A play can be American in the sense that it portrays American characters and American life. In that sense we have an American drama, and beyond any question the most distinctive work of that kind that has been done is Mr. Harrigan's. It could not be mistaken for anything but New York life, and is, with limitations, a faithful portrayal of that life, though it is as rough, dramatically considered, as *Gammer Gurton's Needle* [1566].

I have been looking for a considerable time to see some dramatist appear who shall develop the life of the Middle West, the characters and scenes that have been described by Eggleston. I think that is the field in which we will find the most distinctively American work to be done. If somebody should come up who could treat life in the Middle Western States with the same strength of individual style that Bret Harte formerly had, the yield would be especially rich, and would be more typically American than anything else that could be done.

The dramatists of America have made a good showing of work in the past, considering the youth of our country, and certainly there seems to be every prospect of their doing good work and plenty of it in the future. There have been dramatists here almost from the first of our history, and many of them have sought for materials in America. Naturally the war of the Revolution suggested materials to many, and there was at one time a considerable number of plays founded on incidents of the Revolution. Now, however, there is little interest in Revolutionary plays, and even the plays that treat of the Civil War do not excite any very broad interest in the large cities. [. . .]

In all this I have tried to make it clear that it does not matter whether an American dramatist chooses American material or not. His work, so long as it is added to the volume of work done in America and in the American spirit, belongs to the American drama. As a matter of fact, the dramatists of this country seldom do choose American subjects, but nearly all greatly prefer foreign material. They are entirely right in this, for the work of an artist is not to be restricted artificially. It cannot be, indeed, and the playwrights of all nations and generations have recognized this. They have gone to other countries and other ages for their characters and their stories, and by treating these have made them their own. They have never relied on delineations of national characteristics.

As for the prospects for the American dramatist to-day, there are always chances for the artist who does good work, and the rewards for the dramatist who succeeds are very great. [. . .]

It seems to me that the future of the drama in America is exceedingly bright. The status of the theatre was never as good as it is at present; and it is a remark that I have made before, that attacks upon the theatre nowadays are attacks upon the patrons rather than upon the players. Certainly the very best people we have in American society patronize the theatre to-day, and it is to gratify their tastes that the theatre is made what it is. If, then, the theatre is attacked, the critics are animadverting on the tastes of the best society.

Not only is the drama pure and the theatre respectable, but the moral of actors in this country is unsurpassed by that of any other country or age. With these conditions, and the constant competitive efforts of a small army of dramatic writers to produce the best work, there is no reason to have any misgivings about the future.

Mr. Edward Harrigan Speaks.

[. . .] At the outset of my career I found that whenever I tried to portray a type, I was warmly applauded by the audience, and praised by the press the next day. This, in all probability, is what gave me a decided bent, and has confined all my work to certain fields. It began with the New York "boy," the Irish-American, and our African brother. As these grew in popularity I added the other prominent types which go to make up life in the metropolis, and in every other large city of the Union and Canada. These are the Irishman, Englishman, German, Low German, Chinese, Italian, Russian, and Southern darky. I suppose erelong I shall add the Bohemian, Hungarian, Roumanian, Polak, and Scandinavian. As yet, however, their turn has not come. This system has given my pieces their peculiar polyglot character.

Though I use types and never individuals, I try to be as realistic as possible. Not only must the costuming and accessories be correct, but the speech or dialect, the personal "make-up," the vices and virtues, habits and customs, must be equally accurate in their similarity to the facts. Each drama is a series of photographs of life to-day in the Empire City. As examples, the barroom in one of the Mulligan series was copied from a saloon in Roosevelt Street, the opium den in *Investigation* from a "joint" in Pell Street, and the "dive" in

Waddy Googan from an establishment in the neighborhood of the Bowery.

If I have given undue prominence to the Irish and negro, it is because they form about the most salient features of Gotham humanity, and also because they are the two races who care the most for song and dance. [. . .]

In constructing a plot, I use one that is simple and natural—just like what happens around us every day. Sometimes I'll start with only a germ, and let it develop of its own accord as I write. While doing my best to obtain realism in the plot, I try to avoid that whose sole value is local or temporary, and construct something that will interest and amuse ten or even twenty years hence. With the plot fixed or started, and with the types and places in my mind, it is easy to construct the characters and write the piece. [. . .]

It is seldom I use any material but what I described. Polite society, wealth, and culture possess little or no color and picturesqueness. The chief use I make of them is as a foil to the poor, the workers, and the great middle class. The average gentleman is so stereotyped that he has no value except in those plays where he is a pawn on the chess-board of melodramatic vice or tragic sin. [. . .]

It may be that I have struck a new idea in confining my work to the daily life of the common people. Why some other playwright does not try the same experiment, I cannot say. Their trials and troubles, hopes and fears, joys and sorrows, are more varied and more numerous than those of the Upper Ten. Whoever puts them on the stage appeals to an audience of a million, while the author of *Two Nights in Rome* [Archibald C. Gunter, 1879] or *The Professor* [William Gillette, 1881] addresses scarcely one-tenth as many. And human nature is very much the same the world over. It thins out and loses all strength and flavor under the pressure of riches and luxury. It is most virile and aggressive among those who know only poverty and ignorance. It is also then the most humorous and odd. [. . .]

In the realism which I endeavor to employ I believe in being truthful to the laws which govern society as well as to the types of which it is composed. A playwright drops to a low level when he tries being a moralist, but to a much lower level when he gilds vice and sin and glorifies immorality. All of these are parts of life, and as such are entitled to be represented in the drama. The true realist will depict them as they are. Though he make the drunkard a source of infinite merriment to the multitude, he will not conceal the rags, misery, and disease which follow in his footsteps; though he discover virtue in criminals and tramps, he will not be blind to the qualities which outweigh and crush it down; and above all he will portray the fact that right-doing, kindness, and good-nature are in the majority, and "control the machine." [. . .]

Mr. Bronson Howard Illustrates and Defines.

In defining the American drama I should not limit the field of the dramatist's work any more than I would that of the poet. The American drama is the whole body of the drama as it is written by American dramatists, and it is not by any means confined to plays on American subjects or with American characters. I would certainly resent the idea, if any one maintained it seriously, that a man writing plays was not an American dramatist because he might happen to choose subjects other than American. I have preferred American subjects for my own work, but I do not consider for a moment that I am for that reason any more an American writer than I would have been if I had chosen to construct my plays of foreign material.

I would go as far in this direction as to say that if Dion Boucicault is an American citizen, his plays belong to the American drama, although it is a fact that he is a foreigner by birth, and that he has almost exclusively written of Irish scenes and characters. In a word, the American drama is that volume of plays produced in America by Americans, and the subject-matter of the plays themselves has nothing to do with the question. [. . .]

I should agree with Mr. Daly in saying that there is at present no such thing as a distinctively American school of dramatic art, but I am inclined to think that when there have been fifty American plays produced for one that we have now, there will slowly crystallize a school. It will not, however, happen until then. We now have simply a number of Americans writing plays in the English language. The question whether there will ever arise an American school as distinguished from the English school, as that has come down to us from the earlier writers, will depend entirely on whether there shall come up any special mode of construction or strong peculiarity of work in the way of character delineation or literary work. The mere making of plays with American subjects and plots would not make an American school, though it might constitute a branch of it.

A school is not a mere body of literature by any means. It is literature that contains something characteristic and different from other work which constitutes a school. It is the manner of treatment, and not the subject or field, which makes a school. To illustrate this, it may be said that the German school embraces a sort of farcical comedy, in which they include and combine real life and true sentiment of the German kind. Now real life and true sentiment are to the French mind utterly and entirely irreconcilable. They are like oil and water.

Mr. Daly's own reproductions of foreign plays are ordinarily Americanized before they are presented to the New York public, and we have had a number of other plays that may be called distinctively American, not only in authorship and scene and subject, but in treatment. I would certainly class *Rip Van Winkle* [most successful was Joseph Jefferson's version of Dion Boucicault's stage adaptation, 1866], *Davy Crockett* [by Frank Hitchcock Murdoch, 1872], *The Danites* [by Joaquin Miller, 1877], and *My Partner* [by Bartley Campbell, 1879] among the characteristically American plays.

To take another field, we have seen the success of a thousand, more or less, of trivialities in the way of burlesque plays, that are full of American features, such as the characters that became known by their catchwords of "Front," "Fifty cents all 'round," and the like. Then take the *Gilded Age* [by George Densmore and Mark Twain, 1874]. It is a type of still another class. Colonel Sellers [in *The Gilded Age*] is a great picture of a typical character, and Bardwell Slote [in Benjamin E. Woolf's *The Mighty Dollar*, 1875] is another.

It is, in fact, easy to name many plays that have taken their place among American productions as distinctively national. *Kit* [T.B. De Walden's *Kit, the Arkansas Traveller*, 1870] and [Boucicault's] *The Octoroon* [1859] were two of these, and deserve especial mention, being strong pictures of a class of life that is passing away. The Mississippi River drama could never again be as popular as it was once, for it is no longer a representation of reality. Then Boucicault made the *Streets of New York* strongly American. Of course it wasn't an American play when he took it, but it was one when he presented it here. So with several plays of Daly's. His *Under the Gaslight* [1868] and *Horizon* [1871] were thoroughly American, for, wherever he may take his material, he puts in American characters, and he works with strong American instincts.

In one sense Mr. Harrigan's work is of exceedingly great importance. He has dealt in his plays with one phase of American life, and has done it most ably. It is local, of course, but it is characteristically American, and is of notable character. Its importance lies in the part it plays in the growth of a national drama, and in this direction its influence is very great, and will be felt for a long time.

In addition to all these, John Brougham, Boucicault, and Lester Wallack have brought out a considerable number of plays of strong American character, though very many of these plays were, considered artistically, nothing more than mere skits. One, I remember, was on Mormonism, which is certainly a distinctively American matter. And only very recently Gillette, in *The Professor* [1881], has produced a strongly American play, though he attempted in its construction to combine the German and French schools of treatment. It was a most successful attempt too, and he accomplished it in the most artistic manner. The French are very artistic, and the Germans radically inartistic in their combinations of comedy and farce, but Gillette, copying both schools, achieved a very artistic success.

Of course these instances do not by any means compose the entire list, but they are examples of what I understand to be the work which has been done up to the present time in the direction of developing an American drama. This work is the only suggestion, so far as I know, of what may possibly be done in the future by American playwrights to develop a class of plays that may become a part of a school of dramatic art. As I said, there is not such a school as yet, for the work is not distinctive enough to be classed as a separate school.

As to the future of the American drama, I am afraid the Editor of *Harper's Weekly* will have to ask me an easier one.

Mr. William Gillette Surveys the Field.

[. . .] It is hardly necessary to repeat the truism that the law of the survival of the fittest applies as well to plays, parts, and players as to every other field of life. The stage in every generation is crowded with plays—good, bad, and indifferent. The number of dramatic compositions in English alone must run up far over the hundred thousand mark. Yet of this vast army of the children of the brain but a small percentage escape the law of infant mortality, and a much smaller one achieve what may be termed permanent success. This process of elimination is as active and efficient to-day as ever before. While it is ruthless, and works ruin to hundreds and thousands of incompetents, it is beneficent in the long-run, producing a meritorious dramatic literature, and richly rewarding those authors who by accident, intuition, or hard study conform to its provisions and produce works that are responsive to its demands.

The trouble with most dramatic writers is that while they see and to a large extent appreciate the endless changes in methods, ideas, social relations, and personalities engendered by the progress of society, they do not, on the one hand, realize that the dramatic laws or principles which underlie all work remain unchanged, nor on the other that each age demands for its recreation the presentation in artistic form of the varied elements which constitute and characterize its daily life.

A fair illustration is perhaps afforded by Howard's *Henrietta* [1887], one of the best comedies of the present time. In many respects it is a series of perfect photographs. No descriptive writer could give a better picture of the Wall Street maelstrom, of the inane habits of purposeless young millionaires, and of the wild scramble for wealth through modern methods, in which health, life, honor, reputation, and decency are madly used as collateral security in the market, than is presented in visible form upon the boards by the author of this play.

The slight changes required by dramatic art to produce antitheses and climaxes are effected by the delineation of character in slightly eccentric forms, the dexterous juxtaposition of incidents, and an ever-varying sequence of contrasts, but never by the distortion of facts or the violation of probabilities.

On the other hand, how many plays die still-born from the non-application of this principle! When motives and methods true and natural enough in other years are re-dressed in the modern vernacular, and readorned with modern clothes, habits, and manners, no matter how high the literary merit or how great the skill employed, the audience vaguely feels the incongruity, and resents the unnatural union between opposing and unassimilative types.

In the development of the American drama a promising feature is the tendency toward realism as opposed to conventionalism. By realism should be inferred not actualism, but the artistic representation of reality. This proposition verges on very debatable ground. Every recent essay toward putting the actual upon the boards has met with unbounded applause from the galleries and a portion of the parquet. The success of live horses and a real steam fire-engine in one play, of a fiery steed in *Mazeppa* [originally written by John Howard Payne, who closely followed Léopold and Cuvelier's *Mazeppa; ou, Le Cheval Tartare*] and numerous so-called border dramas, of a long assorted lot of water-tanks in aquiferous spectacles, and of a large healthy cow in a new comedy, seem for the moment indisputable evidence to the contrary. Yet the success of these will not be permanent if we are to judge from the past. Within twenty-five years there have been witnessed dramatic productions in which the elephant, buffalo, lion, bear, dog, and donkey were honored stars. All of these children of the menagerie but one have passed into oblivion, the donkey alone remaining. Perhaps no more appropriate result could have been afforded by the law of the survival of the fittest to express the intrinsic value of actualism as opposed to artistic realism.

It is as impossible to exactly reproduce nature upon the stage as upon the easel. Art must have recourse to the principle of suggestiveness. The mimic clatter of hoofs produces the same idea as the visible gallop of a soldier's charger from Right Upper Entrance to Left Lower Entrance, but it does not excite the fear that the animal will plunge into the bass-drum in the orchestra, or convert a mimic town or forest into a wilderness of shattered framework or ruined canvas. The plunge of D'Artagnan into a painted ocean, or of Monte Cristo into an illusory sea, is more natural and thrilling than the shivering leap of a water-proofed heroine into a tank of cold water in midwinter.

We do not appreciate the extent toward which realism has gone in these latter days. A rural scene in Booth's Theatre, New York, not twenty years ago, consisted of a drop-curtain and eight or ten side-pieces, all stock property, and used indiscriminately to represent an American wilderness, and English grove, or a Roman campagna. [. . .]

In the operatic productions at the Metropolitan Opera-house, the stage setting which characterizes Daly's Theatre, the Madison Square, Palmer's, the Broadway, the Lyceum, and fifty other great houses of amusement which might be mentioned, so thoroughly is this law of artistic realism obeyed that vast fortunes are expended, and an army of skilled artisans and artists employed upon the purely mechanical and material portions of the drama.

In the presentation of plays there is ever a conflict between two tendencies or schools, if the fact will allow the use of the term. In one the author or star, after directing the general outlines of the various parts, allows a liberal discretion to each actor in filling the character which had been intrusted to him. In the other, the author or star supplies himself every detail, and trains and drills the actor until he is mechanically "perfect." The one permits, or tends to permit, the display of originality on the part of the individual performer; the other tends to restrict this to a minimum or to destroy it altogether. [. . .]

Excepting in those cases where the author depicts or caricatures a historical or local character, all parts are essentially types. The better the literary and dramatic work, the more comprehensive is the character drawn. When a part is assigned an actor, his ability is displayed by the manner in which he shapes the character. If commonplace, he gives the type and nothing more. If shrewd, he gains from author, critic, or elsewhere some concrete notion out of the ordinary run, and does what is called good work. But if talented, or, rarer still, a genius, he creates an individuality which, while it belongs to the type the author had in view, rises into a personality which attains success, if not fame. [. . .]

Mr. John Grosvenor Wilson's Plea for the Romantic Drama.

My own bent is strongly toward the romantic drama. The old classification of dramatic literature, tragic, comic, and melodramatic, is as applicable and correct as ever, so far as it goes, but to be comprehensive it should include the romantic, in which lofty sentiment, heroic characters, poetic language, and idealized life are presented with those charms of beautiful presentment that make the acted play a picture as well as a poem.

Yet to-day there is no theatre in America devoted to this class of the drama, and there has been little presentation of it in our country beyond the work of Charles Fechter and some occasional experiments by the great stars of the profession. This I should call one of the peculiarities of the drama in America. In the Latin countries it has long flourished, and Henry Irving's fame in London depends upon his romantic productions rather than his tragedy or comedy. Therefore I look forward to a growth of interest in this form of drama as one of the changes likely to occur in America.

The tendency of to-day, it seems to me, is to overdo the realistic. Real steam-engines, ponds of water with naphtha launches afloat therein, and barns with live hens and geese surrounding them, may be excellent adjuncts, but seem to me insufficient to constitute, as they do, the principal attractions of a certain class of the drama. The unusual rather than the commonplace seems the worthier field for ambitious work, although it is true that to the average man the contemplation of the unusual may be tiresome and difficult; and it must be conceded that a certain level of mediocrity is always more popular than work on a higher level can be made.

Perhaps the most striking example of this that has been seen in this country is the wonderful success of *Uncle Tom's Cabin* [1852], which still draws crowds wherever it is presented, in the city or in the country. That play was founded on the best-advertised novel in the world—a timely and most sensational novel dealing with the old eternal sentiments, and presenting the favorite pictures of vice trampling upon virtue, and virtue finally triumphant.

This fact is, to some extent, a hampering influence in the growth of the American drama; for the theatre, in this country at least, must always be a business enterprise, and the manager must always present what pays. [. . .]

The question then is, "What is the perfect play?" I do not see that there is any difference between an American play and any other, excepting that it is written by an American, and may or may not deal with American subjects. To whatever school the play belongs, it should have certain qualities which do not vary. The curtain should go up on a scene which is the absolute and logical outcome of certain events which are supposed to have occurred prior to the beginning of the story. In other words, the play should begin at a strong situation in the story, and should not be an attempt to present all the circumstances which have led to that situation. The first act should then be the inevitable following out of the opening situation to its legitimate and necessary conclusion.

More than that, the end of the first act, which should be its climax—for it must, if the interest is to be kept up, end with a climax—should be the embryo of the first situation in the second act. So the play should proceed through the chosen number of acts, each one being logical as well as dramatic in action, and each leading naturally to the next one, and every development of character and incident being the natural sequence of everything that has preceded it in the whole play. The close must be, of course, the result of all that has been told, not only in general but in detail. No character must be introduced and dropped before the end, or even at the end, with a lame and insufficient conclusion, for every character in the drama must be of sufficient importance to call for a thorough development and an adequate part in the story.

Nor should any character serve only the purpose of forwarding the action of the play, for I hold that, as in a novel, each individual should be a type representing some section of mankind, not merely presenting personal eccentricities. [. . .] The future of the art in this country must be great, for the opportunities are unlimited, and the intelligence of the American worker in this, as in any other direction, is unsurpassed.

Mr. Steele MacKaye on Stage Setting.

The most pleasing feature of the American drama of to-day is the ever-increasing attention paid to stage setting. This is true in a popular as well as in a technical sense. Never before has so much money and thought been directed toward those details on which artistic success depends.

Yet we are far from not only where we ought to be, but from the proud position occupied by the European stage. This is not due to any lack of public spirit, nor to false economy, but partly to the intellectual carelessness of the American public and partly to the absence of the artistic spirit in the general management of theatres. To-day, just as two thousand years ago, the money-changer sits in the temple. The problem that the manager perpetually considers is, "How can I make the most money in the least time?" He seldom asks, "How can I best present the best play by the best people?"

There are scores of magnificent playhouses which are worthy settings of the noblest dramas of the race. But they are desecrated by being the scene of the dramatic imbecility, the serio-comic absurdity, and the meaningless spectacles of the present day. In one respect the manager is not to be blamed. Human nature does pursue the flying dollar, and doubtless will forever. It is only natural in the race for wealth that a manager should at times yield to the temptation of producing a worthless play which will return to him vast profits. He is to blame for not realizing that the highest art, when properly presented, is in the long-run most remunerative. [. . .]

In the mechanics of stage setting the greatest law is that which Ruskin applied to architecture, "Appropriateness, utility, fidelity." Thus, for example, the artisan makes a library scene of impossible painted bookcases, and the furniture of a parlor such as is displayed in an ordinary shop-window. Another artisan presents a ballroom by crowding together as much handsome furniture and useless decoration as the scene will contain. A true artist will have real books and the paraphernalia of scholarship in the one case, and only the furniture and decorations which good-manners and common-sense allow in the other. The artisan merely imitates a fact, while the artist reproduces the fact itself. [. . .]

Another suggestion in regard to artistic stage setting is the increase of comfort provided for both spectator and player. This includes such arrangements as the double and treble stage, the many ingenious devices for lessening labor, for accelerating the necessary work, for increasing the safety and comfortableness behind the curtain, and developing the aesthetic conditions of life for the actor. In this regard commendable progress has been made; so much so that in many respects the American theatre of to-day is altogether a different world from that of two generations ago.

[. . .] the profession is dividing into two great schools—one whose extreme is Henry Irving and the Comédie Francaise, and the other whose extreme is the dime museum. This differentiation promises to be more rapid in the future than in the past. The public at large are slow to assimilate artistic and social conditions, but having already begun to associate buffoonery and stage vulgarity with vulgarity in actual life, it is no wonder that theatre-goers are now patronizing that class of theatres which present the dramas suited to their individual tastes. Thus, ere many years have gone by, there will be a wide demarcation between the great temples of amusement devoted to art and culture and numberless small and cheap playhouses devoted to the inartistic and commonplace recreations of the unthinking.

[354] A. Hennequin. "Characteristics of the American Drama"
The Arena [1890]

[. . .] Turning now, after this long introduction, to the dramas of England and America at the present time, let us consider what French forms we find developed into English types. Two, and two only: The melodrama and the *comédie*. The French melodrama, condemned by the French sense of artistic form, found no such opposition in England. It appealed rather to the English sense of formlessness, or better, perhaps, to the English love of strong effect, even at the sacrifice of formal and technical perfection. It became, therefore, the basis for one leading type of English and American plays. Examine what American play you will, you find in it some traces of melodrama, some straining after effect by means of exaggerated sentiments, language, or characterization, introduced heedlessly at the expense of artistic moderation and naturalness. Adding to this quality, the social element borrowed from the French *drame*, we may set down as one prevalent type of American plays the social melodrama.

The other principle type is derived, as I have said, from the French *comédie*, a word which is susceptible of a great variety of meanings but which I am here using to include what corresponds in France to our comedy of incidents, and comedy of manners. [. . .] The French *comédies*, therefore, which have had influence in this country, range all the way from dignified comedy, properly so called, to screaming farces. Of these it is the comedies of incidents and the light farce which have left upon our playwrights the most lasting impress.

We have now seen what are the sources from which the American drama draws its models. Let us consider for a moment the environment of the American playwright and the demands upon him by his audience.

In America the theatre is a play-house, the play is a show. Splendid as has been the history of the drama, sacred as are the associations which cluster about the names of the great dramatists,—for the great body of the higher class of English-speaking peoples, theatrical performances are still placed, as they were in the period of dominant Puritanic influence, on a par with bear-baiting and rope walking,—actors are still rated in some quarters but a degree above vagrants and sturdy beggars; the stage is regarded much as a mediæval baron regarded the antics of the court fool. So long as the fellow's sallies were amusing he was given full liberty, but if he dared to speak his mind in seriousness, to the stocks with him! The American audience will consent to be amused by its drama or to be moved to fictitious sorrow, but it will not patiently permit itself to be instructed. It will submit to rank and fustian ineffable, to buffoonery and horse-play unspeakable, but it will not listen to the discussion of a serious social problem. The amusement must be laughable, but nothing more.

Nor will it suffer itself to be instructed or amused in what it calls an immoral way. It likes to see virtue rewarded and vice sent to the penitentiary. [. . .]

This shrinking from the immoral precludes the discussion of what are known as delicate questions—in brief of the one question which forms the central motive of so many French dramas. Adultery may, indeed, be hinted at in American plays, as it may even form an important element of the plot, but it must not be seriously discussed or even presented as a problem. The dramatist must let us see his opinion, and that opinion must be openly, definitely, unhesitatingly condemnatory. In fact, the subject must not be presented as a question at all, but as a sin. [. . .]

What, then, are the requirements of the American drama? We have seen that two main types of plays have come down to us through the French, and we have considered some of the leading peculiarities of the American audiences. Combining these two ideas, we may arrive at the following characteristics as being *in the main* those most likely to prove successful in American plays:—

1. Strong melodramatic situations.
2. Farcical scenes and incidents.
3. Horse-play, song, and dance, etc.
4. Moral sentiments.
5. Poetic justice.

[. . .] We see that up to the present time the efforts of English and American playwrights to satisfy the public have produced mongrel compositions built upon French originals. This is the present state of the American drama. Does not the hope of the future drama lie in the possibility that some dramatist will break away from the French traditions and either return to the earlier source of inspiration, or else find here on native soil the spring whose waters fill us with immortal thirst?

[358] D. Boucicault. "The Future American Drama"
The Arena [1890]

There is not, and there never has been, a literary institution, which could be called the American Drama. We have produced no dramatists essentially American to rival such workers as Fenimore Cooper, Bret Harte, Hawthorne, Mrs. Harriet Beecher Stowe, and others of world-wide reputation in the realms of narrative fiction. So long as our stage could be supplied from the English or French theatres, there appeared no necessity for home-made material. [. . .] What is good enough for London is no longer good enough for New York. [. . .] London and Paris are no longer names to conjure with now and here in 1890, as they were in 1870. But, on the other hand and meanwhile, we find the *Old Homestead* [by G. L. Aiken, 1856], *The Wife* [by David Belasco and Henry C. De Mille, 1887], *Held by the Enemy* [by William Gillette, 1886], the *Charity Ball* [by David Belasco and Henry C. De Mille, 1889], *Shenandoah* [by Bronson Howard, 1888], *The Henrietta* [by Bronson Howard, 1887], the

County Fair [by Charles Barnard and Neil Burgess, 1889], the *Senator* [by David D. Lloyd, 1889], *Paul Kauvar* [by James Steele MacKaye, 1887], and other native American productions have eclipsed their European rivals. Thus within the last two or three years our home-made plays have asserted their value: partly because our playwrights have improved and advanced in their craft, but mainly because the French and English dramatic authors are played out, and so we are thrown upon our own resources. May this attitude so suddenly assumed be regarded as the small beginning of a declaration of dramatic independence on the part of our people? Is it the baby drama of the future? If so, do these works, or any of them, present new features or new form giving promise of a new issue? [. . .]

But the French stage has recently taken a new departure; it has received a new vocation. The drama is no longer an imitation of human passions and weaknesses; it is a philosophical school of sociology, for the illustration and argument of ethical problems! The incidents in this new form should be of natural, ordinary occurrence, without contrivance, the skill of the dramatist being that he should show none. The language may not transcend the commonplace colloquy of every-day intercourse.

It is true, the dramatists of the new school do not profess to compose tragedies or comedies. They write what we denominate domestic dramas, which are to dramatic literature what photographs are to the Fine Arts. No one disputes the correctness to be found in a photograph; it is a minute copy of Nature, but there are qualities in a painting which no mechanical result can supply. I deny that the drama is, or ever was intended to be, a copy of Nature, as the new apostles of naturalism have preached that it should be. [. . .]

But it is not our business, at present, to discuss the question of naturalism in literature, it concerns our subject only to discern how far it is likely to affect the drama, and especially the future drama of America. However, what is called naturalism as we find it exemplified in the works of Zola, his imitators, and followers, may thrive on public censure, when presented in a narrative form; it is otherwise when it challenges public opinion in a theatre. Could there be found an American audience content to tolerate the representation of scenes and the utterance of language so filthy? The drama has been stigmatized as the most profligate form of literature, the stage has been proscribed for indecency and libertinage. I ask, in all sobriety, if we could obtain a theatre full of spectators, all of whom had read Zola in private, would that crowd endure to have the scenes there depicted, presented before them; would they tolerate the language? Would they not drive the scenes from the stage? [. . .]

I believe in the public *en masse*; I believe there is in the mass of minds, when unified on the consideration of any matter, and provided they are free from prejudice on such matter, a mental power, and a justice of opinion that no individual in that crowd could exercise. [. . .]

[. . .] And what is success? It is simply the consensus of those wretched creatures whose opinions we are bound to despise; it is the fiat of the people. I am not to be misguided by Shakespere's contempt for them. Firstly, because there was no public in his time,—of course, I mean an educated mass. And secondly, Shakespere entertained a weak prejudice in favor of rank and birth; he was anti-republican every time.

If we press these circumstances on the attention of the reader, it is because the Future Drama of America is with our people, and with their voice, the Press. With the people mainly because the publication of a play is made in their presence, and their opinions are formed and expressed before they can be influenced by press notices,—the newspapers can only repeat and circulate these opinions, or attempt to modify them by critical protest, but the public verdict is supreme and final. The jury is composed here, as it was composed in Greece, of the people, and the drama is, therefore, made by the collaboration of the people and the poet. And this is as it should be. It behooves us to consider what are the tendencies of the people, for the coming American dramatist will inevitably receive the germinating principle from the intellectual atmosphere he breathes, and not from any impregnation by an effete European source, which is confessedly done with. Is there anything in this new school of naturalism which can affect our future drama? We have discarded the artificialities of the old melodrama, and the epigram in modern comedy is out of fashion. Tragedy for the moment is retired from the stage, and it is very doubtful if in the next generation, say in the year 1920, a single artistic descendant of Booth and Forrest will be in existence. The transcendental drama will probably be regarded with as much curiosity as the unfolding of a mummy,—for such would be now the performance of *Comus* [by John Milton, 1634, published in 1637], or of the *Mourning Bride* [by William Congreve, 1697]. But as Nature never proceeds by leaps, let us endeavor to discern the direction and inclination of the people, and forecast, as well as the present may indicate, the form of the future.

The American community differs essentially from every other of which we have any record. A ready made, polyglot population has inflowed into this land. [. . .] This new people has not had time to fuse thoroughly the races of which it is composed, and as the arts are the product of a mature and virile condition of the brain, they can find no residence here where there is no central organ, which can be recognized as the brain of the nation. In other words, we have no metropolis, no mother city. New York, in population and in wealth, claims to be the third in rank amongst the cities of the world, coming next after London and Paris: but population and wealth do not constitute a metropolis. A metropolis is the mother city of a nation, from whose breast flow the arts and sciences: and in this respect New York comes far behind the puny capitals of European States, which are more important to the human race than we are. They represent something, we represent nothing—except size. The arts in the United States are foreigners that have never become naturalized. [. . .]

There are two cogent reasons why the arts cannot hope for, much less expect, that national support which is extended to them on the continent of Europe. The first is that the shop-keeping English race from which we derive our being, have never regarded the aesthetic side of life as a serious matter, concerning the people in government. The second is the jealousy naturally existing between the States in Congress, when the question arises for the expenditure of any large amount of money to support an establishment to be located in one city. But if New York could afford to expend ten or fifteen millions upon a world's fair—a temporary show of questionable advantage,—why may we not spend a fifth of that amount in the erection of a university of the arts,—a building sheltering music, painting, sculpture, and schools of oratory and the drama? If the Central Park can assign a lot to a zoological garden, for the exhibition of beasts, surely it would give a space for such a Conservatory. It might be made self-supporting, so its first cost might be its only cost. Looked at from a "business" point of view, it would attract from the various States students, male and female, who with their families would furnish an artistic quarter in the city. [. . .]

The condition of the dramatic field in the United States is fully described by Shakespere in Hamlet's lines: "It is an unweeded garden that grows to seed—things rank and foul in Nature possess it merely." Such as the soil is, in intelligence and fine aspirations,—for the American people yield to none in these respects,—it is used to grow the most worthless and gaudy weeds. The prominent features of the theatre are burlesque operetta, and the kind of farce we used to call extravaganza. The money changers have displaced the priests in the temple. The burlesque operetta is a hybrid, produced by a mixture of the old English burlesque, the French opera bouffe, and negro minstrelsy. The prominent comedian is the "end man" who has washed his face,—the leading soprano is the showleg prince of the fairy burlesque of our youth, and the whole is tossed in the French omelette pan, seasoned with waltz music. This piece of nonsense is offered for the serious appreciation of our public as the important subject and feature of our drama!

In the United States there are but four theatres devoted legitimately to the cultivation of the drama; of which three are in New York and one in Boston. And these theatres are the smallest in the cities; so little accommodation is required for the audience likely to patronize the better kind of play. Elsewhere and throughout this great country the Drama is a tramp. The theatres regard her as a transient guest, here to-day, gone to-morrow, or a bag man who brings on show samples of goods. Thus it is in New York, where its principal theatres let lodgings by the week to stars, and managers are merely janitors.

Let the condition of Paris or London be compared with that of New York. There is not in either European capital a single star theatre, that is, a theatre where the season is devoted to a weekly change of entertainment; this practice is reserved for the provinces. Each theatre has its special character and a company of comedians associated with it. But the American cities are provincial, and even in the few small theatres that entertain fixed companies, one depends on the German stage, another relies on English plays in preference to risking the production of American works, which have pushed themselves into notice in the theatres of less pretension, at the risk perhaps of the authors, or of some actor desirous of obtaining a "pedestal" play. He uses New York as a fence on which to post his bills and reap the profits of this advertisement in the provincial towns.

When I visited the United States for the first time in 1853, the drama was in a more promising state. Three theatres, Wallack's, Burton's, Niblo's were representative, and admirably equipped for the performance of comedy and ballet pantomime. In the following year when visiting Philadelphia, I found in one stock company John Gilbert, Lizzie Weston Davenport, Joseph Jefferson, John S. Clarke, A. Davenport, and others of equal calibre, whose names I cannot recall. At that time there was a body of much better actors in the United States than I had left in England, but the drama was imported; no attempt was made at independence in this respect.

The public has changed in this generation, and are eager now to recognize and support a native American drama. The managers fail to recognize this revolution, but they must come to it.

Tragedy and high comedy will always be held in respect on the future American stage, but it seems probable that the drama of modern life, the reflex of the period, will prevail over every other kind of entertainment. This drama will present a character or a group of characters, not a complicated or sensational action, affording a physiological study by way of illustration, not by way of description. The ingenious comedy of intrigue and the drama of incident, the artifice of which resembles a mechanical contrivance, rather than the simple outcome and result of incidents flowing naturally to their catastrophe, has surfeited the audience with dramas and comedies that are really more like tricks on the cards, than exhibiting the game of life. Of this legerdemain, the French stage of the present century affords numerous examples. We are done with it. [. . .]

The drama of the future will be prosaic and positive. Its grandeur will be in its truth—truth in its purity, its delicacy, and tenderness. Pathos will assume the place of passion. The plot, a subject simple and perspicuous, will be designed with one object, not to surprise the spectator with startling incident. The incidents will be merely contrivances to exhibit the characters.

The American mind is rather philosophic and scientific than poetic. It is positive and inquisitive. Its scope is the reach of our senses, and its imagination is bounded by its information. It is sensitive of the ridiculous, so it watches flights of fancy with a smile, and applauds the rocket, but reckons it all up without any emotion, inclining to regard poetic effusion as a kind of fireworks, and rhetoric as fustian.

The dramatic resources of France, England, and Germany, appear to be exhausted. The dramatic power has always exhibited itself in the early periods of a nation's growth; when the race is young and mentally vigorous, the dramatists appeared and flourished. America has not got out of her teens; she is still growing. But that she will take the lead in the nations in intelligence is as certain as that she will surpass them in stature.

There are two features which will probably appear in the near future of our drama. One of these is a theatre where the engrossing subject of the hour will be exhibited, and performed as dramas of the period, illustrating great current events as closely as the pictorial newspapers present such to their readers,—be it the adventures of the discoverers in Equatorial Africa, a Brazilian revolution, or Siberian revolt. In this manner was written the *Relief of Lucknow* [Dion Boucicault's *Jessie Brown; or, The Relief of Lucknow*], produced in 1858. During the siege of Lucknow, while that city was still invested by the Sepoy mutineers, this piece was played in New York. This was called the "contemporaneous" drama. The other kind to which I refer, will incline to deal with the popular problems of the hour, whether social or scientific. Such as hypnotism; the inheritance of criminal proclivities, which Zola, Ibsen, and their followers maintain to be constitutional and irrepressible; the great struggle between labor and capital; representations of the millennium, described by such dreamers as Mr. Bellamy. *The American, who is nothing if not utilitarian, would enjoy a theatre put to such uses*, properly,—that is, by the true dramatic process. Independently of this matter, which will be the *object*, not necessarily the *subject*, of the play, an amusing or interesting action must prevail over every other consideration. And above all the interest must be domestic; for there is as much romance, as much poetry, and frequently more real tragedy in our home life than in all the works of imagination.

[360] A. Hennequin. "The Drama of the Future"
The Arena [1891]

[. . .] I have in mind particularly the very positive assertion of a Western critic, who, in commenting upon some utterances of mine concerning the rules of dramatic construction, says, "People in the plays of the future are going to come on and get off the stage as often and as sensibly as they naturally would and should. The day of the 'heavy,' the 'ingénue' is over. There will be no 'prepared climax' arranged to top off the auditor's expectations with a delightful quiver of emotion. There will be no artificial scissoring off of dramas into acts, so many minutes to the act and so much spasmodic, rhapsodical sensation to each quarter of an hour. Things will go on very much as they do in real life."

We have all heard something like this from other sources. Mr. Howells, in his daintily cynical way, and Mr. Archer, in his brusquely snappish way, have said much the same thing. The old machinery of dramatic technique is to be pitched into the street. Mr. Archer will show Shakespeare the door to make way for Ibsen. Mr. Howells will politely give the *congé* to the spirit of Romantic Drama to make way for—Mr. Howells!

That the drama of the future, if it is to be worth seeing, will be in some respects different from the drama of the present, there can be not the slightest question. [. . .] but what I maintain and propose to show in this paper is that the prophet-critics, whom I have mentioned, have not succeeded in forecasting the nature of the change. In other words, the elements of the drama with which it has been proposed to dispense, are those without which we cannot have any drama at all.

What is it that constitutes a drama? There are two essentials: first, portrayal of life; secondly, action. Take out either element, and you have left a nondescript which may or may not be worth serious attention, but which certainly is not, in any rational sense, a drama. Let us consider the two, throwing emphasis on each in turn.

The drama is a portrayal of life, but it is a portrayal by means of action. It will need, therefore, *characters* in whom this active life shall be made manifest, and a *stage* upon which these characters shall be marshalled before the eyes of the spectators. Whatever changes may take place in the nature of the drama, these two features, we may be sure, will always be retained.

Now, if we inquire into the character of the drama as it actually exists at the present time; that is, as it is known by actors and stage managers, not as it is theorized by those who have gained their experience from the orchestra chair, we shall find that all characters as they are assigned to actors, are classified under a few general heads. [. . .] The cast of a stock company, for example, may comprise a leading man, a first old man, a comedian, a second old man, a light comedian, a juvenile, a leading lady, a first old woman, a soubrette, and an ingénue. This is one of the things which the modern playwright must take into consideration. As things are now constituted, it is well for him, if he hopes ever to see his play produced, not to put in characters haphazard, but to see that he has these various classes in their proper proportion. And this is where our friends, the prophets, utter their first note of warning. All these conventional characters, they tell us, are becoming, or have already become, painfully antiquated. There shall be no more ingénues, neither any engaging of leading heavies. The dramatist of the future will no longer be trammelled by these fetters of an ancient tradition, but will be free to choose and arrange his *dramatis personae* to suit his own sweet will.

I wish the dramatist of the next generation all possible freedom, but that he will escape this particular constraint, if it be one, I cannot for an instant concede. Were these names mere theoretical terms arbitrarily devised by the ingenuity of some bookish critic, then we might expect to see them superseded by the next new fashion of the hour. They are not, however, of this character. They are names for classifications that have their correspondences in the actual world, of which the mimic world of the stage is the counterpart. Go out into the world and seek your characters, say the leaders of the new school. Very well, let us take our stand on this street corner, where the stream of humanity whirls past in bewildering multifariousness of race, age, and temperament. At first all is confusion. No two persons seem alike. [. . .] We begin involuntarily to try to assign each individual to some general type, and if we study the throng long enough and carefully enough, we shall soon be able to do so with all. Now if the observer have the dramatic faculty, and in addition be familiar with the conventional names of the stock characters of the drama, he will be surprised to find how readily they may be applied to the persons whom he sees passing before him. Let him but think of the passers-by as characters in a play, and each will at once fall into his proper category. [. . .]

The drama as a portrayal of life calls not only for characters, but for a stage. We have it on excellent authority, that all the world is a stage; and not a few heralds of the new order of dramatic things imagine, I should say, that it is upon this stage that the drama of the future is to be presented. If I understand them rightly, they propose that what are known as "theatrical conventions" shall give way to the realities of actual life. By theatrical conventions in the best sense is meant those peculiarities of dramatic representations which grow out of the conditions of the environment, the architectural arrangement of the theatre and the like, and which seem violations of the logic of ordinary life. [. . .] The question of stage realism is an old one, as old at any rate as Aristotle; but it seems to me that no one has come nearer the truth than [. . .] Charles Lamb. In his essay on "Stage Illusions" [see *The Works of Charles Lamb*, ed. William Macdonald, 12 vols. (London: Dent, 1903), 2: 29–30] he says: "The actor who plays the annoyed man must a little desert nature; he must, in short, be thinking of the audience, and express only so much dissatisfaction and peevishness as is consistent with the pleasure of comedy. In other words, his perplexity must seem half put on. [. . .] In some cases a sort of compromise may take place, and all the purposes of dramatic delight be attained by a judicious understanding, not too openly announced, between the ladies and gentlemen—on both sides of the curtain."

[. . .] "A judicious understanding, not too openly announced, between the ladies and gentlemen on both sides of the curtain,"—is not that what all proper stage convention comes to? We, of the audience, recognize the fact that you, of the stage, are not at home in your own houses. We understand well enough that you are talking to us in an unnaturally loud voice out of the centre of a great awkward, complex machine full of ropes, pulleys, traps, and ladders, and painted canvases. We know well enough that your daggers are made of lath, and your champagne of cold tea, and that your faces are covered with paint. We know very well when you say, "An hour has passed," that in reality it has not been fifteen minutes. But we shall not complain. We have a judicious understanding with you. You, on your side, agree to do the best you can to entertain us with the means at hand; we on our side agree to make allowances for the conventional character of the instrument through which you bring before us the conception of the dramatist. [. . .]

It is not hard to explain how this idea that the drama is to throw away its conventional elements has arisen. It has come about, I take it, through the theorizing of men who are accustomed to writing novels and stories, but are not at home in stageland. When they read plays or try to write them, they imagine the lines are being read, not as being acted and heard. They think of men and women as moving about in the freer world of the novel, not as taking their carefully learned steps upon the boards of a theatre. The plays that such men write strike the novel-reader as admirable. What character! What nobleness of sentiment! But the actor who is called upon to interpret them, and without whose aid they cannot come to a dramatic birth, reads them with contracted eyebrows. "Very pretty story, but not adapted for the stage," is the verdict in nine cases out of ten; and if this verdict is appealed from, the higher court of the public rarely fails to confirm it with costs to the unlucky dramatist. [. . .]

The stage remaining what it is (and practically it has suffered no change worth speaking of since the days of the mystery and miracle plays), the dramas of the future, so far as their forms are determined, will be governed by the same laws of dramatic construction which prevail at the present day. Whether the play is realistic or idealistic, psychological or meteorological, it will as of old have its lines, its monologues, its exposition, its stage business, its climax and its catastrophe. It will have its conventionalities just as a picture will always have perspective. It will have characters that are artless and simple, and characters that are malignant, call them ingénue and villain, or whatever you like. It will have a stage with its "exteriors" and "interiors," "entrances," "wings," "traps," and "flats." It will have special features and devices of dialogue for the purpose of conveying certain kinds of information to the audience. It will have its own conventional time, which will go fast or slow as the dramatist shall choose. It will be rendered by actors who will employ overloud tones of voice and make exaggerated gestures and pretend to do all sorts of things, which they do not do in fact. They will have set times for coming and going off, and if one character plays two parts he will have time allowed him to make a change of dress and "make-up." So it has always been; so, we may be very sure, it always will be. [. . .]

[361] [Herne's *Margaret Fleming*: "An Epoch–Marking Drama"]
The Arena [1891]

A movement destined, I think, to be in a degree epoch-marking in the dramatic annals of the American stage, was inaugurated by Mr. James A. Herne, on the fourth of May, in Boston, in the production of his remarkable realistic drama, *Margaret Fleming*, at Chickering Hall. The play is a bold innovation, so much so that no theatre in the city would produce it, although the various managers who examined it declared it to be as strong as and no less powerful than any American drama yet written. [. . .] The superb acting of Mr. and Mrs. Herne contributed much to the success of the play; curiosity also doubtless attracted many, yet beyond and above this was the deep appreciation of a thoughtful and intelligent constituency, who saw in this drama the marvellous possibilities of the stage for improvement as well as entertainment. They also saw real life depicted. The absence of empty lines and stilted phrases so common in conventional drama was refreshing and interesting to those who believe that the drama has a mission other than merely to amuse. *Margaret Fleming* is nothing if not artistic from the standpoint of the realist. Its fidelity to life as we find it—to existing conditions and types of society,—is wonderful. Its dramatic strength is none the less marked. But aside from and above all this, for me it has a far greater merit—utility. I have no sympathy with the flippant, effeminate, and senile cry, "Art for art's sake" [. . .].

The theatre may be made the most potent engine for progress and reform. We are living in the midst of the most splendid age which has dawned since humanity first fronted the morning, dimly conscious of its innate power and the possibilities that lay imbedded in its being; an era of life, growth, warfare. On the one hand are ancient thought and prejudice, on the other the inspiration of greater liberty and a nobler manhood. On the one hand selfishness, sensuality, vulgar ostentation, avarice, luxury, and moral effeminacy crying, "Art for art's sake," demanding amusements that will aid in dissipating any moral strength or deep thought that still lingers in the mind, and literature that shall enable one to kill time without the slightest suspicion of intellectual exertion; physical, mental, and moral ennui, with an assumed lofty contempt for utility. On the other hand we have the gathering forces of the dawn, demanding "art for progress," declaring that beauty must be the hand-maid of duty; that art must wait on justice, liberty, fraternity, nobility, morality, and intellectual honesty,—in a word the forces in league with light must compel the beautiful to make radiant the pathway of the future. In the union of art and utility lies the supreme excellence of *Margaret Fleming*, it deals with one of the most pressing problems of our present civilization; it is the most powerful plea for an equal standard of morals for men and women that I have ever heard. This thought, it is true, like the entire drama, is anything but conventional; it breathes the spirit of the coming day.

[363] H. Garland. "Mr. and Mrs. Herne"
The Arena [1891]

In May last, in a small hall in Boston [Chickering Hall], on a stage of planking, hung with drapery, was produced one of the most radical plays from a native author ever performed in America. Mr. and Mrs. James A. Herne, unable to obtain a hearing in the theatres for their play, which had been endorsed by some of the best known literary men of the day, were forced to hire a hall, and produce *Margaret Fleming* bare of all mechanical illusion, and shorn of all its scenic and atmospheric effects. Everybody, even their friends, prophesied disaster. In such surroundings failure seemed certain. But a few who knew the play and its authors better, felt confident that there was a public for them. It was a notable event, and the fame of *Margaret Fleming* is still on its travels across the dramatic world.

There were two reasons for this result, the magnificent art of Mrs. Herne, which "created illusion by its utter simplicity and absolute truth to life," and second, because the play was, in fact, as one critic said, "an epoch-marking play." It could afford to dispense with canvas, bunch-lights, machinery, as it dispensed with conventional plot and epithet, and as its actors discarded declamation and mere noise. [...]

One of the most noticeable and gratifying results of Mr. and Mrs. Herne's performance was the forced abandonment by the critics of conventional standards of criticism. Every thoughtful word, even by those most severe, was made from the realist's standpoint. It forced a comparison with life and that was a distinct gain.

The critics got at last the point of view of those who praise an imperfect play simply for its honesty of purpose, and its tendency. My own criticism of *Margaret Fleming* is that it lacks the simplicity of life. It has too much of plot. Things converge too much, and here and there things happen. Measured by the standard of truth it fails at two or three points in its construction, though its treatment is markedly direct and honest. Measured by any play on the American stage, it stands above them all in purpose, in execution, in power, and is worthy to stand for the new drama. It was exposed to the severest test, and came out of it triumphantly. What the effect will be upon the American drama, it would be hard to say. Certainly whether great or small, that influence will be toward progress, an influence that is altogether good.

Already it has precipitated the discussion of an independent American theatre, where plays of advanced thought and native atmosphere can be produced. It has given courage to many who (being in the minority) had given up the idea of ever having a play after their ideal. It has cleared the air and showed the way out of the *cul de sac* into which monopoly seemed to have driven plays and players. It demonstrated that a small theatre makes the production of literary plays possible, and the whole field is opening to the

American dramatist. The fact that the lovers of truth and art are in the minority, no longer cuts a figure. The small theatre makes a theatre for the minority not only possible, but inevitable. [. . .]

[364] E. Fuller. "An Independent Theatre"
Lippincott's Monthly Magazine [1892]

[. . .] Since the ideals which the American advocates of an Independent Theatre hold are still but vaguely defined, it is perhaps fair to take the concrete instance furnished by the production of [James A. Herne's] *Margaret Fleming* [1891] as coming near to a realization of them. We know that, in the words of one writer, "the laying bare of the social problem" is proposed as an important end. No one who has seen *Margaret Fleming*, either in New York or in Boston, will accuse the author of undue reserve. It is described as a plea for purity in man, and it "lays bare the social problem" with a frankness hard to distinguish from indecency. The story may be briefly summarized. Philip Fleming, married to Margaret, has had an intrigue with another woman, who bears him a child, forgives him, and dies. The wife comes upon the scene, finds the child crying for sustenance, and after a severe mental struggle catches it to her breast and nurses it. This is the real climax of the play, and a sweet and decent climax it is. Then Margaret is stricken blind and goes mad, but recovers her wits in time to lecture her husband *à la* Nora Helmer in *A Doll's House*, and to tell him how she loathes him and can never forgive him. And this, save for some repulsive studies of depravity in the minor characters, is all there is to Mr. Herne's "unconventional" study of social life in America, the lesson of which appears to be that if a man ought to be pure a woman ought to be vindictive. To unaccustomed nostrils the moral stench of the play is intolerable, whether foot-baths or the state of the infant stomach, adultery or insanity, are under discussion. I do not mean to plead for the ethical standard of the Young Person. But I do not think that art will ever make any progress by overstepping the bounds of taste, or that the theatre can be reformed by revolt against the principles to which all our great dramatists in the past have held.

And yet there is a field for the establishment of an Independent Theatre, if by that is meant a theatre sufficiently endowed to be independent of any consideration outside of those suggested by art. If our reformers will lead off in this direction, they will find many followers, even among such inferior cattle as actors and critics. As government aid seems to be out of the question, such a theatre must depend upon private liberality. In the present state of the public taste, it is a safe rule that the profit from a play is in inverse ratio to its excellence. A large annual deficit, therefore, would have to be counted upon, at least at the outset. Are there any wealthy men who would be willing to spend their money in this way? It has been shown how much private effort may do for musical culture; and universities and hospitals and libraries are founded almost every month in the year. Will there rise up some munificent patron of dramatic art? And if this should come to pass, upon what lines should the endowed theatre be conducted? It would be fatal to give it over to fads, as I fear that most of the advocates of the Independent Theatre would wish to do. [. . .] The man at the head of the new institution should combine with courage and with culture a practical knowledge of the playhouse and long experience in theatrical management. [. . .] The next requisite would be a carefully-chosen company of actors [. . .]. The vicious "star" system has made such a company more and more difficult to get together; but it can be done, and the training which the new theatre would give might in time furnish outside managers with more skilful artists than modern hodge-podge methods are likely to develop. For now one man in his time no longer plays many parts; and whatever talent he has gets an eccentric and abnormal twist, until manner becomes mere mannerism. Our endowed theatre would help to obviate this evil.

The production of good plays—new or old—is even of more consequence than the training of good actors. Although this age exalts the interpreter at the expense of the creator, "the play's the thing" after all. [. . .] An Independent Theatre should not be the mouth-piece of a school; it should rest firmly upon the traditions of art, in which case it would have to give the pseudo-realism of the time the cold shoulder. In brief, the development of the drama and not the exploitation of sociological fads should be its object. And it would have the unacted classical drama to draw upon. [. . .]

Are these the objects which the promoters of the Independent Theatre purpose to accomplish? If they are, then no sincere friend of the drama will withhold earnest and cordial support. Unfortunately, none of that band of enthusiasts has done or said anything so far to inspire the belief that such support is asked or can be given. [. . .]

The demand that life shall be set forth "as we see it" is another of those observations the bearing of which depends upon their application. The point from which we take our survey chiefly determines the value of our record. It is not so much the object as the medium which we must consider. Life as it is, in the customary sense of this overworked phrase, is an impossibility in art. Those who think differently have the eye of the naturalist, not the eye of the artist. The criticism which extols a play for trivial realities that have no aesthetic value is as profitless as that which applauds a live ox and a genuine buzz-saw; and it is as childish as that of the uneducated person who declares that a certain painting suits him because the flowers look as if he could pluck them. The theatre is little likely to be advanced by pseudo-realism of this type. If the Independent Theatre has nothing better to offer, if its purposes are not as large as the noble art which it is anxious to restore, then we may as well look for our aesthetic redemption to the writers of the popular burlesque. They at least give us bad art without pretending that it is good.

[369] H. Modjeska. "Endowed Theatres and the American Stage"
Forum [1892]

[. . .] It seems to me that there is no danger in America which can be said to threaten the future existence of the stage. In this country new theatres are built every day; every day new stars appear on the histrionic horizon; every day new companies and new combinations are formed. This is not surprising, for the stage offers a large field for financial investment and speculation. One can get a higher rent from a theatre than from almost any other kind of building. The work of the theatrical manager is comparatively very easy, as it consists mostly of "filling dates"; that is, of finding enough so-called attractions to give performances during the whole of the theatrical season. Such work does not require any artistic or literary education or any preliminary training. There is also in this land of possibilities and ambitions a vast number of candidates for histrionic honors, and their prospects seem always bright. But the future of the stage and the future of dramatic art and dramatic literature are very different from each other.

The increasing number of theatres and of theatrical organizations in America proves only one thing; that is, the increase in the public desire here for theatrical performances. The population of the cities and even of the minor towns here grows at a wonderful rate; besides, the general welfare and the natural need of recreation after a day's hard work or after a day of idleness are certainly incentives for some outside excitement. This is, however, not the ultimate *desideratum* of dramatic art. No harm is done if a manager fill his pockets or if an actor or actress acquire a fortune. But is this the manner in which a higher standard of dramatic art can be attained? Are pastime on one side and speculation on the other the only objects for which the theatre exists? Is there not a higher object than either of these?

When I came to America, there were many things in the theatrical methods and customs prevailing here that puzzled me. The first thing I noticed as strange was the manner in which theatrical performances were advertised. Huge posters, lithographs, quotations from the press on the bills, pictures of Shakespeare standing side by side with advertisements of patent medicines and dog-shows were placed in such a way as to catch the eye of every passer-by and disfigure the walls. This brutal custom of bringing the people to the theatre by means of elaborate prints and a bragging style struck me very disagreeably at first, but little by little I came to understand that it was adopted and sanctioned by even the best actors of this country, for the reason that it was the only way to attract the public. On the continent in Europe, however, the people are always on the lookout for everything that is going on in the artistic world, and a small sheet of paper is sufficient to notify them of performances. Another surprise awaited me when I took up a newspaper and looking eagerly for theatrical notices found them under the heading of "Amusements," and, to cap the climax, discovered, just beneath an elaborate criticism on the performance of *Julius Caesar*, an account of a show of trained monkeys. [...]

One of the strongest proofs of the relatively small importance of the theatres in the United States is the lack of buildings built solely for the drama. In Europe, theatres bear the character of public buildings and are situated in a square with plenty of space around them. Here nearly all of them are crowded between the shops in business streets. They present externally very slight indication of their exceptional character, except by means of a signboard and a frame with photographs of actors and actresses exposed in the open lobby. In some large cities the manager of to-day attempts by adorning the front entrances of his building to give it something of an artistic air; but in the majority of towns the lack of respect for the appearance of the theatre is appalling. Very often one has to pass through a drug store to the stage, and both of those establishments are frequently under the same management. The arrangements behind the scenes are still worse, and though I have learned not to expect too much, I cannot be reconciled to the appearance of the stage entrances and to the condition of the dressing-rooms. [...] These inconveniences and drawbacks, however, are trifles in comparison with the greater evils which affect the character of dramatic art in this country, the main one of which is a complete lack of stock companies.

In place of stock companies we have the modern system of travelling stars and combinations. There is nothing more detrimental to the actor, nothing more injurious to the advancement and development of his art, than the constant shifting on his part from one place to the other, and, what is still worse, the run of the same play hundreds of times, until the actor's work becomes nothing more than a mechanical and weary reproduction of his part night after night, and his only desire is that it may soon be over. [...]

Why do the great actors of this country travel from place to place instead of remaining in the large cities? There is one main reason: the lack of an endowed theatre, where the principal talent of the country, having an assured sustenance, may, without regard to the future, be devoted exclusively to artistic pursuits. Great actors would thus create a standard which would be authoritative in matters of dramatic art. It would be impossible for a single person, even of the most prominent standing, to keep up in any of the American cities a stock company devoted purely to legitimate drama and comedy. [...] It is true that there are several stock companies in New York. The organizations of Augustin Daly, [Albert Marshall] Palmer, and [Daniel] Frohman, as well as the cheerful home of local comedy under [Edward] Harrigan, answer in part to the wants that permanent theatres ought to supply. There is also a stock company of old standing and reputation in Boston—the Boston Museum. All these companies contain excellent talent; they are conducted with sagacity and artistic knowledge; they possess a public of their own. And yet we see that even they lose sometimes their best actors or sublet their theatres to inferior organizations; that they are compelled to make long runs of pieces of poor intrinsic merit, mostly translations, and that only occasionally they can afford to give performances of a legitimate order. Is there no remedy for this degraded condition of American dramatic art?

There is no remedy except in the establishment of endowed theatres independent of the money question. The supremacy of such institutions, supplied with superior talent, artistic management, and elevated repertory, would soon be acknowledged by a public so quick to appreciate as the American people. This would naturally improve the taste and necessarily react upon the conduct of other theatres. There is no question that they would attract a great many persons who, disgusted with present conditions, rarely or never go to the playhouse. Such theatres, if obliged by the provisions of their endowment to produce the classic works of dramatic literature, would at the same time offer a ready hospitality to the best modern plays and bring to the front new authors, exciting emulation among the foremost writers of the country. A few great actors and innumerable so-called stars and combinations cannot furnish opportunities for the development of dramatic literature. The plays now written are mostly well or ill fitted dresses, made to order for each individual star, pieces of one part; or else they are conglomerations of scenic effects adapted to the capacity of the company, where the author sometimes has little to do, the ingenious actors having burdened the lines with their own inventions. [. . .]

Instead of being itself a guide in matters of refinement and art, the stage of to-day is guided merely by the question of attractiveness and knows no higher aim than the receipts of the box-office; instead of trying to improve the public taste, it panders to the tastes of the majority. [. . .] Is there anything more noticeable than the increasing vulgarity, falsely called realism, of the plays that nowadays achieve the greatest success? [. . .]

An endowed theatre is conducted on the basis of a stock company selected from the foremost talent of the country. The actor remains there for the greatest part of his life; at the end of his services, when old age or infirmity disables him for further work, he is granted a pension. The manager is not a speculator, but a responsible employee, chosen on account of fitness for his duties. In many of those institutions the plays are accepted or refused by a committee composed of the most prominent members of the company, sometimes in conjunction with a few select literary advisers. "Runs" of plays night after night are practically unknown. A successful piece is placed in the permanent repertory, to be repeated several times weekly or monthly. The rule is a continual change of bill. The companies are numerous; therefore there is no necessity for an actor to play every night. The regulations of the endowment usually prescribe the production of standard works at certain intervals. [. . .] Besides the endowed theatres, there exist in the larger cities, mainly in the capitals, many private ones that have to support themselves, and are therefore conducted more on a business basis. But such is the prestige of the endowed theatres that the others are compelled to follow the example set by them, and thus avoid the complete anarchy which is the result of our American system.

Starring is not wholly unknown on the European continent, but it is singularly modified and restrained. Actors and actresses who have achieved a notable success, whose fame has reached beyond the limits of their own town or country, are granted now and then a few months' vacation, during which they are invited by other theatres to appear as "guests" in conjunction with the stock companies. Such was, I understand, the practice in this country as long as the stock companies existed. [. . .]

As to the *personnel* of endowed theatres, there would be no difficulty in forming it. Dramatic talent is not rare here. The prevalent mixture of races, the inherent quickness and subtlety of perception, the nervous and emotional temperament, as well as the innate sense of humor and observation among Americans—all these elements seem exceedingly propitious to the development of native dramatic talent. [. . .]

As our mode of government places entirely out of question any idea of State or municipal support, it is not to be expected that in the present state of the public mind, where the theatre is considered mostly as an amusement and very often as a precursor of Hades, public subscriptions could be solicited with any prospect of success. The only chance is to find among the rich, the very rich, of this country men both enlightened and generous enough to endow such theatres with private donations. [. . .]

It is not unreasonable to hope that soon we shall see a Maecenas of dramatic art, inspired by a noble ambition, not only erecting in one of the larger cities of America a theatre worthy of the high purposes for which it is founded, but also devoting a sufficient capital to assure its independence. Such an endowment would certainly be duplicated in time in other cities, because nothing is more contagious than good example. This is the only hope which sustains the courage of those who long to see the American stage in the place it ought to fill.

[370] A. M. Palmer. "Why Theatrical Managers Reject Plays"
Forum [1893]

[. . .] Several of our young dramatists who were, five years ago, floundering in the experimental stage and doing work which, while it promised something, actually performed little, have, since that time, brought forth some good plays with characters in them genuinely American, moved by American motives, using decent American language and living in a true American atmosphere. These plays are as yet few in number, but they reveal talent in the writers, and also, what is still more valuable to the cause of American playwrights, they reveal the existence of good dramatic types and of strong dramatic conditions in our own home circles. The prominent evil tendency of the American writer has been to look for his types among his countrymen of the baser sort, who never by any possibility pronounce English words properly and who seem to take the greatest pains to speak slang and utter vulgarisms and to act as if good manners were a reproach instead of an accomplishment.

It is true that the plays in which these characters appear often have an underlying poetic sentiment and even a strong dramatic force in some of their incidents, but they are a weariness and a vexation to those who believe that it is not un-American to speak correctly and to behave decently. Let our young writers, and our older ones too, for that matter, abandon for a while the men and women who talk through their noses, the *habitants* of the realistic New England kitchens, and of the realistic, but not always agreeable New England hencoops and barns, the precocious children who talk baseball slang and "sass" their parents, and the thousand and one *outré* and (to the refined mind) disagreeable characters and things with which the "American" play is generally crowded, and give us in their places the gentle, the strong, the correctly-talking and the correctly-behaving characters of which surely our American life furnishes numberless types. [. . .]

[371] B. O. Flower. "Mask or Mirror. The Vital Difference Between Artificiality and Veritism on the Stage"
The Arena [1893]

The theatre of recent years has been a mask rather than a mirror; that is to say, it has been afflicted with the gangrene of artificiality. [. . .] In other words, only the surface has been ruffled; the almost unfathomable depths of the soul have not been stirred. The pictures and voicings have lacked the true ring of life's verities in anything like a full or vital way. [. . .] and this is one of the chief reasons why the theatre has failed to wield a more decisive influence upon public opinion. Only that which is true, only that which is real, or, if ideal, is in perfect alignment with the eternal verities as found in life, can produce a lasting impression on the deeper emotions of humanity. [. . .]

The power of the work of our modern school of veritists or realists lies in its fidelity to life as it is; and though I do not think that Ibsen, Tolstoi, Howells, or Garland have ascended the mountain quite far enough to sweep the whole horizon, they are doing magnificent work, and work which is vital because it is true. [. . .]

Perhaps nowhere has the artificiality bred of imitation been more pronounced than in the drama. [. . .] The great expense incident to staging a play properly; the timidity of managers, who are, as a rule, wedded to conservatism; the critics, whose education has been entirely along the lines of the past, and who, as a rule, are very jealous for the old traditions; and lastly a public sentiment, which, when discriminating, is usually prejudiced in the direction of conventionalism, render it well-nigh impossible to present a dramatic work which is strongly unconventional. It is therefore far more than a personal triumph when a dramatist succeeds in spite of these obstacles. [. . .]

A play reflecting nature in a real and wholesome manner was enacted during the most of the past winter. I refer to Mr. James A. Herne's New England comedy-drama, *Shore Acres* [1892], which recently won such a signal success in Boston. The cordial reception given this play calls for more than a passing notice, because its successful presentation was a victory of far-reaching significance for the drama. It demonstrated the falsity of certain claims which have long fettered dramatic progress and prevented the stage from wielding a decisively educational influence, which might have been exerted had the drama been loyal to truth rather than the slave of traditionalism. [. . .]

Had the play been simply a clever conventional drama, the success would merely have been a marked tribute to the genius and ability of Mr. Herne, in his double *rôle* of dramatist and actor; but the far wider significance of the triumph will be readily appreciated when we remember that *Shore Acres* is a radically unconventional drama, which boldly ignores many of the most cherished traditions of the conventional stage, and radiates an atmosphere charged with truth and rendered luminous, not by the fire-fly glow of empty words, but by the divine radiance of noble deeds shining through simple, humble lives; and, moreover, it is a play without a plot or a villain, dealing entirely with the lowly ones of earth—merely a section, as it were, taken from the every-day life of some poor farmers and fishermen living on the coast of Maine.

It has been claimed that no play which dealt with humble life, which ignored plot and excluded the vulgarities of the variety stage and the cheap jokes and claptrap of the minstrel and melodrama could succeed. The success of *Shore Acres* completely refutes this calumny against a theatre-going public; while those who have persistently asserted that in order to satisfy public taste, plotless and villainless dramas which make no illegitimate bids for the applause of the gallery, must be relieved by gorgeous stage setting and fashionable dressing in which rich gowns cut perilously low in front, and ridiculously long behind, make up for what is wanting in other artificial features, have been shown that beyond the tricks of conventionalism, beyond the devices of artificiality, rises ART, which, when true, appeals to something deeper and finer than the surface whims of humanity, and which, even when she concerns herself with the humblest life, provided she is true in her delineations, proves absorbingly fascinating to all those in whom the current of human emotions flows in the deep nature-ordained channels, instead of over the shallow crust of conventionality.

It was not to be expected that *Shore Acres* would please the froth or the dregs of society, for the denizens of these strata, through education, environment, and the atmosphere of life, become unnatural; they live behind a mask, and to them the mask is more engaging than the mirror. The erotic atmosphere of a fashionable society drama, heavy with artificial perfumes and shadowing forth luxurious ease, intrigue, and the fever of a superficial existence, representing puppets of passion, connoisseurs of wines, and ornamented by inane scions of foreign aristocracies, best satisfies the butterflies of fashion; while plays dealing with plot and passion, in which villains are invincible until the final act is reached, and where the young are nightly shown how safes are blown open by professional burglars, and various other crimes are committed with ease and dexterity, appeal to another class whose point of view renders life's true visage as unreal as it is to the flippant children of fashion's careless world. To the dwellers in both of these social strata *Shore Acres* failed to appeal; while from the earnest feeling multitude who ever recognize the voice of truth whenever spoken, and who appreciate true art because their souls are sufficiently near the pulsating breast of nature to recognize the face of truth, it found a ready welcome. [. . .]

> [In a footnote:] The realistic atmosphere of the play is indicated by an incident which occurred one night when I was witnessing the performance. Behind me sat a lady and gentleman who appeared to be greatly interested in the production; the gentleman, however, seemed much worried because, as he observed a number of times, he could not recollect any "Berry lighthouse" along the shore. To each of them, as apparently to the vast audience, it was history rather than fiction which was being unfolded. Many illustrations of a similar character might be cited to emphasize the peculiar influence which this play exerted in taking hold of the real self of the auditor.

[. . .] The popular or conventional pseudo-idealism of the past has been essentially immoral because it has been untrue, strained, and unnatural; or when possible it has been so divorced from the real as to carry little vital truth to the brain of those to whom it has appealed. Realistic idealism, when hand in hand with veritism, gives to life a moral uplift, subtle and illusive in character, but most potential for lasting good. It is the soul of progress—the inspiration of noble endeavor—the touch which floods the present with light, and reveals the next upward step.

Realism is vitally important; she depicts life as it is today; she is true, impartial, and mercilessly candid. But vital idealism complements realism [. . .]. The relation between realism and vital idealism in the utilitarian economy may be compared to two influences acting upon the inmates of a building which is on fire. Realism sounds the alarm, she describes the true condition; while idealism leads the awakened victims from a death-trap to a place of safety. [. . .]

[381] J. A. Herne. "Art for Truth's Sake in the Drama"
The Arena [1897]

[. . .] During the first twenty years of my career as an actor the literature of the stage was limited. We had any quantity of plays, but not much literature, and absolutely no differentiation or characterization. [. . .] in the main we relied upon what was called "the *standard drama*," containing any number of miscellaneous plays of more or less merit by any number of miscellaneous authors of more or less merit. We had tragedy, melodrama, domestic drama, spectacle, and farce. The standard drama of that day was a drama of plot rather than of purpose. The dramatist was concerned first of all with his plot. [. . .] And so, while it is true that we had some excellent plays, they each had a plot, a hero, and a villain, and always ended with virtue triumphant. The hero always married the heroine, and the villain was always foiled before the final curtain fell. The characters in these plays were of a necessity more or less artificial.

The system then in vogue was the "star system," that is, a star actor travelled from city to city and presented the plays of his repertoire with the assistance of the local stock company, instead of with his own company, as is the custom now. We had some marvellous actors in those days, when you consider the material they had to work with. In many instances they actually made those artificial characters human, and those plotty plays real.

The stage sword-combat was one of the essentials of the standard melodrama, the authors having no less an authority than Shakspere for precedent. We used to gather in the wings to watch two tragedians fight the combat in the last act of Shakspere's *Richard III* or *Macbeth*, a very laughable affair to me now, but very real to me then; and those actors, although they had studied and rehearsed every blow, and knew just when and where to strike, thrust, parry, and guard, were very much in earnest when night came and the battle was on. [. . .]

[. . .] One [tragedian] I have in mind who, whenever he played Richard III or Macbeth, used to place extra swords at both wings of the stage, in order that the fight might not be curtailed through the breaking of a sword. With him an actor might omit some of Shakspere's lines, but he must not miss a blow of the combat. [. . .]

It is generally held that the province of the drama is to amuse. I claim that it has a higher purpose—that its mission is to interest and to instruct. It should not *preach* objectively, but it should teach subjectively; and so I stand for truth in the drama, because it is elemental, it gets to the bottom of a question. It strikes at unequal standards and unjust systems. It is as unyielding as it is honest. It is as tender as it is inflexible. It has supreme faith in man. It believes that that which was good in the beginning cannot be bad at the end. It sets forth clearly that the concern of one is the concern of all. It stands for the higher development and thus the individual liberty of the human race.

[388] W. D. Howells. "A Subscription Theatre"
Literature [1899]

[. . .] I should, for my part, very gladly see the experiment of a subscription theatre attempted here. Of course, a true American of the sort whose truth is to our principles rather than our interests might feel that such a theatre would not be thoroughly American. A thoroughly American theatre, in his eyes, would be one which was protected by a tariff, and which should rise spontaneously in virtue of prohibitive duties levied upon all plays of foreign origin. With such a theatre in the hands of a patriotic trust, and with a patriotic union of actors vigilant to see that no alien performers were suffered to take part in the production of our native dramas, we should have something thoroughly American. We have already the apparatus for such a theatre on one side in the theatrical syndicate which now controls nine-tenths of the playhouses throughout the country, and we have in past times had something like it on the other side in the disposition of certain actors to apply our alien labour law to the importation of foreign histrionic talent.

But as yet no theatre trust and no actors' union have met on the common ground open to them; and a subscription theatre, though not so thoroughly American, would not be so opposite to the American spirit as a State or city theatre. If it were founded by a number of rich men it would be their enterprise; it would be in the hands of a trust, and in the hands of a trust we always feel ourselves so much safer, or at least so much more at home, than we feel in our own hands, possibly because we are so much more accustomed to be there. The course from a city or a State theatre to the division of property and all the well-known horrors of socialism would be rapid and direct; while the disadvantages of a subscription theatre would be only such as we are used to in some other things. They would not occur so promptly, however, to the mind of a critic fresh from a land of more economic freedom, and it may therefore be worth while to point some of them out.

With us the rich form some such class as the nobles in other countries; and they are too new to their importance to hold it in personal contempt, as long-descended aristocrats safely may and sometimes do hold theirs; they have not yet had time to grow the pseudo-liberality which sometimes distinguished eccentric noblemen. They stand by their order more relentlessly, and their devotion to the social framework which holds them in place is vigilant and intense. In a theatre founded and controlled by them, no play criticizing or satirizing society could be favoured, and no play recognizing or representing occasional if not essential truth in regard to our industrial conditions would be permitted. To be forbidden it need not be a play celebrating a successful strike, or depicting a case of cruel exploitation, or the methods of a combine; it need only be a play calling attention to the conditions. It is not imaginable that their management would approve of such a play as Ibsen's *Enemy of the People* [1882], or *Die Weber* [1892] of Hauptmann, or even *Die Ehre* [1889] of Sudermann. If Mr. Herne wrote a play dealing as frankly with life in a mining town or a factory town as his *Griffith Davenport* [1899] deals with life on a Virginia plantation, it could never pass the censorship of such a body of subscribers. Mr. Bernard Shaw's satire of *Arms and the Man*, if they felt its irony and realized its implications, could not be given twice in their subscription theatre, which would in nowise be a free theatre. No dramatist who knew American conditions and American character could write freely for a theatre sustained by the subscriptions of a limited number of rich men, unless he were of their thinking. If some dramatist who did not know our conditions and character, and were not of the subscriber's thinking, wrote freely, he would learn an interesting lesson from the fate of his play in their hands. What has happened in some of our highest institutions of learning would happen in any subscription theatre, unless the subscriptions were kept so low as to diffuse the enterprise among a number too great to be governed by the instinct of wealth.

[. . .] With a subscription of twenty-five dollars they could have as many plays, from dramatists who also spoke their minds; and if the experiment were tried in ten or twenty places we should have at once a free theatre, where good work could make that appeal to the public which it can now do only on almost impossible terms. How long we should have it is another question, much involved in the temperamental impatience of our public.

[390] H. Potter. "The Drama of the Twentieth Century"
The Arena [1900]

[. . .] we have a stage but recently emancipated from the reproach of impropriety—its literary inheritance unsuited to our age and country, its traditions all foreign and of the past. We have a stage that openly honors idle luxury and the emptiness of title and aristocracy: where aristocracy means not what the word expresses, "the best and noblest," but merely the richest, and often the worst. We have a stage where the workers have no place, where the thinkers have no place, where noble ideals have very little part, but which is chiefly a faithful reflection of the baser, the more sordid and artificial elements of modern life. Before the stage of to-day lies one of the grandest opportunities ever offered to humanity: that it once more resume its ancient office, become again the educator of the people, the best friend of the proletariat, remembering always that all hope for art that does not rest on the elevation of the masses is a house built on sand—is basically unsound. The twentieth-century stage [. . .] faces the future as one recovering from a long illness, before whom life lies mapped out anew [. . .].

[. . .] The old individuality of the artisan, who with a joyful independence labored at his task, elaborating the details and perfecting the workmanship to the limit of his skill and knowledge, finding in the completeness of his work the interest and satisfaction of life, and experiencing in some degree the ecstasy of creation, though that which he made were no more than a chest or a pair of shoes—this has passed away, and the toilers of to-day are in danger of becoming almost as much machines as the engines they attend. Meanwhile individuality of thought, independent of authority and tradition, is increasing with giant strides. Men *will* think, and the overworked and underpaid man, if his brain be not too near ossification through the monotony of his toil, will nourish thoughts of discontent, of hatred, of revenge. The question faces us, Must the age of mechanical invention be also the apotheosis of commercial slavery—a death in life for the toilers? The solution of the problem seems to lie, at least in part, in shortening the hours of labor and providing for the laborer, in his leisure time, amusements that shall be stimulating in a healthy way. The first reform is the duty of the State; the second is the mission of the Stage. [. . .]

In the evolution of the new drama certain things will have to be eliminated. There will, for instance, be no representations of murders, of suicides, of torture-chambers, and no painful death scenes dragged out with disgusting detail and realism until the nerves of the audience are all unstrung and their health impaired. If such things occur necessarily in the course of the play they will be mentioned or indicated, never illustrated or described. The reformed stage will offer no object-lessons in vice, nor will it seek to impose on its audience the dreadful immovable fear and expectation of death. The teaching of revenge will bear no part in it; but the unity of cause and effect, the indissoluble relation between the doer and the deed—this will be shown as plainly as if the Greek Nemesis presided over every stage. It will illustrate unmistakably the truth of the axiom that "all which is hidden shall be revealed;" that impatience, indolence of mind or body, and restlessness publish themselves as unerringly to a perceptive eye, if not as obtrusively, as do the grosser sins of vice, drunkenness, or dishonesty. Its lesson will be unmistakable that there are no privileges in the universe, and that the broken man is the man that has striven to break the law.

The glorification of a fretful lawless passion, or of a Napoleonic crime, will be excluded from the stage of the new era, and Reason will no longer be insulted by the assertion that petty crimes are despicable whilst enormous crimes are magnificent. The idea that work is misery, and contemptible, will disappear in the evolution of the stage. It is one of the legacies of a materialistic past—the past that thought preaching was religion. The drama of the future will never preach, but it will be didactic in its essence as all good art must be: thus it will exhibit religion as the art of living by law, the law of high thinking and right doing, and, recognizing the fact that effort (employment) is one-half of character—builds the character, first of the individual and then of the nation—it will never show the toiler despicable or ridiculous merely because he is a toiler, and will paint no aureole round the head of the idle incumbent of inherited dignities. Work even to the young may be made as interesting as play; in fact, children are most happy in their play when they believe themselves to be at work. [. . .] The new hero who awaits his introducer will be a worker. He will not be the man that wins laurels by the slaughter of his fellow-creatures, whether beast or human [. . .]. He will be the heroic scientist, devoting his life to the betterment of humanity; he will be the heroic physician, who braves death to keep it away from others; the philanthropist, who rescues brothers and sisters from despair, and fates worse than death; the unlettered, untaught man that fights fire or earth or water, and endures toil, privation, poverty, and suffering in single-hearted devotion to duty. There is no novelty in the thought, which yet will bear emphasizing anew, that heroism on the stage is always popular; all that is needed here is to broaden the general conception of heroic action. [. . .]

The new hero will necessarily carry his own environment with him onto the new stage, and people will then begin to realize that the talk of the shop, the store, the market-place, the field, the prairie, and the waterside is at least as elevating, as interesting, and much more naturally dramatic, than is the talk of the club, the reception, or the hotel. The great success of plays like [Joseph Arthur's] *Blue Jeans* [1890] and [Denman Thompson and George W. Ryer's] *The Old Homestead* [1886] shows clearly that the *heart* of the people is not, as indeed it could not be, divorced from the *life* of the people. It is but a short time since we realized the idealism of a piston-rod, of a dynamo, of a locomotive, of a telegraph wire; but already we have outgrown the foolish old complaint that steam and electricity have banished romance from the world. The ideal aspect; the inner heart of science; its tragedies and comedies; the pathos and beauty that belong to the laboratory, the mine, the diggings, the ranch, the farm, the fishing-boat—all await the man of genius who shall come with the courage of his convictions, ready to tell what he sees as he sees it and win the whole world to stand by his side and see out of his eyes [. . .].

War and bloodshed will find no place in the twentieth-century drama, as before long they will find none on the stage of the civilized world; and thus the histrionic will assume its proper place among the arts and appear in the vanguard of progress, instead of reluctantly dragged along in the rear. The wild flowers of national life—myth, legend, song, folk-lore—will form a part of the dower of the new drama [. . .].

It is true that people cannot now be taught, as were the people of the ages we are accustomed to call heroic, absolutely or principally through the ear. Such a method would be neither desirable nor possible, since the invention of printing has accustomed the world to teaching conveyed in signs and object-lessons. Where the ancient stage had one means of expression and influence, the modern will possess many, for every play will be built scientifically and will conform to the mystical laws of color, number, and sound, which, unseen and heretofore unsuspected, yet underlie the manifested universe—laws that rule Nature and guide human nature.

What hope, it will be asked, is there for the working of such a metamorphosis in the face of private interests and private cowardice? The prophecy has been made that before the middle of the twentieth century many places of public amusement—opera-houses, academies of music, athletic grounds, etc.—will be provided at public expense. The schools for training artists and actors will then be public institutions, free as are now our common schools, and the only qualification for entrance will be ability of a marked order. This will come in the ordinary progress of evolution—that grand march of humanity which, within fifty years, has built our public schools and made of them usually the most imposing and expensive features of their town; has made free public baths and libraries; and in less than ten years has given us free kindergartens and lecture-courses, and is now on the verge of widely extended municipal ownership in different directions. In such practical fashion our rulers have expressed their conviction that education and hygienic facilities for the people are necessary to the well-being and even to the continued existence of a republic. The recognition of the ethical and educational value of amusements is but one short step further. Free amusements will always be cheaper in the end than free prisons and poorhouses. The new version of the old aphorism will be, "*Let me make the amusements of the people and I care not who may make their laws.*"

Limited in aspiration and effort to the slow growth of humanity, the expression of any ideal will come by degrees that often appear painfully slow. Yet, though far off it may seem to be, in the near future shines the realization of this nineteenth-century ideal—a theater where the actors, the audience, the very hall shall be in harmonious vibration: *a conditioned stage with a conditioned audience.* In the erection of such a playhouse only the true artist could bear a part. From the architect to the laborer, the men who worked upon it would have turned their backs forever on the baser side of life; would have realized that work worthily performed becomes worship; would have formed a conception of the brotherhood of man, and have realized that fear, despair, treachery, violence, and melancholy are only different ways of spelling the one word *selfishness.* Such a theater would have to be built like Solomon's Temple—without the sound of a hammer, *i.e.*, by men of peace, in the days of peace, with thoughts of peace. It would have to be *isolated* and *insulated*: isolated from all strife, struggle, and competition, if such still pollute the atmosphere of its far-off city; apart from centers of traffic, from railroads and the noise and bustle of commercialism, situated in parks or woods, where the tones of Nature and of art might blend in one harmonious whole to the God of beauty and harmony. It would have to be insulated by an interior lined with glass and silk—non-conductors that would not retain the personality of the audience. [. . .]

[398] H. G. Rhodes. "The American Invasion of the London Stage"
The Cosmopolitan [1902]

The commercial invasion of England by America is now a household word from the Atlantic to the Pacific: the artistic invasion receives very little attention from us. Yet the latter should, perhaps, please our vanity as much as the former, even though it may not do quite so much toward filling our pockets. The invasion of the London stage by American actresses and actors is the part of our attempt at foreign conquest along artistic lines which is most apparent to the British public. Yet London views its visitors so far only with pleasure and with no envy. There has been no serious disturbance of the theatrical labor market. Occasionally one hears an English actress laughingly protest that she can get no engagement because she hasn't a New York reputation. But the Americans, although on the whole notably prominent, are still only a small part of the whole body of players, and the annual emigration of English actors and actresses to the United States to join permanently the ranks of American players more than balances the account. [. . .]

Yet it will take more than this mere interchange to account for the attitude of Americans toward English theatrical life. There are a certain number of Americans who began their career upon the London stage, and a greater number who, having once tasted the pleasures of English theatrical life, are unwilling to abandon it and return to their native land.

An actor's life in England is less nomadic than that of his American brother. For the man or woman in the higher ranks of the profession London is England, the provinces are comparatively unimportant. They have their theaters, of course, and a great number of provincial actors who are always hoping and longing for a London engagement. But once you have become a London actor, your visits to the provinces are rare and brief. You act in a piece through its run in the metropolis, then you go to another London theater and appear in a fresh piece. You do not, as in America, go on tour with the piece. That is usually relegated to a secondary company. Engagements in London are for "the run of the piece," not for a season of forty weeks, as in America. This makes the life, perhaps, more precarious than in America, but it also makes it more varied, and it allows the actor to have a home in London. American players can have summer, holiday homes; that is all. But the London actor can have a place of his own the year round, his own belongings, a place to bring up his children, and all the comforts that come from having one's own kitchen and one's own fireside.

Furthermore he gets more practice in his art, because he has more different parts to play. The play is rare that runs a whole year in London; so during the time an American would be occupied with one rôle a London actor plays many parts. Unquestionably this means more work and that great tedium of rehearsals which, although the public does not always realize it, is sometimes the greatest part of an actor's toil. But as more work means more opportunity, this but adds to the attraction of the London stage for the American. [...]
[A discussion of several American actresses and actors on London stages follows.]

[399] G. W. Shinn. "The Actors' Church Alliance"
The Arena [1902]

[Shinn was Honorary Vice-President of The Actors' Church Alliance.]
[...] Briefly stated, *one of the fundamental principles of this Alliance is that the stage is an honorable profession in which a man may serve his God and his fellow-men. Another is that the stage ministers to an innocent craving of our nature for recreation; still further, that it is an ally of the Church in aiding the happiness of the people, as it deepens in their minds the great lessons that may be drawn from pictures of human life.* [...]

One of the practical directions in which the energies of the Alliance are directed just now is toward the suppression of Sunday performances. A few years ago these were forbidden by law. Such laws are still unrepealed in some of the States, but they are not enforced. The people generally do not realize how intolerable is the bondage in which the actor is held who has to play seven days a week. Well-nigh the whole profession protests against it, and some of their leading men and women are appealing to the Christian Church to help them in their efforts to secure a day of rest. It would be strange if such an appeal should go unheeded, but the greed of managers and the unreasoning demands of the public have thus far prevented any considerable change. The theaters of all sorts are wide open on Sundays in many of our cities. They should all be closed. The religious sentiment of the people should be strong enough to close them out of respect for the day itself, but this plea of the actors for a period of needed rest added to that should certainly secure very prompt results.
[See also *[416]*.]

[400] J. Corbin. "The American Drama"
Forum [1902]

[...] Beyond question the syndicate has brought great material benefit to the American theatre. Under the old system not many of the independent managers had a sufficient reserve of capital to undertake elaborate and expensive productions, and when they did undertake them the chance of failure was considerable. The force of factitious rivalry made it difficult or impossible to secure the best actors, to arrange the most economical lines of travel, and to secure the best available theatres. The trust, on the other hand, has plenty of ready money to invest in anything that promises gain, either immediate or remote. It is able to make instant use of all the lucrative plays produced, and to place the entire available stock of actors to the best common profit. It is able to arrange tours at the outset of the season so as to keep all the best theatres filled, and to keep all the best companies continually employed. If, in the course of the season, it becomes necessary to alter existing arrangements, the shifts are made with the utmost speed and economy. As for the actors, in the history of the American stage it seems certain that they have never been so well assured of continuous employment and proper pay, of ease and comfort in travelling—of all the material conditions, in short, that minister to happiness and self-respect. Never before have plays been so well cast as a whole, or the productions so well rehearsed, nor has the standard of elegance and fitness in scenery and in costume ever before been so high. Never have the best plays produced the world over been so profitably placed before the theatre-going public throughout the land. In short, never has the commercial organization of the drama been so fortunate.

As against this, the theatre has undeniably suffered in all the essentials of high art. The fact that most of the plays produced are imported from abroad reduces the art of the stage-manager to the humble function of reproducing slavishly the foreign production, with the result that intellectual stage management has become almost extinct. One Broadway manager, it is true, Mr. Daniel Frohman [the brother of Charles Frohman of the syndicate], is an artist of high ideals and intelligence. His productions at the Lyceum Theatre and at Daly's Theatre are invariably excellent. He has not infrequently discovered in English plays merits that were not recognized in London. Sometimes, too, his production of a play is markedly superior to the English production, as in the case of Pinero's delightful comedietta, *Trelawney of the Wells* [1898].

He is, however, a solitary exception. [. . .]

Under the régime of the syndicate the art of the actor suffers quite as much as that of the stage manager. The whole system rests on the assumption that each play shall run months together in New York, and then months, and even years, on the road. Thus the actors—from those who speak a few lines only to the stars of the company—are doomed to spend a short lifetime with a single part. In the old days of the stock company all hands had many new parts every season, sometimes many new parts each week. [. . .]

[. . .] the most economical management of the syndicate booking is secured in the case of plays that are reasonably certain of long runs. So the mediocre novelty is given life, and the master works of the past are dead to the stage.

It has sometimes been said that the prevalence on our stage of plays of foreign origin is prejudicial to the native drama. When the whole world is laid under tribute, the native playwright has, it is true, to face a keen competition. But against this is the fact that a play on an American subject and American characters has a popular appeal many times as strong as a play dealing with foreign themes and foreign actors. Such actors as W. H. Crane and N. C. Goodwin show a decided preference for American plays, the grounds of their preference being presumably of a purely commercial nature. Moreover, the importation of the best plays from abroad tends to educate the public, and the playwrights too. The chief drawback in the production of good American plays is the fact that all subjects are tabooed except such as, by appealing to the great theatre-going public, are inviting to the theatrical speculator. [. . .]

The dramatic situation [. . .] is not without some faint glimmer of hope. By a curious working of economic forces, the result of the operations of the syndicate has been to multiply many times the number of stock companies. The perfection of the organization of syndicate booking has made it impossible for many of the minor theatres in the larger cities to exist, as they did formerly, on what is known as travelling attractions. To avoid closing their doors they have gathered together companies which revive at popular prices the best old plays, from [J. Madison Morton's] *Box and Cox* [1847] to *Hamlet*. The sanguine mind may still hope that these stock companies will revive the glories of the past generation; but the hope is apparently doomed to prove vain. The theatres of the stock companies are usually situated in unfashionable districts and their clientèles are of the humble sort; so that the maximum charge for the afternoon is twenty-five cents and for the evening fifty cents. In order to make both ends meet, the management is forced to give two performances daily, and to change the bill weekly. At this rate it is obviously not possible to make the scenery and costumes adequate. The labors of the stock actors are so severe that many of them break down and even die in the harness from physical exhaustion; but even at this it is not possible properly to rehearse a production. It is true that these stock companies train up actors in a way that nothing else does; but the fact is as much a source of weakness as of strength, for as soon as an actor attains any considerable degree of excellence, he is tempted to join the syndicate companies by the prospect of less arduous work, greater pay, and greater luxury. One substantial benefit, however, has resulted from the work of the cheap stock company theatres. They have shown beyond question that the public taste is still sound enough to justify repeated revivals of the good old plays.

The stock companies controlled by the syndicate reach a higher level of excellence, but they offer less ground for hope. As far as character actors are concerned they do very well, and for this reason they sometimes give excellent all-round performances. But they find one grave difficulty. It is an incident of the amiable limitations of the theatre-going public that handsome and agreeable lovers are at a premium; and as soon as one of the stock companies produces an attractive leading juvenile the operation of purely commercial considerations drives him out on the road as a star. [. . .]

The loss of the stock companies does not end here; for as it is necessary that all these popular stars should have popular parts to play, the stock companies are apt to lose the most attractive new dramas. Both as to their companies and as to their repertory the stock companies are thus narrowly limited. In point of fact it can scarcely be said that they have a repertory. Every year the runs of new plays are pushed to the utmost limit, with the result that revivals are few and far between. [. . .] Clearly, the whole force of the syndicate organization works against the production of old plays.

Of all the hopeful signs of the times the most hopeful is the enterprise of the actors themselves. The natural ambition of an artist is to do the best work only, and from year to year of late the leading American players have struck out along new lines [in classic roles]. [. . .]

[. . .] That the upward tendency among American actors will carry the drama far seems very unlikely. As long as the theatre continues to be managed along purely commercial lines, their struggles must be very much like those of the proverbial aspirant who tried to pull himself up by his boot straps. Yet, taking the record of several years together, it is evident that the number of those who are looking for a freer artistic life is on the increase, and also that a very considerable proportion of the great theatre-going public is ready to enjoy the best and to pay for it. [. . .]

[. . .] As for the experiment of the independent theatres of the past, they should warn us that it is not wise to rely on cliques, however enthusiastic, and much less on individuals—theirs is the sort of elevator that is sure to break. Any movement toward higher organization should be as far as possible the expression of the genius of the best element in the great theatre-going public. And it should, as far as possible, rest on a sound and permanent commercial basis. To ask this is clearly to ask a great deal. Yet a problem of precisely similar nature has been already solved. We have at hand an admirable example of how the drama of a great and widely disseminated nation may be elevated with safety. [. . .]

[A description of the theater system in Germany follows.]

As for America, or at least English-speaking America, no one who knows the conservative power of established organization, even of the worst, will look for any early duplication of this system. As far as the German-speaking public is concerned, the system is to be seen in full operation: there are vigorous and successful repertory theatres in New York, Philadelphia, Chicago, and Milwaukee, and every season great German actors [. . .] make the tour of all these theatres as guests. But it will be many years, it is to be feared, before this admirable example is imitated by the English-speaking public. The syndicate would, of course, oppose any plan to this end. [. . .]

There are, to be sure, grave obstacles. In each city it will be necessary to have at the outset an endowment of half a million dollars, and perhaps more; and in case of mishap or mismanagement it may be necessary to call on private subscriptions for aid. But no people in the world are as liberal in public munificence as we in America. The nation that has freely contributed hundreds of millions to its universities has only to realize the educational power of the drama, and its civilizing influence upon manners, in order to do at least as well by it as has been done by the crowned heads of Germany. A similar obstacle is to be met in the case of the managers. One result of the operations of the syndicate, as has been pointed out, is that the art of stage management is almost dead. But the country that has already shown the highest intelligence in so many fields of science and art will scarcely fail in stage management when the opportunity arises. At any rate, the experience of past years has shown that actors are increasingly anxious to play the best parts, and that a large and increasing element in the great theatre-going public is ready to encourage them. When there is a strong and vital upward tendency the final triumph of good sense is only a matter of time [. . .].

[416] G. W. Shinn. "Church and Stage after Five Years"
The Arena [1904]

[. . .] We must not think of the Alliance [The Actors' Church Alliance] as organized simply to correct abuses which are found on the Stage but also to correct the narrowness and the prejudice which have kept the Church, or so many of its members, from recognizing the usefulness of the theater as an institution and which have led to most unbrotherly treatment of members of this calling. The benefits to accrue from this Alliance are not all on one side. The evils to be corrected are not confined to one side.

[. . .] *It is part of the mission of the Alliance to improve the popular taste and by encouraging the production of wholesome plays, to gratify the fondness for dramatic representations without injuring the moral sense of those who witness them.* The old plan of condemning all play-acting and putting a stigma upon the theater itself has not worked well in the past. It is surely a better plan to use proper discrimination, to admit that the theater is capable of providing wholesome recreation and useful instruction and to encourage it to do its best. [. . .]

It will be seen at once what possibilities for good there are for having men in the large towns and cities who are ready to visit sick members of this profession, to hold religious services for them and to show friendliness and interest in every proper way. One result of the appointment of these Chaplains, which will become more and more evident to the players as time goes on, will

be to relieve that terrible feeling of loneliness and friendlessness which so often assails the people of the stage as they go from place to place, knowing no one, and feeling that they are regarded with suspicion even by many of those who come to see them act. Now they are sure of some sympathetic friends whenever they reach a town or city where Chaplains have been appointed, and if they are overtaken by illness or misfortune of any kind there are persons to whom they can appeal. [. . .]
[See also *[399]*.]

[418] D. Frohman. "The Tendencies of the American Stage"
The Cosmopolitan [1904]

[. . .] Plays of historical interest have been popular with us from the time of our earliest playhouses, but there is a Gallic flavor to them—an antiquated chivalry and romance—with which we moderns are not in sympathy. Our emotions, or rather the forms of our emotions, are advanced as much as our manners and customs, and though the canons of a good play hold good for all nations and all times, there are certain side requirements to an American play which are subservient to the dramatic interests of any race.

The first requirement of a play is a love-story. It may be romantic love, modern, or, so far as period is concerned, of any age, because the theme is of universal interest. The story and its complications need not be new, though their treatment must be fresh, and every year requires a more novel, though not necessarily outré, setting than the last. The love-story must be clear and distinct in the mind of the dramatist, and he must find an obstacle in its course. This obstacle, reasonably, convincingly, ingeniously, he must remove. He need seek no newer obstacles than those that William Shakespeare has stated in *A Midsummer Night's Dream*, or which Milton has laid down in *Paradise Lost*, as interposing between lovers, whether they may be man and maiden or husband and wife. Thus far the themes and the situation are universal. The task of the modern American dramatist is to seize on these and make them local and national. In order to do this he must take types of character which this country has produced, place them in an environment which is recognizably true and make them act in a characteristic manner under the influence of the emotions and passions which are universal.

The fault with some of our so-called American plays is that, while the characters are dressed like Americans and talk like them, they are simply disguised French and German people undergoing the trials and tribulations incident upon the conditions of France and Germany. This is probably because so many of our plays are borrowed from and adapted from the plays of other countries. Now, French and American plays proceed quite differently. French dramatists find situations and develop character from them. The American tendency is to draw certain characters together and develop a situation from the clash or harmony of such a meeting. [. . .]

American conditions do not demand such intense extremities. It is not that we are not romantic, and, I hope, capable of chivalry, even when we know that such chivalry is not going to pay. Indeed, I venture to assert that under a quiet and practicable exterior exists a deep sentiment for the graceful things in life, an exterior which furnishes just the sort of contrast which is so dramatically effective in a hero, coolness in danger—often more telling than the brandishing volubility of other nations—a disposition to do heroic things without pausing to recognize that they are great, and a strong feeling for domesticity and peace or other much-maligned sentiment.

And the American girl? Where can we find a more interesting subject for a play? The intelligent descendant of the rather severe régime of the Puritan frequently carries under a somewhat reserved manner all the intensity of a woman of southern Europe. The modern society girl! What unsuspected depths may not lie under that light and frivolous manner which she assumes as armor, what capacity for self-sacrifice and a heroic constancy of affection which would make her a thrilling heroine? Take the parvenue's daughter living in an artificial atmosphere—ambitious, wistful, proud, who learns through genuine love how to emancipate herself for her conditions. With such leading characters, and added to them the genuine types which our varied social order furnishes, you have a group which Sardou might envy the American playwright for its freshness and its opportunities. The accession of sudden wealth, its effect on character and circumstance—here is a fruitful and typical theme for the American dramatist. The tendency to-day—if without contradicting myself I may be permitted to acknowledge such a tendency—is for the home subject. Surely there are no affairs more thrilling to us than our own? And we must have a love-interest because our plays demand realism, and it is love which is the most real thing in life. Unless a love-story shines like a radiating sun through a play, that play will die; for an important factor to reckon with is that the majority of the audience are young and unmarried. Therefore in the healthy play—and it is only of this play, since it is the only successful kind, that I am speaking—when the hero and heroine are man and wife, it is better from a dramatic point of view that the audience meet with them first unmarried, because this increases the sympathy and interest in the love-story. For the author's task is easier if he deals with those whose matrimonial markets have not been made.

Debatable plays, problems, fantasies of the character dear to the heart of Ibsen, Bernard Shaw and the rest of them, are never financially successful in America. These are relegated to special audiences, whose predilections favor subjects that treat frequently either of abstract interests, or the harsher phases of life.

But the play I would recommend as the most inclusive and exclusive example of a brilliantly good play is *As You Like It*. Setting aside the imaginativeness and poetry of the lines—which will never again be equaled—I would recommend to all playwrights a close and thoughtful study of the construction. [...]

[...] Pit against this the managerial impossibilities of *Hamlet*—a magnificent piece of literature, a scholarly study, a brilliant collection of rhetoric, but no play. Jefferson said that Shakespeare undoubtedly sat constantly at the prompt-table at his rehearsals. I could go further and say that *Hamlet* might have been written as a stopgap. The characters, which were undoubtedly preconceived character-studies, are strung together, hanging limply from an old-fashioned peg, jostling against one another like stray individuals in a crowd and exposing their inmost hearts without rime or reason. [...] Except for its intellectual character, its Jove-like reflections on human nature, what would be a modern manager's impression to-day if confronted by the manuscript of a play like *Hamlet* if proffered for its theme and its purely technical construction?

But what a fruitful source of study are many of the plays, a few of which I select at random, that contain the various qualities I have mentioned, all of them sound, sane and convincing in theme, plot, character and treatment: the psychology, construction and plot of [Dion Boucicault's] *Led Astray* [1873] and *The Ironmaster* [Pinero's 1884 adaptation of Georges Ohnet's *Le Maître des Forges*]; the romantic chivalry and character-study in [Edward Bulwer-Lytton's] *The Lady of Lyons* [1838] and *The Prisoner of Zenda* [Edward Rose's 1896 adaptation of Anthony Hope's novel]; the modern spirit, the dialogue and general wholesomeness of [Bronson Howard's] *The Henrietta* [1887] and [Howard's] *The Banker's Daughter* [1878] (the latter marking almost a new era in the management of its plot); the old Lyceum play of *The Wife* [by David Belasco and Henry C. De Mille, 1887]—a splendid variant of this theme; [William Gillette's] *Held by the Enemy* [1886] and [Gillette's] *Secret Service* [1895], embodying character-study, the intense theatric quality, and the note of modern interest, which always appeals to the audiences of to-day; [Augustus Thomas's] *Alabama* [1891] as a study of American types; and for the pastoral drama, a class of play of fadeless popularity, note such works as [Denman Thompson and George W. Ryer's] *The Old Homestead* [1886], [James A. Herne's] *Shore Acres* [1892], [Lottie B. Parker's] *Way Down East* [1898] and [George Ade's] *The County Chairman* [1903].

American audiences in particular look for vivacity and rapid sequence. French and German audiences deprecate action at the expense of reflection. They prefer food for thought. Americans are perhaps too busy to be appreciative of dramatic art. It is not that they do not want esthetic pictures, but that, being busy men and women, they have not the leisure indispensable for a full appreciation of them.

The manager who produces plays which may be and are discussed with interest and affection in a man's home is certain of success. Life, not as it is, but as it should be, is the motive that should be entertained. There is much that is beautiful and real at the same time—much that should furnish good, sound, convincing and interesting material for a successful American play.

[419] D. Belasco. "The Theatrical Syndicate. One Side"
The Cosmopolitan [1904]

[. . .] That the methods of the theatrical syndicate are mainly responsible for the decadence of the drama here in America, is a proposition which may be easily proved by an analysis of the situation. When the syndicate was formed, some seven or eight years ago, its declared intent and purpose was primarily the placing of all theatrical transactions with which it had to do upon a strictly business footing—a purpose laudable enough and sufficiently harmless in itself, but one which was destined to develop potentialities of quite another order. In brief, it was thought to organize the booking of attractions throughout the country, to systematize the haphazard methods which had hitherto prevailed in this department, and to concentrate the work connected with the various enterprises coming under syndicate jurisdiction, in such a way as best to serve the business interests of the six members who composed that body.

These members were Mr. Al. Hayman, who is not a producer; Mr. Charles Frohman, who controls many New York theaters and who is among the most prolific of producers; Messrs. Nixon & Zimmerman, who have several theaters in Philadelphia, and Messrs. Klaw & Erlanger, who at the time of the formation of the theatrical syndicate were conducting a booking-agency on their own account. Messrs. Klaw & Erlanger, however, were a valuable adjunct to the forces of the trust, in that they undertook to bring under the control of the syndicate all theaters in which they had hitherto booked attractions for a commission.

[. . .] The beginnings of the enterprise were comparatively small, albeit they were sure. Some thirty-odd playhouses in the principal cities of the United States, from Boston to San Francisco and as far south as New Orleans, came, without a murmur from their managers, under the control of the theatrical syndicate. This control was thus easily secured owing to the tempting prospect held out to the theater-owners. It was represented to them, and rightly represented, that they would be relieved of the necessity and work of securing attractions for their houses, and that this work would be done through the booking-office of the syndicate, acting as a sort of theatrical clearing-house. [. . .] From thirty, the number of theaters in the control of the syndicate has augmented to over five hundred, and the number of managers who are under its thumb has increased in a proportionate ratio. The representations of the theatrical syndicate were true enough as far as they went, but how far did they go? Managers of theaters were told the truth, but not the whole truth—that is, not until they were well within the syndicate web. As soon, however, as they had been safely entangled, and had had time to look about them, seeing their brother flies in a like predicament, the "whole truth" was vouchsafed in a manner not to be mistaken. And the whole truth was that they were allowed to keep their houses clean and well lighted, but were to have no voice whatsoever in the choice of attractions to be played under their own roofs. Further than this, a strict taboo was placed upon the attractions of those managers who refused to abide by syndicate methods or to accept syndicate terms. [. . .]

[. . .] The influence of the theatrical trust extends now to the remotest hamlet (provided the hamlet happens to have a playhouse, or a hall where plays may be given), and the owners and managers of from five to seven hundred theaters in the United States of America are reduced to the status of servants—not public servants, as in a sense they should be, but servants of an organization whose representatives say to them, "Take what is given you, or you will get nothing!" [. . .]

The syndicate, having secured its corner in the theatrical market, now held the key to the situation. Very few first-rate, or even second-rate, theaters remaining in the hands of the independent owners, it is manifest that the syndicate was in a position to dictate in any way it chose, not only to theater-owners, but to the managers of attractions who came to it for bookings. Thus the control of the theaters meant the control of attractions, and the control of attractions meant the subjugation of the theater-owners throughout the United States. The theatrical trust had completed its circular web; it remained only to develop the branching strands. [. . .]

With the business of their booking-agency already flourishing in a minor way, Messrs. Klaw & Erlanger had the advantage of their associates at the start. This advantage they took care to maintain and increase until, gradually overriding the other members of the organization, they have come to be looked upon as the head and front of the trust in themselves. It was inevitable, therefore, that the policy to be developed and carried out should turn either for good or for ill according to the conscience, integrity and refinement of Messrs. Klaw & Erlanger, and it is to be regretted that with such vast opportunities for good at their command, they had neither the necessary ability nor the necessary culture to conduct their transactions with that due consideration for the artistic side of their profession which alone raises it above the business of a pork-packer.

That the theatrical situation here in America to-day is the calamitous result of these gentlemen's methods, is a truth which can hardly be gainsaid when we look facts in the face. The almost limitless resources at the beck and call of the trust have gradually enabled it to destroy competition in such a way that, with very few exceptions, the entire army of independent producers is now either bankrupt or in the employ of the syndicate. Men of artistic ability, of discriminating judgment, whose work was beneficial to the community at large, whose productions were an educational force, have been obliged to sink their individualities, either by submitting to the dictates of a business organization and practically becoming its servants, or by forsaking their profession and carrying themselves and their energies into other fields. The policy of the syndicate made an alternative impossible, for if the manager of a successful play, which may have cost from thirty to seventy thousand dollars to produce, refused to accede to the dictates of the trust, his production was relegated to the warehouse for want of theaters to put it in. In other words, it was the syndicate policy to force managers of successful plays into literally presenting them with an interest in their productions—a policy which it was able to exercise owing to its control of all the principal theaters in America. Practically, the syndicate said, "Give us an interest in your production, or we cannot give you a route!" And an interest in the production did not mean a fair and reasonable percentage; it meant an exacting tribute—a third, and in some cases half, of the total profits. At the same time, it must be understood that the syndicate assumed no risks whatever, so that if the play of an independent manager failed, the loss fell solely upon the producer. [. . .]

[. . .] they [members of the trust] began to make productions on their own account—began to enter into competition with the very managers and producers whose interests they were morally bound to serve. Holding absolute control of the situation, these managers elected to compete with their own customers. The majority of available theaters about the country being at their command, they doubtless asked why they should not further utilize the monopoly, to become themselves proprietors of attractions.

The case had both an artistic and an ethical aspect. On the artistic side, in a man who has hitherto been solely connected with business pursuits, the attempt to select stars, to judge manuscripts and to produce plays must be considered a brave adventure; while from an ethical point of view, the experiment which the booking members of the syndicate now proposed to themselves would have been a dangerous one, even to the most ticklish conscience. In the first place, it is to be remembered that these gentlemen were in a position to know every business detail connected with the enterprises of their customers, and in the second, that they could, if they wished, take advantage of this knowledge to book their own attractions accordingly. There was the temptation to usurp the best time for themselves; the temptation to monopolize the "business" of a city by sending a powerful attraction in their control to play against some less profitable work which they were, nevertheless, paid to book; and there was the temptation to furnish poor routes and poor time to rival managers, while reserving the better territory and the more desirable dates for plays of their own. [. . .]

Not only are the methods of these managers, as above outlined, significant of their unhealthy influence, but so also is the policy they adopt in dealing with those who attempt to defy their authority. From time to time, certain men have arisen with hearts full of hope for the future of the American stage, and a fine regard for its artistic importance. These rebels to the syndicate have found themselves unable to tolerate the arbitrary and dictatorial methods of a coterie of individuals who, whatever else may be said of them, cannot be allowed to have achieved their extraordinary power through any great qualities of mind. One by one, however, the rebels have been overcome—either crushed out or bought off by the trust, so that now the only really independent managers left in the field are Mrs. Harrison Grey Fiske and myself. As we have each a theater of his own in New York city, the syndicate realizes its inability to dictate to us as it dictates to others, and, in consequence, it has made us the objects of its bitterest assaults. Of late, however, I appear to have been a chief target, and for this reason, perhaps I may be permitted to cite one or two personal instances, as a further illustration of the policy of the theatrical trust. [. . .]

[. . .] The greater evil, the greatest evil of all, is the debasing influence exercised by certain members of the syndicate on the American stage. It is the influence of the greed of gain and of the lack of culture displayed by managers, who have no veneration, save a commercial one, for the traditions of the past; no thought, save a commercial one, for the possibilities of the future; no care, save a commercial one, for the potentialities of the present. We have heard very much about commercialism of late—much that was wise and much, perhaps, that was foolish; but it remains an undoubted truth that no pursuit classified as an art can be revolutionized and classified as a business. [. . .]

Aside from this purely commercial aspect of the case, it cannot be too often insisted upon that another evil effect of syndicate methods is the tendency to submerge individuals and thus to destroy competition. But by destroying competition, you destroy originality; by destroying competition, you make the creation of a standard of excellence well-nigh impossible. What, then, is the result? The result is a plethora of foreign failures, of indifferently dramatized novels, of inane and tiresome musical comedy. The result is the degradation of the national stage—the decadence of the national drama.

Fortunately, the remedy for such a condition of affairs lies with the public, and in view of the present season alone, it can hardly be doubted that the public is already applying that remedy with a high hand. It is with theatricals as it is with politics—in the last event the public is the arbitrator. Moreover, the meteoric rise of the syndicate and consequent decline in the art of the stage should give promise of an equally speedy dissolution, when the time is ripe; for decay, whether it be social or esthetic, of nations or of an art, is generally sure in proportion to its slowness. May we not, then, console ourselves with the thought that when the worm is removed from the root, the flower will bloom again?

[See also [428].]

[420] M. Klaw. "The Theatrical Syndicate. The Other Side"
The Cosmopolitan [1904]

[. . .] The theater in the United States is not a public institution, and it is about time some one said so.

An attempt is made now and then to draw a parallel between the theater and, for example, the railroad, as illustrations of public institutions. There is this difference between them: The railroad takes up the public highway, which is yours and mine and everybody's. The theater, on the other hand, does not take up one inch that it does not pay for—and in most cases it pays twice as much as anybody else would pay for the same thing. In America there are no governmental subsidies for theaters. Private capital has built every playhouse in the land.

The theater is not primarily an educator of the public. Many good folk think it is, but this is not so. It is not so, because there hasn't been any demand by the public that it should be educated. Let the demand once become apparent, and the desired response will immediately follow. The theater is governed by the rules and observances of all other commercial enterprises. It is not out to dictate to public taste. It is out to satisfy the public demand. While even such a purely business undertaking must be hedged about with the essential suggestions of artistic requirement, I do not believe the public demands of us that we give over our commercialism. Moreover, the public would have no such right. What the public has the right to ask of the manager is that he shall give it good, clean, decent entertainment of a wholesome sort. That is as far as the public should go. And it is the duty of the manager to label his wares, honestly and clearly, that they may not be mistaken, just as it is the obligation of every other merchant to display indications of the character of the contents of his establishment.

The primary inspiration of the theatrical syndicate was the fact that local managers, through a lack of organization, were rapidly approaching bankruptcy. I know of no better way to express the situation than as dog-eat-dog methods. Exaggerated receipts were constantly published, and the glittering results thus shown induced outside capital to invest in theatricals and the building of theaters followed. The frenzied rivalry could have but one result—managers and lessees of theaters saw their money fading away, with no apparent chance to stem the tide, for none would give an inch, and so all suffered. When, as frequently happened, two theaters would go up in a single town capable of supporting only one, it meant the ruin of the managers of both.

There is no more clashing of dates, under the arrangement effected by the theatrical syndicate. Everybody is making money, as should be the case. The audiences in the interior towns are witnessing as strong attractions as New Yorkers are given, and there is no longer any conflict of rival interests. [. . .]

The theatrical syndicate has brought order out of chaos, legitimate profit out of ruinous rivalry. Under its operations the actor has received a higher salary than was ever his, the producing manager has been assured a better percentage on his investment, and the local manager has won the success which comes from the booking of accepted metropolitan favorites. I know of no one, generally speaking, who has been worked an injury by the commercialization of the stage in America. Practically every first-class theatrical manager is now a member of it, and never in the history of theatricals have they all been so prosperous.

[434] C. H. Meltzer. "The New Theater"
The Independent [1907]

[. . .] While they are talking and dreaming of a National Theater in England, Americans have begun to build one. True, it will be known, when completed, as the "New"—not as the "National " Theater. But the purposes of the projected playhouse will be no less broad for lack of a name which would, perhaps, have been misleading; as the money for building it will be provided, not by a sceptical and reluctant government, but by a group of public spirited and enlightened capitalists. [. . .]

Like other men with brains, Mr. Heinrich Conried, director of the Metropolitan Opera House, had long hoped to be the promotor, and, perhaps, manager, of a theater in which literature, drama and the art of acting should find free and full expression here, regardless of the customary financial drawbacks. [. . .]

The chief purposes of the New Theater, as they have been explained to the writer by some of the founders and by the Administrator-General [Conried], are to promote the best interests of the stage, and to improve the public taste, by the organization of a permanent company of trained actors, who will interpret (in English) the best standard plays in the dramatic literature of the world, and, from time to time, will appear in new works by American and foreign authors. The founders (and Mr. Conried) are convinced that the stimulating example set by the New Theater will rapidly develop the unquestionable talent of American dramatists, help to reform acting, and result in the creation of a dignified and admirable American drama. [. . .]

[436] J. Corbin. "The Dawn of the American Drama"
Atlantic Monthly [1907]

[. . .] Quite boldly, then, I prophesy the dawn of the American drama; and quite confidently, too, for the drama has already dawned. [. . .] The present season, I am persuaded, has been the most notable in the history of our stage;

and every indication points to a brighter day to come. [. . .]

If the drama is dawning, the fact is in a large measure due to the organization of independent managers into what is in effect an anti-syndicate; for though the Fafnir of monopoly may lie gorged with possessions, fate will not allow it to sleep. It is a mistake, I think, to regard this as the sole cause. Shortly before his death, the late Kirke La Shelle, one of the ablest and most intelligent of our managers, remarked that native playwrights were beginning to write in the technique of the European masters, and that the time was at hand when we should have a vigorous drama. On hearing the remark, one of the syndicate dramatists asked somewhat skeptically who these new playwrights were, and where were their plays. It was the wrong time for scoffing. The Shubert brothers had already established a formidable circuit of first class theatres in the leading American cities, and had secured the cooperation of other independent managers, who had openly revolted against the arbitrary authority and the financial exactions of the syndicate booking agency,—among them Mr. and Mrs. Fiske, David Belasco, and Walter N. Lawrence. Actors, too, and among them the ablest and most prominent, seceded to the anti-syndicate. There was an urgent need of plays.

Meantime another powerful factor had been introduced into the situation. The supply of foreign pieces, by monopolizing which the syndicate had built up its strength, was failing. As for plays from the Continent, two influences combined to invalidate them. The growth of native feeling in our audiences rendered the old method of false and specious adaption powerless; and, with the growth of realism and the literary sense abroad, the plays themselves were becoming more and more difficult to transpose into terms of American life. [. . .] The newer order of dramatists—Ibsen, Sudermann, Hauptmann, Capus, Brieux, Donnay, Lavedan and others—were on the whole impossible, at once because of their greater intellectuality, their more local and individual presentation of life, and the gloominess or unmorality of their themes. [. . .]

There has been an attempt to make the public believe that the anti-syndicate is inspired by a lofty devotion to dramatic art; but in part at least this is manifest buncombe. The most powerful factors in the combination, the Shuberts, are quite of the type of the syndicate managers. They have been more daring in their reliance on fresh talent, but there has been nothing to show that this has been the result of anything higher than commercial necessity. [. . .] In short, the conditions governing the dramatic world continue all but as purely commercial as they have been. I am stating a fact, not preferring a charge. If any one is to blame for the commercialism of the drama, it is not the merchants who purvey it, but ourselves, who have rested content with no better than the average public demands. [. . .]

[437] W. Mailly. "The Season's Social Drama"
The Arena [1907]

If evidence were needed that a change is taking place in the character of the drama being presented on the American stage, the record of the New York season just closed furnishes it. Never have so many plays dealing with subjects of social interest and significance been seen in this city during any one season, and since New York is the theatrical center of the United States, it is safe to say that this indicates a general condition. "The serious drama," said a man associated with national theatrical journalism for many years, "is forging to the front rapidly, and it is the most hopeful sign in the dramatic world to-day."

We can all echo that; but the change is coming none too soon, though it had to come sooner or later. The theater had to reflect the changing social conditions and respond to the quickening social conscience of the time. The economic revolution that has internationalized industry, popularized education, and brought humanity into closer relationship, is working a revolution in the thought and outlook of the great masses of the people. As science, literature, music and art are being impregnated with the spirit of change and advance, so the theater also, "that compound of all the arts," is at last thrilling with the impulse of the new era of social unity and consciousness.

[. . .] The same spirit of unrest and investigation and criticism which permeates the whole of modern society, and which has expressed itself to some degree in the current literature of the time, must also find expression in the drama, if the drama is to fulfill its true function as the interpreter and illuminator of its age. Those who lament the passing of Romanticism and the oncoming of Realism as degrading to the stage are setting their faces against the forces of progress at work in every phase of human activity.

The English-speaking stage has remained the most conservative, and, therefore, the most backward, of any in the world, until its adherence to conventional forms has become a humiliation to those who realize that the drama, to be vital and significant, must deal with the concrete things which concern humanity. The complex and cosmopolitan life of to-day presents ever new problems to the people, problems which they cannot escape from, try as they will. The notion that the chief function of the theater is to provide such an avenue of escape is being dissipated. The enjoyment of farce and musical comedy or resplendent scenic productions is but temporary, and is quickly followed by a rude return to the harsh realities of life—besides leaving the mind nothing but husks to feed upon.

Problems are not settled or evaded in that way. Gradually it is becoming recognized that the theater has a higher mission than merely that of amusement-purveyor to the thoughtless or frivolous. Men and women who are tired and jaded with the merciless commercial struggle are turning to the theater for intellectual stimulus and spiritual satisfaction, and are looking for plays treating with the questions which beset them daily and for which their minds and souls are yearning for a solution. [. . .]

The most important contribution of an American dramatist to our stage this year was [William Vaughn Moody's] *The Great Divide* [1906], which, in a way, marks the dividing line between the past and the future of our stage. [. . .]

[453] G. J. Nathan. "The United States of Playwrights"
The Bookman [1909]

It has been said that if you turn to the person who happens to be sitting next to you in a subway, elevated or surface car in New York and ask him how the play he is writing is getting along, his reply nine times out of ten will assure you that your presumption was correct. Yes, he is writing a play. For statistics indicate that a veritable tidal wave of plays has flooded recently as is flooding still into the metropolitan play brokers' and managers' offices. Not only from New York, but from cities and villages in every State of the Union, dramatic compositions of more or less merit have clogged the mails on the producers' desks, until there has been recorded for the year ended June 1st, 1909, the high water mark of unsolicited play manuscripts. It is said that approximately 13,000 plays were received from confident authors from all over the country during the period of time mentioned. The consensus of the estimates of the dramatic bureaus and managers places the figure several thousand higher than the figure for the year previous.

That only about three per cent. of the huge annual influx of voluntarily submitted plays ever reaches the producing stage is a further disclosure arrived at by averaging the estimates of the various persons to whom the manuscripts are sent. Some place the figures as high as five per cent., while others state that two per cent. might be a fairer estimate. Specialising in the matter of statistics bearing on unsolicited manuscript, it may be interesting to note that one of the leading New York play agents received exactly 1,702 dramatic compositions during the last year from novices living in thirty different States; that Henry B. Harris, the theatrical producer, received 251 plays from unknown playwrights during a single week in January of this year; that Charles Frohman's mail never fails to bring annually in at least eleven or twelve hundred plays from writers of whom he has never heard; and that Henry W. Savage has been deluged during the last few months with a hitherto not even remotely approached number of gratuitously submitted manuscripts.

Theatrical producers say that never before has the entire country been attacked with the play-writing mania to the extent it has been recently. And, in this connection, it is curious to record the fact—established by a compilation of statistics from many sources—that the particular communities that lead in the list of amateur playwrights who have sent in their products to the producing centre are Washington, D.C., Brooklyn, N.Y., and Los Angeles, Cal. From each of these cities alone several hundred dramatic compositions were received in the time mentioned.

The recent wholesale writing of plays in every section of the United States is not without its explanation, for all the producers concur in the opinion that it has been brought about by the considerable number of articles that have been published broadcast telling of the great fortunes that have been made by such playwrights as Augustus Thomas, Clyde Fitch, Eugene Walter, *et al.* Articles on this topic—the huge revenue that is accrued from successful plays—have been printed and reprinted so frequently in journals of the villages as well as the cities that it is not to be wondered at that so many persons have seized their untried pens and have rushed into what they have come to believe is the easiest and most fertile field of fortune.

In answer to the question: "Do the great majority of these persons know anything at all of even the fundamentals of dramatic construction?" the managers and agents who read the manuscripts unanimously agree in the negative. Only in rare instances does a play arrive in the daily mails that carries within it a vestige of the knowledge of the science of drama making. Almost all the plays, furthermore, are extremely artificial and utterly devoid of the quality known as human interest. It is said that statistics prove that more than one-half of the works of the tyro dramatists are of the romantic trend. *The Three Musketeers* is believed to have furnished more inspiration to amateur playwrights than any other story.

Novices revel in romantic themes and disguised "Musketeers" pour into the managers and agents under a great diversity of titles. The romantic plays that have been evolved by hopeful writers the country over contain romance with a vengeance, many of them being made up entirely of love scenes between the hero and heroine with a long series of duels thrown in for good measure. Two other favourite themes are the long lost sister and the eventual discovery of her identity by her brother, who, in the meantime, has fallen in love with her, and the wayward son and his subsequent reconciliation with his family. [. . .]

Theodore Burt Sayre, perhaps the best known play reader in America, has been looking over the tens of thousands of plays that have been submitted by amateur dramatists to Charles Frohman for the last ten years, and his observations, accordingly, must be regarded as being based on considerable experience. He says, "Mr. Frohman receives plays written on everything from paper bags to wrapping paper. [. . .] Most of them are as untrue to life as one could imagine. [. . .] If the novice playwrights would remember what I have termed the three S-entials, I am sure their efforts would stand a much greater chance for success."

The three "S-entials" in play construction, as Mr. Sayre puts it, are sympathy, suspense and surprise. [. . .]

Henry W. Savage recently took time to reply at length to an aspiring dramatist who had complained to him that he (Mr. Savage) had returned three plays to him with no detailed explanation as to why they had been rejected. Mr. Savage's tabulated advice to this man and, he says, to all other tyros, was and is as follows:

I. Write a clean love story—the kind that, when you were a boy, made you curl up in a corner and continue reading while the folks went to dinner.
II. Write something new, even if you never saw it on the stage before. It might go.
III. Do not select as a subject any current news topic.
IV. Do not attempt to write about anything with which you are not familiar.
V. Make your characters natural. To be so, they must do only what men and women do in real life, and not what the story books say they do.
VI. Make your characters speak good English.
VII. Do not use stilted words.
VIII. Do not say, "I have found the papers with the old man's will secreted," etc.
IX. Do not preach. The public can secure free seats in a church.
X. Remember that an audience has imagination and that it reads newspapers and has real human intelligence.
XI. Avoid soliloquies.
XII. Do not put too much in your play.
XIII. Do not distribute your scenes so widely that you have one on an island, another at Herald Square and a third in Chicago.
XIV. Make the action of your play take place all in one day if possible.

[. . .]

[454] C. Hamilton. "Over–Production in the American Theatre"
Forum [1909]

Dramatic Art and the Theatre Business

[. . .] At the present time, the dramatic art in America is suffering from a very unusual economic condition, which is unsound from the business standpoint, and which is likely, in the long run, to weary and to alienate the more thoughtful class of theatre-goers. This condition may be indicated by the one word—*over-production*. Some years ago, when the theatre trust was organized, its leaders perceived that the surest way to win a monopoly of the theatre business was to get control of the leading theatre-buildings throughout the country and then refuse to house in them the productions of any independent manager who opposed them. By this procedure on the part of the theatre trust, the few managers who maintained their independence were forced to build theatres in those cities where they wished their attractions to appear. When, a few years later, the organized opposition to the original theatre trust grew, to such dimensions as to become in fact a second trust, it could carry on its campaign only by building a new chain of theatres to house its productions in those cities whose already existing theatres were in the hands of the original syndicate. As a result of this warfare between the two trusts, nearly all the chief cities of the country are now saddled with more theatre-buildings than they can naturally and easily support. [. . .] In New York itself this condition is even more exaggerated. Nearly every season some of the minor producing managers shift their allegiance from one trust to the other; and since they seldom seem to know very far in advance just where they will stand when they may wish to make their next production in New York, the only way in which they can assure themselves of a Broadway booking is to build and hold a theatre of their own. Hence, in the last few years, there has been an epidemic of theatre building in New York. And this, it should be carefully observed, has resulted from a false economic condition; for new theatres have been built, not in order to supply a natural demand from the theatre-going population, but in defiance of the limits imposed by that demand.

A theatre-building is a great expense to its owners. It always occupies land in one of the most costly sections of a city; and in New York this consideration is of especial importance. The building itself represents a large investment. These two items alone make it ruinous for the owners to let the building stand idle for any lengthy period. They must keep it open as many weeks as possible throughout the year; and if play after play fails upon its stage, they must still seek other entertainments to attract sufficient money to cover the otherwise dead loss of the rent. Hence there exists at the present in America a false demand for plays—a demand, that is to say, which is occasioned not by the natural need of the theatre-going population but by the frantic need on the part of warring managers to keep their theatres open. It is, of course, impossible to find enough first-class plays to meet this fictitious demand; and the managers are therefore obliged to buy up quantities of second-class plays, which they know to be inferior and which they do not expect the public to approve, because it will cost them less to present these inferior attractions to a small business than it would cost to shut down some of their superfluous theatres.

In New York, nobody will go to the theatre in July, and most of the playhouses are forced to close. Practically speaking, nobody will go to the theatre in August either, except the fairly large floating population from such towns as Omaha and Kansas City that drifts to the metropolis at that uncomfortable season for purposes of business, or sight-seeing, or both. A few years ago, the theatres of New York remained closed until the middle of September. This year most of them opened with a rush at the beginning of August. The managers apparently decided that they could save the rent of their theatre-buildings for that month by shovelling on the stage some sort of entertainment which might attract the visitor from Kansas City and show him the interior of a Broadway playhouse. It is obvious that no manager would waste at such a season a production which he fully believed to be first class; any play which he knew absolutely to be good he would naturally save for one of the four best months for new productions—October, November, January, or February; and the logical inference is, therefore, that the managers themselves knew very well that their August offerings were second class. We are thus confronted with the anomalous condition of a business man offering for sale, at the regular price, goods which he knows to be inferior, because he thinks that there are just enough costumers available who are sufficiently uncritical not to detect the cheat. Thereby he hopes, in the off season, to cover the rent of an edifice which he has built, in defiance of sound economic principles, in a community that is not prepared to support it throughout the year. No very deep knowledge of economics is necessary to perceive that this must become, in the long run, a ruinous business policy. Too many theatres showing too many plays too many months in the year cannot finally make money; and this falsity in the economic situation reacts against the dramatic art itself and against the public's appreciation of that art. Good work suffers by the constant accompaniment of bad work which is advertised in exactly the same phrases; and the public, which is forced to see five bad plays in order to find one good one, grows weary and loses faith. The way to improve our dramatic art is to reform the economics of our theatre business. We should produce fewer plays, and better ones. We should seek by scientific investigation to determine just how many theatres our cities can support, and how many weeks in the year they may legitimately be expected to support them. Having thus determined the real demand for plays that comes from the theatre-going population, the managers should then bestir themselves to secure sufficient good plays to satisfy that demand. That, surely, is the limit of sound and legitimate business. The arbitrary creation of a further, false demand, and the feverish grasping at a fictitious supply, are evidences of unsound economic methods, which are certain, in the long run, to fail.

[456] [The Arrival of the Moving–Picture Shows]
Scribner's Magazine [1909]

[. . .] The American who claims for his own a certain degree of what Boston women reverently call "culture," is allowed [. . .] to be a rather impossible person in his dramatic standards. The idea of a play as the vehicle of a "star" in an emotional or, better yet, a "character" part, is about as far as he goes in his appreciation of drama. Why, then, is the newest form dramatic art has taken left to the office-boy and the cash-girl and the submerged nine-tenths to enjoy? Enjoy it they, at least, do, and get better value for their money than do the patrons of real theatres. The price is five cents, or at most ten; [. . .] think what you are saving on your entertainment, even as compared with a place at the "polite vaudeville" theatre round the corner—to say nothing at all of anything so extravagant as attendance at the playhouse where they are giving a dramatized "best-seller"!

It is only when you tell the Prosperous Person that there are a rising ten thousand of moving-picture establishments that he "takes notice"; it is the figures that talk to him. What all of us should realize is that this new department of the modern drama is—relatively—a virgin soil. Who knows what crops it may yet raise? And why assume that depravity—gross vulgarity even—is necessarily bound up in it? [. . .] After all, why *not* can our drama, when all's said and done? And if the canning's to be done, it had best be well done. Caruso and the rest are not above singing into operatic cans that we open up in our flat houses. Canned drama is only the next step. This is the age of the machine.

They have come to stay, the moving-picture shows—as an institution, that is. There may well be too many houses in operation at the present moment; a process of elimination is to be expected as this business becomes better and better organized. What I insist on is the propriety of it, all things considered. [. . .]

[457] "The Theatre of Ideas"
The Nation [1910]

[. . .] Our old friends, "questions of the day," still hold the stage, but the old zest is not there, and, by all accounts, neither are the old box office receipts. We have had successful plays of late that have dealt neither with capital and labor, nor with dishonest bosses, nor with the iniquities of Wall Street. We have had plays of late that have attempted to deal with social questions of high importance, and have not been very successful. The trend seems to be away from the drama of what the advertisements describe as the burning question of the hour. [. . .]

But there is one question of the day that has been generally overlooked. And that is, that when all is said and done, a stupid and ill-built play is a bad play, and no amount of contemporary social or political significance can make it anything but a bad play. The theatre among us has never suffered from a superfluity of ideas to an extent that would justify our sniffing at them. But there is all the difference in the world between putting ideas on the stage in adequate form, and putting on the stage in any form anything that the newspapers and militant magazines may be talking about; whether it be

Christian Science or dress reform, child labor or breakfast foods. It is impossible to deny that the drift has been towards making the theatre a universal forum. It is also impossible to deny that the thing cannot be done, and that we are beginning to find it out. [. . .] Is it really essential that the evils of tabacco-smoking or the bad effects of dancing on the heart should be discussed upon the stage? [. . .]

[459] C. Hamilton. "The Younger American Playwrights"
The Bookman [1910]

Only a dozen years ago a play of contemporary American life by a comparatively unknown American author was a rarity upon the New York stage; most of the offerings were importations or adaptions from abroad, or else dramatisations of popular novels, mainly foreign; and the few original American plays were the work of half a dozen men who had somehow gotten themselves established in our theatre and were untroubled by any emphatic knocking of the younger generation at the door. Nowadays the aspect of our stage is different. Considerably more than half the plays that are produced during a season in New York are plays dealing with America to-day; and of these the greater number are written by men and women whose names were totally unknown half a dozen years ago. [. . .] In the artistic sense, our new playwrights have succeeded in the great aim of entertainment and have revealed many glimpses of life which are new and true. But should we, therefore, be justified in boasting that we have at present an American Drama, in the sense that there is a French Drama, a German Drama, a Norwegian Drama, even a British Drama? [. . .]

[. . .] For the fact seems to be that Mr. Thomas is just now our only dramatist, without a second, and that the large and interesting group of American playwrights, each of whom evinces some special and particular claim to third place in the hierarchy, are only dramatists in the making, some of whom may rise to leadership and win the worthier appellation, while others will merely continue to render service in the ranks, without promotion. A playwright is a man who writes entertaining and successful plays; a dramatist is a playwright who teaches while he entertains, adds to the sum total of national thought by evolving, formulating, and expounding truths which theretofore have lain latent in the national consciousness; he must be not an artist only, but a seer also—not a follower merely, but a leader as well; he must master the stage as a medium of expression and he must use it to express ideas. It is in this high sense that Mr. Thomas is at present our only dramatist; but there is decided promise in the work of many of our new and growing group of playwrights. [. . .]

Perhaps the main merit of our younger American playwrights is the remarkable freshness, vividness, and accuracy of their observation of many interesting phases of American life. They have clear and eager eyes for what is going on about them. [. . .] But this gift of observation, which has grown prevalent among our playwrights, has hardly seemed in any instance to be supplemented by a deeply penetrant vision. Our playwrights record facts; they rarely reveal truths. They give us a glimpse of living; they seldom open a vista upon life. It is not unfair to say that, for all their accuracy of observation, they have not achieved an understanding of American life. Understanding may be defined as apprehension plus comprehension. Our playwrights evidence the former; they do not, as a rule, reveal the latter. We know already how life looks; we want to be told what life is: and our new playwrights cannot tell us, because they do not know. They have grasped the materials, but have not reached the themes, of the great drama of American life. [. . .]

Again, our younger playwrights have shown a surprising gift for sketching the details of character, and have populated our stage with a multitude of minor figures that are real [. . .] [that] are not the old conventional puppets of the stage, but are convincingly alive. They think and feel and act and talk like actual people. Step on their toes, and they will swear—or beg your pardon. And yet, on the other hand, no single large and memorable character emerges from any of these plays to live afterward within our recollection. Our new playwrights sketch characters; they do not draw them. Their skill confines itself to the rendering of minor figures; they seem incapable of that sustained effort of imagination which results in the creation of a figure at once living and large. They deftly note those specific and individual characteristics which define a person sharply and set him apart from his fellows; but they fail of imagining those generic and broadly human characteristics which make a person typical of multitudes and unite him to his fellows. [. . .] We have had many plays of American business; but we have imagined no great American business man. We have had several plays of American politics; but we have created no great American politician. We have written countless plays about the West; but is there a single character in any of them who is sufficiently typical and resumptive to step bodily out of the story and walk living through [the] halls of memory [. . .].

Our new dramatic authors have shown an easy aptitude for story-telling. [. . .] But this particular gift is just as likely to be dangerous as to be helpful. In the theatre it is more important to build a story firmly than to ripple through it fluently. Many of our plays are too narrative in arrangement. Our authors allow themselves to dally along alluring by-paths of invention, instead of rigorously excluding all material that is not emphatically pertinent to the theme. [. . .] We hear very little earnest discussion among our playwrights about the technical aspects of their art. They do not develop ideas of how plays should be written—ideas for which they are willing to argue and to work. In America the drama suffers because of the absence of dramatic criticism. Not only does it receive hardly any help from the newspaper and magazine reviewers, but our playwrights themselves seem to take very little critical interest in the problems of their art. We have no school of dramatic authors, because our authors are not willing to go to school. We make no concerted and organised effort to improve the technique of our drama, because we carelessly assume that whatever is good enough is good enough. What we need is a leader—to follow or to revolt from, as we choose. The British drama has such a leader in Sir Arthur Pinero. [. . .] Our playwrights wander apart and do their work as best they may, without striving to aid or to combat each other. Just as our plays, referred to life, are not about anything, because they are lacking in themes, so our stage, referred to art, is not about anything, because it is lacking in tendencies. We shall not really do things in our theatre until we find out what it is we want to do.

[. . .] If adherence to actuality be the best ideal of dramatic writing, then we must set the dialogue of our younger playwrights very high indeed. In life, people actually talk as Miss Crother's people talk upon the stage. But Sir Arthur Pinero's characters do not talk as people talk in life; they merely seem to do so. Most of our playwrights write habitually in slang, to accentuate the sense of actuality. Mr. Henry Arthur Jones does not write in slang; and yet we have not equalled the spontaneity and liveliness of his dialogue in *The Liars* [1897]. Our new writers are too desperately afraid of seeming literary. It is true that one or two of them, like Mr. Moody and Mr. Percy MacKaye, have erred upon the other side. [William Vaughn Moody's] *The Great Divide* [1906] was weighted down with writing; and Mr. MacKaye, in *Mater* [1908], marred a really fine comedy by embroidering it with verbal conceits and forcing all the characters to speak the language of a Harvard senior showing off. But can we not touch and hold a note between over-writing and under-writing? If we refuse to be so literary as Mr. MacKaye, must we be so slangy as Mr. [Paul] Armstrong and Mr. [James] Forbes? At present the best things that are said in our plays are said in a language that, while fresh and emphatic at the moment, will be out of date and hardly intelligible a dozen years from now. Would it not be wiser to mould a more permanent medium of speech to the service of our laudable purpose to seem natural? Might it not be helpful if, like the European playwrights, we should publish our plays and submit our dialogue to the exacting test of print?

Let us now sum up the ground that we have covered in the foregoing analysis. We have seen that our younger playwrights have been quick to observe facts, but slow to reveal truths, they have been reporters rather than creators; they have apprehended, but not comprehended, the possibilities of drama in the life of America to-day. Their plays have lacked themes. They have sketched a multitude of living minor characters, but have drawn scarcely any major characters that are sufficiently resumptive and important to be remembered apart from the plays in which they figured. They have told stories fluently, but have not built them firmly. They have written dialogue that is natural but not permanent. They have lacked the vision to realise the profound and underlying aspects of our life, the imagination to create large and lasting characters, the technical training and the critical application to develop a mastery of structure, and the serious literary purpose to achieve an enduring ideal of writing. Thus succinctly stated in summary, this criticism seems an excessively severe arraignment of the work of our younger playwrights. We must hasten, therefore, to remember that each of them has been free of many of the faults which have been enumerated as prevalent among the group considered as a whole, and that most of them at moments have risen superior even to the merits that have been indicated as characteristic of them all.

And if our rising playwrights have not yet developed a national drama that is worthy of the name, we must remember also that the outlook for the future—even for the immediate future—is very hopeful. There is an opinion prevalent at present among the dramatists and the dramatic critics in London that the next great development of drama in the English language will take place in America rather than in England. The opinion is based on the almost unlimited opportunities offered to new playwrights by the multiplicity of our theatres, on the high degree of education and intelligence that is common to our audiences throughout the country, and on the inexhaustible richness of our national life in themes hitherto unexploited on the stage. This is a fair statement of the opportunity that stands before us, and of which we have not yet availed ourselves. We have not written nearly enough good plays to fill our thousands and thousands of theatres; we have written down to our audiences instead of up to them; and the great themes that lie latent in our national life we have scarcely touched at all. [. . .] Some of the playwrights now before us may develop the technical mastery and the penetrant vision, the high seriousness and the imagination, the art and the message, that must go to the making of the next American dramatist; and if not, others surely will arise. The conditions are ripe, and all that is needed is the men; and it is one of the miracles of destiny that when great work is ready to be done, the necessary men arise to do it.

[469] "Another Stage Experiment"
The Nation [1911]

For its first experiment, the Chicago Theatre Society, which was recently organized under the presidency of Hamlin Garland, announces a season of "joyous" drama. The phrase is a happy one, possibly even more so than the user of it was aware. For to Mr. Garland the principal function of the "joyous" drama would be to wean the American people away from the puerilities of the musical "show." [. . .] Reformers of the theatre too often make the mistake of leaping from the musical-comedy level to the Ibsen level, and thus supply an opening for scornful girding at the "highbrows." What reformers too often fail to perceive is that there can be truth and art in the lightest of comedies; and that truth in art is what the American theatre needs most. As a people we dislike, on the stage, what is truthful and what is disagreeable. When you give us Ibsen, you give us both. What the Chicago experiment seems to be on the point of doing is to omit the disagreeable treatment for the present. It is a council of wisdom. [. . .]

Our greatest need for the present is not to be educated in the subtleties of the human soul and human conduct, but to be rescued from the posturings and the melodramatics that travesty the broadest facts of human conduct. [. . .] It is the overoiled arm of coincidence that typifies the vice of our drama. From seeing people happen to be in places, where they have no right to be, and turn out to be what they have no right to be, one gets easily accustomed to seeing them perform unnatural heroics, take unnatural postures, and exhibit unnatural virtues and vices. Many plays succeed because they are "dainty," "sweet," and "clean." No one would grudge them their success if to these qualities they added a touch of truth and life. But too often the "charming" play is as false in its mechanism as the would-be realistic play. Our serious plays suffer from an excess of melodrama. Most of our light plays suffer from an excess of what we think is "life" but is not.

Here, then, is the chance for the "joyous" drama. If it can only free us from the belief that when we enter a theatre we have left the probabilities of life and character behind, it will have done the work that lies closest to its hand. There is no insistence here on the intellectual drama, nor even on the drama that settles the same questions of the day that the newspapers settle every day. The captains of industry and stock-exchange villains and honest young district attorneys who have latterly invaded the stage illustrate admirably that debasement of standards which we have described as melodramatics. Multi-millionaires and Trusts and private secretaries and stenographers are undeniably real things, and the audience consequently takes it for granted that the play must be a realistic play. But if the captain of industry displays the intelligence of a rabbit, if the good young business man reveals the virtues of an Ivanhoe, and the heroine who frustrates the captain of industry reveals chiefly a fascinating smile and a touch of hysterics—it is from that species of the "drama of life" that the "joyous" drama can deliver us. Give us comedy of the lightest, if you will, but a comedy of human beings and not of lay-figures.

[484] C. Hamilton. "Timely Topics in the Theatre"
The Bookman [1913]

The American drama at the present time seems to be hovering in a state of transition between that initial period during which it was made up of mere theatrical machinery and discussed no topics of serious importance to the public, and that still future period during which it will ascend to the revelation of permanent realities of life. Meanwhile, it is devoted mainly to an exhibition of the events of the hour and a discussion of the topics of the day.

Our most successful playwrights, for the moment, are those who hold their noses close to their newspapers. They gather what is being talked about in the daily press and set it forth upon the stage before a public that naturally wants to see what it has been reading of for many months. As one topic after another is promoted to the first pages of our journals, it also comes forward in our theatres and assumes the centre of the stage. Three or four seasons ago, the favourite subject for discussion in our drama was the iniquity of big business, last year it was the methods used by malefactors to evade our laws, and this fall it seems to be the white slave traffic. An interest in these public evils having previously been worked up in the press, our playwrights have taken advantage of the occasion to show the public what the public has been reading about.

There is no surer avenue than this to immediate success within the theatre; and yet it is scarcely necessary for the critic to point out that in thus allying their work with journalism our playwrights are withholding it from literature. Our one most serious handicap to the development of a national drama that shall have some value as literature is the craze of our theatre for keeping, as the phrase is, up to date. [. . .]

[. . .] our American drama at the present time [. . .] deals with types of character that are local instead of being universal, and discuss themes that, instead of being permanent, are merely temporary. Our playwrights think too little of the ultimate aim of art and too much of the immediate aim of social reform. Reform is the only enterprise that annihilates its own existence by success; and, when once a current topic has been settled, there can arise no reason for reopening discussion of the point. The more successful our journalistic plays may be, the more quickly must they go to a grave of their own digging. But a drama that expounds the great recurrent problems of humanity may remain as immortal as the human race itself.

On the other hand, however, in these years while we are waiting for the great American drama that is to be, it is surely better that our playwrights should attack the social problems of the hour than that they should discuss no problems whatsoever. Our theatre has advanced far from that initial period when it merely discoursed sweet nothings to awaken easy tears. [. . .]

This opinion, which is based upon a very earnest interest in the development of the American drama through its present mood of journalism to its future mood of literature, has recently been opposed by a certain portion of the public. These people, who, only a year ago, applauded the timely and fashionable plays in which a slippery evasion of the law was speciously set forth in the light of a virtue to be emulated, have been shocked by the shift of journalistic attention to those devices by which innocent young girls are allured, against their will, into a life of shame. They have been so shocked that they have written letters to the newspapers deploring what they call the "immorality" of two plays [Bayard Veiller's *The Fight*, 1912, and George Scarborough's *The Lure*, 1913] in which the white slave trade is discussed, either as the main theme, or as a subsidiary feature, of the action; and those same newspapers which for months have been printing on their leading pages the very facts out of which these dramas have been fabricated have come forth with Victorian editorials in which a whole thesaurus has been ransacked to furnish synonyms for the adjective "indecent" to hurl against these plays. [. . .]

In the midst of such a hullabaloo as this, it seems useless for the critic of the drama to reiterate the axiom that the morality of a play depends not at all upon its subject-matter but upon the integrity and sanity of mind with which that subject-matter is set forth. The only test of morals in the drama is the test of truthfulness. A play is immoral if, in defiance of the laws of civilised society, it makes a hero of a gentlemanly burglar, or if it extols the undeniable picturesqueness of the crime of arson without also reminding the audience of its inconvenience to the neighbours; but it is not immoral if it sets forth sexual iniquity as a thing to be abhorred. This point is obvious to any thinking mind; but it never seems to occur to city-magistrates. "What is the play about?" is asked by these officials. "Incest" (let us imagine) is the answer. "That's indecent; arrest the manager," remarks the moral magistrate. The play in question, incidentally, is *Oedipus the King*. [. . .]

[485] J. Corbin. "The New Revolt against Broadway"
Scribner's Magazine [1913]

[. . .] For many years there has been a revolt against Broadway and all that it stands for. We are familiar enough with the cry that the drama has been debased by being commercialized. To-day, after all allowances are made for the exaggerations of humor, or of despair, the fact is clear enough that the drama has become not only inartistic but uncommercial.

This fact has given the revolt a new point of attack. In times past the demands of the more intelligent public could be safely disregarded, and the result was that remonstrance was loud—and none too good-tempered. Of late the manager has become willing to listen to the voice of the intelligent. And so the voice of the intelligent has become gentle, their attitude helpful and kind. Yet the revolt is none the less a revolt for being well-directed and well-mannered.

The concrete result is that New York, Chicago, Boston, Philadelphia, and many other centres, have organizations, the object of which is to co-operate with the managers in making good plays succeed. Already the movement has more than justified itself; but if we take into account the inner needs and ultimate possibilities of the situation it will be evident, I think, that as yet it is only in its first tentative beginnings. Out of the despair of the manager has risen a hope for art-loving playgoers. Whether or not the automobile public continues in its devotion to the "movies," the people who are behind the drama-league movement foresee a time when an increasing number of good plays will be offered to the patronage of intelligent public not only in the big cities but in the one-night stands.

The movement has of late received an impetus from the formation of an organization along thoroughly new lines in the theatrical metropolis. Before many seasons are past, it is hoped, the methods of the New York organization will be understood and powerfully aided in every city and town in the land.

To gain a clear idea of these methods it is necessary to trace the origin of the conditions which they have been devised to meet. [. . .]

[. . .] The crying need in the business of the theatre is some means by which good plays can command at once the attendance of a considerable body of well-placed people—people whose judgments spread abroad in rapidly widening circles. To launch it successfully it is as necessary to have an artistic audience on the spot as an artistic performance.

The readiest means to insure this was hit upon, in a large measure accidentally, almost a decade ago by the People's Institute of New York. Led by the late Charles Sprague Smith, it was doing a very important social and educational work on the lower East Side. In special it recognized clearly that, properly conducted, the drama is one of the most powerful of all means toward informing the mind and developing right social instincts. It was Mr. Smith's ambition eventually to establish a theatre devoted to popular art. As a first step he devised a plan for insuring that whatever was of value in the current drama should be made accessible to his people. He organized a drama committee and made arrangements with the managers by which the plays it recommended should be opened to work-men, school-children, and teachers at half-prices.

From the point of view of Broadway there was little philanthropy in the scheme. Even at that time the managers were aware that there was a desperate need to get the public into their houses during the first weeks of a run. Many a play was tided over to success by the People's Institute sale of tickets at half-price. In one case of which I have knowledge a piece that had started on the dolorous path to the storehouse became so successful that the author—whose profits are only a percentage of those of the manager—received an offer, which he refused, of seventy-five thousand dollars for his royalties. The play was *The Man of the Hour* [1906]; and its author, Mr. George Broadhurst, who had tried for several years in vain to get recognition as something more than a writer of farce, was started on a career of rather phenomenal success. [. . .]

In a modified form the MacDowell Club took up the work. This is an organization devoted to music and the allied arts which has a very large membership among people of means and intelligence. Its peculiar aim was to facilitate the production of good plays by helping them to succeed. It asked no concession from box-office prices—not even the usual first-night courtesies. When a production did not come up to the committee's standards, it took no action. When it did, it sent out a bulletin to the club members, a large body of whom were pledged to go to every play recommended during the first three weeks of its run, discuss it as widely as possible, and urge others to attend. When a play had some special point of novelty or artistic value, as for example *Sumurûn* [by Friedrich Freksa, presented by Max Reinhardt at the Casino Theatre, New York, 16 Jan. 1912] or *The Yellow Jacket* [by J. Harry Benrimo and George C. Hazelton, 1912], the MacDowell Club gave a conference on the subject, with brief addresses and an informal discussion. Similar work was taken up by the Woman's Cosmopolitan Club in New York and by drama leagues in many cities. [. . .]

If the various leagues are to have any real power and authority, they must be able not only to recommend attendance but to command it; and here the leaguers encountered a very grave difficulty. When a play is successful—and most good plays still are—all the seats on the forward part of the floor are sold through the ticket agencies at an advance of half a dollar each, so that those who wish to pay only the box-office price can get nothing in front of the tenth row. [. . .]

In a word, it is impossible to insure that the league members attend plays which have been recommended without first insuring that they shall be able to secure seats from which they can see them and hear them.

The Drama Society of New York has hit upon a scheme which promises to solve the difficulty and to make the organization a power for incalculable good. Instead of relying on the informal pledges of its members it requires a guarantee that they will actually support the plays which its committee designates. Concretely it imposes a yearly membership fee of forty dollars.

For this it gives ample return. The member receives the bulletins of the league, free admission to two or three "conferences" on dramatic subjects of the hour, and a pair of seats on the forward part of the floor to each of ten productions recommended by the committee as artistically worthy of support, whether or not they bid fair to prove popular. [. . .]

Meantime the drama leagues throughout the country have developed an almost national organization, led by the very able and active Chicago centre. Unlike the Drama Society of New York they merely recommend attendance, the members buying tickets or not, as they see fit. Yet the influence which they exert through their bulletins is very large. Chicago is also the home of The

Theatre Society, a novel organization which is rapidly developing its activities. In its first year it supported a stock company, the Drama Players, which made nine productions, some of them of the very highest order artistically. [...]
Already many small cities have drama leagues. [...]

[488] S. Cheney. "The American Playwright and the Drama of Sincerity"
Forum [1914]

[...] the American dramatist of to-day *is* a failure if judged by his contemporaries on the other side of the Atlantic.

In answering *wherein* American plays fail, one may sum up the indictment in three counts: first, that they have too much untempered strength, and not enough depth and subtlety; second, that they lack the poetic touch, the sense of beauty; and third, that they too often are marred by the attempt to give the public what it wants, chiefly in comic relief and in melodramatic turns. [...]

Having recognized some of the qualities wherein they have failed, one may well ask *why* they have failed. The causes are many, but it is worth while to trace one or two of the principal ones.

The lack of subtlety and lack of depth are due in some measure to the fact that our playwrights have been recruited largely from the ranks of newspaper writers. To mention only a few who come to mind immediately: Eugene Walter, Augustus Thomas, George Ade, William C. De Mille, and A. E. Thomas. The newspaper men have brought to the theatre an admirable directness and a "dramatic sense." But necessarily they have been trained to see rapidly the surface aspects of life, rather than to ponder deeply on the underlying motives and causes. They have the reportorial instinct for outward sensational situation, but not the dramatist's insight into motivation and character growth. They display a wonderful facility in grasping vital stories and setting them forth in quick, forceful strokes; but they too seldom free themselves from journalistic haste and shallowness.

Another large group of writers for the theatre—and especially of the older men—have been brought up within the playhouse, and find it difficult to get away from what is inherently theatric. They have witnessed so many times the effectiveness of the old stock situations that they mistake them for the dramatic elements of life. Men like David Belasco, who were schooled in the theatre of the eighties and nineties, cannot bring themselves to part with the melodramatic poses, the comic relief figures, and the distracting naturalisms of the setting, that were so large a part of the stock in trade of the past generation of playwrights. [...]

A very potent cause for the failure of the American dramatist is that he generally is too close to the glittering lights and glittering dollars of Broadway. There is in his hurried life a constant temptation to commercialize his talents.

Again and again men of solid promise have lowered their ideals to produce plays that were melodramatic, or farcical, or sentimentally sweet enough to catch the "popular" taste; and others have turned their hands to the fashioning of musical comedy librettos, to satisfy the jaded appetites of the tired business man. [. . .]

A more fundamental reason for the failure of the American playwright is that in the American theatres the play has not been the thing. The drama has been of secondary importance to the acting and the setting; the work of the playwright secondary to that of the manager, producer and actor. Fortunately the condition is passing, but without doubt it has had a retarding effect upon the growth of a vital American drama. [. . .] We are at last learning that it is the playwright's art that is truly creative, and that the actor's work should be interpretative. The dramatist should be recognized as the artist, the actor as the tool for the accomplishment of that artist's purpose. The average American play has been buried, too, under all sorts of "scenic effects" and superadded vaudeville "stunts." The manager has counted as so much clear gain any trick of setting or any added incident that would bring a laugh or a round of applause from the audience, without regard to relevance or organic connection with the essential plot. The practice has tended to degrade the production to vaudeville standards, and to discourage the writing of plays of unified structure, designed to evoke a single sustained mood. Both the star system and the managers' craze for "stage effects" have contributed substantially to the failure of the American playwright. [. . .]

Certainly the outlook *is* promising. [. . .]

The American playwright has developed the beginnings of a great drama, of an American drama of sincerity. He has touched on the surface of the rich mine of native material; but he has not as yet worked with the exquisite balance of poet and dramatic craftsman—with high purpose and the sense of inner beauty. In this year of our Lord nineteen-fourteen, one can only say definitely that he is progressing; for the rest, one may only wait and watch and pray—and utter words of encouragement. But brooding over all the signs, one need not stretch the imagination too far to see emerging out of the future the man of wide vision, the poet who yet is the perfect technician, who will weave the material of the time into a gripping story, at the same time revealing the beauty of his own imagination. With that figure in mind one need not weep too copiously over the failure of the American playwright.

[490] F. Kiper. "Some American Plays. From the Feminist Viewpoint"
Forum [1914]

[. . .] One must frankly confess at the outset that it is by the unconscious rather than the conscious method that the American dramatists are revealing themselves in regard to the woman movement. We have at present no Ibsens, Shaws, Björnsons, Strindbergs, Brieuxs. In a drama whose themes are almost entirely those of contemporary social life, few among our playwrights are attempting to interpret to us the meaning of the growing divorce "evil," of the suffrage agitation, of women in the professions, of young girls in industry, of the sudden awakening of the sheltered woman to a knowledge of prostitution and venereal diseases. Almost none among our clever writers for the stage are bringing to these vital themes a conscious philosophy or an informed understanding. Yet the woman movement is undoubtedly, if perhaps the class-consciousness in the labor struggle be excepted, the one most important tendency of the century. It is important because it deals not with a limited and selected class of society, but with the very fundamentals of society—the relation of the sexes and consequently the next generation. Race-suicide, the double standard of morals, the taints of heredity, these are not side issues, but of relevancy to all of national existence.

It is the enviable privilege of the dramatist "to popularize the pressing questions of the time." That is, he must be an interpreter to the people of what they have heretofore vaguely sensed, of what is already implicit in the public mind, but through him is realized with vividness. The drama, being preeminently a social art and dependent not on the selected audience but on the average, develops correlatively with the developing social and artistic consciousness of a people. We of America must therefore remember, in our indictment of American dramatists, what Whitman has said of another art, "To have great poets there must be great audiences too."

That the great, or at least the receptive audiences are coming into being in America is a fact to all but the most pessimistic among the critics of dramatic tendencies. America is really beginning to take its drama seriously, to consider its plays as something more than "shows" for the pleasing of the immature minded. [. . .] I hold no brief for the thesis play as such—even the thesis play of trans-Atlantic importation. But surely until the American audience ceases to demand only cant and provincialism, prudishness and sentimentality, America can produce no dramatists of import—minds that are conscious of large issues and that have the ability to fuse at white heat into one, thesis, plot, characterization.

To many it appears that even now the time is ripe for a new birth and that there are the stirrings of parturition. Already several worthy plays have come out of America and there is springing up a veritable crop of young dramatists with a feeling for the stage and the craftsman's facility. While we are awaiting our big American playwrights—and perhaps the next decade will welcome them!—it is of interest to the feminist to hear what the present writers of the theatre have to say about American women. [. . .] [Analyses of plays by Augustus Thomas, Joseph Medill Patterson, Eugene Walter, Edward Sheldon and Rachel Crothers, George Broadhurst, Percy MacKaye, and Charles Rann Kennedy follow.]

[...] It may be true enough that the idealization and worship of women is a purifying influence for men—but such worship is rather hard on the women. Less satisfying aesthetically, but more convenient in this work-a-day world, is it, to be able to doff one's wings occasionally. The literature that will be written by woman as a revealer of that so-called mystery, herself, will probably not sentimentalize feminity. She knows that there is no sacrosanct or magic quality in femaleness, either for angelic or demoniac power—other than that sacredness of individual worth that accrues to every human being by the mere fact of being human. There will be an increasing number of women playwrights in America as the doors of occupational and educational opportunity are thrown wider. It is to be hoped that they will feel impelled—they and their brother-writers,—to set forth sincerely and honestly, yet with vital passion, those problems in the development and freedom of women that the modern age has termed the problems of feminism.

[494] W. D. Howells. "The Plays of Eugène Brieux"
The North American Review [1915]

[...] with a really good play one really does not need the stage, or at least need it, so to speak, necessitously. It is a luxury, it is perhaps a superfluity of naughtiness; [...] I have a passion for reading plays which seems to grow upon me at the time of life when one hates to go out after dinner to the theater. If the theater would come to me, very well, I would not refuse its help in the interpretation of a dramatist; but I can get on without it; and if it insists, it must give me a seat on the center aisle of the orchestra, not farther than eight rows back. [...] In my arm-chair at home I do not have to suffer any waits between the acts; nobody crushes across my knees coming in or going out, or makes me rise to let him by; there are no draughts; I have no anxiety as to the hat of the lady in front of me, whether I shall have the courage to ask her to take it off if she forgets to do so. The dramatist has not me at his mercy, but I have him at mine, and I can shut him off, or up, at an instant's notice. [...]

It is not so easy to tell what a dramatist means as what a novelist means. That is one reason for dramatists forbearing the use of problems in plots. The novelist may (if he is an inartistic novelist, especially) go inside of his characters or behind them and push them the way he would have them go, or tell what they think and what they feel, and explain their circumstance to the last detail; but the dramatist, having got his people on their legs, has to let them do their own walking and talking, with the help of a few sign-board suggestions in the way of stage directions. [...] They are all like that, the good dramatists of our time, of every time that was not a rotten time. [...] They have no scruple in luring you to the theater and then letting you realize that you are as in a church, under a machine-gun fire of homilies from a pulpit that calls itself a stage. You may say it is a fraud, that you supposed you were coming to a musical comedy, but you ought to have known who was asking you. [. . .]

The primal purpose of a play is to illustrate life or to reproduce it. This done, the secondary, or moral, purposes fulfil themselves—that is, they teach, they impart the convictions of the dramatist if he has any, and if he has none he is no dramatist, but a contriver of emotional acts analogous to the feats of the trapeze or of ground-and-lofty tumbling. [. . .]

[496] "The Theatre Adrift"
The Nation [1915]

In ten years, if the moving pictures continue their triumphal progress, the spoken drama will be dead. When Mr. W. A. Brady made this gloomy prophesy the other night he used the word "spoken" in a very general sense, in contradistinction to the silent or screen drama. [. . .]

[. . .] Is there a legitimate field for the spoken play in this country, which the movies can never occupy? Common-sense would argue that there is such a field. An art some twenty-five hundred years old cannot conceivably perish as sudden as the managers predict. When a crisis in the spoken drama supervenes, the tendency of the business men of the theatre is to look for external causes. Some time ago it was the automobile. Then it was auction bridge and the tango. Now it is the motion pictures. It must be frail virtue that succumbs before every fad of the moment. It seldom occurs to these practical men to ask whether they themselves are not largely responsible; but to-day there is very evidently a busy searching of hearts along Broadway. All this bother about price-cutting, and ticket agencies, and alliances made and broken the same day, indicates both the existence of a crisis and its cause. Big Business in the theatre has struck a slump. The revelations in court about circuits and syndicates and territorial delimitations and booking privileges read very much like a proceeding under the Sherman Anti-Trust law. The same methods that have brought so many railways into the hands of a receiver have operated in the theatre.

Under the influence of Big Business, the spoken drama has undergone an evolution which did make it exceedingly vulnerable to the competition of the movies. Managers in buying a play wanted naturally the play that promised big profits, and such a play must be one of a very wide appeal. A long run in New York city, such as would satisfy the wildest dreams of the European playwright, was not enough. The play must run in the provinces, and employ several road companies. [. . .] Writing, then, for a nation-wide audience, the dramatist has been compelled to go very thin on character, ideas, dialogue, to concentrate on action, and action reduced to its elementary term. The spoken drama has been reduced to a minimum of speech. It became largely a matter of pistol-waving on the one hand and crude sex appeal on the other. And when it comes to pistol-waving, the photo-play can beat the living theatre at the game. If the spoken drama is to compete with the screen-play on the mere ground of action, then Mr. Brady is right, and there is no reason why the badly written, psychologically worthless spoken play should survive.

But once you give up your dreams of huge profits and agree to call a play successful which will appeal not to the millions, but only to the tens of thousands, the outlook for the spoken drama is far from hopeless. [. . .] The real play is impossible if you persist in thinking of indefinite runs and half a dozen road companies. How can even half a dozen road companies compare with the movie film which shows simultaneously in a hundred theatres? [. . .]

At any rate, the film play in itself need not be an enemy of the true drama. The film play may yet turn out to be a blessing in disguise. If it weans away from the theatre the men who think of profits in war stocks, there might be a chance for the managers content with lesser profits to be made in furnishing real plays to the public. By satisfying the elementary appetite for "action," it may yet drive pistol-waving from the theatre and leave the stage clear for a real spoken drama. People will go to the movies for one thing and to the theatre for another. And the dramatist who is relieved from the demand for something "doing" every minute may give us plays that are spoken in a more real sense than the "spoken" drama of crooks and detectives.

4

Chronological List of Dramatic Criticism in American Periodicals, 1746–1915

An italicized number preceding an entry indicates that the text is reprinted, at least in part, in this collection.

[1] "On Theatrical Entertainment." *The American Magazine and Historical Chronicle* (Boston) 3 (Aug. 1746): 356–58.
[2] "The Antigallican No. II." *The American Magazine and Monthly Chronicle for the British Colonies* (Philadelphia) 1.3 (Dec. 1757): 116–19.
[3] "Theatrical Representations not condemned; the harmless Recreations of the over-righteous indulged; and a high-strained Compliment to uncharitable Clergymen." *The New England Magazine of Knowledge and Pleasure* (Boston) 1.2 (Oct. 1758): 37–38.
[4] Tisdale, Joseph. "The Speech of Joseph Tisdale, Esq. in the House of Representatives, June 1767, against the Bill then before the House, for preventing Stage Plays, and other Theatrical Entertainments." Boston, 1767.
[5] Hill, Richard. *An Address to Persons of Fashion, containing some particulars relating to Balls; and a Few Occasional Hints Concerning Playhouses, Card-Tables, etc.* Boston, 1767.
[6] "Extract from the Votes and Proceedings of the American Continental Congress." *The Boston Gazette and Country Journal*, 7 Nov. 1774: n.p.
[7] "Report of a committee of the assembly of Pennsylvania, to whom had been referred a petition of messrs. Hallam and Henry, praying to have a bill passed to licence a theatre in or near Philadelphia." *The American Museum, or, Universal Magazine* (Philadelphia) 5.2 (Feb. 1789): 185–90.
[8] "The Contrast." *The Universal Asylum and Columbian Magazine* (Philadelphia) 5 (Aug. 1790): 117–20.

[9] "Effects of the Stage on the Manners of a People, and the propriety of encouraging and establishing a virtuous Theatre. By a Bostonian." *The Massachusetts Magazine* (Boston) 4 (Oct. 1792): 633–34.

[10] "A Defence of the Stage." *The Thespian Oracle, Or Monthly Mirror* (Philadelphia) 1 (Jan. 1798): 1–2.

[11] Philo. "On the Effects of Theatric Exhibitions." *The Weekly Magazine of Original Essays, Fugitive Pieces, and Interesting Intelligence* (Philadelphia) 1 (21 Apr. 1798): 357–60.

[12] Antiphilus. "To the Editor." *The Weekly Magazine of Original Essays, Fugitive Pieces, and Interesting Intelligence* (Philadelphia) 1 (28 Apr. 1798): 394–97.

[13] WDNI. "On Theatric Exhibitions." *The Weekly Magazine of Original Essays, Fugitive Pieces, and Interesting Intelligence* (Philadelphia) 2 (23 June 1798): 230–31.

[14] A Sober Enquirer. "More of the Theatre." *The Weekly Magazine of Original Essays, Fugitive Pieces, and Interesting Intelligence* (Philadelphia) 2 (30 June 1798): 262–63.

[15] W.D. "Encore." *The Weekly Magazine of Original Essays, Fugitive Pieces, and Interesting Intelligence* (Philadelphia) 3 (11 Aug. 1798): 41–42.

[16] "Theatrical Register." *The Monthly Magazine, and American Review* (New York) 3.6 (Dec. 1800): 455.

[17] "The Drama—Theatrical Review No. I." *The Port Folio* (Philadelphia) 1 (3 Jan. 1801): 4.

[18] "The Drama—Theatrical Review No. III." *The Port Folio* (Philadelphia) 1 (17 Jan. 1801): 21.

[19] "Winstanley's *Hypocrite* unmasked." *The American Review, and Literary Journal* (New York) 1.1 (Jan.–Mar. 1801): 64–67.

[20] Irving, Washington. *Letters of Jonathan Oldstyle, Gent.* Ed. Bruce I. Granger and Martha Hartzog. Boston: Twayne, 1977, 8–31 [Letters III through VIII originally published in *The Morning Chronicle* (New York), 1 Dec. 1802–8 Feb. 1803].

[21] "Theatrical Register." *The Weekly Visitor, or Ladies' Miscellany* (New York) 1 (19 Mar. 1803): 191.

[22] *The Evening Fire–Side* 1 (5 Jan. 1805): 30.

[23] "On Stage Players." *Portland Magazine* 1 (18 May 1805): 5–6.

[24] H. "All the World is but a Stage." *The Companion and Weekly Miscellany* (Baltimore) 2 (23 Nov. 1805): 26–27.

[25] *The Theatrical Censor* (Philadelphia) 1 (9 Dec. 1805): 1–4.

[26] "Remarks on the Theatre." *The Thespian Mirror* (New York) 1 (28 Dec. 1805): 2–4.

[27] "The Drama." *The Repository and Ladies' Weekly Museum* (Philadelphia) 6 (4 Jan. 1806): 23.

[28] "To the Benevolent." *The Thespian Mirror* (New York) 1 (18 Jan. 1806): 29–30.
[29] [Field, Robert.] "The Dramatick Works of William Dunlap, in ten volumes, vol. I containing—The Father of an only Child, Leicester, Fontaineville, Abbey, Darbey's Return." *The Monthly Anthology, and Boston Review* 3 (Oct. 1806): 550–51.
[30] "The Ordeal ... No. 1." *The Emerald, or, Miscellany of Literature* (Boston) 1 (18 Oct. 1806): 294–95.
[31] [Sargent, Winthrop.] "*The Battle of the Eutaw Springs, and Evacuation of Charleston, or the glorious 14th of December, 1782, a national drama in five acts.* By William Ioor, of St. George, Dorchester, South Carolina, &c. &c." *The Monthly Anthology, and Boston Review* 4 (Mar. 1807): 163.
[32] Amicus. "Thoughts on the Propriety of Establishing a Theatre in this City. No. I." *The Guardian* (Albany) 1 (26 Dec. 1807): 22.
[33] Candidus. "To 'Amicus.'" *The Guardian* (Albany) 1 (2 Jan. 1808): 26.
[34] Amicus. "Thoughts on the Propriety of Establishing a Theatre in this City. No. II." *The Guardian* (Albany) 1 (2 Jan. 1808): 26–27.
[35] Philo–Amicus. "A Few Words to 'Candidus.'" *The Guardian* (Albany) 1 (9 Jan. 1808): 30.
[36] Candidus. "To 'Amicus.' No. II." *The Guardian* (Albany) 1 (9 Jan. 1808): 31.
[37] Philo–Candidus. "To 'Philo–Amicus.'" *The Guardian* (Albany) 1 (16 Jan. 1808): 34–35.
[38] "Boston Theatre." *The Ordeal* (Boston) 1 (7 Jan. 1809): 13–16.
[39] "The Drama." *Something* (Boston) 1 (18 Nov. 1809): 6–8.
[40] *The Rambler's Magazine* (New York) 2 (1809–10): 9–11.
[41] "The History of the Stage. Chapter I. Objections to the Stage Considered and Refuted." *The Mirror of Taste and Dramatic Censor* (Philadelphia) 1.1 (Jan. 1810): 9–23.
[42] [Letter to the editor] *The Mirror of Taste and Dramatic Censor* (Philadelphia) 1.1 (Jan. 1810): 103–5.
[43] "The Drama—A Plain Statement." *The Cabinet* (Boston) 1 (12 Jan. 1811): 25–28.
[44] "The Drama—A Plain Statement." *The Cabinet* (Boston) 1 (19 Jan. 1811): 36–39.
[45] Histrio–Mastix. "Histrio Mastix—To the Editor." *The Cynick* (Philadelphia) 1 (28 Sept. 1811): 19–29.
[46] "Theatrical Recorder." *The Comet* (Boston) 26 Oct. 1811: 14–15.
[47] "*George Barnwell* and *The Forty Thieves.*" *The Comet* (Boston) 7 Dec. 1811: 92–94.
[48] "*Bunker Hill*—Musick mad—High Life below Stairs." *The Comet* (Boston) 28 Dec. 1811: 129–30.

[49] Edwards, John. *An address, to all play-actors, play-hunters, legislators, governors, magistrates, clergy, churchmen, deists, and the world at large.* New York, 1812.

[50] Verus. "For the Repertory." *The Philadelphia Repertory* 2 (1 Feb. 1812): 292–93.

[51] Verus. "For the Repertory." *The Philadelphia Repertory* 2 (8 Feb. 1812): 300–301.

[52] Hamilton. "On Theatres." *The Philadelphia Repertory* 2 (7 Mar. 1812): 333–34.

[53] Verus. "For the Repertory." *The Philadelphia Repertory* 2 (21 Mar. 1812): 348–49.

[54] "Wanted." *The Polyanthos* (Boston) n.s. 1 (Apr. 1812): 215.

[55] "American Dramatists." *The Polyanthos* (Boston) 2 (Sept. 1813): 281–88.

[56] "The Theatre." *The Stranger* (Albany) 1 (29 Jan. 1814): 249–52.

[57] "The Theatre." *The Stranger* (Albany) 1 (12 Feb. 1814): 257–59.

[58] "The Theatre." *The Stranger* (Albany) 1 (26 Feb. 1814): 277–79.

[59] A. "The Battle of New Orleans." *The Portico* (Baltimore) 1.2 (Feb. 1816): 93–99.

[60] "American Literature." *The National Register* (Washington) 1 (22 June 1816): 258–59.

[61] "Drama." *The National Register* (Washington) 1 (27 July 1816): 339–40.

[62] "Boston Theatre." *The Boston Weekly Magazine* 1 (26 Oct. 1816): 10.

[63] "Thespian Corps." *The Weekly Recorder* (Chillicothe, OH) 3 (27 Nov. 1816): 142.

[64] "Theatrical Defeat." *The Weekly Recorder* (Chillicothe, OH) 3 (29 Nov. 1816): 142.

[65] "A Brief Account of the Boston Stage." *The Boston Weekly Magazine* 1 (30 Nov. 1816): 29–30.

[66] "A Brief Account of the Boston Stage." *The Boston Weekly Magazine* 1 (28 Dec. 1816): 46.

[67] "Boston Theatre ." *The Boston Weekly Magazine* 1 (25 Jan. 1817): 61–62.

[68] S. "The American Drama." *The Portico* (Baltimore) 3.5 (May 1817): 370–73.

[69] "Boston Theatre." *The Boston Weekly Magazine* 1 (7 June 1817): 138–39.

[70] "Boston Theatre." *The Boston Weekly Magazine* 1 (21 June 1817): 145–46.

[71] "Thespian Register." *The American Monthly Magazine and Critical Review* (New York) 1.3 (July 1817): 209–10.

[72] "Boston Theatre." *The Boston Weekly Magazine* 1 (5 July 1817): 153–54.

[73] "The American Drama." *The National Register* (Washington) 4 (12 July 1817): 30–32.

[74] "Boston Theatre." *The Boston Weekly Magazine* 1 (19 July 1817): 161–62.

[75] "Thespian Register." *The American Monthly Magazine and Critical Review* (New York) 1.4 (Aug. 1817): 298–302.
[76] "Theatrical." *New England Galaxy* (Boston) 1 (26 Dec. 1817): n. p.
[77] "Boston Theatre." *The Boston Weekly Magazine* 2 (27 Dec. 1817): 45–46.
[78] "Dramatic Censor." *The American Monthly Magazine and Critical Review* (New York) 2.4 (Feb. 1818): 299.
[79] "Weekly Theatrical Register." *The Boston Weekly Magazine* 2 (28 Feb. 1818): 83.
[80] "Weekly Theatrical Register." *The Boston Weekly Magazine* 2 (7 Mar. 1818): 85–86.
[81] "Weekly Theatrical Register." *The Boston Weekly Magazine* 2 (14 Mar. 1818): 91.
[82] "The Drama." *The National Register* (Washington) 7 (10 Apr. 1819): 225–27.
[83] "The Drama." *New England Galaxy & Masonic Magazine* (Boston) 3 (4 Feb. 1820): 65.
[84] Viator. "A Tragedy More Interesting Than a Prayer–Meeting." *Boston Recorder* 8 (5 Apr. 1823): 54.
[85] "Theatrical." *The Boston Weekly Magazine* n.s. 1 (11 Sept. 1824): 103.
[86] Alpha. "Theatrical Amusement." *The New–York Mirror* 2 (18 Sept. 1824): 61.
[87] "Theatrical." *The Boston Weekly Magazine* n.s. 1 (16 Oct. 1824): 123.
[88] "Theatrical." *The Boston Weekly Magazine* n.s. 1 (23 Oct. 1824): 127.
[89] "Theatrical—George Barnwell." *The Boston Weekly Magazine* n.s. 1 (30 Oct. 1824): 131.
[90] Z.A.K. "Actors." *The New–York Mirror* 2 (20 Nov. 1824): 133–34.
[91] "Theatrical." *The Boston Weekly Magazine* n.s. 1 (27 Nov. 1824): 145.
[92] "The Drama." *The American Athenaeum* (New York) 1 (28 July 1825): 119.
[93] "The Drama." *The American Athenaeum* (New York) 1 (18 Aug. 1825): 150.
[94] Menander. "National Drama." *The New–York Mirror* 3 (15 Oct. 1825): 93.
[95] "The Drama." *The American Athenaeum* (New York) 1 (27 Oct. 1825): 271.
[96] "The Drama." *The New York Literary Gazette and American Athenaeum* 2 (18 Mar. 1826): 22.
[97] "The Theatre." *Boston Recorder and Religious Telegraph* 11 (6 Oct. 1826): 159.
[98] "The German Drama." *The New York Literary Gazette and American Athenaeum* 3 (23 Dec. 1826): 189–90.
[99] "The Drama." *The Albion* (New York) 5 (13 Jan. 1827): 248.
[100] "The Drama." *The Albion* (New York) 5 (3 Feb. 1827): 272.

[101] Thespis. "Morality of the Stage—No. I." *The Correspondent* (New York) 1 (10 Mar. 1827): 100–102.

[102] Thespis. "Morality of the Stage—No. II." *The Correspondent* (New York) 1 (17 Mar. 1827): 119–20.

[103] "The Drama, versus The Saints." *The Correspondent* (New York) 1 (7 Apr. 1827): 173–75.

[104] [Paulding, James Kirke.] "American Drama." *The American Quarterly Review* (Philadelphia) 1.2 (June 1827): 331–57.

[105] "The Drama." *The Albion* (New York) 6 (16 June 1827): 8.

[106] "The Theatre." *Boston Recorder and Religious Telegraph* 12 (13 July 1827): 111.

[107] "The Drama." *The Albion* (New York) 6 (14 July 1827): 40.

[108] "The Drama." *The Albion* (New York) 6 (19 Oct. 1827): 152.

[109] "The Drama." *The Albion* (New York) 6 (24 Nov. 1827): 192.

[110] "The Theatre." *Boston Recorder and Religious Telegraph* 12 (14 Dec. 1827): 200.

[111] "The Drama." *The Albion* (New York) 6 (26 Jan. 1828): 264.

[112] "The Drama." *The Albion* (New York) 6 (16 Feb. 1828): 288.

[113] "The Drama." *The Critic* (New York) 1 (22 Nov. 1828): 62–64.

[114] "The Diorama at the Bowery Theatre." *The Critic* (New York) 1 (13 Dec. 1828): 104.

[115] D. "The Theatre." *Hopkinsian Magazine* (Providence) 3.14 (Feb. 1829): 325–29.

[116] "The Modern Drama." *The Philadelphia Monthly Magazine* n.s. 1.5 (Mar. 1829): 297–309.

[117] "The Modern Drama." *The Philadelphia Monthly Magazine* n.s. 1.6 (Apr. 1829): 369–76.

[118] "Bowery Theatre. *The West Indian.*" *The Critic* (New York) 1 (4 Apr. 1829): 351–52.

[119] "American Opera House. Jonathan in England." *The Critic* (New York) 2 (13 June 1829): 88.

[120] "Theatrical Portraits." *The New–York Mirror* 6 (13 June 1829): 391.

[121] "The Drama As It Is." *The New–York Mirror* 7 (21 Nov. 1829): 160.

[122] C. "An Evening at the Theatre." *The New–York Mirror* 7 (13 Feb. 1830): 252.

[123] Watchman, Ch. "Theatrical Exhibitions." *Boston Recorder* 15 (7 July 1830): 108.

[124] [Paulding, James Kirke.] "Dramatic Literature." *The American Quarterly Review* (Philadelphia) 8.15 (Sept. 1830): 134–61.

[125] "Tablet of Green–Room Gossip." *The Euterpeiad* (New York) 1 (15 Oct. 1830): 106–7.

[126] "The Theatre." *The Spirit of the Pilgrims* 3.11 (Nov. 1830): 597–601.

[127] "The Expurgation of the Theatre." *Boston Recorder* 15 (24 Nov. 1830): 182.
[128] "The Expurgation of the Theatre." *Boston Recorder* 15 (1 Dec. 1830): 192.
[129] "The New York Stage." *The New-York Mirror* 9 (15 Oct. 1831): 115.
[130] "Glances at the Stage." *The New-York Mirror* 10 (27 Oct. 1832): 133–34.
[131] [Hopkinson, Joseph.] "*A History of the American Theatre.* By William Dunlap . . ." *The American Quarterly Review* (Philadelphia) 12.24 (Dec. 1832): 509–31.
[132] "A Specimen of the Acted Drama." *New-England Magazine* (Boston) 6 (Feb. 1834): 106–8.
[133] "The Broker of Bogota." *The New-York Mirror* 11 (1 Mar. 1834): 277.
[134] L. "Directions How to Make a Tragedy." *The New-York Mirror* 11 (8 Mar. 1834): 287.
[135] "Decline of the Modern Drama." *New-England Magazine* (Boston) 8 (Feb. 1835): 105–7.
[136] "A Chapter on Dramatizing Novels." *The New-York Mirror* 12 (28 Feb. 1835): 278.
[137] "The Theatre." *The Literary Gazette* (Concord, NH) 2 (12 June 1835): 40.
[138] H. "The Drama." *The Knickerbocker* (New York) 7.1 (Jan. 1836): 7–12.
[139] "The Bowery Theatre." *The New-York Mirror* 13 (5 Mar. 1836): 286–87.
[140] "Dramatic and Histrionic Talent." *Spirit of the Times* (New York) 6 (2 July 1836): 156.
[141] D. "A Talk about Theatricals." *The American Monthly Magazine* (New York) n.s. 3 (Apr. 1837): 344–48.
[142] "The Drama." *The Ladies' Companion* (New York) 6 (Apr. 1837): 300–302.
[143] "To the Literati of the United States." *Spirit of the Times* (New York) 7 (3 June 1837): 121.
[144] "French Theatricals." *The New-York Mirror* 15 (9 Dec. 1837): 190.
[145] "Mirabilia Exempla." *Burton's Gentleman's Magazine and American Monthly Review* (Philadelphia) 2.2 (Feb. 1838): 129–31.
[146] "Theatrical Puffs." *The New-York Mirror* 15 (9 June 1838): 394.
[147] "Our Theatres." *The New-Yorker* 6 (10 Nov. 1838): 125–26.
[148] "The Drama." *The New-York Mirror* 17 (8 Feb. 1840): 262.
[149] "Dangers of the Theatre." *Boston Recorder* 25 (14 Feb. 1840): 28.
[150] Cibber, Colley. "American Actors and Dramatic Authors." *Spirit of the Times* (New York) 10 (7 Mar. 1840): 12.

[151] "A Lay Sermon." *The Knickerbocker* (New York) 15.4 (Apr. 1840): 274–79 [reprinted in *American Masonic Register and Literary Companion* (Albany) 1 (11 Apr. 1840): 250].

[152] "The Drama versus the Ballet." *The New-York Mirror* 18 (18 July 1840): 30.

[153] "Theatricals." *The Ladies' Companion* (New York) 14 (Feb. 1841): 199.

[154] "Lectures vs. Theatres." *The New-Yorker* 11 (20 Mar. 1841): 13.

[155] "The Drama." *The Knickerbocker* (New York) 17.5 (May 1841): 441–42.

[156] Jones, William A. "Theatrical Criticism." *Arcturus* (New York) 2.7 (June 1841): 26–30.

[157] "Theatricals." *The Ladies' Companion* (New York) 15 (July 1841): 149–50.

[158] "The Drama." *The Dramatic Mirror and Literary Companion* (New York and Philadelphia) 1 (4 Sept. 1841): 28.

[159] "The Stage." *The Dramatic Mirror and Literary Companion* (New York and Philadelphia) 1 (25 Sept. 1841): 52.

[160] "Prospects of the American Stage." *Arcturus* (New York) 2.11 (Oct. 1841): 279–85.

[161] "The Morality of the Stage." *The Dramatic Mirror and Literary Companion* (New York and Philadelphia) 1 (30 Oct. 1841): 92–93.

[162] "Theatricals." *The Ladies' Companion* (New York) 16 (Nov. 1841): 51.

[163] "Drunkards of the Dramatic Profession." *The Dramatic Mirror and Literary Companion* (New York and Philadelphia) 1 (27 Nov. 1841): 124–25.

[164] "The Drama, Ourselves, the Mirror, Stars, &, &." *The Dramatic Mirror and Literary Companion* (New York and Philadelphia) 1 (1 Jan. 1842): 164–65.

[165] "The Stage." *The New-York Mirror* 20 (1 Jan. 1842): 5.

[166] "The Drama." *The Dramatic Mirror and Literary Companion* (New York and Philadelphia) 1 (8 Jan. 1842): 172.

[167] "Temperance and the Stage." *The Dramatic Mirror and Literary Companion* (New York and Philadelphia) 2 (26 Mar. 1842): 54.

[168] "The Drama in New York." *The Dramatic Mirror and Literary Companion* (New York and Philadelphia) 2 (23 Apr. 1842): 76.

[169] "Theatricals." *The Ladies' Companion* (New York) 17 (July 1842): 172–73.

[170] "The Decline of the Drama." *Brother Jonathan* (New York) 2 (16 July 1842): 324.

[171] "The Drama." *The Albion* (New York) 1 (20 Aug. 1842): 404.

[172] "Theatricals." *The Ladies' Companion* (New York) 17 (Sept. 1842): 283.

[173] "Things Theatrical." *Spirit of the Times* (New York) 12 (10 Sept. 1842): 336.

[174] H. "The Drama." *The Knickerbocker* (New York) 21.1 (Jan. 1843): 84–87.
[175] "The Drama." *The Albion* (New York) 2 (25 Mar. 1843): 152.
[176] Smith, Sol. "A Friendly Letter to the Rev. Dr. Beecher." *Spirit of the Times* (New York) 13 (26 Aug. 1843): 312.
[177] "Rambling Thoughts on the Drama." *Brother Jonathan* (New York) 6 (14 Oct. 1843): 188–89.
[178] "The Drama." *Brother Jonathan* (New York) 6 (4 Nov. 1843): 278.
[179] "The Drama." *The Albion* (New York) 3 (10 Aug. 1844): 387–88.
[180] "The Drama." *The Albion* (New York) 3 (21 Sept. 1844): 456.
[181] "Bowery Theatre." *The Albion* (New York) 3 (16 Nov. 1844): 556.
[182] "The Drama." *The Albion* (New York) 4 (11 Jan. 1845): 23.
[183] "The Drama." *Broadway Journal* (New York) 1 (11 Jan. 1845): 30.
[184] "The Drama." *The Albion* (New York) 4 (8 Feb. 1845): 72.
[185] "The Drama." *The Albion* (New York) 4 (22 Mar. 1845): 144.
[186] "The Drama." *The Albion* (New York) 4 (29 Mar. 1845): 156.
[187] [Poe, Edgar Allan.] "The New Comedy by Mrs. Mowatt." *Broadway Journal* (New York) 1 (29 Mar. 1845): 203–5 [abridged version reprinted in *The American Theatre As Seen by Its Critics, 1752–1934*. Ed. Montrose J. Moses and John Mason Brown. New York: Cooper Square, 1967, 59–63].
[188] "Things Theatrical." *Spirit of the Times* (New York) 15 (29 Mar. 1845): 56.
[189] "Mr. Forrest's Second Reception in England." *The United States Democratic Review* (New York) 16 (Apr. 1845): 385–87.
[190] "The New Comedy of Fashion." *The United States Democratic Review* (New York) 16 (Apr. 1845): 411–12.
[191] "The Drama." *The Albion* (New York) 4 (5 Apr. 1845): 164.
[192] "The Drama." *The Anglo American* (New York) 4 (5 Apr. 1845): 571.
[193] [Poe, Edgar Allan.] "Prospects of the Drama—Mrs. Mowatt's Comedy." *Broadway Journal* (New York) 1 (5 Apr. 1845): 219–20 [reprinted in *The American Theatre As Seen by Its Critics, 1752–1934*. Ed. Montrose J. Moses and John Mason Brown. New York: Cooper Square, 1967, 63–66].
[194] "The Broadway Theatre." *Broadway Journal* (New York) 1 (10 May 1845): 301.
[195] "Editor's Table." *Arthur's Ladies' Magazine of Elegant Literature and the Fine Arts* (Philadelphia) 3 (June 1845): 287–88.
[196] "Bowery Theatre." *The Albion* (New York) 4 (27 Sept. 1845): 468.
[197] "The Drama." *Broadway Journal* (New York) 2 (18 Oct. 1845): 232.
[198] "The Drama." *Broadway Journal* (New York) 2 (15 Nov. 1845): 290–91.
[199] "The Drama." *The Anglo American* (New York) 6 (10 Jan. 1846): 284–85.
[200] "The Drama." *The Albion* (New York) 5 (17 Jan. 1846): 35.
[201] "The Drama." *The Albion* (New York) 5 (21 Jan. 1846): 48.

282   The Dawning of American Drama

[202] "The Theatre and its Influences." *Spirit of the Times* (New York) 15 (24 Jan. 1846): 569.

[203] "American Actors in England." *The United States Democratic Review* (New York) 19 (Sept. 1846): 186–92.

[204] Whitman, Walt. "As a Very Average Proof." *The Brooklyn Daily Eagle*, 7 Oct. 1846 [reprinted in Whitman. *The Gathering of the Forces*. Ed. Cleveland Rodgers and John Black. 2 vols. New York: Putnam's, 1920. Vol. 2: 341–42].

[205] "The Drama." *The Albion* (New York) 5 (5 Dec. 1846): 588.

[206] Whitman, Walt. " 'The Gladiator'—Mr. Forrest—Acting." *The Brooklyn Daily Eagle*, 26 Dec. 1846 [reprinted in Whitman. *The Gathering of the Forces*. Ed. Cleveland Rodgers and John Black. 2 vols. New York: Putnam's, 1920. Vol. 2: 330–34; and in *The American Theatre As Seen by Its Critics, 1752-1934*. Ed. Montrose J. Moses and John Mason Brown. New York: Cooper Square, 1969, 69–70].

[207] Whitman, Walt. "Miserable State of the Stage.—Why Can't We Have Something Worth the Name of American Drama!" *The Brooklyn Daily Eagle*, 8 Feb. 1847 [reprinted in Whitman. *The Gathering of the Forces*. Ed. Cleveland Rodgers and John Black. 2 vols. New York: Putnam's, 1920. Vol. 2: 310–14; and in *The American Theatre As Seen by Its Critics, 1752-1934*. Ed. Montrose J. Moses and John Mason Brown. New York: Cooper Square, 1969, 70–72].

[208] Whitman, Walt. "Why Do Theatres Languish? And How Shall the American Stage Be Resuscitated?" *The Brooklyn Daily Eagle*, 12 Feb. 1847 [reprinted in Whitman. *The Gathering of the Forces*. Ed. Cleveland Rodgers and John Black. 2 vols. New York: Putnam's, 1920. Vol. 2: 314–18].

[209] "The Drama." *The Albion* (New York) 6 (27 Feb. 1847): 108.

[210] "The Drama." *The Literary World* (New York) 1 (27 Feb. 1847): 88–89.

[211] "The Drama." *The Albion* (New York) 6 (17 Apr. 1847): 192.

[212] "The Drama." *The Albion* (New York) 6 (8 May 1847): 228.

[213] "Things Theatrical." *Spirit of the Times* (New York) 18 (22 Apr. 1848): 108.

[214] "Drama." *The Albion* (New York) 7 (13 May 1848): 236.

[215] "Drama." *The Albion* (New York) 7 (20 May 1848): 248.

[216] "Drama." *The Albion* (New York) 7 (2 Sept. 1848): 428.

[217] "Broadway Theatre." *The Albion* (New York) 7 (23 Sept. 1848): 464.

[218] "Mr. Forrest and Mr. Macready." *The Literary World* (New York) 96 (2 Dec. 1848): 877–78; reprinted in *Spirit of the Times* 18 (9 Dec. 1848): 496–97.

[219] "Drama." *The Albion* (New York) 8 (20 Jan. 1849): 32.

[220] "Dramatic Copyright." *Spirit of the Times* (New York) 18 (20 Jan. 1849): 576.

[221] "Drama." *The Albion* (New York) 8 (3 Feb. 1849): 56.
[222] "Drama." *The Albion* (New York) 8 (24 Feb. 1849): 92.
[223] "Drama." *The Albion* (New York) 8 (21 Apr. 1849): 188.
[224] "Things Theatrical." *Spirit of the Times* (New York) 19 (21 Apr. 1849): 108.
[225] *The New York Evening Post*, 10 May 1849: 2.
[226] "Alarming Riot at the Astor Place Theatre." *The New York Evening Post*, 11 May 1849: 2.
[227] "Mr. Macready's Re-Appearance." *The Albion* (New York) 8 (12 May 1849): 224.
[228] "The Riot." *The New York Evening Post*, 12 May 1849: 2.
[229] "General News. Terrible Riot in the City." *The Independent* (New York and Boston) 1 (17 May 1849): 95.
[230] "Drama." *The Albion* (New York) 8 (1 Sept. 1849): 416.
[231] "Silsbee, the Yankee Comedian." *Spirit of the Times* (New York) 19 (17 Nov. 1849): 468.
[232] "Drama." *The Albion* (New York) 8 (1 Dec. 1849): 572.
[233] "Drama." *The Albion* (New York) 8 (29 Dec. 1849): 620.
[234] "Theatrical Humbugs." *Spirit of the Times* (New York) 19 (29 Dec. 1849): 540.
[235] "Drama." *The Albion* (New York) 9 (9 Feb. 1850): 68.
[236] "Drama." *The Albion* (New York) 9 (2 Mar. 1850): 104.
[237] "Drama." *The Albion* (New York) 9 (16 Mar. 1850): 128.
[238] "Theatres, Stars, and Managers." *Spirit of the Times* (New York) 20 (4 May 1850): 128.
[239] "Drama." *The Albion* (New York) 9 (11 May 1850): 224.
[240] "Decline of the Drama." *The Prompter's Whistle* (New York) 2 (14 Sept. 1850): 34–36.
[241] "Drama." *The Albion* (New York) 10 (1 Nov. 1851): 524.
[242] "Prize Dramas." *The Literary World* (New York) 9 (15 Nov. 1851): 390.
[243] "The Modern American Drama." *The American Whig Review* (New York) n.s. 9.2 (Feb. 1852): 176–82.
[244] "The Drama and Vicious Plays." *The Literary World* (New York) 10 (14 Feb. 1852): 125–26.
[245] "The American Drama." *The American Whig Review* (New York) n.s. 9.3 (Mar. 1852): 228–35.
[246] "Reform in Theatres." *Spirit of the Times* (New York) 22 (21 Aug. 1852): 321.
[247] "Places of Public Amusement. Theatres and Concert Rooms." *Putnam's Monthly Magazine* (New York) 3.14 (Feb. 1854): 141–52.
[248] "New Theatre and Opera House." *Gleason's Pictorial Drawing-Room Companion* (Boston) 6 (22 Apr. 1854): 253.

[249] "Drop the Curtain." *The United States Democratic Review* (New York) 34.1 (Aug. 1854): 121–27.
[250] Alba. "Drama." *The Albion* (New York) 14 (27 Jan. 1855): 44.
[251] "Letter from Acorn." *Spirit of the Times* (New York) 25 (17 Mar. 1855): 49.
[252] "Shakspeare Darkeyized—Macbeth in High Colors. From 'Doesticks: What he says.'" *Spirit of the Times* (New York) 25 (11 Aug. 1855): 303–4.
[253] "Letter from Acorn." *Spirit of the Times* (New York) 26 (6 Sept. 1856): 349–50.
[254] Alba. "Drama." *The Albion* (New York) 15 (25 Oct. 1856): 512.
[255] Desdichado. "Drama." *The Albion* (New York) 15 (1 Nov. 1856): 524.
[256] Hamilton. "Drama." *The Albion* (New York) 15 (15 Nov. 1856): 547–48.
[257] Hamilton. "Drama." *The Albion* (New York) 15 (22 Nov. 1856): 560.
[258] Hamilton. "Drama." *The Albion* (New York) 15 (6 Dec. 1856): 584.
[259] "A National Drama." *Putnam's Monthly Magazine* (New York) 9 (Feb. 1857): 148–51.
[260] "The Drama, the Pulpit and the Press." *The Albion* (New York) 35 (25 Apr. 1857): 199.
[261] "Dr. Bellows on the Theatre." *The Albion* (New York) 35 (2 May 1857): 209–10.
[262] "The Rev. Dr. Bellows's Lecture on 'The Pulpit and the Stage.'" *Spirit of the Times* (New York) 27 (31 Oct. 1857): 449.
[263] "The Drama in America." *The United States Democratic Review* (New York) 40 (Dec. 1857): 554–60.
[264] "The American Drama." *Emerson's Magazine and Putnam's Monthly* (New York) 6 (Mar. 1858): 304–12.
[265] "The Drama." *The United States Democratic Review* (New York) 42 (July 1858): 16–39.
[266] "The Decline of the Drama. Retirement of Mr. Forrest." *Spirit of the Times* (New York) 28 (13 Nov. 1858): 473.
[267] Hamilton. "Drama." *The Albion* (New York) 37 (3 Sept. 1859): 427.
[268] Hamilton. "Drama." *The Albion* (New York) 37 (29 Oct. 1859): 523.
[269] "The Octoroon. A Disgrace to the North, a Libel on the South." *Spirit of the Times* (New York) 29 (17 Dec. 1859): 529.
[270] "Things Theatrical." *Spirit of the Times* (New York) 29 (24 Dec. 1859): 552.
[271] "On the Stage." *The Albion* (New York) 37 (31 Dec. 1859): 626–27.
[272] Conway, M. D. "The Citizen and the Drama." *The Dial* (Cincinnati) 1.12 (Dec. 1860) [reprinted in *The Dial: A Monthly Magazine for Literature, Philosophy and Religion.* Ed. M. D. Conway. New York, 1860, 762–73].
[273] Mercutio. "Drama." *The Albion* (New York) 41 (24 Oct. 1863): 511.

[274] "Management—With a Specimen." *The Round Table* (New York) 1 (26 Dec. 1863): 29.
[275] "Dramatic Critics in New York." *The Round Table* (New York) 1 (2 Jan. 1864): 43–44.
[276] "The Theaters and the Newspapers." *The Round Table* (New York) 1 (9 Jan. 1864): 59–60.
[277] Mercutio. "Drama." *The Albion* (New York) 42 (19 Mar. 1864): 139.
[278] "Spiking the Guns of the Press." *The Round Table* (New York) 1 (9 Apr. 1864): 264–65.
[279] "The Drama in Richmond." *The Magnolia Weekly* (Richmond) 2 (16 Apr. 1864): 232.
[280] "The New Richmond Theatre." *The Magnolia Weekly* (Richmond) 2 (30 Apr. 1864): 248.
[281] "Theatrical Benefits Exposed." *The Round Table* (New York) 2 (9 July 1864): 59–60.
[282] Mercutio. "Drama." *The Albion* (New York) 43 (1 July 1865): 307.
[283] "About Theaters and the Drama." *The Round Table* (New York) n.s. 6 (14 Oct. 1865): 91.
[284] Mercutio. "Drama." *The Albion* (New York) 44 (3 Feb. 1866): 55.
[285] Mercutio. "Drama." *The Albion* (New York) 44 (17 Mar. 1866): 127.
[286] "The Theatres." *The Nation* (New York) 2 (5 Apr. 1866): 428–29.
[287] Mercutio. "Drama." *The Albion* (New York) 44 (26 May 1866): 247.
[288] "Drama." *The Albion* (New York) 45 (5 Jan. 1867): 7.
[289] "The Stage—As It Is and Should Be." *The Round Table* (New York) 5 (5 Jan. 1867): 4.
[290] Logan, Olive. "The Drunken Drama." *The Galaxy* (New York) 4 (Dec. 1867): 934–41 [See also Chapter 8: "About the Drunken Drama," in Logan. *Apropos of Women and Theatres*. New York, 1869].
[291] Logan, Olive. "American and Foreign Theatres." *The Galaxy* (New York) 5 (Jan. 1868): 22–27.
[292] "The Naughty Drama." *The Round Table* (New York) 7 (14 Mar. 1868): 165–66.
[293] "Table–Talk." *Appleton's Journal* (New York) 1 (3 Apr. 1869): 25.
[294] Howells, William D. "The New Taste in Theatricals." *Atlantic Monthly* (New York) 23 (May 1869): 635–44.
[295] "Table–Talk." *Appleton's Journal* (New York) 1 (1 May 1869): 154.
[296] "The Stage and Nature." *Putnam's Magazine* (New York) n.s. 4 (July 1869): 63–71.
[297] "Drama." *The Albion* (New York) 47 (31 July 1869): 450.
[298] "Table–Talk." *Appleton's Journal* (New York) 2 (28 Aug. 1869): 57–58.
[299] Field, Kate. "Dramatic Criticism." *The Aldine Press* (New York) 3.2 (Feb. 1870): 20.
[300] "Table–Talk." *Appleton's Journal* (New York) 3 (5 Feb. 1870): 163–64.

[301] "Table–Talk." *Appleton's Journal* (New York) 3 (9 Apr. 1870): 413–14.
[302] "Table–Talk." *Appleton's Journal* (New York) 4 (30 July 1870): 142.
[303] "Table–Talk." *Appleton's Journal* (New York) 5 (21 Jan. 1871): 82–83.
[304] "Table–Talk." *Appleton's Journal* (New York) 5 (3 June 1871): 658–59.
[305] "Music and Drama." *The Albion* (New York) 49 (9 Sept. 1871): 572.
[306] "Theaters and Theater–going." *Scribner's Monthly* (New York) 4.2 (June 1872): 238–39.
[307] "About Acting." *Scribner's Monthly* (New York) 4.5 (Sept. 1872): 639–40.
[308] "Table–Talk." *Appleton's Journal* (New York) 8 (19 Oct. 1872): 442.
[309] "Dramatic Prospects." *Scribner's Monthly* (New York) 5.1 (Nov. 1872): 131–32.
[310] "Plays and Players." *The Galaxy* (New York) 15.3 (Mar. 1873): 410–12.
[311] "Music and the Drama." *Appleton's Journal* (New York) 10 (27 Dec. 1873): 828–29.
[312] "The Metropolitan Stage." *The Aldine* (New York) 7.2 (Feb. 1874): 47.
[313] "Music and the Drama—Boucicault's Latest." *Appleton's Journal* (New York) 12 (29 Aug. 1874): 285–86.
[314] "Music and the Drama." *Appleton's Journal* (New York) 13 (2 Jan. 1875): 23–24.
[315] "Music and the Drama." *Appleton's Journal* (New York) 13 (30 Jan. 1875): 154–55.
[316] Matthews, Brander. "The Decline of the Drama." *The Galaxy* (New York) 19.2 (Feb. 1875): 225–31.
[317] [Dr. Holland.] "Theaters and Theater–going." *Scribner's Monthly* (New York) 9.4 (Feb. 1875): 501–2.
[318] "Music and the Drama." *Appleton's Journal* (New York) 13 (20 Feb. 1875): 250–51.
[319] "Editor's Table." *Appleton's Journal* (New York) 13 (6 Mar. 1875): 309.
[320] "Music and the Drama." *Appleton's Journal* (New York) 14 (18 Sept. 1875): 378.
[321] "Music and the Drama." *Appleton's Journal* (New York) 14 (25 Sept. 1875): 412.
[322] Bunce, O. B. "*Julius Caesar* at Booth's Theatre." *Appleton's Journal* (New York) 15 (22 Jan. 1876): 115–17.
[323] "Editor's Table." *Appleton's Journal* (New York) 15 (19 Feb. 1876): 246.
[324] "Editor's Table." *Appleton's Journal* (New York) n.s. 2 (Feb. 1877): 185–86.
[325] Boucicault, Dion. "The Decline of the Drama." *The North American Review* (Boston) 125 (Sept. 1877): 235–45.
[326] "*Rip Van Winkle*." *Appleton's Journal* (New York) n.s. 4 (Feb. 1878): 146–51.

[327] *The Nation* (New York) 28 (9 Jan. 1879): 34.
[328] Matthews, Brander. "The American on the Stage." *Scribner's Monthly* (New York) 18.3 (July 1879): 321–33.
[329] "The Drama." *Scribner's Monthly* (New York) 21.4 (Feb. 1881): 632–33.
[330] *The Critic* (New York) 1 (26 Feb. 1881): 50.
[331] "The Drama." *The Critic* (New York) 2 (17 June 1882): 169.
[332] "The Drama." *The Critic* (New York) 2 (15 July 1882): 195–96.
[333] MacKaye, Steele. "Safety in Theaters." *The North American Review* (Boston) 135 (Nov. 1882): 461–70.
[334] "The Drama." *The Critic* (New York) 3 (28 Apr. 1883): 201–2.
[335] Buckley, J. M., John Gilbert, A. M. Palmer, and William Winter. "The Moral Influence of the Drama." *The North American Review* (Boston) 136 (June 1883): 581–606.
[336] "The Drama—Past and Present." *Oriole Tidings* (Baltimore) 1 (6 Oct. 1883): n.p.
[337] "Things Theatrical. A Few General Remarks on the Drama by a New York Manager." *Oriole Tidings* (Baltimore) 2 (30 Aug. 1884): n.p.
[338] Smile, Seemie. "The Morality of the Modern Stage." *Oriole Tidings* (Baltimore) 2 (20 Dec. 1884): n.p.
[339] Magnus, Julian. "A Plea for Reality in Plays." *Century Illustrated Magazine* (New York) 31.1 (Nov. 1885): 155–56.
[340] G. J. H. "The Decline of the Stage." *Oriole Tidings* (Baltimore) 3 (6 Feb. 1886): n.p.
[341] Hutton, Laurence. "The American Play." *Lippincott's Monthly Magazine* (Philadelphia) 37 (Mar. 1886): 289–98 [rev. version in Hutton. *Curiosities of the American Stage*. New York, 1891, 4–8].
[342] Daly, Augustin. "The American Dramatist." *The North American Review* (Boston) 142 (May 1886): 485–92.
[343] Howells, William D. "Editor's Study." *Harper's New Monthly Magazine* (New York) 73 (July 1886): 314–19 [partly reprinted in *W. D. Howells As Critic*. Ed. E. H. Cady. London: Routledge, 1973, 84–88].
[344] Magnus, Julian. "The Condition of the American Stage." *The North American Review* (Boston) 144 (Feb. 1887): 169–78.
[345] Magnus, Julian. "Wanted—A Representative Theatre." *The North American Review* (Boston) 145 (Nov. 1887): 568–70.
[346] "The Lime Light Man." *The Stage* (Philadelphia) 3 (13 Oct. 1888): 5.
[347] "The Lime Light Man." *The Stage* (Philadelphia) 4 (20 Oct. 1888): 5.
[348] Daly, Augustin, et al. "American Playwrights on the American Drama." *Harper's Weekly* (New York) 33 (2 Feb. 1889): 97–100.
[349] Matthews, Brander. "The Dramatic Outlook in America." *Harper's New Monthly Magazine* (New York) 78 (May 1889): 924–30 [reprinted in Matthews. *Studies of the Stage*. New York, 1894, 39–76].

[350] "How Actors Are Engaged. The Player's Business Life." *The Stage* (Philadelphia) 38 (15 June 1889): 11–12.

[351] "The American Dramatist." *The Stage* (Philadelphia) 39 (22 June 1889): 10–11.

[352] Howells, William D. "Editor's Study." *Harper's New Monthly Magazine* (New York) 79 (July 1889): 314–19.

[353] Warner, Charles Dudley. "Literature and the Stage." *The Critic* (New York) 15 (7 Dec. 1889): 285–86.

[354] Hennequin, Alfred. "Characteristics of the American Drama." *The Arena* (Boston) 1 (May 1890): 700–709.

[355] Garland, Hamlin. "Ibsen As a Dramatist." *The Arena* (Boston) 2 (June 1890): 72–82 [shortened version in Garland. *Crumbling Idols*. Ed. Jane Johnson. Cambridge, MA: Belknap Press, 1960, 81–93].

[356] Hutton, Laurence. "The American Burlesque." *Harper's New Monthly Magazine* (New York) 81 (June 1890): 59–74.

[357] Howells, William D. "Editor's Study." *Harper's New Monthly Magazine* (New York) 81 (June 1890): 152–57 [reprinted in *W. D. Howells As Critic*. Ed. E. H. Cady. London: Routledge, 1973, 178–82].

[358] Boucicault, Dion. "The Future American Drama." *The Arena* (Boston) 2 (Nov. 1890): 641–52.

[359] Waddle, Charles Carey. "The American Amateur Stage." *The Cosmopolitan* (New York) 10.1 (Nov. 1890): 12–25.

[360] Hennequin, Alfred. "The Drama of the Future." *The Arena* (Boston) 3 (Mar. 1891): 385–93.

[361] "An Epoch–Marking Drama." *The Arena* (Boston) 4 (July 1891): 247–49.

[362] Howells, William D. "Editor's Study." *Harper's New Monthly Magazine* (New York) 83 (Aug. 1891): 476–79.

[363] Garland, Hamlin. "Mr. and Mrs. Herne." *The Arena* (Boston) 4 (Oct. 1891): 543–60.

[364] Fuller, Edward. "An Independent Theatre." *Lippincott's Monthly Magazine* (Philadelphia) 49 (Mar. 1892): 371–75.

[365] Ford, James L. "The Independent or Free Theatre of New York." *Lippincott's Monthly Magazine* (Philadelphia) 49 (Mar. 1892): 375–78.

[366] Maynard, Cora. "The Theatre of Today." *The Cosmopolitan* (New York) 12.6 (Apr. 1892): 725–32.

[367] Herne, James A. "Old Stock Days in the Theatre." *The Arena* (Boston) 6 (Sept. 1892): 401–16.

[368] Mansfield, Richard. "A Plain Talk on the Drama." *The North American Review* (Boston) 155 (Sept. 1892): 308–14.

[369] Modjeska, Helena. "Endowed Theatres and the American Stage." *Forum* (New York) 14 (Nov. 1892): 337–44.

[370] Palmer, A. M. "Why Theatrical Managers Reject Plays." *Forum* (New York) 15 (July 1893): 614–20.
[371] Flower, B. O. "Mask or Mirror. The Vital Difference Between Artificiality and Veritism on the Stage." *The Arena* (Boston) 8 (Aug. 1893): 304–13.
[372] Mathews, F. Annie Aymar. "A Plea for the Play-Writer." *Godey's Magazine* (New York) 127 (Oct. 1893): 466–68.
[373] De Cordova, Rudolph. "The Stage As a Career: An Actor's Experience." *Forum* (New York) 17 (July 1894): 622–32.
[374] Speed, Jno. Gilmer. "A Week in New York Theatres." *Forum* (New York) 19 (Mar. 1895): 118–28.
[375] Speed, Jno. Gilmer. "The Theater As a Civilizing Influence." *The Outlook* (New York) 51 (13 Apr. 1895): 599–600.
[376] Monroe, Lucy. "Chicago Letter." *The Critic* (New York) 27 (6 July 1895): 16.
[377] Fuller, Edward. "The Decadent Drama." *Lippincott's Monthly Magazine* (Philadelphia) 56 (Sept. 1895): 423–26.
[378] Wingate, Charles E. L. "Boston Notes." *The Critic* (New York) 27 (7 Dec. 1895): 393.
[379] Howells, William D. "Life and Letters." *Harper's Weekly* (New York) 40 (22 Feb. 1896): 175.
[380] Howells, William D. "Life and Letters." *Harper's Weekly* (New York) 40 (29 Feb. 1896): 199.
[381] Herne, James A. "Art for Truth's Sake in the Drama." *The Arena* (Boston) 17 (Feb. 1897): 361–70 [reprinted in *American Drama and Its Critics*. Ed. Alan S. Downer. Chicago: University of Chicago Press, 1965, 1–9].
[382] Clarke, Joseph I. C. "A National Theatre." *Harper's Weekly* (New York) 41 (8 May 1897): 463.
[383] Pyle, Ingram A. "The American Drama." *Lippincott's Monthly Magazine* (Philadelphia) 60 (July 1897): 130–33.
[384] Howells, William D. "Suggestions of a Patriotic Play." *Literature* (New York) n.s. 1 (24 Feb. 1899): 145–46.
[385] Hapgood, Norman. "The Upbuilding of the Theatre." *Atlantic Monthly* (New York) 83 (Mar. 1899): 419–25.
[386] Hapgood, Norman. "A Theory of Dramatic Criticism." *Forum* (New York) 27 (Mar. 1899): 120–28.
[387] Henderson, W. J. "The Business of a Theatre." *Scribner's Magazine* (New York) 25.3 (Mar. 1899): 297–314.
[388] Howells, William D. "A Subscription Theatre." *Literature* (New York) n.s. 1 (14 Apr. 1899): 313.
[389] La Shelle, Kirk. "The Theatrical Advance Agent." *The Cosmopolitan* (New York) 28.3 (Jan. 1900): 325–30.

[390] Potter, Helen. "The Drama of the Twentieth Century." *The Arena* (Boston) 23 (Feb. 1900): 157–66.

[391] Peck, Harry Thurston. "The Drama of Disintegration." *The Cosmopolitan* (New York) 28.5 (Mar. 1900): 513–15.

[392] Hapgood, Norman. "The Syndicate." In Hapgood. *The Stage in America 1897–1900.* New York: Macmillan, 1901, 6–38.

[393] Hapgood, Norman. "Our Only High Class Theatre." In Hapgood. *The Stage in America 1897–1900.* New York: Macmillan, 1901, 134–49.

[394] Kobbé, Gustav. "Events of the Dramatic Season." *Forum* (New York) 31 (May 1901): 298–305.

[395] Garland, Hamlin, et al. "James A. Herne: Actor, Dramatist, and Man." *The Arena* (Boston) 26 (Sept. 1901): 282–91.

[396] Stearns, Richard. "The Drama's Tendency toward the Unintellectual." *The Cosmopolitan* (New York) 32.1 (Nov. 1901): 65–74.

[397] Howells, William D. "Editor's Easy Chair." *Harper's Monthly Magazine* (New York) 104 (Mar. 1902): 670–74.

[398] Rhodes, H. G. "The American Invasion of the London Stage." *The Cosmopolitan* (New York) 33.1 (May 1902): 25–32.

[399] Shinn, George Wolfe. "The Actors' Church Alliance." *The Arena* (Boston) 28 (July 1902): 15–22.

[400] Corbin, John. "The American Drama." *Forum* (New York) 34 (July 1902): 63–76.

[401] Bathon, Wingrove. "The Winter's Drama." *The Cosmopolitan* (New York) 33.6 (Oct. 1902): 625–34.

[402] Ford, James L. "A Plea for the Free Theater." *Munsey's Magazine* (New York) 28.1 (Oct. 1902): 148–52.

[403] "The Future of the Drama." *The Nation* (New York) 76 (19 Feb. 1903): 147.

[404] Gaffney, Fannie Humphreys. "Modern Dramatic Realism." *The Arena* (Boston) 29 (Apr. 1903): 391–96.

[405] Hackett, James K. "A University for the Drama." *The Independent* (New York and Boston) 55 (23 Apr. 1903): 973–74.

[406] Davies, Henry. "The Stage As a Moral Institution." *The Critic* (New York) 43.1 (July 1903): 24–28.

[407] McCracken, Elizabeth. "The Copyrighting of Plays." *The Bookman* (New York) 18.1 (Sept. 1903): 83–86.

[408] Price, L. Guernsey. "American Undergraduate Dramatics." *The Bookman* (New York) 18.4 (Dec. 1903): 373–88.

[409] Boyesen, Hjalmar Hjorth. "The Odd and Eccentric in the Drama." *The Cosmopolitan* (New York) 36.3 (Jan. 1904): 279–88.

[410] Field, Louise M. "A Defence of the Stage To-Day." *The Critic* (New York) 44.1 (Jan. 1904): 87–88.

[411] Howells, William D. "Some New American Plays." *Harper's Weekly* (New York) 48 (16 Jan. 1904): 88, 90 [reprinted in *American Drama and Its Critics.* Ed. Alan S. Downer. Chicago: University of Chicago Press, 1965, 10–17].
[412] "An Attempt to Regenerate the Drama." *The Independent* (New York and Boston) 56 (11 Feb. 1904): 324–25.
[413] "The Movement for an Endowed National Art Theater for America." *The Arena* (Boston) 31 (June 1904): 641–45.
[414] Gaige, Roscoe C. "Staging a College Play." *The Cosmopolitan* (New York) 37.2 (June 1904): 227–34.
[415] Mackay, F. F. et al. "A National Art Theater for America." *The Arena* (Boston) 32 (July 1904): 48–53.
[416] Shinn, George Wolfe. "Church and Stage after Five Years." *The Arena* (Boston) 32 (Sept. 1904): 284–87.
[417] "The Stage Does Not Believe in the Negro on the Stage." *The Stage* (New York) 1 (24 Sept. 1904): 2–3.
[418] Frohman, Daniel. "The Tendencies of the American Stage." *The Cosmopolitan* (New York) 38.1 (Nov. 1904): 15–22.
[419] Belasco, David. "The Theatrical Syndicate. One Side." *The Cosmopolitan* (New York) 38.2 (Dec. 1904): 193–98.
[420] Klaw, Marc. "The Theatrical Syndicate. The Other Side." *The Cosmopolitan* (New York) 38.2 (Dec. 1904): 199–201.
[421] "A Plea for the White Performer." *The Stage* (New York) 2 (24 Dec. 1904): 16.
[422] "Vultures in the Guise of Agents." *The Stage* (New York) 2 (7 Jan. 1905): 16.
[423] Metcalfe, James S. "Financing the National Theatre." *The North American Review* (Boston) 180 (Feb. 1905): 198–209.
[424] Zangwill, Israel. "The Future of Vaudeville in America." *The Cosmopolitan* (New York) 38.6 (Apr. 1905): 639–46.
[425] Hennessy, Roland Burke. "An Open Letter to Whom It May Concern." *The Stage* (New York) 3 (15 July 1905): 9.
[426] F. J. W. "The National Theatre Chimera." *The Stage* (New York) 4 (19 Aug. 1905): 7.
[427] Davies, Acton. "That Uncertain Person—the American Dramatist." *The Cosmopolitan* (New York) 40.1 (Nov. 1905): 81–88.
[428] Belasco, David. "Art for Business' Sake." *The Cosmopolitan* (New York) 40.2 (Dec. 1905): 231–39.
[429] "Confessions of a Dramatic Critic." *The Independent* (New York and Boston) 60 (1 Mar. 1906): 492–97.
[430] Moses, Montrose J. "The American Dramatists." *The Independent* (New York and Boston) 61 (27 Sept. 1906): 735–43.

[431] "A National Necessity." *The St. Louis Dramatic News* 1 (12 Dec. 1906): 4.

[432] Dale, Alan. "The Indelicacy of Modern Plays: How Our Sense of Modesty Is Becoming Dulled through the Marked Tendency of Many of the Season's New Dramas in the Direction of Too Great Candor." *The Cosmopolitan* (New York) 42.3 (Jan. 1907): 316–25.

[433] Meltzer, Charles Henry. "On the Printing of Plays." *The Independent* (New York and Boston) 62 (3 Jan. 1907): 20–23.

[434] Meltzer, Charles Henry. "The New Theater." *The Independent* (New York and Boston) 62 (17 Jan. 1907): 133–34.

[435] Flower, B. O. "The Theater As a Potential Factor for Higher Civilization, and a Typical Play Illustrating Its Power." *The Arena* (Boston) 37 (May 1907): 497–509.

[436] Corbin, John. "The Dawn of the American Drama." *Atlantic Monthly* (New York) 99.5 (May 1907): 632–44.

[437] Mailly, William. "The Season's Social Drama." *The Arena* (Boston) 38 (July 1907): 35–46.

[438] Eaton, Walter Pritchard. "Our Infant Industry." In Eaton. *The American Stage of To–Day*. Boston: Small, 1908, 6–26.

[439] Frohman, Daniel. "The Theaters and the Panic." *The Independent* (New York and Boston) 64 (30 Jan. 1908): 252–53.

[440] Colby, Frank Moore. "A Model for Dramatic Critics." *Forum* (New York) 39 (Apr. 1908): 550–51.

[441] Hamilton, Clayton. "Certain Lessons of the Recent Season." *Forum* (New York) 40 (July 1908): 43–49.

[442] "The New Theatre." *The Bookman* (New York) 28.1 (Sept. 1908): 1–3.

[443] "A Declaration!" *New York Star* 1 (14 Nov. 1908): 7.

[444] Hamilton, Clayton. "Holding the Mirror up to Nature." *Forum* (New York) 40 (Dec. 1908): 537–38 [reprinted in Hamilton. *The Theory of the Theatre*. New York: Holt, 1910, 184–92].

[445] MacKaye, Percy. "The Drama of Democracy." In MacKaye. *The Playhouse and the Play*. New York: Macmillan, 1909. Reprinted 1968, 89–120.

[446] [Spanner, Richard]. "What Ails Our Stage? The Meaning of the Onslaught on Indecent Plays in New York." *The St. Louis Dramatic News* 5 (17 Feb. 1909): 4.

[447] C. G. "Is Drama Regarded Seriously? Another Aspect of the Burning Question: What Ails Our Stage?" *The St. Louis Dramatic News* 5 (24 Feb. 1909): 4.

[448] C. G. "Why Our Stage Is Physical: Another Contribution to the Flagrant Query: What Ails Our Stage?" *The St. Louis Dramatic News* 5 (3 Mar. 1909): 4.

[449] C. G. "Some Dramatic Impossibilities: Continuance of the Current Contention: What Ails Our Stage?" *The St. Louis Dramatic News* 5 (10 Mar. 1909): 4.

[450] Hamilton, Clayton. "The Paucity of Themes in the American Theatre." *Forum* (New York) 41 (June 1909): 544–46 [partly reprinted as "Themes in the Theatre," in Hamilton. *The Theory of the Theatre*. New York: Holt, 1910, 228–32; and in *The American Theatre As Seen by Its Critics, 1752–1934*. Ed. Montrose J. Moses and John Mason Brown. New York: Cooper Square, 1967, 191–93].

[451] "The New Theatre's Enemies: Sinister Opposition Encountered in New York by an Advancing Movement." *The St. Louis Dramatic News* 6 (9 June 1909): 10.

[452] Lyons, Rabbi Alexander. "The Purification of the Stage. An Opportunity for the American Jew." *The St. Louis Dramatic News* 6 (18 Aug. 1909): 8.

[453] Nathan, George Jean. "The United States of Playwrights." *The Bookman* (New York) 30.1 (Sept. 1909): 35–38.

[454] Hamilton, Clayton. "Over–Production in the American Theatre." *Forum* (New York) 42 (Oct. 1909): 353–56 [partly reprinted as "Dramatic Art and the Theatre Business," in Hamilton. *The Theory of the Theatre*. New York: Holt, 1910, 161–68].

[455] Phelps, William Lyon. "The New Theater." *The Independent* (New York and Boston) 67 (28 Oct. 1909): 957–62.

[456] "Plays without Words." *Scribner's Magazine* (New York) 46.1 (Nov. 1909): 121–22.

[457] "The Theatre of Ideas." *The Nation* (New York) 90 (20 Jan. 1910): 69–70.

[458] Andrews, Charlton. "Dr. Sheldon and the Theater." *The Independent* (New York and Boston) 68 (5 May 1910): 971–73.

[459] Hamilton, Clayton. "The Younger American Playwrights." *The Bookman* (New York) 32.3 (Nov. 1910): 249–57.

[460] Hamilton, Clayton. "Plays, Home–Made and Imported." *The Bookman* (New York) 32.6 (Feb. 1911): 594–607.

[461] MacKaye, Percy. "The Civic Theatre: Suggestions Regarding Its Scope and Organization." *The Drama* (Chicago) 1 (Feb. 1911): 98–115.

[462] "The Drama League of America." *The Drama* (Chicago) 1 (Feb. 1911): 116–22.

[463] "The California Grove Play." *The Drama* (Chicago) 1 (Feb. 1911): 131–35.

[464] "The New Theatre and a Moral." *The Nation* (New York) 92 (9 Mar. 1911): 250.

[465] Moses, Montrose J. "The Disintegration of the Theatre." *Forum* (New York) 45 (Apr. 1911): 465–71.

[466] Williams, J. E. "The Formula of the American Drama." *The Drama* (Chicago) 2 (May 1911): 212–21.
[467] Guthrie, William Norman. "Editorial: The Formula of the American Drama." *The Drama* (Chicago) 2 (May 1911): 222–43.
[468] Moses, Montrose J. "The Regeneration of the Theatre." *Forum* (New York) 45 (May 1911): 584–88.
[469] "Another Stage Experiment." *The Nation* (New York) 93 (13 July 1911): 41.
[470] Garland, Hamlin. " 'Starring' the Play." *The Nation* (New York) 93 (20 July 1911): 54.
[471] Van Landingham, H. A. "University Training for Playwrights." *The Drama* (Chicago) 3 (Aug. 1911): 136–44.
[472] Wegefarth, W. Dayton. "The Decline of Lurid Melodrama." *Lippincott's Monthly Magazine* (Philadelphia) 88 (Sept. 1911): 427–28.
[473] Hamilton, Clayton. "Organising an Audience." *The Bookman* (New York) 34.2 (Oct. 1911): 161–66 [reprinted in Hamilton. *Studies in Stagecraft*. New York: Holt, 1914, 257–72].
[474] Moses, Montrose J. "American Professors of Dramatic Literature." *The Independent* (New York and Boston) 71 (12 Oct. 1911): 813–16.
[475] Hamilton, Clayton. "The Drama of Illusion." *The Bookman* (New York) 34.4 (Dec. 1911): 358–70 [reprinted in Hamilton. *Studies in Stragecraft*. New York: Holt, 1914, 34–42].
[476] Heydrick, Benjamin A. "The Drama." *The Chautauquan* (Meadville, PA) 65.1 (Dec. 1911): 25–48.
[477] Hamilton, Clayton. "The Function of Dramatic Criticism." *The Bookman* (New York) 35.1 (Mar. 1912): 26–31 [reprinted in Hamilton. *Studies in Stagecraft*. New York: Holt, 1914, 273–87].
[478] Grau, Robert. "The Prosperity of American Playwrights." *Lippincott's Monthly Magazine* (Philadelphia) 89 (Apr. 1912): 617–19.
[479] Burton, Richard. "The Theatre and the People." *The Drama* (Chicago) 6 (May 1912): 169–90.
[480] Young, Stark. "Some American Dramatic Material." *The Drama* (Chicago) 6 (May 1912): 210–21.
[481] Grau, Robert. "Science and the Theatre." *Lippincott's Monthly Magazine* (Philadelphia) 90 (Nov. 1912): 637–38.
[482] "The Theatrical Situation." *The Nation* (New York) 96 (6 Feb. 1913): 136–37.
[483] Howells, William D. "Editor's Easy Chair." *Harper's Monthly Magazine* (New York) 126 (May 1913): 958–61.
[484] Hamilton, Clayton. "Timely Topics in the Theatre." *The Bookman* (New York) 38.2 (Oct. 1913): 129–36.
[485] Corbin, John. "The New Revolt against Broadway." *Scribner's Magazine* (New York) 54.4 (Oct. 1913): 516–23.

[486] F. J. M., Jr. "The Stage vs. the Drama." *The Nation* (New York) 97 (18 Dec. 1913): 596–99.

[487] "Three Years of the Drama League." *The Nation* (New York) 98 (26 Mar. 1914): 322–23.

[488] Cheney, Sheldon. "The American Playwright and the Drama of Sincerity." *Forum* (New York) 51 (Apr. 1914): 498–512 [reprinted as part of Chapter 1 in Cheney. *The New Movement in the Theatre*. New York: Kennerley, 1914].

[489] Hamilton, Clayton. "What Is Wrong with the American Drama." *The Bookman* (New York) 39.3 (May 1914): 314–19 [reprinted in Hamilton. *Problems of the Playwright*. New York: Holt, 1917, 312–28].

[490] Kiper, Florence. "Some American Plays. From the Feminist Viewpoint." *Forum* (New York) 51 (June 1914): 921–31.

[491] "The Theatre for Amusement." *The Nation* (New York) 99 (2 July 1914): 7.

[492] McLaws, Lafayette. "A Master of Playwrights." *The North American Review* (Boston) 200 (Sept. 1914): 459–67.

[493] Burton, Richard. "The Drama League of America." *The Nation* (New York) 99 (3 Dec. 1914): 668–69.

[494] Howells, William D. "The Plays of Eugène Brieux." *The North American Review* (Boston) 201 (Mar. 1915): 402–11.

[495] "The Violation of Theatrical Neutrality by the Experimental Amateur." *Current Opinion* (New York) 58.5 (May 1915): 334–35.

[496] "The Theatre Adrift." *The Nation* (New York) 101 (28 Oct. 1915): 512.

5

Alphabetical List of the Periodicals Consulted

I have listed only the bibliographical data necessary to identify a particular journal. If the title of a journal varies, the main entry is under its earliest title. For further bibliographical information, see Jean Hoornstra and Trudy Heath, eds., *American Periodicals 1741–1900: An Index to the Microfilm Collections: American Periodicals 18th Century; American Periodicals 1800–1850; American Periodicals 1850–1900, Civil War and Reconstruction* (Ann Arbor: University of Michigan Press, 1979); Carl J. Stratman, *American Theatrical Periodicals, 1798–1967: A Bibliographical Guide* (Durhman, NC: Duke University Press, 1970); and, of course, the *Union List of Serials in Libraries of the United States and Canada*.

\ indicates: the title was changed to . . .

* indicates that the periodical contains relevant material and that articles from it are listed in Chapter 4.

The Aeronaut (New York) 1–13 (1816–1822)
The Albion (New York) 1–54 (1822–1876).
The Album and Ladies' Weekly Gazette \ *The Philadelphia Album and Ladies' Literary Gazette* \ *The Philadelphia Album and Ladies' Literary Port Folio* 1–8 (1826–1834)
The Aldine Press \ *The Aldine* (New York) 3–9 (1870–1879)
The American Athenaeum (New York) 1 (1825–1826)
The American Magazine and Historical Chronicle (Boston) 1–3 (1743–1746)
The American Magazine and Monthly Chronicle for the British Colonies (Philadelphia) 1 (1757–1758)
**American Masonic Register and Literary Companion* (Albany) 1–8 (1839–1847)
The American Monthly Knickerbocker. See *The Knickerbocker*

The American Monthly Magazine (Boston) 1–3 (1829–1831)
**The American Monthly Magazine* (New York) 1–6 (1833–1836); n.s. 1–6 (1836–1838)
**The American Monthly Magazine* (Philadelphia) 1–2 (1824)
**The American Monthly Magazine and Critical Review* (New York) 1–4 (1817–1819)
**The American Museum; or, Repository of Ancient and Modern Fugitive Piece* \ *The American Museum, or, Universal Magazine* (Philadelphia) 1–12 (1787–1792)
**The American Quarterly Review* (Philadelphia) 1–22 (1827–1837)
**The American Review, and Literary Journal* (New York) 1–2 (1801–1802)
**The American Review: A Whig Journal* \ *The American Whig Review* (New York) 1–16 (1845–1852)
The American Whig Review. See *The American Review: A Whig Journal*
The Analectic Magazine (Philadelphia) 1–14 (1813–1819); n.s. 1–2 (1820)
**The Anglo American* (New York) 1–10 (1843–1847)
**Appleton's Journal* (New York) 1–15 (1869–1876); n.s. 1–11 (1876–1881)
*Arcturus (New York) 1–3 (1840–1842)
*The Arena (Boston) 1–41 (1889–1909)
The Ariel (Philadelphia) 1–6 (1827–1832)
Arthur's Ladies' Magazine of Elegant Literature and the Fine Arts. See *Ladies' Magazine of Literature, Fashion and Fine Arts*
Arthur's Magazine. See *Ladies' Magazine of Literature, Fashion and Fine Arts*
Atlantic Journal, and Friend of Knowledge (Philadelphia) 1–8 (1832–1833)
*Atlantic Monthly (Boston) 1–116 (1857–1915)
Ballou's Pictorial Drawing-Room Companion. See *Gleason's Pictorial Drawing-Room Companion*
The Baltimore Repertory of Papers on Literary and Other Topics 1 (1811)
The Baltimore Weekly Magazine 1 (1800–1801)
*The Bookman (New York) 1–45 (1895–1917)
**The Boston Lyceum* 1–2 (1827)
The Boston Magazine (1802–1806). See *The Boston Weekly Magazine*
Boston Monthly Magazine 1–2 (1825–1826)
The Boston Quarterly Review 1–5 (1838–1842)
Boston Recorder. See *Recorder*
Boston Recorder and Religious Telegraph. See *Recorder*
The Boston Spectator 1 (1814–1815)
The Boston Weekly Magazine \ *The Boston Magazine* 1–3 (1802–1805); n.s. 1 (1805–1806)
**The Boston Weekly Magazine* 1–3 (1816–1819); n.s. 1 (1824)
*Broadway Journal (New York) 1–2 (1845–1846)
*Brother Jonathan (New York) 1–6 (1842–1843)

Brownson's Quarterly Review (Boston) 1–3 (1844–1846); n.s. 1–6 (1847–1852); 3d s. 1–3 (1853–55); (New York) 1–4 (1856–1859); 2d–3d s. 1–4 (1860–1863); national s. 1 (1864); last s. 1–3 (1873–1875)
**Burton's Gentleman's Magazine and American Monthly Review* (Philadelphia) 1–7 (1837–1840)
*The Cabinet (Boston) no. 1–10 (1811)
Century Illustrated Magazine. See *Scribner's Monthly*
**The Columbian Magazine \ The Universal Asylum and Columbian Magazine* (Philadelphia) 1–9 (1786–1792)
*The Comet (Boston) no. 1–13 (1811–1812)
**The Companion and Weekly Miscellany* (Baltimore) 1–2 (1804–1806)
**The Correspondent* (New York) 1–5 (1827–1829)
*The Corsair (New York) 1 (1839–1840)
*The Cosmopolitan (New York) 1–42 (1886–1907)
The Critic (Philadelphia) no. 1–20 (1820)
*The Critic (New York) 1–2 (1828–1829)
*The Critic (New York) 1–49 (1881–1906)
*The Cynick (Philadelphia) 1 (1811)
Democratic Review. See *The United States Democratic Review*
Democrat's Review. See *The United States Democratic Review*
The Dial (Boston) 1–4 (1840–1844)
*The Dial (Cincinnati) 1 (1860)
*The Drama (Chicago: The Drama League of America) 1–20 (1911–1915)
**The Dramatic Mirror, and Literary Companion* (New York and Philadelphia) 1–2 (1841–1842)
**The Emerald, or, Miscellany of Literature* (Boston) 1–2 (1806–1807); n.s. 1 (1807–1808)
Emerson's Magazine and Putnam's Monthly. See *The United States Magazine of Science, Art, Manufactures, Agriculture, Commerce and Trade*
Emerson's United States Magazine. See *The United States Magazine of Science, Art, Manufactures, Agriculture, Commerce and Trade*
*The Escritoir (Albany) 1 (1826–1827)
The Euterpeiad (Boston) 1–3 (1820–1823); n.s. 1 (1823)
*The Euterpeiad (New York) 1–2 (1830–1831)
The Evangelical and Literary Magazine. See *The Virginia Evangelical and Literary Magazine*
**The Evening Fire–Side* (Philadelphia) 1–2 (1804–1806)
Examiner and Hesperian. See *Literary Examiner and Western Monthly Review*
*The Eye (Philadelphia) 1–2 (1808)
Figaro! Or Corbyn's Chronicle of Amusements (New York) 1 (1850)
The Fly; or, Juvenile Miscellany (Boston) 1 (1805–1806)
*Forum (New York) 1–54 (1886–1915)
The Friend (Albany) 1 (1815–1816)

The Galaxy (New York) 1–25 (1866–1878)
Gentleman's Magazine. See *Burton's Gentleman's Magazine*
Gleason's Pictorial Drawing–Room Companion \ Ballou's Pictorial Drawing–Room Companion (Boston) 1–17 (1851–1859)
Godey's Lady's Book. See *Lady's Book*
Godey's Lady's Book and Magazine. See *Lady's Book*
Godey's Magazine and Lady's Book. See *Lady's Book*
Graham's Magazine. See *Burton's Gentleman's Magazine*
The Guardian (Albany) 1 (1807–1808)
Hopkinsian Magazine (Providence) 1–4 (1824–1832)
The Independent (New York) 1–86 (1848–1916)
The Irish Shield (Philadelphia) 1–4 (1829–1831)
The Knickerbocker; or, New York Monthly Magazine \ The Knickerbocker Monthly \ The American Monthly Knickerbocker (New York) 1–64 (1833–1864)
The Knickerbocker Monthly. See *The Knickerbocker; or, New York Monthly Magazine*
The Ladies' Companion (New York) 1–20 (1834–1844)
The Ladies' Literary Cabinet (New York) 1 (1819); n.s. 1–7 (1819–1822)
Ladies' Literary Portfolio (Philadelphia) 1 (1828–1829)
Ladies' Magazine of Literature, Fashion and Fine Arts \ Arthur's Ladies' Magazine of Elegant Literature and the Fine Arts \ Arthur's Magazine (Philadelphia) 1–5 (1844–1846)
Ladies Port Folio (Boston) 1–2 (1820)
Lady's Book \ Monthly Magazine of Belles–Lettres and the Arts, the Lady's Book \ Godey's Lady's Book \ Godey's Magazine and Lady's Book \ Godey's Lady's Book and Magazine, etc. (New York) 1–137 (1830–1898)
The Lady's Miscellany; or, The Weekly Visitor. See *The Weekly Visitor, or Ladies' Miscellany*
The Lady's Monitor (New York) 1 (1801–1802)
The Lady's Weekly Miscellany. See *The Weekly Visitor, or Ladies' Miscellany*
Lippincott's Magazine \ Lippincott's Monthly Magazine \ McBride's Magazine (Philadelphia) 1–97 (1868–1916)
Lippincott's Monthly Magazine. See *Lippincott's Magazine*
Literary and Evangelical Magazine. See *The Virginia Evangelical and Literary Magazine*
Literary Examiner and Western Monthly Review \ Examiner and Hesperian (Pittsburgh) 1–2 (1839–1840)
The Literary Gazette (Concord, NH) 1–2 (1834–1835)
The Literary Gazette (Philadelphia) 1 (1821)
The Literary Gazette and American Athenaeum. See *The New York Literary Gazette and Phi Beta Kappa Repository*

The Literary Magazine, and American Register (Philadelphia) 1–8 (1803–1807)
**The Literary World* (New York) 1–13 (1847–1853)
McBride's Magazine. See *Lippincott's Magazine*
**The Magnolia Weekly* (Richmond) 1–3 (1862–1865)
**The Massachusetts Magazine* (Boston) 1–8 (1789–1796)
The Minerva (New York) 1–2 (1822–1824); n.s. 1–3 (1824–1825)
**The Mirror of Taste and Dramatic Censor* (Philadelphia) 1–4 (1810–1811)
**The Monthly Anthology, and Boston Review* 1–10 (1803–1811)
**The Monthly Magazine, and American Review* (New York) 1–3 (1799–1800)
Monthly Magazine of Belles–Lettres and the Arts, the Lady's Book. See *Lady's Book*
The Monthly Recorder (New York) 1 (1813)
The Monthly Register, Magazine, and Review of the United States (New York) 1–4 (1805–1807)
The Moralist (New York) 1 (1814)
**The Morning Chronicle* (New York) (1802–1807)
*The Nation (New York) 1–103 (1865–1916)
**The National Register* (Washington) 1–10 (1816–1820)
The New American Magazine (Woodbridge, NJ) no. 1–27 (1785–1760)
**New England Galaxy* (Boston) 1–21 (1817–1838); n.s. 1 (1838–1839)
**New–England Magazine* (Boston) 1–9 (1831–1835)
**The New England Magazine of Knowledge and Pleasure* (Boston) no. 1–3 (1758–1759)
New York Literary Gazette no. 1–24 (1839)
New York Literary Gazette and Journal of Belles Lettres, Arts, Sciences no. 1–19 (1834–1835)
The New York Literary Gazette and American Athenaeum. See *The New York Literary Gazette and Phi Beta Kappa Repository*
**The New York Literary Gazette and Phi Beta Kappa Repository \ The New York Literary Gazette and American Athenaeum \ The Literary Gazette and American Athenaeum* 1–3 (1825–1827)
The New–York Magazine, or Literary Repository 1–6 (1790–1795); n.s. 1–2 (1796–1797)
**The New–York Mirror* 1–20 (1823–1842)
**The New York Review* 1–10 (1837–1842)
*New York Star 1–2 (1908–1909)
**The New–Yorker* 1–11 (1836–1841)
The North American Quarterly Magazine (Philadelphia) 1–9 (1832–1838)
**The North American Review* (Boston) 1–202 (1815–1915)
*The Observer (Baltimore) 1–2 (1806–1807)
Opera Glass (New York) 1 (1828)
*The Ordeal (Boston) 1 (1809)

Oriole Tidings (Baltimore) 1–3 (1883–1886)
Parlour Review, and Journal of Music, Literature, and the Fine Arts (Philadelphia) no. 1–10 (1838)
The Philadelphia Album and Ladies' Literary Gazette. See *The Album and Ladies' Weekly Gazette*
The Philadelphia Album and Ladies' Literary Port Folio. See *The Album and Ladies' Weekly Gazette*
The Philadelphia Magazine, and Weekly Repertory 1 (1818)
**The Philadelphia Monthly Magazine* 1–2 (1827–1828); n.s. 1–6 (1828–1830)
The Philadelphia Monthly Magazine; or, Universal Repository of Knowledge and Entertainment 1–2 (1798)
**The Philadelphia Repertory* 1–2 (1810–1812)
The Philadelphia Repository and Weekly Register \ *The Repository and Ladies' Weekly Museum* 1–6 (1800–1806)
The Pioneer (Pittsburgh) 1 (1812)
The Play Bill (Philadelphia) 1–2 (1876–1877)
*The Polyanthos (Boston) 1–5 (1805–1807); n.s. 1–2 (1812); 3d s. 1–4 (1812–1814)
*The Port Folio (Philadelphia) 1–5 (1801–1805); n.s. 1–6 (1806–1808); n.s. [i.e., 3d s.] 1–8 (1809–1812); 3d s. [i.e., 4th s.] 1–6 (1813–1815); 4th s. [i.e., 5th s.] 1–20 (1816–1825); Hall's 2d s. 1–2 (1826–1827)
*The Portico (Baltimore) 1–5 (1816–1818)
**Portland Magazine* (Portland, ME) 1 (1805)
The Prompter (Philadelphia) 1 (1866–1867)
**The Prompter's Whistle* (New York) 1–4 (1850)
Puritan Recorder. See *Recorder*
Putnam's Magazine. See *Putnam's Monthly Magazine of American Literature, Science, and Art*
**Putnam's Monthly Magazine of American Literature, Science, and Art* \ *Putnam's Magazine* (New York) 1–10 (1853–1857); n.s. 1–6 (1868–1870)
**The Rambler's Magazine* (New York) 1–2 (1809–1810)
*Recorder \ *Boston Recorder* \ *Recorder and Telegraph* \ *Boston Recorder and Religious Telegraph* \ *Puritan Recorder* 1–35 (1816–1850)
Recorder and Telegraph. See *Recorder*
The Repository and Ladies' Weekly Museum. See *The Philadelphia Repository and Weekly Register*
*The Round Table (New York) 1–10 (1863–1869)
**The St. Louis Dramatic News* 1–6 (1906–1909)
*Salmagundi (New York) no. 1–20 (1807–1808); 2d s. no. 1–13 (1819–1820)
**Scribner's Magazine* (New York) 1–61 (1887–1917)
**Scribner's Monthly* \ *Century Illustrated Magazine* (New York) 1–91 (1870–1915)
*Something (Boston) 1 (1809–1810)

The Spirit of the Pilgrims (Boston) 1–6 (1828–1833)
Spirit of the Times (New York) 1–31 (1831–1861)
The Stage (New York) 1–4 (1904–1906)
The Stage (Philadelphia) 1–3 (1888–1890)
The Stranger (Albany) 1 (1813–1814)
The Theatrical Budget, Or Actor's Regalio (New York) 1–n.s. no. 6 (1823–1828)
The Theatrical Censor (Philadelphia) no. 1–17 (1805–1806)
The Thespian Mirror (New York) 1 (1805–1806)
The Thespian Monitor, and Dramatick Miscellany (Philadelphia) 1 (1809)
The Thespian Oracle, Or Monthly Mirror (Philadelphia) 1 (1798)
The Town (New York) 1 (1807)
The United States Democratic Review (Washington; New York) 1–43 (1837–1859)
The United States Magazine. See *The United States Magazine of Science, Art, Manufactures, Agriculture, Commerce and Trade*
The United States Magazine and Democratic Review. See *The United States Democratic Review*
The United States Magazine of Science, Art, Manufactures, Agriculture, Commerce and Trade \ *The United States Magazine* \ *Emerson's United States Magazine* \ *Emerson's Magazine and Putnam's Monthly* (New York) 1–7 (1854–1858)
The United States Review. See *The United States Democratic Review*
The Universal Asylum and Columbian Magazine. See *The Columbian Magazine*
Vanity Fair (New York) 1–7 (1859–1863)
The Virginia Evangelical and Literary Magazine \ The Evangelical and Literary Magazine \ Literary and Evangelical Magazine (Richmond) 1–11 (1818–1828)
The Weekly Magazine of Original Essays, Fugitive Pieces, and Interesting Intelligence (Philadelphia) 1–4 (1798–1799)
The Weekly Recorder (Chillicothe, OH) 1–7 (1814–1821)
The Weekly Visitor, or Ladies' Miscellany \ *The Lady's Weekly Miscellany* \ *The Lady's Miscellany; or, The Weekly Visitor* (New York) 1–15 (1802–1812)

6

Selected Bibliography on the History of the American Drama and Theatre before 1915

Andrews, Charlton. *The Drama To-Day*. Philadelphia: Lippincott, 1913.
Angotti, Vincent L. "American Dramatic Criticism, 1800–1830." Ph. D. diss., University of Kansas, 1967.
Archer, Stephen M. *American Actors and Actresses: A Guide to Information Sources*. Detroit: Gale, 1983.
Bailey, Claudia Jean. *A Guide to Reference and Bibliography for Theatre Research*. 2d ed. Columbus: Ohio State University Libraries, 1983.
Baker, Blanche M. *Dramatic Bibliography: An Annotated List of Books on the History and Criticism of the Drama and Stage and on the Allied Arts of the Theatre*. New York: Wilson, 1933.
———. *Theater and Allied Arts: A Guide to Books Dealing with the History, Criticism, and Technique of the Drama and Theatre, and Related Arts and Crafts*. New York: Wilson, 1952.
Barnes, Noreen C., and Laurie J. Wolf. "Actresses of All Work: Nineteenth-Century Sources on Women in Nineteenth-Century American Theatre." *Performing Arts Resources* 12 (1987): 98–134.
Barrett, Daniel. "Recent Collections of Nineteenth-Century Theatre Materials on Microform." *Nineteenth-Century Theatre* 17 (1989): 66–81.
Bronner, Edwin. *The Encyclopedia of the American Theatre 1900–1975*. South Brunswick, NJ: Barnes, 1980.
Brown, Thomas Allston. *History of the American Stage*. New York: Franklin, 1870. Reprint. 1969.
Browne, Walter. *Who's Who on the Stage; The Dramatic Reference Book and Biographical Dictionary of the Theatre, Containing Records of the Careers of Actors, Actresses, Managers, and Playwrights of the American Stage*. New York: Browne, 1906.
Bryan, George B. *Stage Lives: A Bibliography and Index to Theatrical Biographies in English*. Westport, CT: Greenwood, 1985.

Buratti, David. "*The Spirit of the Times*: Its Theatrical Criticism and Theories as a Reflection of Cultural Attitudes." Ph. D. diss., Indiana University, 1977.
Burton, Richard. *The New American Drama*. New York: Crowell, 1913.
Carter, Huntley. *The New Spirit in Drama and Art*. London: Palmer, 1912.
Charvat, William. *The Origins of American Critical Thought, 1810–1835*. Philadelphia: University of Pennsylvania Press, 1936.
Cheney, Sheldon. *The Art Theatre*. New York: Knopf, 1917.
———. *The New Movement in the Theatre*. New York: Kennerley, 1914. Reprint. 1971.
Chielens, Edward E. *American Literary Magazines: The 18th and 19th Centuries*. New York: Greenwood, 1986.
———. *The Literary Journal in America to 1900: A Guide to Information Sources*. Detroit: Gale, 1975.
Christophersen, Merrill G. "Early American Dramatic Criticism." *Southern Speech Journal* 21 (Spring 1956): 195–203.
Craig, Edward Gordon. *On the Art of the Theater*. Chicago: Browne's Bookstore, 1911.
Dickinson, Thomas H. *The Case of American Drama*. Boston: Houghton, 1915.
———. *The Insurgent Theatre*. New York: Huebsch, 1917.
Dormon, James H., Jr. *Theater in the Ante Bellum South, 1815–1861*. Chapel Hill: University of North Carolina Press, 1967.
Dramatic Index: Covering Articles and Illustrations Concerning the Stage and Its Players in the Periodicals of America and England and Including the Dramatic Books of the Year. 41 vols. Boston: Faxon, 1910–1952.
Dunlap, William. *History of the American Theatre*. 2d ed. New York, 1832. Reprint. New York: Franklin, 1963 [3 vols. in 1].
Eaton, Walter Prichard. *The Actor's Heritage: Scenes from the Theatre of Yesterday and the Day Before*. Boston: Atlantic Monthly, 1924.
———. *The American Stage of To–Day*. Boston: Small, 1908.
———. *At the New Theatre and Others. The American Stage: Its Problems and Performances, 1908–1910*. Boston: Small, 1910.
———. *Plays and Players: Leaves from a Critic's Scrapbook*. Cincinnati: Stewart, 1916.
Eddleman, Floyd Eugene. *American Drama Criticism: Interpretations 1890–1977*. 2d ed. Hamden, CT: Shoe String, 1979. *Supplement I*, 1984. *Supplement II*, 1989.
Edgar, Neal L. *A History and Bibliography of American Magazines, 1810–1820*. Metuchen, NJ: Scarecrow, 1975.
Falk, Armand E. "Theatrical Criticism in the *New York Evening Post*, 1801–1830." Ph. D. diss., Michigan State University, 1968.
Gilder, Rosamond. *A Theatre Library: A Bibliography of One Hundred Books Relating to the Theatre*. New York: Theatre Arts, 1932.

Gohdes, Clarence. *Literature and Theater of the States and Regions of the U.S.A.: An Historical Bibliography*. Durham, NC: Duke University Press, 1967.
Grimsted, David. *Melodrama Unveiled: American Theater and Culture, 1800–1850*. Chicago: University of Chicago Press, 1968.
Hamar, Clifford E. "American Theatre History: A Geographical Index." *ETJ* 1 (1949): 164–94.
Hamilton, Clayton. *Problems of the Playwright*. New York: Holt, 1917.
———. *Studies in Stagecraft*. New York: Holt, 1914.
———. *The Theory of the Theatre*. New York: Holt, 1910.
———. *The Theory of the Theatre and Other Principles of Dramatic Criticism*. New York: Holt, 1939.
Hapgood, Norman. *The Stage in America, 1897–1900*. New York: Macmillan, 1901.
Henderson, Archibald. *The Changing Drama*. New York: Holt, 1914.
Hornblow, Arthur. *A History of the Theatre in America from Its Beginnings to the Present Time*. 2 vols. Philadelphia: Lippincott, 1919. Reprint. New York: Blom, 1965.
Hudson, Frederic. *Journalism in the United States, from 1690 to 1872*. New York: Harper, 1873. Reprint. Grosse Pointe: Michigan Scholarly Press, 1968.
Johnson, Albert E., and W. H. Crain, Jr. "Dictionary of American Drama Critics, 1850–1910." *Theatre Annual* 13 (1955): 65–89.
Johnson, Claudia D., and Vernon E. *Nineteenth–Century Theatrical Memoirs*. Westport, CT: Greenwood, 1982.
Kribbs, Jayne K. *An Annotated Bibliography of American Literary Periodicals, 1741–1850*. Boston: Hall, 1977.
Larson, Carl F. W. *American Regional Theatre History to 1900: A Bibliography*. Metuchen, NJ: Scarecrow, 1979.
Laufe, Abe. *The Wicked Stage: A History of Theater Censorship and Harassment in the United States*. New York: Ungar, 1978.
Litto, Fredric M. *American Dissertations on the Drama and the Theatre*. Kent, OH: Kent State University Press, 1969.
Long, Eugene Hudson. *American Drama from Its Beginnings to the Present*. New York: Appleton, 1970.
Mackay, Constance D'Arcy. *The Little Theatre in the United States*. New York: Holt, 1917.
MacKaye, Percy. *The Civic Theatre in Relation to the Redemption of Leisure: A Book of Suggestions*. New York: Kennerley, 1912.
———. *The Playhouse and the Play, and Other Addresses Concerning the Theatre and Democracy in America*. New York: Macmillan, 1909.
Marks, Patricia. *American Literary and Drama Reviews: An Index to Late Nineteenth–Century Periodicals*. Boston: Hall, 1984.

Marshall, Thomas F. "Beyond New York: A Bibliography of the 19th–Century American Stage from the Atlantic to the Mississippi." *Theatre Research* 3 (1961): 208–17.
Matthews, Brander. *The Development of the Drama*. New York: Scribner's, 1903.
———. *The Historical Novel, and Other Essays*. New York: Scribner's, 1901.
———. *Playwrights on Playmaking, and Other Essays*. New York: Scribner's, 1923.
———. *The Principles of Playmaking, and Other Discussions of the Drama*. New York: Harper, 1919.
———. *Studies of the Stage*. New York: Scribner's, 1894.
Meserve, Walter J. *American Drama to 1900: A Guide to Information Sources*. Detroit: Gale, 1980.
———. *An Emerging Entertainment: The Drama of the American People to 1828*. Bloomington: Indiana University Press, 1977.
———. *Heralds of Promise: The Drama of the American People during the Age of Jackson, 1829–1849*. New York: Greenwood, 1986.
Miller, Tice L. *Bohemians and Critics: American Theatre Criticism in the Nineteenth Century*. Metuchen, NJ: Scarecrow, 1981.
Mott, Frank Luther. *A History of American Magazines*. 5 vols. Cambridge: Harvard University Press, 1938–1968.
Moyer, Ronald L. *American Actors, 1861–1910: An Annotated Bibliography of Books Published in the United States in English from 1861 through 1976*. Troy, NY: Whitston, 1979.
Mullin, Donald. *Victorian Actors and Actresses in Review: A Dictionary of Contemporary Views of Representative British and American Actors and Actresses, 1837–1901*. Westport, CT: Greenwood, 1983.
The New York Times Theatre Reviews 1870–1919. 6 vols. New York: New York Times, 1975.
Ortolani, Benito. *International Bibliography of Theatre, 1982*. New York: Theatre Research Data Center, 1985.
———. *International Bibliography of Theatre, 1983*. New York: Theatre Research Data Center, 1986.
———. *International Bibliography of Theatre, 1984*. New York: Theatre Research Data Center, 1987.
———. *International Bibliography of Theatre, 1985*. New York: Theatre Research Data Center, 1989.
———. *International Bibliography of Theatre, 1986*. New York: Theatre Research Data Center, 1990.
———. *International Bibliography of Theatre, 1987*. New York: Theatre Research Data Center, 1992.

Palmer, Helen H., and Anne Jane Dyson. *American Drama Criticism. Interpretations, 1890–1965 Inclusive, of American Drama since the First Play Produced in America*. Hamden, CT: Shoe String, 1967. Supplement I, 1970.
Pence, James Harry. *The Magazine and the Drama: An Index*. New York, 1896.
Poole's Index to Periodical Literature. New York, 1848. 3d ed. Boston, 1892, plus numerous supplements and revised editions.
Quinn, Arthur Hobson. *A History of the American Drama from the Beginning to the Civil War*. 2d ed. New York: Crofts, 1943.
———. *A History of the American Drama from the Civil War to the Present Day*. Rev. ed. New York: Crofts, 1936.
Rankin, Hugh F. *The Theater in Colonial America*. Chapel Hill: University of North Carolina Press, 1965.
Rigdon, Walter E. *The Biographical Encyclopaedia and Who's Who of the American Theatre*. New York: Heineman, 1966.
Robinson, Alice M., et al. *Notable Women in the American Theatre: A Biographical Dictionary*. Westport, CT: Greenwood, 1989.
Rothman, John. *The Origin and Development of Dramatic Criticism in the "New York Times," 1851–1880*. New York: Arno, 1953. Reprint. 1970.
Ruhl, Arthur. *Second Nights: People and Ideas of the Theatre To–Day*. New York: Scribner's, 1914 [with an essay on "The Great American Play"].
Ryan, Pat M. *American Drama Bibliography: A Checklist of Publications in English*. Fort Wayne, IN: Fort Wayne Public Library, 1969.
Salem, James M. *A Guide to Critical Reviews. Part I: American Drama, 1909–1969*. 2d ed. Metuchen, NJ: Scarecrow, 1973.
Salvaggio, Odette C. "American Dramatic Criticism, 1830–1860." Ph. D. diss., Florida State University, 1979.
Sederholm, Frederick L. "The Development of Theories of Dramatic Comedy in America Through 1830." Ph. D. diss., State University of Iowa, 1961.
Seilhamer, George O. *History of the American Theatre*. 3 vols. New York, 1888–1891. Reprint. New York: Blom, 1968.
Stratman, Carl J. *American Theatrical Periodicals, 1789–1967: A Bibliographical Guide*. Durham, NC: Duke University Press, 1970.
———. *Bibliography of the American Theatre: Excluding New York City*. Chicago: Loyola University Press, 1965.
———. "The Theatre in New York: Addenda." *BNYPL* 70 (1966): 389–407.
Syle, Louis Dupont. *Essays in Dramatic Criticism; with Impressions of Some Modern Plays*. New York, 1898 [with a chapter on "The Future of the Drama"].
Wearing, J. P. *American and British Theatrical Biography: A Directory*. Metuchen, NJ: Scarecrow, 1979.

Wemyss, Francis C. *Chronology of the American Stage from 1752 to 1852.* New York, 1852. Reprint. New York: Blom, 1968.

Wilmeth, Don B. *American and English Popular Entertainment: A Guide to Information Sources.* Detroit: Gale, 1980.

———. *The American Stage to World War I: A Guide to Information Sources.* Detroit: Gale, 1978.

Wilson, Garff B. *A History of American Acting.* Bloomington: Indiana University Press, 1966.

———. *Three Hundred Years of American Drama and Theatre: From* Ye Bear and Ye Cubb *to* Hair. Englewood Cliffs, NJ: Prentice, 1973.

Winter, William. *Vagrant Memories.* New York: Doran, 1915.

———. *The Wallet of Time.* 2 vols. New York: Moffat, 1913.

Young, William C. *Documents of American Theater History: Famous Actors and Actresses on the American Stage.* 2 vols. New York: Bowker, 1975.

———. *Documents of American Theater History: Famous American Playhouses: 1716–1971.* 2 vols. Chicago: American Library Assn., 1973.

7

Index of Names and Key Terms

I have indexed all the texts listed in Chapter 4, not only the texts and excerpts included in my collection. Primarily I indexed those passages that contribute to the overall topic of my collection—in other words, those that try to describe, define, or improve the American drama and theatre. Passages dealing with other themes, such as ancient, Elizabethan, or British theatre and drama were not indexed. Numbers refer to the items in Chapter 4, and italics indicate that the text to which the index number refers is represented in this collection. However, an italicized index number may refer to a passage not reprinted in my collection. In general I have indexed persons only if their achievement is in some way discussed, not if they are just mentioned in passing. Consequently, the authors of the articles in the bibliography are not listed in the index.

accuracy, historical. SEE realism
acting, style of, *82, 180*, 206, 232, 233, 239, 296, 298, 307
actors and actresses, 5, *11*, 20, 23, 27, 41, 87, 90, 103, 108, *110*, 159, 161, 163, 166, 172, *177*, 233, 240, *247*, 296, 301, 350, 425; American, 140, 145, 147, 164, 263, 368, 373, 374; American in England, 203, *398*; children as, 117, *121*; drunk, 290; on strike, *297*. SEE ALSO star actors and star system

Actors' Church Alliance, *399, 416*
actors' fund, 28, 350
Addams, Jane, 461, 479
Addison, Joseph, *325*
Ade, George, 427, 430; *The County Chairman*, 411
advertising, 148, *267*, 276, *369*, 443, *485*
agents, 350, 389, 422
Aldrich, Thomas B., 392
amateur playwrights, *370, 453*
amateur stage, 359, 495
American drama. SEE national drama

American Dramatic Fund Association, *220, 223,* 224, 260, 261
American Dramatists' Club, 455
American and European drama and theatre, *68, 73, 96,* 183, 291, 302, 312, 332, *369, 398,* 411, 428, 460, 483
Americanization, *268*
amusement outside the theatre, 111, *112,* 154, 155, 168, 169, 170
Andrews, George H.: *The Count of Monte Cristo,* 219
animals on stage, 69, *121, 141*
Archer, William, *360, 388,* 489
audience, 473; behavior of, 42, 92, 122, 159, 274; social status of, 70, 283, 337, *344, 354,* 385, 401. SEE ALSO riots

Baker, Benjamin A.: *A Glance at New York,* 328; *New York As It Is,* 213
Baker, George P., 471, 473, 474; and his students, 492
Ballard, Frederick: *Believe Me, Xantippe,* 484
Bannister, N.H.: *Putnam, 179,* 196
Barker, James Nelson: *The Indian Princess,* 55, *341; Marmion,* 60, 61, *104; Superstition, 104*
Barras, C.M.: *The Black Crook,* 289, 292
Barrie, James M.: *The Little Minister,* 407
Bataille, Henry: *The Foolish Virgin,* 460
Bateman, Mrs. S. F.: *Self,* 255
Beecher, Henry Ward, 176
Belasco, David, 427, 430, *436, 488; The Charity Ball,* 357; *The Darling of the Gods, 419; The Return of Peter Grimm,* 475
Bellows, Henry Whitney, 260, 261, 262, *264, 265*
benefits, 281
Bentley, Walter E., *399*
Bernstein, Henri: *The Thief,* 441
Berr, Georges: *The Million,* 475
Bird, Robert M.: *The Broker of Bogota, 133; The Gladiator,* 140, 206, *220,* 340
black Americans and theatre, *247, 252,* 417, 421
Black Rangers, The, 196
blasphemy on the stage, 71, 137
Bohemian Club, 463
Boker, George H.: *Anne Boleyn, 245; The Betrothal, 245; Calaynos, 243, 245*
Booth, Edwin, *300, 381*
Booth, Junius Brutus, *264,* 290
Boucicault, Dion, 249, 302, 308, 328, *381; Belle Lamar,* 313; *The Octoroon, 269, 270; Old Heads and Young Hearts,* 182
Brady, William A., *496*
Broadhurst, George H., *488; Bought and Paid For, 490; The Man of the Hour, 436, 437,* 438, 476, *485; The Price,* 475
Brooks, Joseph, 392
Brougham, John: *Columbus,* 356; *Pocahontas,* 356
Brown, David P.: *Sertorius, 124*
Buchanan, Robert: *'Squire Kate,* 383
Bunce, Oliver B.: *Love in '76, 341*
Burgess, Gelett: *The Cave Man,* 475
Burgess, Neil: *The County Fair,* 352; *Vim,* 352
Burk, John D.: *Bunker Hill, 16,* 48, *341*

burlesque, *174*, 294, 356
Burton, William E., 249, 356
Byron, Henry J.: *Married in Haste*, 323

Caldwell, Anne: *The Nest Egg*, 460
Carleton, Henry G.: *The Butterflies*, 476
Carter, Mrs. Leslie, *419*
Carton, Richard C., 391
censorship, 57, 339, 372, 375, 380, *388*, 391
Chanfrau, Francis, 249, 328
Christmas Play Association, 461
church and the theatre, *1*, *4*, *24*, 35, 37, 50, 63, *84*, 94, 149, 176, *247*, 260, 261, 262, *264*, *265*, *272*, 317, 335, 336, *399*, 415, *416*, 452, 458, 467, 479
Church Street Colored Theatre, New York, *252*
Civic Theatre, 461
Civil War, *279*, 280
Clarke, Joseph I. C., 413
Clemens, Samuel L., 461; *The Gilded Age*, 328, 476
clubs, theatrical, 359, 462, 463, 471, 473, 479, *485*
Cohan, George M., 489
Collier, William: *I'll Be Hanged If I Do*, 460
combination system, *344*
comedy, 182, 190, 294, *303*, *315*, 320, 321, 343
Conrad, R. T.: *Aylmere*, 157; *Jack Cade*, *162*, *212*, *220*
Conried, Heinrich, 392, 393, *434*
Cooke, George Frederick, *43*, *44*
Cooper, James F., 328
Cooper, Thomas A., *78*
copyright, *40*, 140, 145, *220*, 241, *243*, *245*, 251, 253, 263, 372, 407, 476
Craig, Gordon, 486
Craig, John, 471
criticism, 17, *19*, 20, 25, 56, 77, *83*, *99*, 107, 109, *125*, 129, *146*, *156*, 204, 208, 260, 275, 276, 278, *282*, 289, 299, 357, 368, 386, 429, 440, 468, 473, 477, 479, *485*, 489
critics. SEE criticism
Crothers, Rachel: *A Man's World*, *490*; *The Three of Us*, *436*, 438
Cushman, Charlotte, 168, 189, *191*, *198*, 203, 232, 233, *264*

Daly, Augustin, 339, *344*, *348*, 383, 392; *Divorce*, *305*; *Horizon*, *341*
Davis, Owen: *The Family Cupboard*, 484
Davis, Richard H., 430
decline of the drama and theatre, 62, 69, *78*, 93, *104*, *112*, 118, *121*, *141*, 153, 155, 158, 159, 161, 168, 169, 170, *174*, 175, 184, 219, 224, 240, *246*, *264*, 266, 271, *286*, 289, *325*, 336, 337, 340, *344*, 374, 377, 385, 393, 396, 410, 482, 486; denied, 171, *316*, 336, 338, 349, 479
democracy and theatre, 7, *16*, 45, 94, 95, *160*, 248, *272*, *400*, 409, 445, 461, 467, 479
Dickinson. SEE Dickson
Dickson, James H., 74
didacticism. SEE theatre as institution of education and instruction
Dinneford, William, *194*
diorama, 114
drama as literature, 349, 353, 406, 433, 438, 441, 449, 468, 479,

488
Drama League of America, 462, 473, 479, *485*, 487, 493
Drama Players, 475
Drama Society, *485*
dramatizations. SEE novels dramatized
drinking and theatre, 34, 88, 127, 149, 163, 167, 290
Dunlap, William: *André, 124*; *The Battle of New Orleans, 99*; *The Father of an Only Child, 104*; *Pizarro in Peru*, 46; *The Stranger, 98*; *A Trip to Niagara*, 114; *Works*, 29

Eaton, Charles, 147
Educational Theatre, 461
Elizabethan drama, *215*, 263, *325*
Ellett, Elizabeth F.: *Wissmuth & Co., 211*
endowed theatre, 331, *369*, 378, 382, 385, 402, 403, 413, 415, 423
Erlanger, Abraham L. SEE Syndicate

Fairfax, Marion: *The Talker, 490*
Faversham, William, 396
feminism. SEE women
Feuillet, Octave: *Led Astray*, 311
Field, Eugene, 389
Field, Joseph M.: *Such As It Is, 173*
Field, T.M., 328
Finn, H.J., 147
Fiske, Minnie M., 392, 396, *400*, *419*, *436*
Fitch, Clyde, 427, 430, *436*, 438, 489; *Beau Brummel*, 362; *The City*, 476; *The Climbers*, 476; *Glad of It*, 411; *Her Own Way*, 411; *The Truth, 436*

Florence, William J., 328, 356
Fonson, Frantz: *Suzanne*, 460
Forbes, James: *The Chorus Lady, 436*
Forrest, Edwin, *135*, 140, 157, *162*, 178, 183, 189, *198*, 203, 205, *212*, *216*, 217, 218, *220*, 225, 226, 227, 228, *229*, 238, 266, *381*
Fox, George L., 356
Free Theatre, 365, 402. SEE ALSO independent theatre
Frohman, Charles, *459*, 465. SEE ALSO Syndicate
Frohman, Daniel, *400*, *436*, 455, 481
future of the drama, 193, *342*, *348*, *358*, 368, *390*, 403, 466, *496*

Galsworthy, John: *The Silver Box, 437*
Garland, Hamlin, *469*, 470
German drama and theatre, *98*, 393, *400*
Gill, William: *Old Jed Prouty*, 357
Gillette, William, *348*, 396, 427, 430, *436*, 438, 460; *Secret Service, 436*; *Too Much Johnson*, 374
Godfrey, Thomas: *The Prince of Parthia, 104*
Goodwin, Nathaniel C., 392
Gordin, Jacob: *The Kreutzer Sonata, 437*
green room, 274
Grice, C.E.: *The Battle of New Orleans*, 59, *61*
Grove Play, 463
Guy Mannering, 62

Hackett, James H., 119, 328
Hallam, Lewis, *7*

Hamblin, Thomas, *194*, 224
Harper, Joseph *66*; arrested, *65*
Harrigan, Edward, *348*, 352, 362; *Dan's Tribulations*, 343; *The Leather Patch*, 343; *Waddy Googan*, 352
Hauptmann, Gerhart: *The Sunken Bell*, 433; *The Weavers*, 433
Hayman, Al. SEE Syndicate
Hazelton, George C.: *Mistress Nell*, *419*
Heijermanns, Hermann: *The Good Hope*, *437*
Henry, John, 7
Herne, James A., *381*, 392, 395; *Drifting Apart*, 357; *Margaret Fleming*, *361*, 362, *363*, *364*, 365; *Shore Acres*, *371*, 383, 438
Hichens, Robert: *The Garden of Allah*, 475
Hill, George H., 140, 328
history on the stage, 59, 157, *248*
Hodgkinson, John, 70
Hopwood, Avery: *Nobody's Widow*, 460
Howard, Bronson, *344*, *348*, 362, 427, 430; *Aristocracy*, 476; *Diamonds*, *309*; *The Henrietta*, *436*, 476; *One of Our Girls*, 343; *Saratoga*, *303*, 321; *Shenandoah*, 357
Howells, William D., 330, *360*, 392; *Conterfeit Presentment*, 327
Hoyt, Charles H.: *A Midnight Bell* 351, 352; *A Stranger in New York*, 396

Ibsen, H., 355, *358*, *364*, 366, 433, 445; *The Lady from the Sea*, 475
immorality of drama, stage, and theatre, *1*, 5, *7*, *11*, 14, 22, 23, 33, 37, 49, 52, 63, *64*, *73*, 87, *97*, 106, *110*, *115*, 126, 127, 128, 137, 166, 170, *194*, 207, 260, 283, *285*, 289, 292, 306, 335, 375, 377, 404, 432, 446, 452, *484*
independent theatre, *364*, 365, 376, 385, 402
Indians, 38
Ioor, William: *The Battle of Eutaw Springs*, 31
Irving, Henry, 392

James, Henry, 330; *Daisy Miller*, 334
Jefferson, Joseph, 356, 392; *Rip Van Winkle*, 298, *326*, 328, 383
Jews, 452
Jones, George, 143
Jones, Henry A.: *The Hypocrites*, *437*; *Mrs. Dane's Defence*, 407, *490*; *We Can't Be As Bad As All That*, 460
Jones, Joseph S.: *The People's Lawyer*, 328

Kennedy, Charles R. :*The Necessary Evil*, *490*; *The Servant in the House*, 441
Kester, Paul: *Sweet Nell of Old Drury*, *419*
Klaw, Marc. SEE Syndicate
Klein, Charles, 430, *488*; *The Daughters of Men*, 435, *436*, *437*; *The Lion and the Mouse*, 435, *436*, 438, 476; *Maggie Pepper*, 483; *Potash and Perlmutter*, *484*

Lake Erie, 58
Leffingwell, M.W., 356

Lester, C.E.: *Kate Woodhull*, *222*
Lillo, George: *George Barnwell*, 47, *76*, *89*, *115*, 290
Lincoln, Florence: *The End of the Bridge*, 471
Lloyd, David D.: *The Senator*, 357
Logan, Cornelius A., 328
Longfellow, Henry W.: *Evangeline*, 356; *The Spanish Student*, *245*
Luska, Sidney: *Mrs. Peixada*, 343
Lytton, Edward Bulwer, *139*

MacDowell Club, 471, *485*
MacKaye, James S.: *Paul Kauvar*, 351
MacKaye, Percy, *488*; *Jeanne d'Arc*, *436*; *Tomorrow*, *490*
Macready, William C., 189, 203, 218, 225, 226, 227, 228, *229*, 238
Maeterlinck, Maurice: *Mary Magdalene*, 460; *Sister Beatrice*, 475
managers, 25, *43*, *44*, 45, *61*, 69, 70, 74, *104*, *113*, 140, 159, *174*, 240, 249, *264*, 274, *325*, 343, *344*, 368, *370*, 374, 387, 396, 403, 404, 415, 428, 446, 447, 448, 486, 489, *496*; women as, 168
Mansfield, Richard, 392
Marble, Dan, *198*, 328
Marlowe, Julia, 396
Marshall, E. A., 249
Mathews, Cornelius: *Jacob Leisler*, *214*, *245*; *Witchcraft*, *243*, *245*
Matthews, Brander, 392, 474
Mayo, Frank, 328
Medina, Louisa H., *139*, 140, 142
melodrama, *21*, 38, 70, *96*, *121*, 166, *174*, 219, *310*, 331, 337, 338, *354*, *381*, *469*, 472

Merrick, Leonard: *The Impostor*, 460
Miller, Joaquin: *The Danites*, 476
Mitchell, Langdon. *The New York Idea*, *436*, *437*
Mitchell, William, 356
Moffat, Graham: *Bunty Pulls the Strings*, 475
Monroe, James, 71
Montgomery, James: *The Aviator*, 460
Moody, William V.: *The Great Divide*, *436*, *437*, 438, 476
morality of drama, stage, and theatre, *3*, *7*, *9*, 15, 17, *24*, 26, *32*, 35, 41, 50, 85, 90, 102, 103, *110*, *116*, 118, 122, *247*, 317, *324*, *329*, 335, 336, 338, 366, 458
Morton, Charles: *Women of the Day*, *315*
Morton, Thomas: *Education*, 74
motion picture shows, *456*, 481, 491, 493, *496*
Mowatt, Anna C. O.: *Armand*, *245*; *Fashion*, *185*, *186*, 187, *188*, 190, *191*, *192*, 193, *195*, *198*, *220*, *221*, *245*
Murdoch, Frank Hitchcock: *Davy Crockett*, 328, *341*
Murdoch, James E., 197, *198*
music, 20, *287*

National Art Theater Society, 413, 415
national characters, *8*, 328, 349, 351, 352, *484*. SEE ALSO stock characters
national drama and theatre, 38, 55, 60, *61*, *67*, *104*, *116*, *124*, 131, *141*, 147, 150, *160*, 183, 190, 197, 207, 208, 210, *211*, 217,

235, *243*, *245*, 249, 259, 263, *264*, *265*, 273, 294, *304*, 311, *316*, 320, 327, *341*, *342*, *344*, 348, 349, *358*, 374, *400*, 410, *418*, 427, 431, *436*, 438, 445, *459*, 465, 466, 467, 468, 473, 476, 489; material for 8, *104*, *113*, 119, *144*, *221*, 235, 257, 313, *314*, 332, *342*, *348*, 351, 352, *354*, *390*, 450, *457*, *459*, 466, 476, 480
National Theatre, concept of, *345*, 382, 403, 413, 415, 423, 426, *434*
nationalism. SEE patriotism
native drama. SEE national drama and theatre
naturalness. SEE realism
Neighborhood Playhouse, 495
New Theater, *434*, 442, 451, 455, 464, 467, 474, 479
newspapers. SEE press
Nixon–Nirdlinger, Samuel F. SEE Syndicate
novels dramatized, 136, *139*, 353, 394, 396, 406, 407

opera bouffe, 391
originality, *315*, 441
Otway, Thomas: *Venice Preserv'd*, 95
Owens, John E., 328

Palmer, A. M., 352, *364*, 365
Parker, Louis N.: *Pomander Walk*, 460
patriotism, *16*, 20, 38, 48, 55, 58, *61*, *99*, *104*, *124*, *160*, 181, *196*, 214, *222*, 384
Patterson, Joseph M.: *The Fourth Estate*, 467; *Rebellion*, 490
Paulding, James K.: *American Comedies*, 210; *The Lion of the West*, 328
Paulding, William I.: *American Comedies*, 210
Payne, John Howard, 117, 140; *Richelieu*, 284
People's Institute, *485*
performances, prohibition of, *65*, 66, *91*, 123, *247*, 399
Pettitt, Henry: *Taken from Life*, 331
Phillips, Stephen, 433; *Herod*, 407
Pilgrims, The, 38
Pinero, Arthur W.: *Sweet Lavender*, 407
playbills. SEE advertising
plays, adaptation of, 46, *199*, *200*; as mirror of life, *11*, 258, *325*, *360*, 476; characteristics of good, *133*, *418*, *453*; pernicious effects of, *7*, 391
playwrights, 234; American, 140, 249, 255, 257, 427, 430, *436*, 438, *453*, *459*, 476, 478, *485*, *488*; novelists as, *334*; potential, 330
poetic drama, 445, 449
poetic justice, 250, *354*
politics in drama, *162*, 203
Potter, Paul, 427
Pratt, W. W.: *Ten Nights in a Bar Room*, 290
press, *13*, *264*, *325*, 403, 468, *484*, *488*. SEE ALSO criticism
prize tragedies, 131, 143, 217, 242
prostitutes in the theatre, 51, 127
provincialism, American, 256
publication of plays, 433, 473. SEE ALSO copyright
puffing. SEE criticism

Quakers, *7*

racism, 417, 421
Raymond, John T., 328
realism, 20, 38, 48, 59, *72*, 75, *79*, 130, *132*, *173*, 205, 206, *212*, *214*, 230, 284, *285*, 291, 296, *300*, *304*, 308, *309*, *310*, *315*, 323, *325*, 336, 339, 343, 346, 347, *348*, 355, 357, *358*, *360*, 362, *363*, *364*, 366, *370*, *371*, 374, 383, 393, 404, 406, 409, 427, *437*, 438, 444, 466, *469*, 475
Reinhardt, Max. SEE *Sumurûn*
Revolution, The, 181
riots, 18, 20, *54*, *81*, 213, 218; Astor Place, 226, 227, 228, *229*
Robertson, Agnes, *269*, *270*
Robertson, Thomas W., 302, 339
Rosenfeld, Sydney, 412
Rostand, Edmond: *L'Aiglon*, 407; *Cyrano de Bergerac*, 407; *La Samaritaine*, 460

Sardou, Victorien: *Madame Sans-Gêne*, 407
Sargent, Epes, *198*
Sargent, Franklin H., 365
satire on America, *303*
Scarborough, George: *The Lure*, 484
scenery, 62, 70, *72*, *174*, *199*, *264*, 284, 293, 295, *300*, *304*, *310*, 318, 322, 335, 379, 385, 396, 441, 467, 468, 475, 486. SEE ALSO realism
Scott, Sir Walter, 136, *139*, 328
Scribe, Eugène, 486
Shakespeare, William, *100*, *199*, *200*, 203, 205, 219, *243*, *247*, *264*, *268*, 273, *288*, 295, 296, *325*, 336, 338, 340, 396, *418*, 444, 486; as spectacle, 201, 254, 318, 322; on the black stage, *252*; polyglot performance, *288*
Shaw, George Bernard, *457*; *Mrs. Warren's Profession*, *437*, *484*; *Widowers' Houses*, *437*
Sheldon, Charles M., 458
Sheldon, Edward, *488*; *The High Road*, *490*; *The Nigger*, 480
Shubert brothers, *436*, 465
Silsbee, J. S., 231
Simpson, Edmund, *194*
Smith, Charles S., *485*
Smith, Elizabeth O., *245*
Smith, Richard P.: *The Eighth of January*, *124*
Smith, Solomon, 140, 176
Smith, W. H.: *The Drunkard*, 290
Smith, Winchell: *The Only Son*, 475
soliloquies, *80*
Sophocles: *Oedipus the King*, 484
South, *279*, *280*, 476, 480
spectacle, *112*, 118, *121*, *132*, 148, 184, 201, 219, 292, 409, 467
Sperry, J. A.: *Extremes*, 236, 237, *245*
star actors and star system, 93, *104*, *112*, 117, *135*, 140, 152, 153, 155, 158, 164, 207, 224, 240, 263, *265*, 340, *369*, 396, 441, *488*; salaries of, 238
stereotyped plot, *134*, *196*, *381*, 467
stock characters, 59, 119, 130, 152, 231, 328, *341*, 351, 352, 353, *360*, 367, *381*, 466, 467
stock company, 340, *344*, *369*, *400*, 403, 412, *485*
Stone, John A.: *Metamora*, *135*, 140, 203, *341*
Stowe, Harriet Beecher: *Uncle Tom's Cabin*, 247, 269

Index of Names and Key Terms 319

subscription theatre, *388*, 401
subsidized theatre. SEE endowed theatre
Sumurûn, 485
Swan, Mark L.: *Her Own Money*, 484
Syndicate, 392, *400*, 402, 403, *419*, *420*, 428, *436*, 451, *454*, 455, 465, 479, 481, *485*. SEE ALSO Shubert brothers

tariff on theatrical imports, 105, *388*
Taylor, Tom: *The Election*, *268*; *Joan of Arc*, *304*
temperance drama, 290, *326*
theatre: as business, 387, 389, *420*, 428, *454*; as institution of education and instruction, 9, 7, *13*, 15, 25, 26, *30*, 41, 53, *67*, 86, *101*, *116*, 166, 205, 359, 366, *381*, *390*, 406, 415, 435, 449, 466; as mirror of society and life, *12*, 41, 103, *120*, *160*, 165, 209, *272*, 306, *326*, *344*, 349, 366, *437*, 439, 447, 448, 449, 466, 467, 468; as necessary amusement, 41, *390*, 409; closed, *6*, *64*; effects of, 5, 7, 9, *11*, 35, 36, 37, 50, 52, 53, 56, 58, 122, 149, 202, 244, *272*, 277, 290; and safety, 333; suggestions for improvement of, *39*, *112*, *151*, 152, 165, 169, *246*, 263, 307, 335, *400*, 404, 406, *454*, 489; usefulness of, *4*, 9, *12*, *32*, *101*, *116*, *138*, 171, *246*, *272*, *361*; ventilation of, 319; and waste, 5, 23, 88
Theatre Society, *469*, 470
Theatrical Syndicate, Theatrical Trust. SEE Syndicate

Thomas, Augustus, 427, 430, *436*, 438, *459*, *469*, *488*; *Alabama*, 476; *As a Man Thinks*, *490*; *The Other Girl*, 411, *436*; *The Witching Hour*, 441, 485
Thompson, Denman, 362; *The Old Homestead*, 352, 476; *Our New Minister*, 411
Thompson, Lydia, 356
Tree, Ellen, *146*
Trust. SEE Syndicate
Twain, Mark. SEE Clemens, Samuel L.
Tyler, Royall: *The Contrast*, *8*, 328, *341*, 349

unities, 397, 486
university and the drama or theatre, *358*, 405, 406, 408, 414, 471, 473, 474, 492

vaudeville, 424, 445
Veiller, Bayard: *The Fight*, *484*
verisimilitude, veritism. SEE realism
von Weber, Carl M: *Der Freischütz*, *141*
vulgarity. SEE immorality

Wallack, James W., 249
Wallack, Lester, 331
Walter, Eugene, *488*; *The Easiest Way*, 452, 476, *490*; *Fine Feathers*, *490*; *Paid in Full*, 438, 441, 480, *490*; *The Wolf*, 438
Ware, Mr. SEE Sperry, J. A.
Warfield, David, *419*
Washington Square Players, 495
Waterson, Mr.: *Battle of Orleans*, *61*
Wheatley, William, 232

Wilkins, E. G. P.: *Young New York*, 258
Willis, Nathaniel P.: *Bianca Visconti*, 245; *Tortesa the Usurer*, 245
Wilson, Francis, 392
Winstanley, W.: *The Hypocrite Unmasked*, 19
Wise, Thomas E.: *A Gentleman from Mississippi*, 476
women, 39, 145, *191*, *264*, *272*, *404*, *425*, *452*, *473*, *490*; as managers, 168; as playwrights, *245*
Woodworth, Samuel: *The Forest Rose*, 328
Woolf, Benjamin E.: *The Mighty Dollar*, 320, 328

Young, William: *The Japanese Nightingale*, *419*

Zimmerman, J. Fred. SEE Syndicate
Zola, Emile, *358*

About the Editor and Compiler

JÜRGEN C. WOLTER is Professor of English at Bergische Universität, Gesamthochschule Wuppertal. He has published extensively on American theatre in books and journals.